Demon Diary

Volume 2

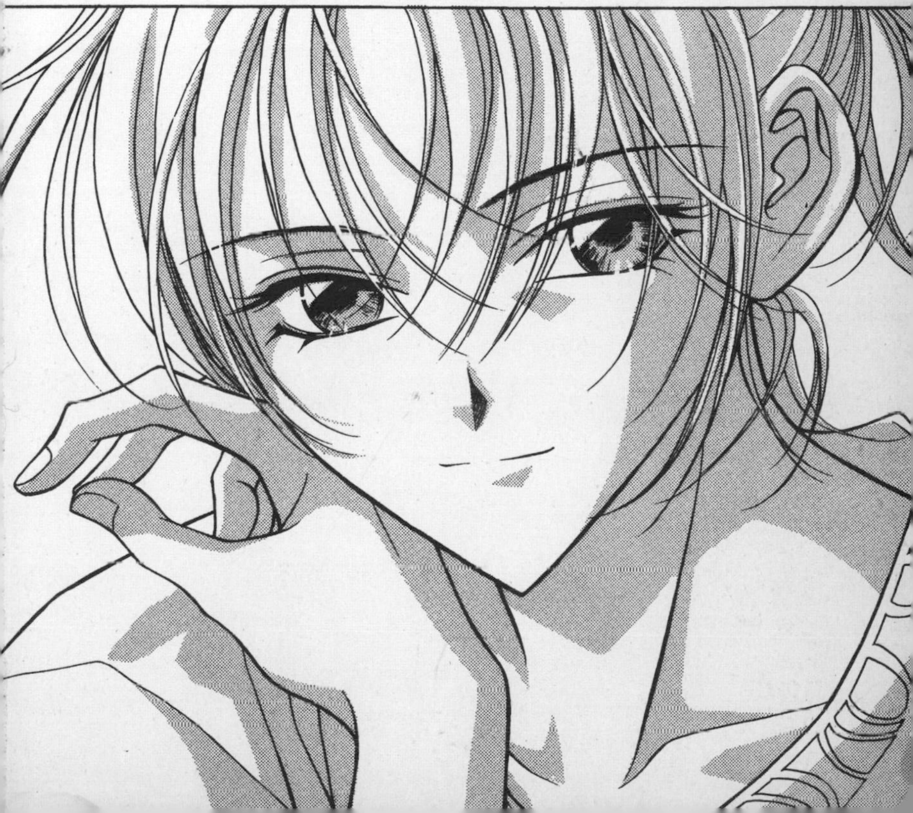

ALSO AVAILABLE FROM ⊛TOKYOPOP®

DEMON DIARY

Art by Kara
Story by Lee Yun Hee

Volume 2

Los Angeles • Tokyo • London

Translator - Lauren Na
English Adaption - Kelly Sue DeConnick
Contributing Editor - Robert Buscemi
Retouch and Lettering - Monalisa de Asis and John Lo
Cover Layout - Aaron Suhr

Editor - Elizabeth Hurchalla
Managing Editor - Jill Freshney
Production Coordinator - Antonio DePietro
Production Manager - Jennifer Miller
Art Director - Matt Alford
Editorial Director - Jeremy Ross
VP of Production & Manufacturing - Ron Klamert
President & C.O.O. - John Parker
Publisher & C.E.O. - Stuart Levy

Email: editor@TOKYOPOP.com
Come visit us online at www.TOKYOPOP.com

A 🐰**TOKYOPOP**® Manga
TOKYOPOP® is an imprint of Mixx Entertainment, Inc.
5900 Wilshire Blvd., Suite 2000, Los Angeles, CA 90036

MAWAN-ILGI 1 ©2000 by KARA. All rights reserved.
First published in KOREA in 2000 by SIGONGSA Co., Ltd.
English translation rights arranged by SIGONGSA Co., Ltd.

English text ©2003 by Mixx Entertainment, Inc.
TOKYOPOP is a registered trademark of Mixx Entertainment, Inc.

ISBN: 1-59182-155-X

First TOKYOPOP® printing: July 2003

10 9 8 7 6 5 4 3 2 1
Printed in Canada

THE STORY SO FAR

RAENEF IS THE BLACK SHEEP OF THE DEMON COURT, WITH MINIMAL KNOWLEDGE OF MAGIC AND COURTLY ETIQUETTE. IN ORDER TO HELP HIM CLAIM HIS BIRTHRIGHT AS A DEMON LORD, THE GODS SEND HIM THE WISE AND NOBLE DEMON TEACHER ECLIPSE TO BE HIS TUTOR. AS RAENEF AND ECLIPSE BEGIN THEIR JOURNEY OF DISCOVERY, THEY FIND THAT THE BONDS OF FRIENDSHIP ARE STRONGER THAN THE TEACHER/STUDENT RELATIONSHIP.

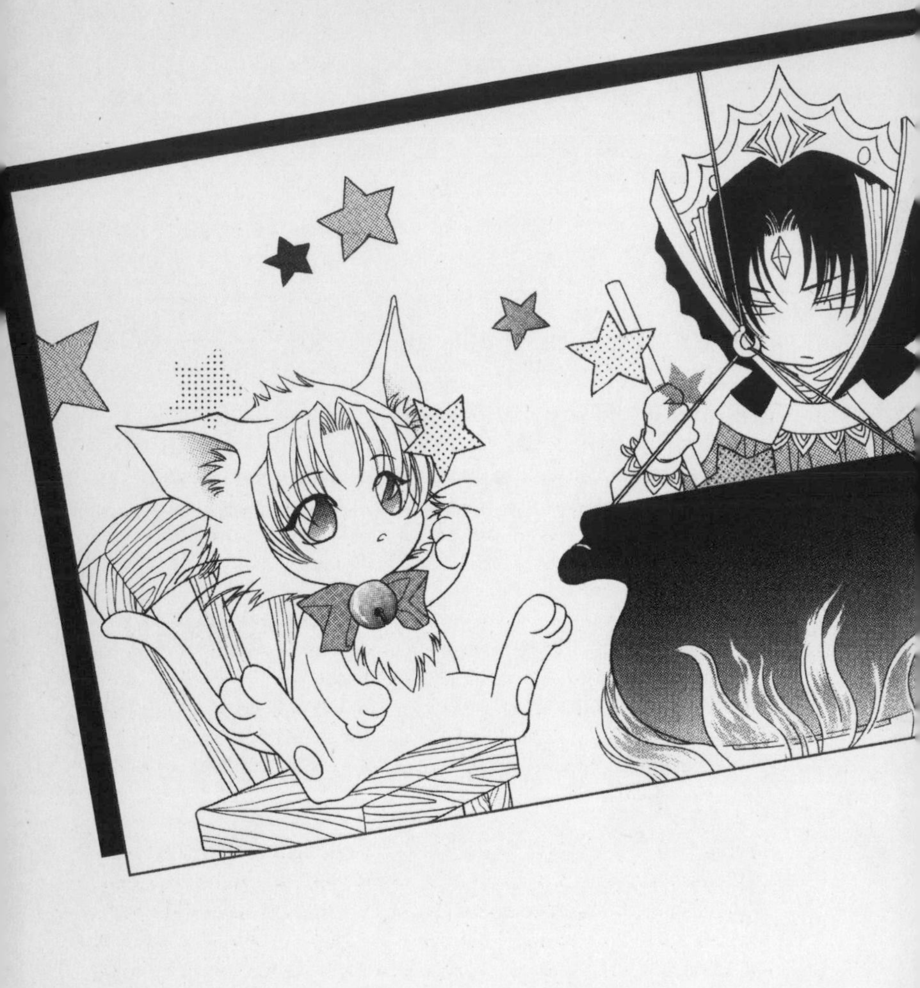

Well, it's been one year since my professional debut as Kara, and, thanks in no small part to the love and support of my fans and publisher, J am pleased and proud to present to you: Demon Diary Volume 2!

Sadly, the writer for volume 1, Lee Chi Hyong, is busy getting ready for his high school entrance exams, so he has had to leave the book. (J know, right? J had no clue. He was introduced to me as a student, so J naturally thought he was in college. Amazing!) Fortunately, Lee Yun Hee has done a fabulous job picking up where Lee Chi Hyong left off, and J am grateful to her for her excellent work.

Where are we with Volume 2? Well, it looks as though Eclipse is adjusting to life with Raenef. Raenef, on the other hand, is going to need to buckle down and start paying attention if he ever hopes to become a proper demon lord. (From where J'm sitting, it looks like Raenef is having more of an effect on Eclipse than the other way around!)

Please continue to love and watch over Demon Diary.

Now, without further ado …

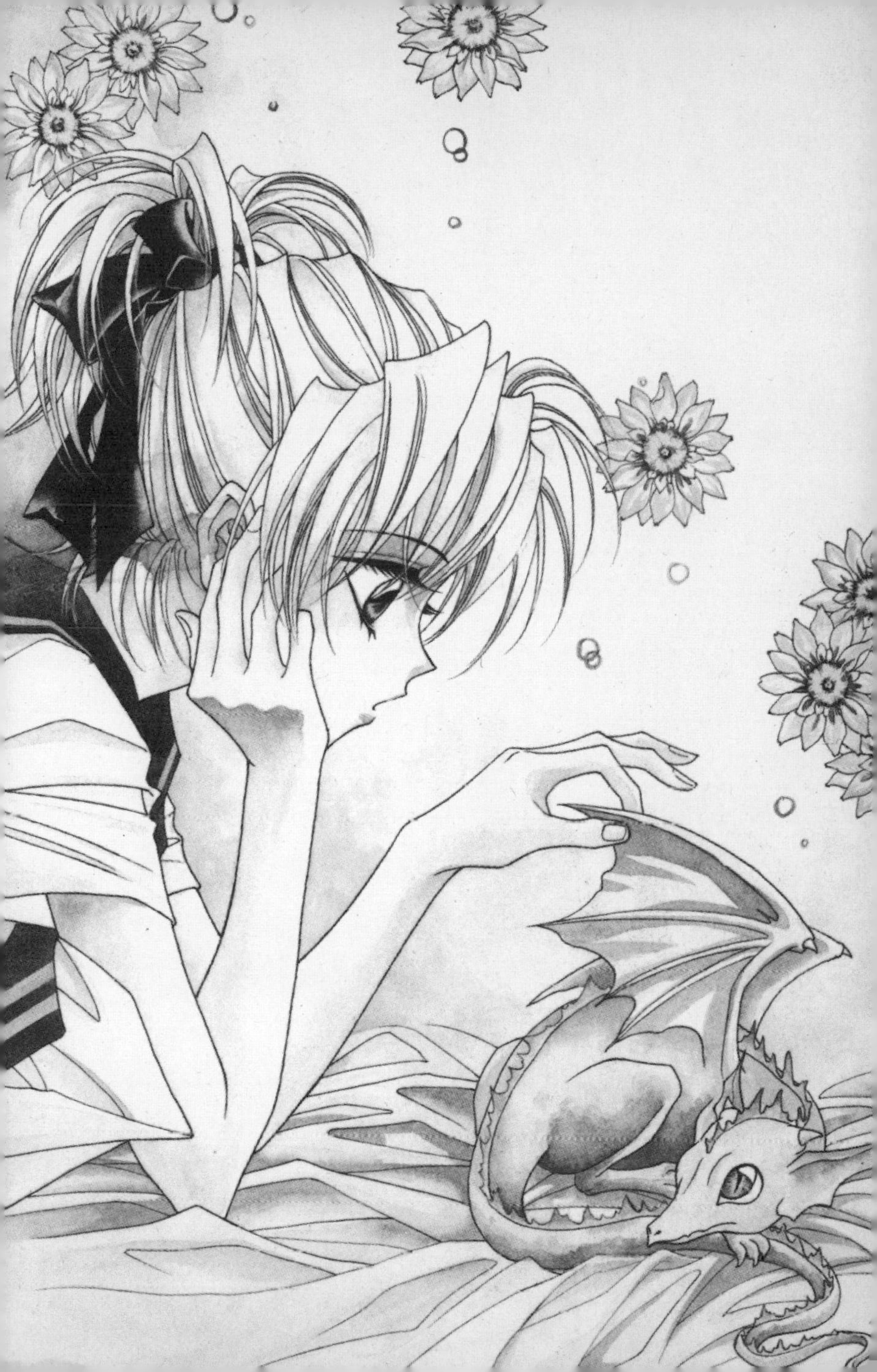

마왕일기

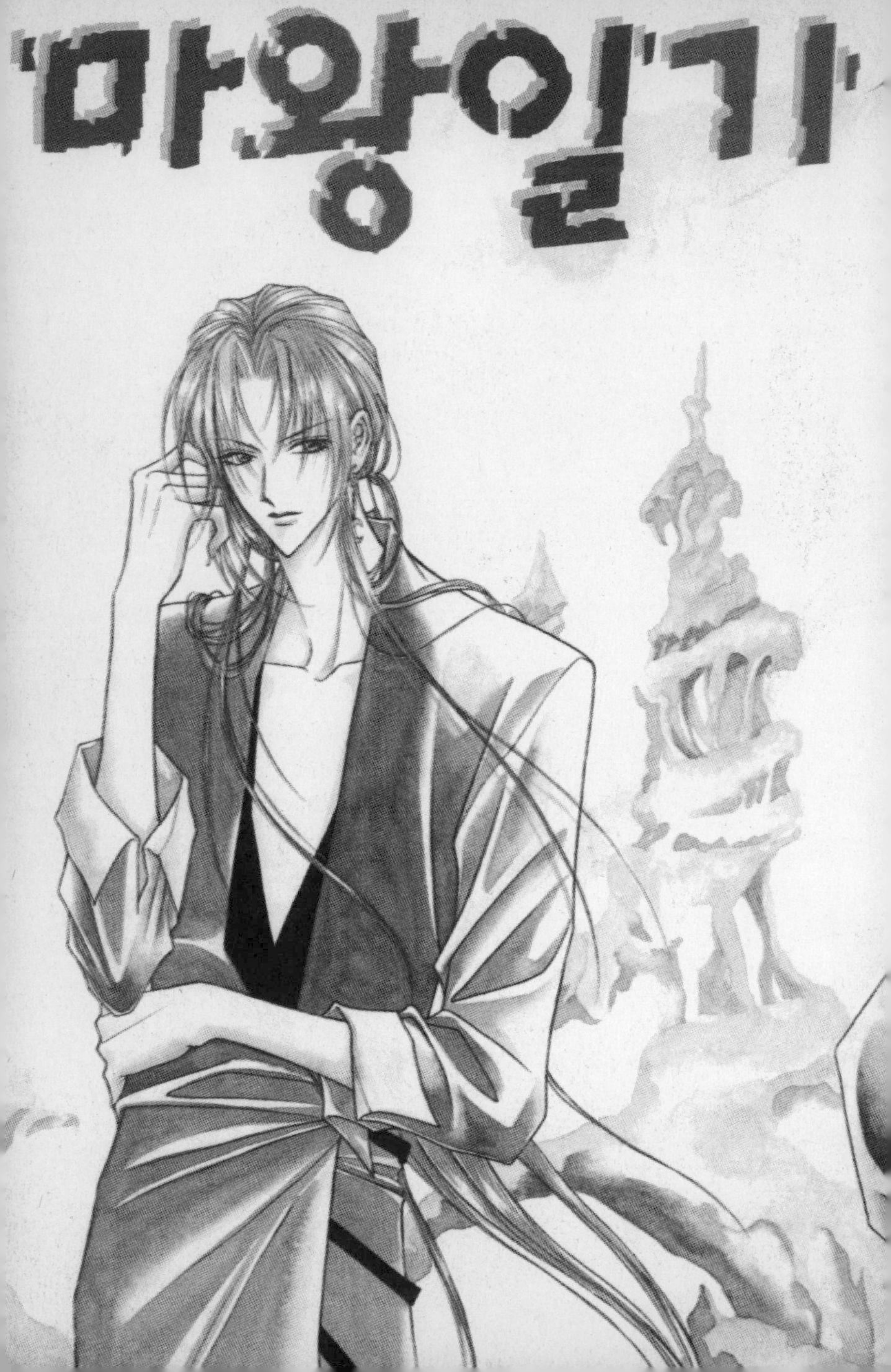

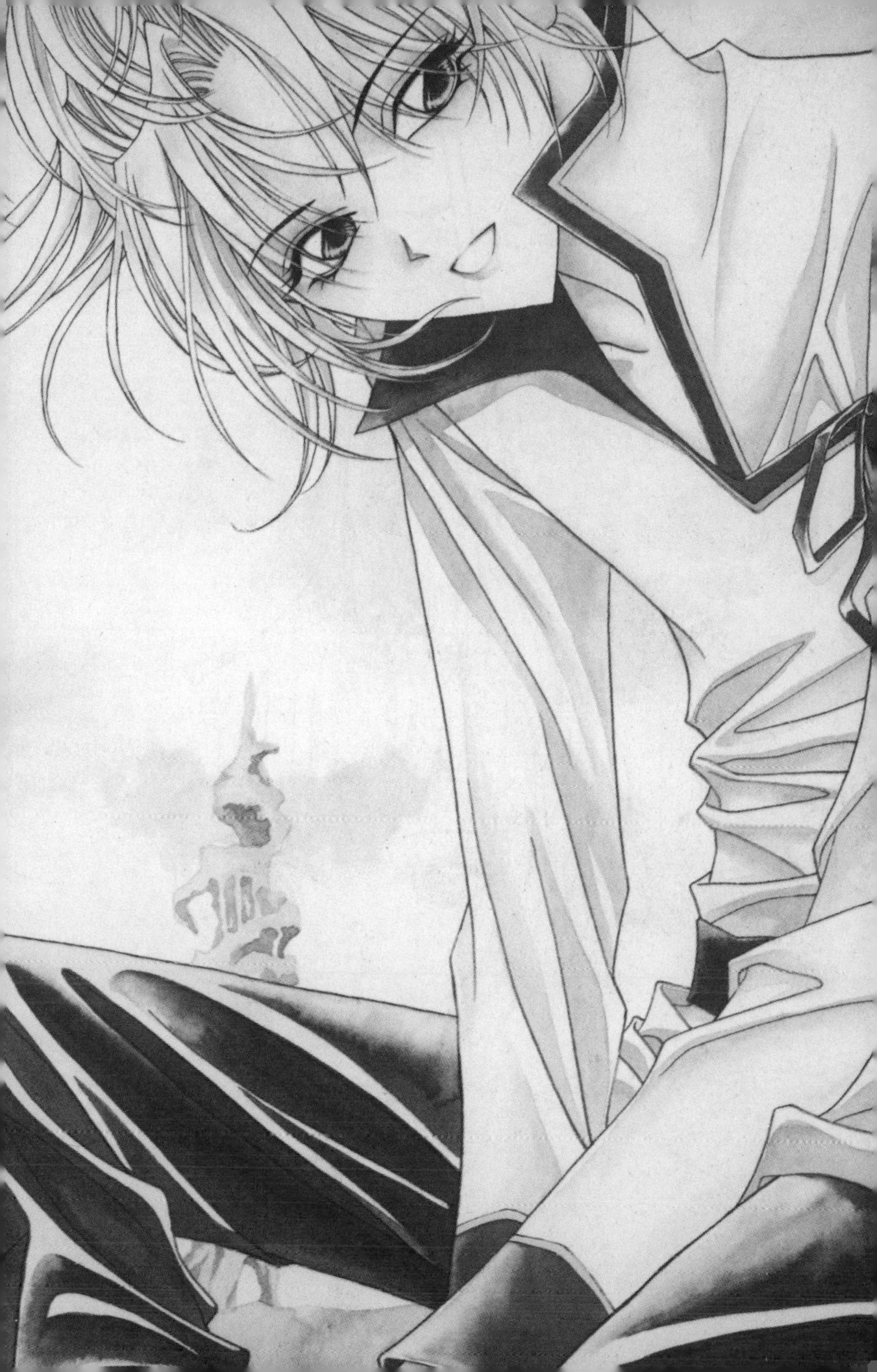

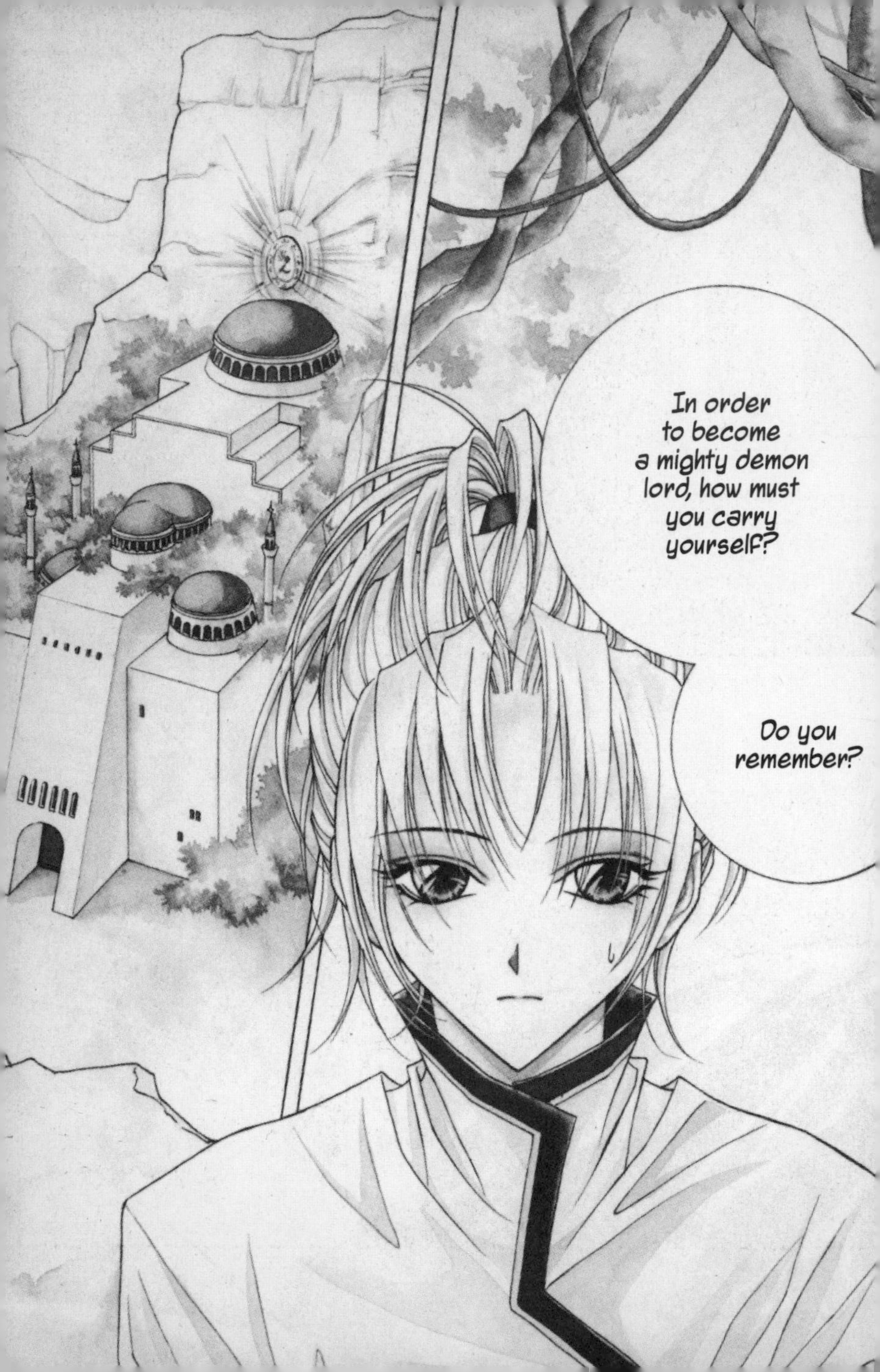
In order to become a mighty demon lord, how must you carry yourself?
Do you remember?

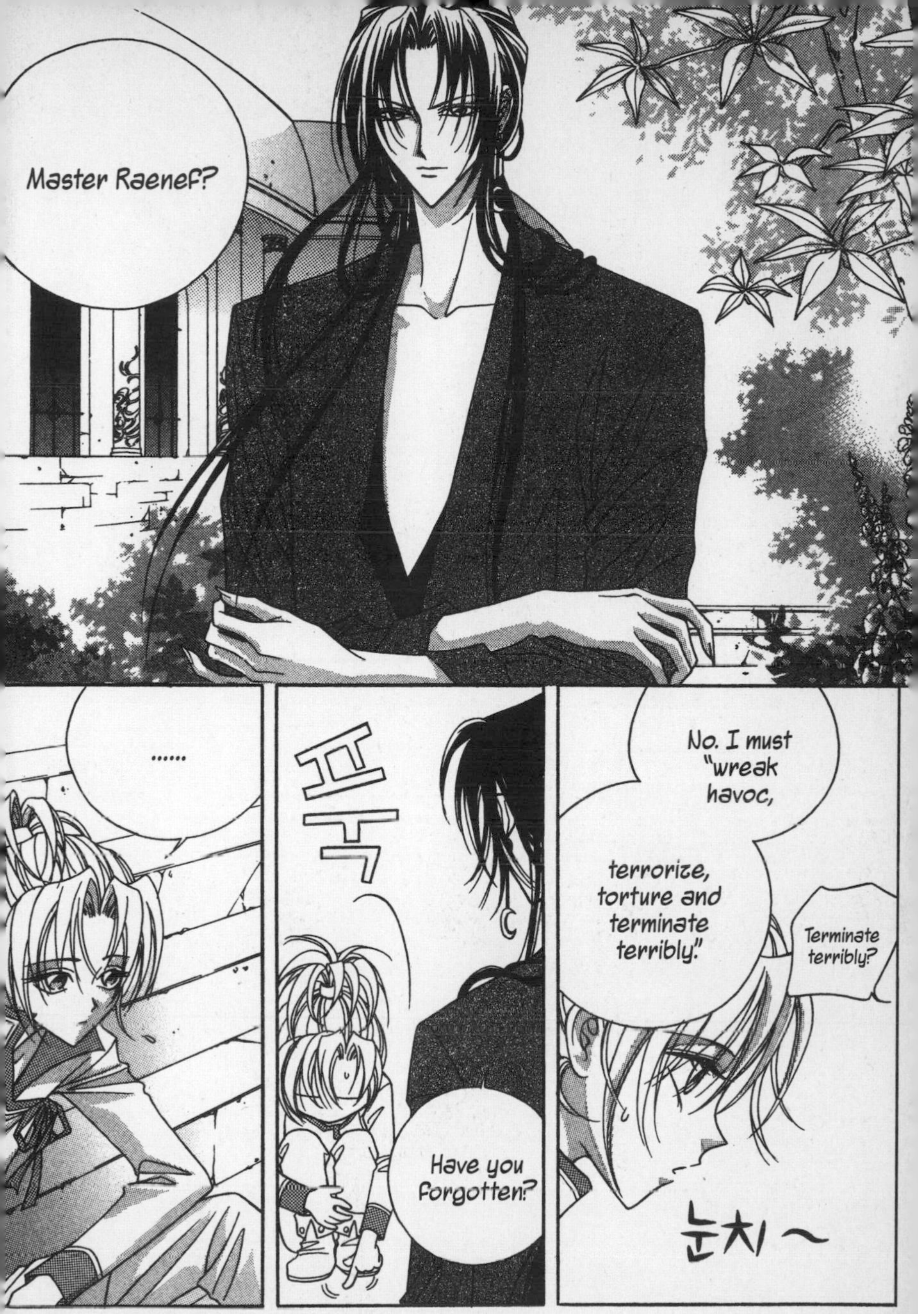

Master Raenef?
......
Have you forgotten?
No. I must "wreak havoc,
terrorize, torture and terminate terribly."
Terminate terribly?
눈치~

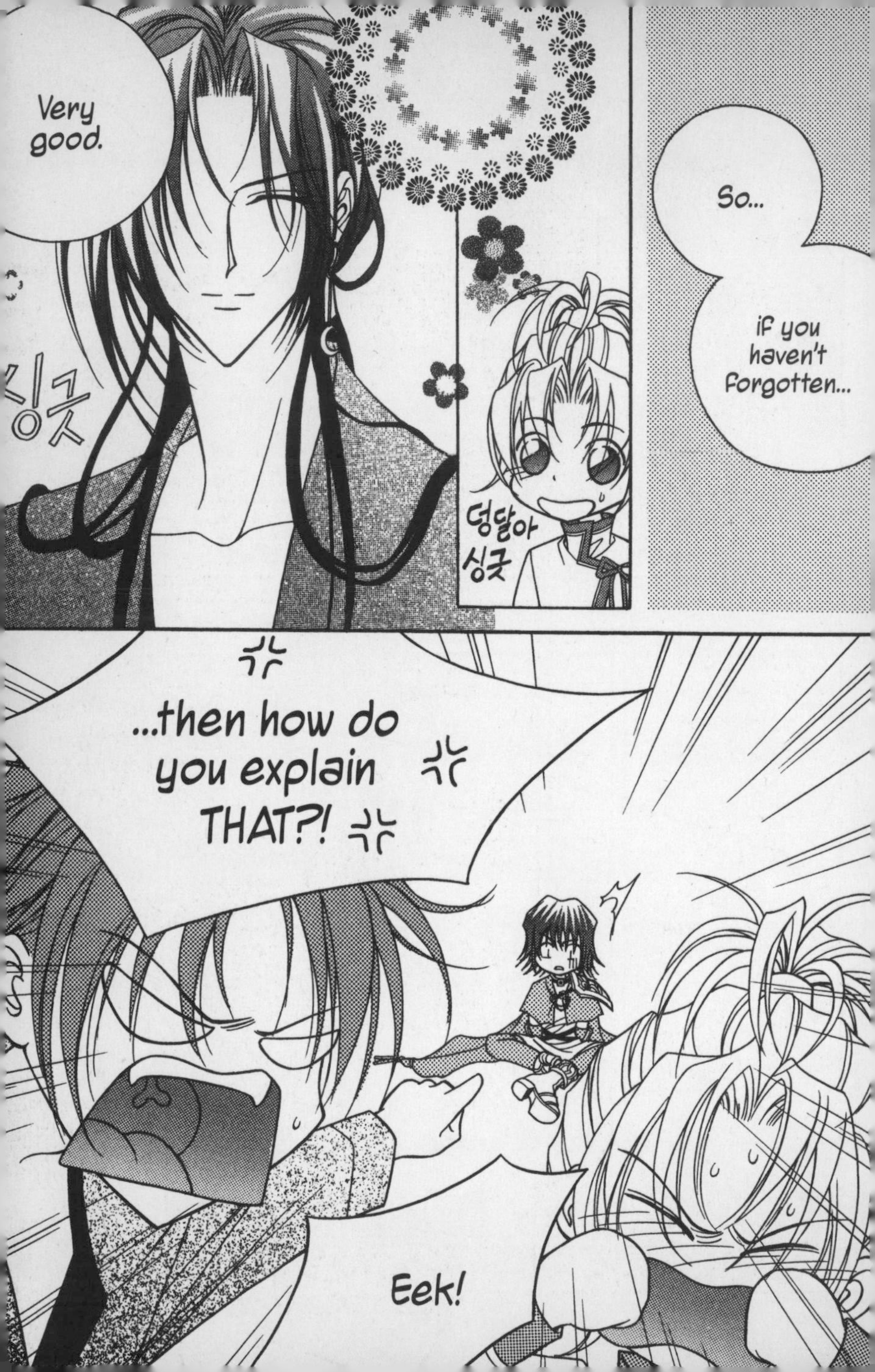
So...
if you haven't forgotten...
덩달아 싱긋
Very good.
싱긋
...then how do you explain THAT?!
Eek!

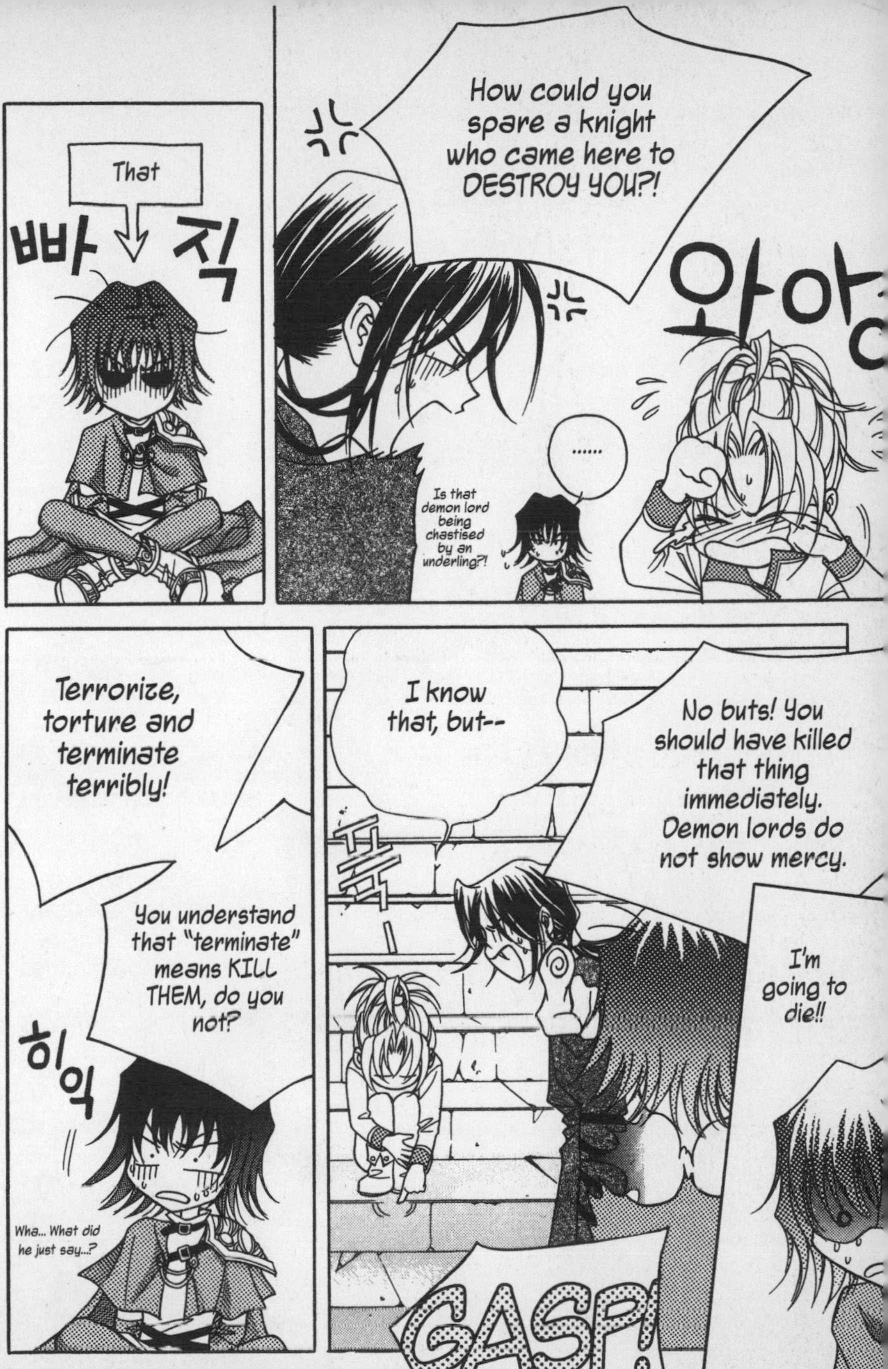
That
빠직
How could you spare a knight who came here to DESTROY YOU?!
와아아
......
Is that demon lord being chastised by an underling?!
Terrorize, torture and terminate terribly!
You understand that "terminate" means KILL THEM, do you not?
히익
Wha... What did he just say...?
I know that, but--
No buts! You should have killed that thing immediately. Demon lords do not show mercy.
I'm going to die!!
GASP!

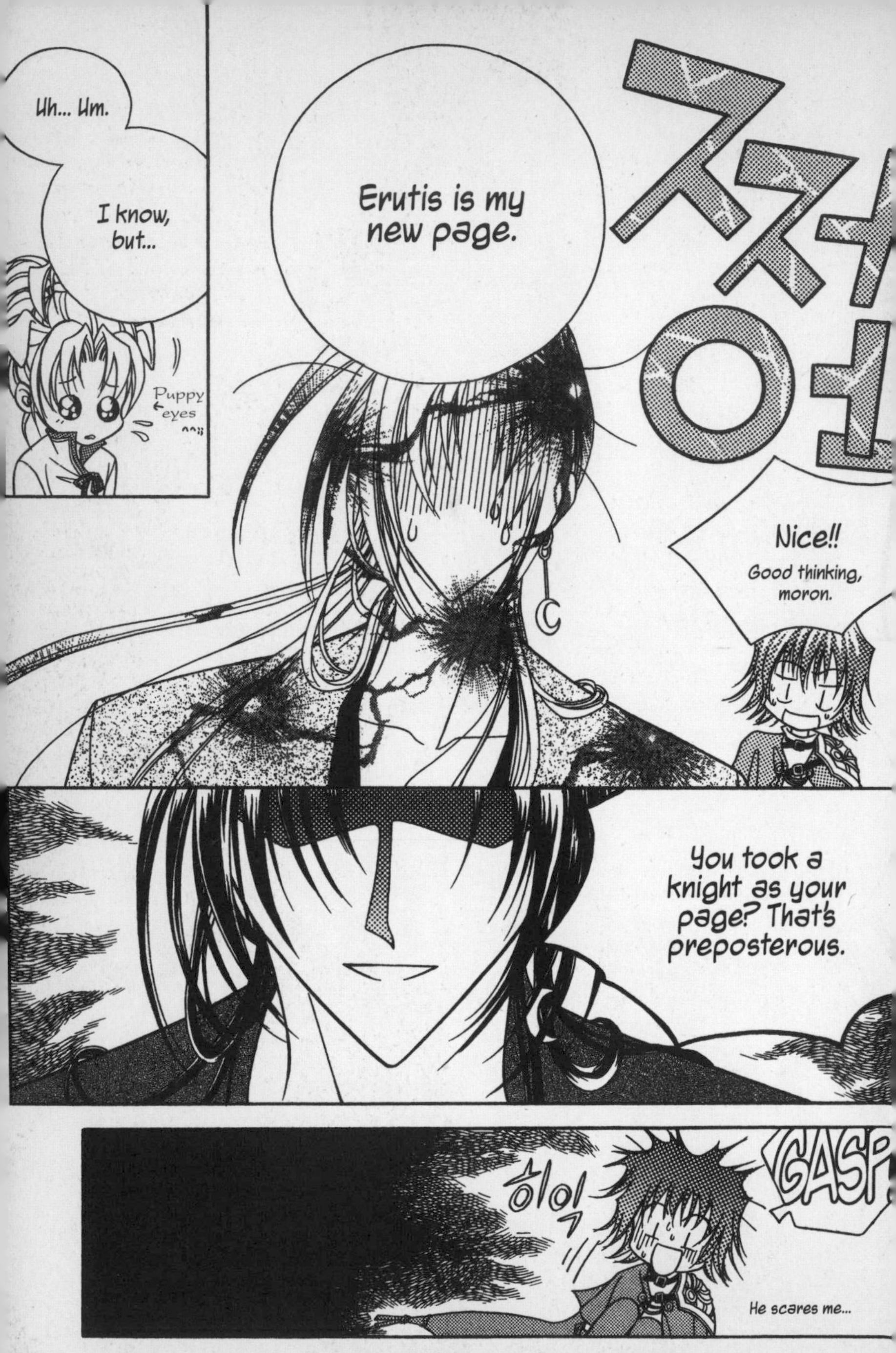
Uh... Um.
I know, but...
Puppy eyes ^^;;
Erutis is my new page.
Nice!!
Good thinking, moron.
You took a knight as your page? That's preposterous.
GASP
He scares me...

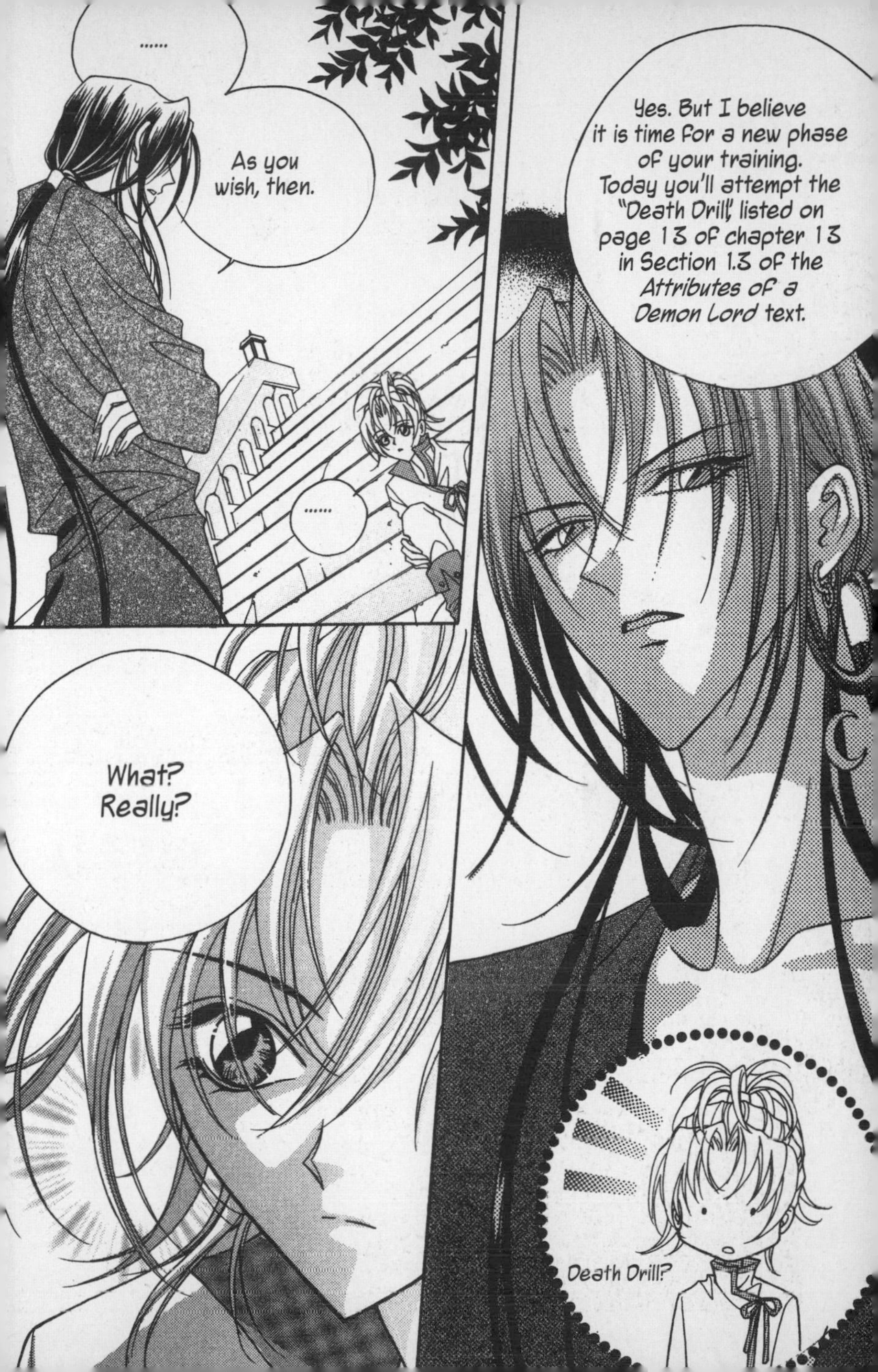
......
As you wish, then.
......
What? Really?
Yes. But I believe it is time for a new phase of your training. Today you'll attempt the "Death Drill," listed on page 13 of chapter 13 in Section 1.3 of the *Attributes of a Demon Lord* text.
Death Drill?

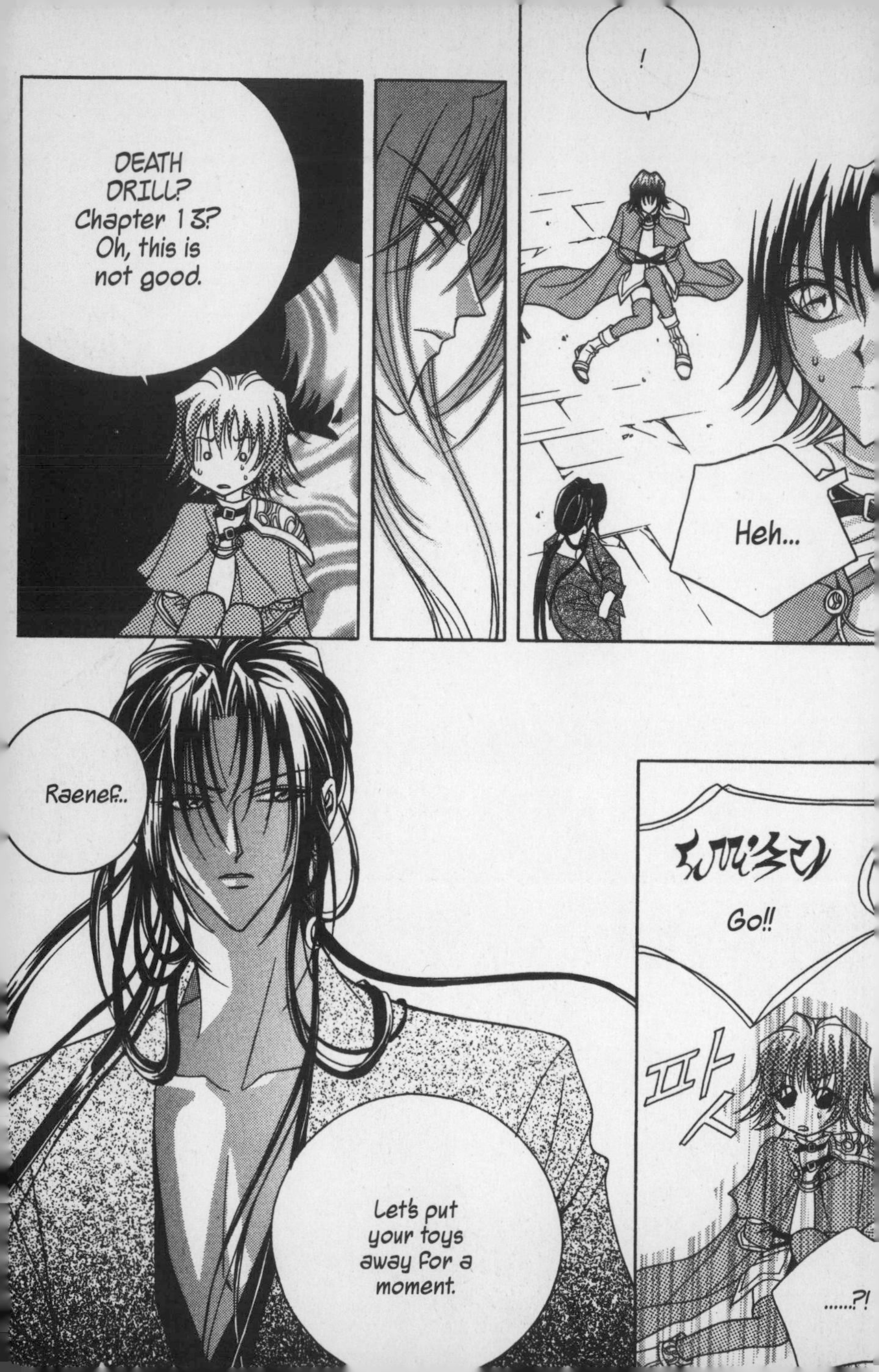

!
Heh...
DEATH DRILL? Chapter 13? Oh, this is not good.
Go!!
......?!
Raenef..
Let's put your toys away for a moment.

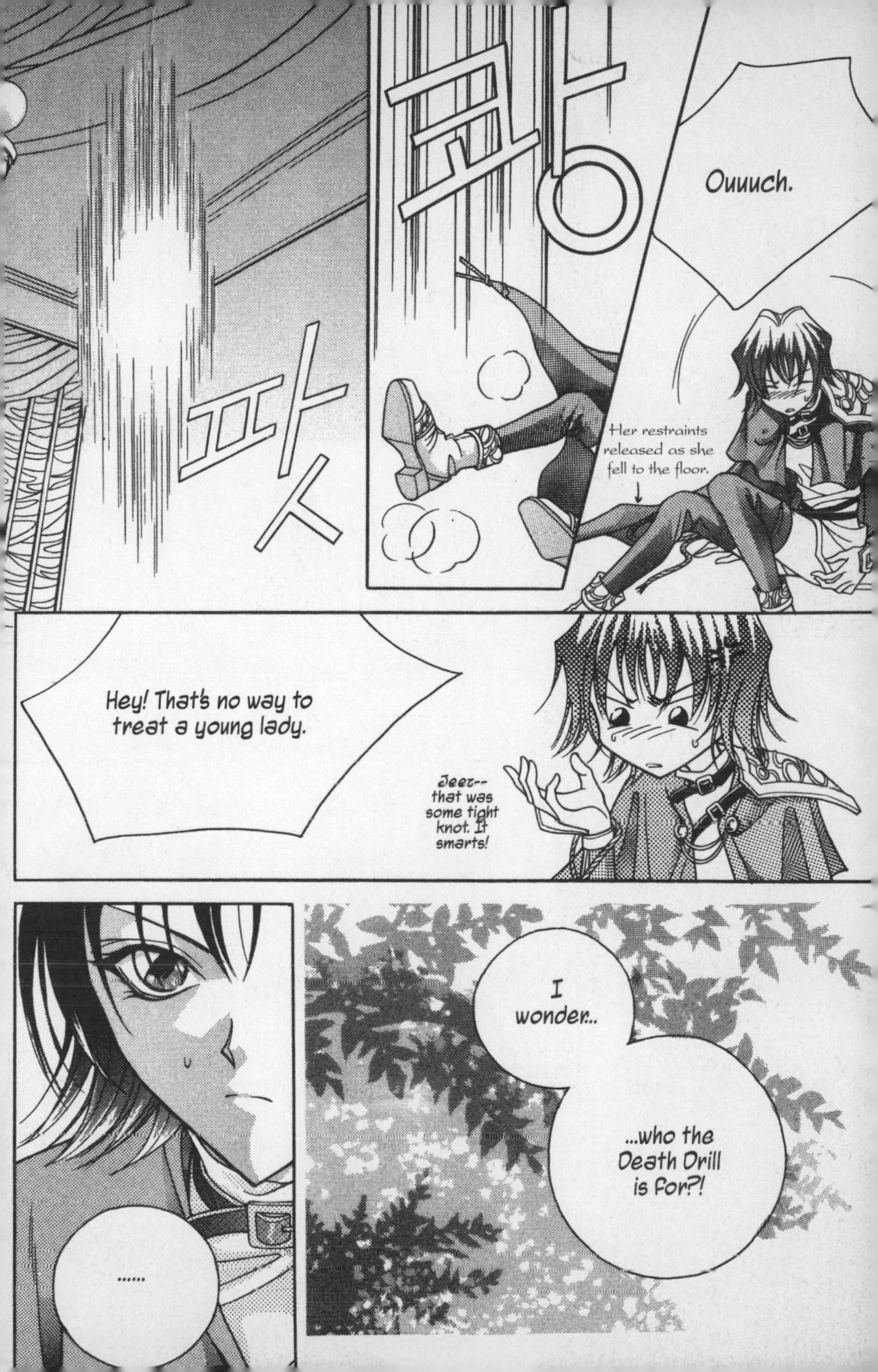

팟
쾅
Ouuuch.
Her restraints released as she fell to the floor.
Hey! That's no way to treat a young lady.
Jeez-- that was some tight knot. It smarts!
......
I wonder...
...who the Death Drill is for?!

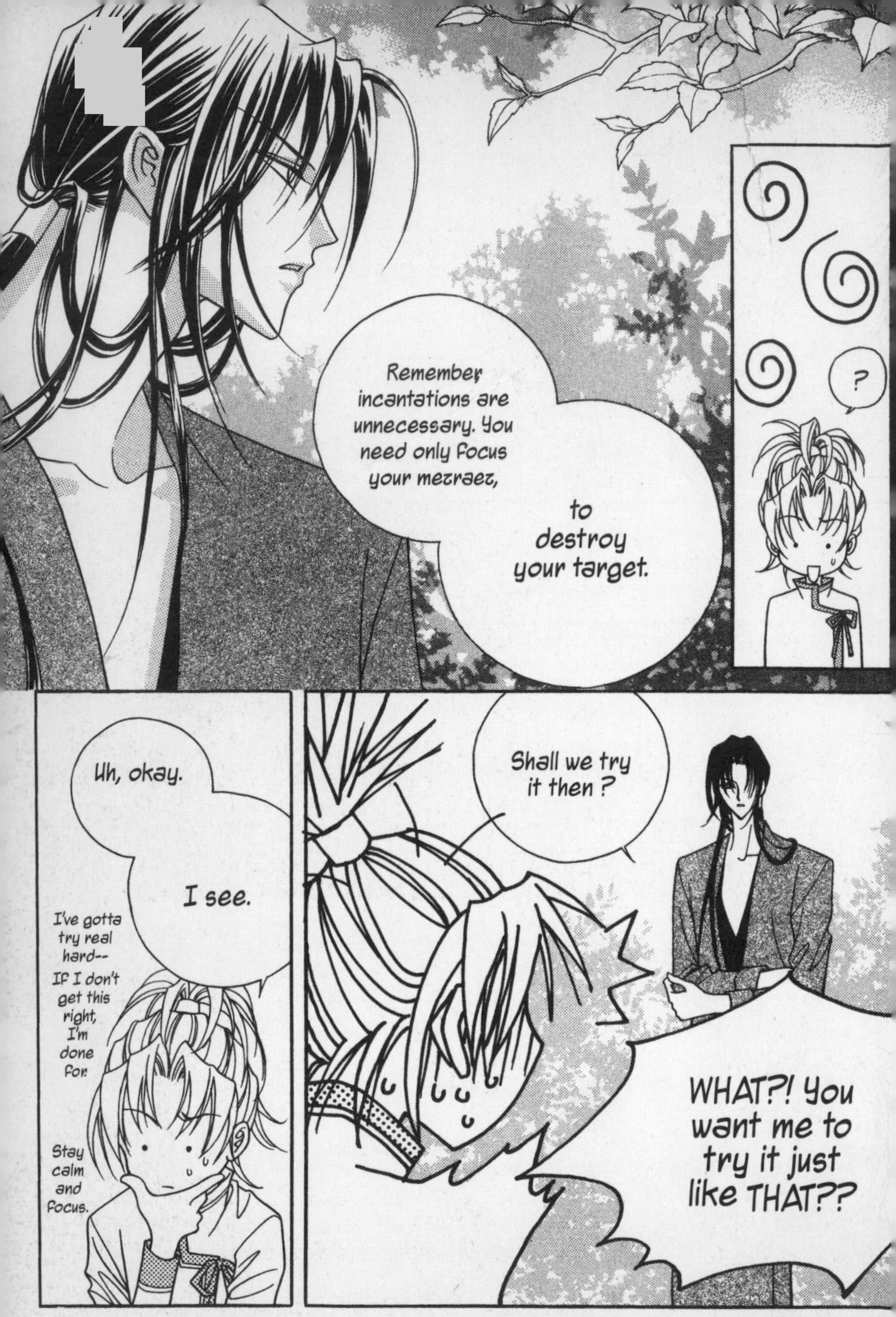
Remember, incantations are unnecessary. You need only focus your mezraez,
to destroy your target.
?
Uh, okay.
I see.
I've gotta try real hard-- If I don't get this right, I'm done for.
Stay calm and focus.
Shall we try it then?
WHAT?! You want me to try it just like THAT??

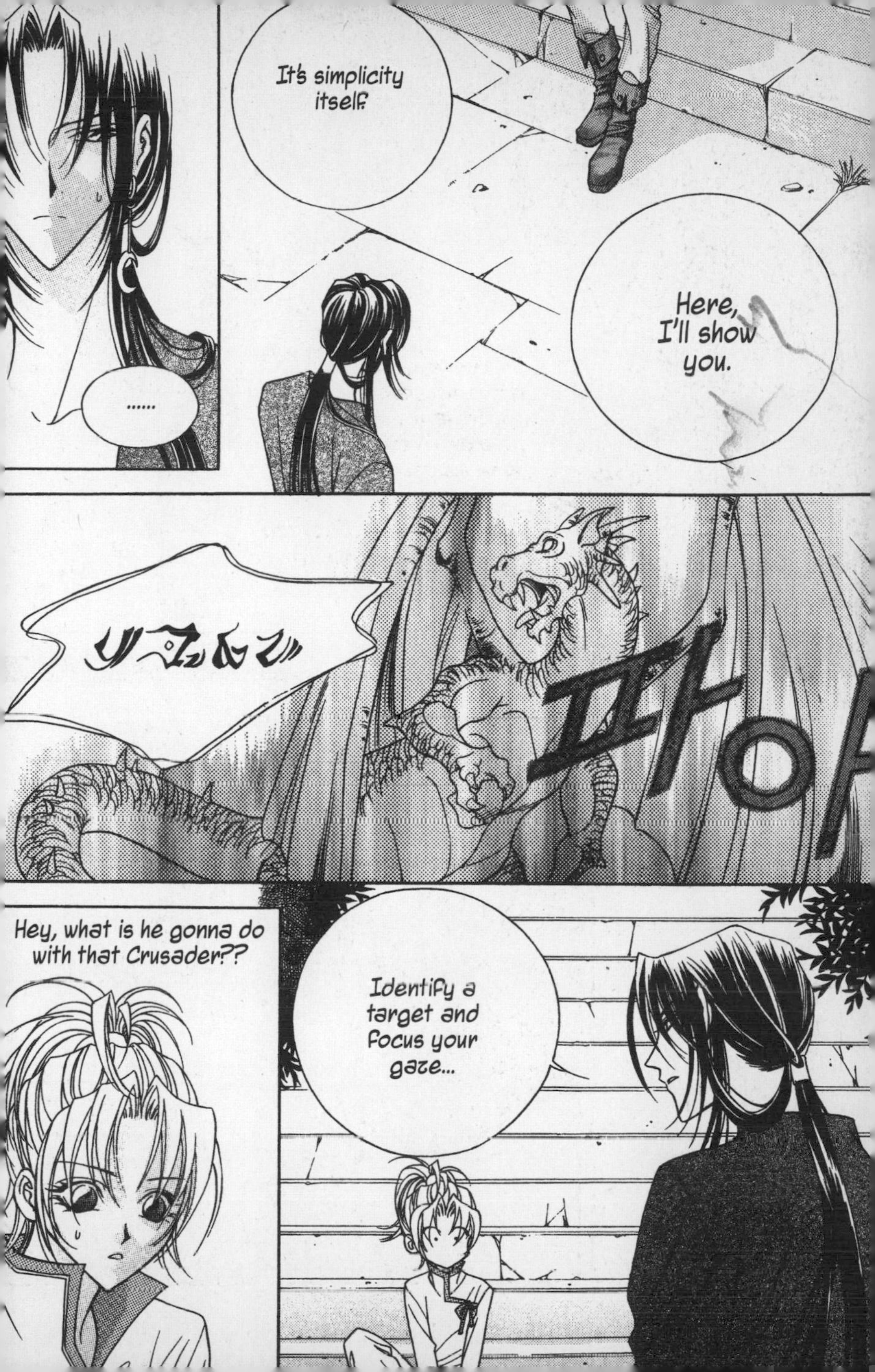
It's simplicity itself.
Here, I'll show you.
......
Identify a target and focus your gaze...
Hey, what is he gonna do with that Crusader??

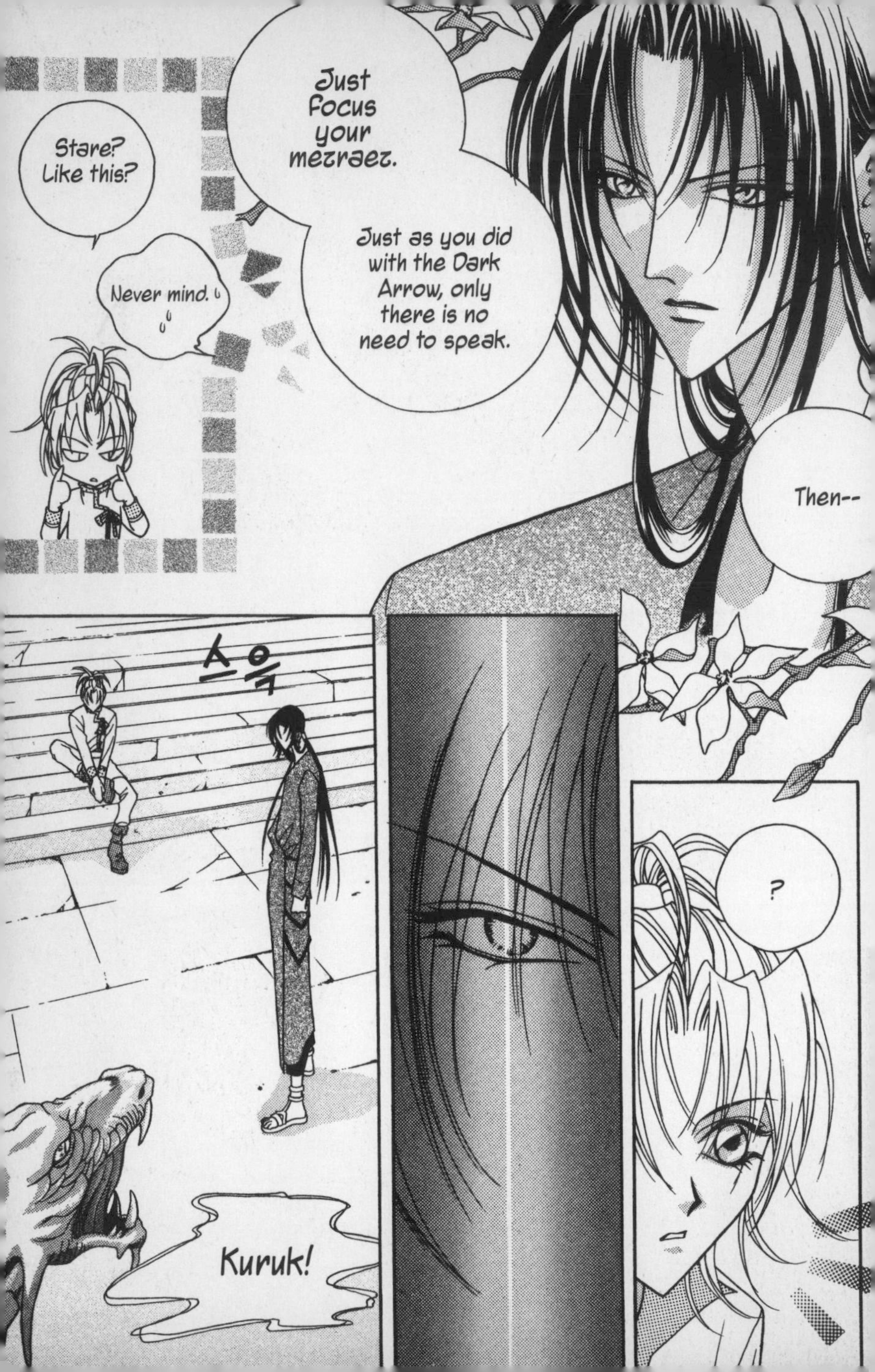

Just focus your mezraez.
Stare? Like this?
Never mind.
Just as you did with the Dark Arrow, only there is no need to speak.
Then--
스윽
?
Kuruk!

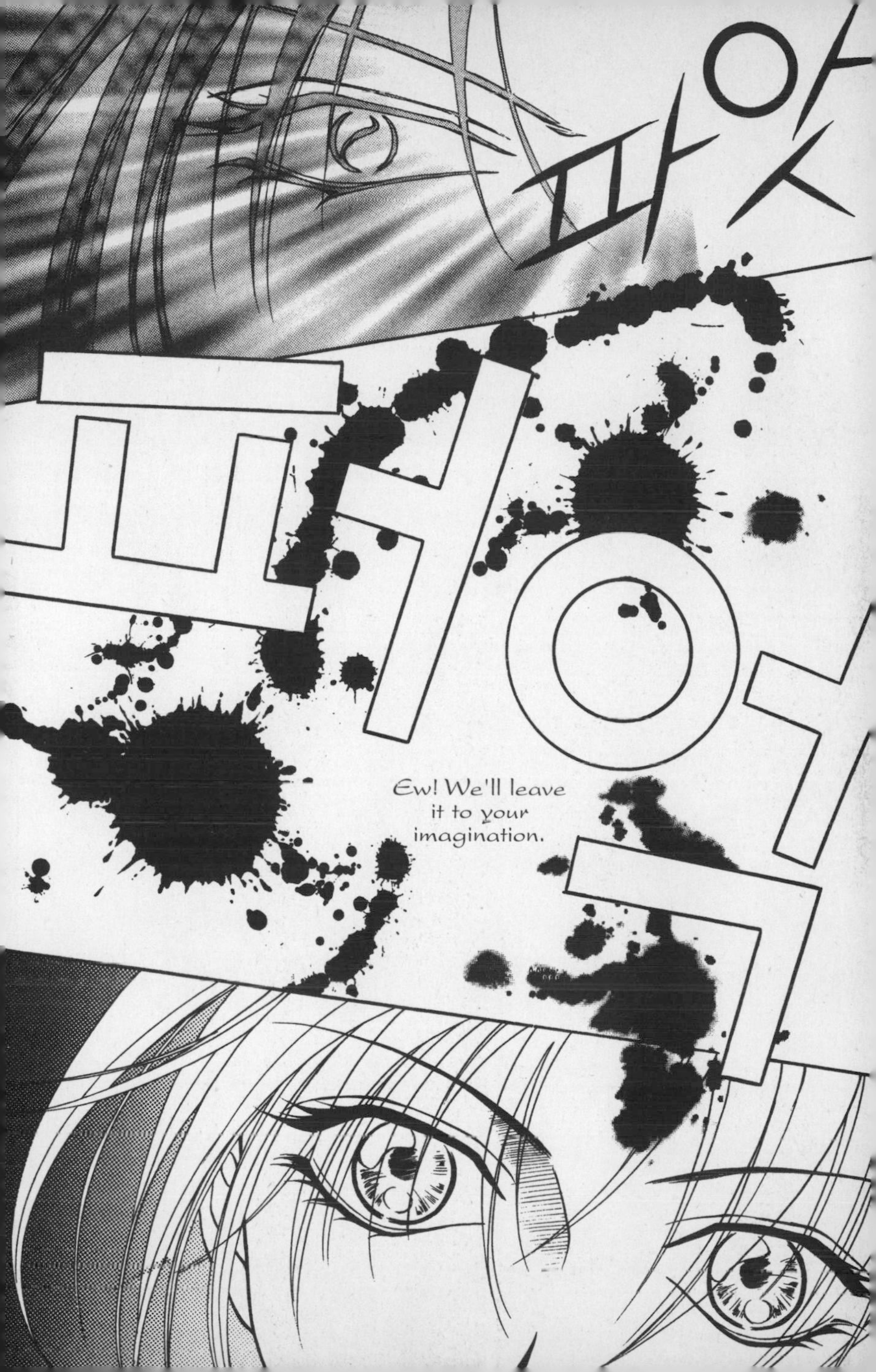
파앗
Ew! We'll leave it to your imagination.

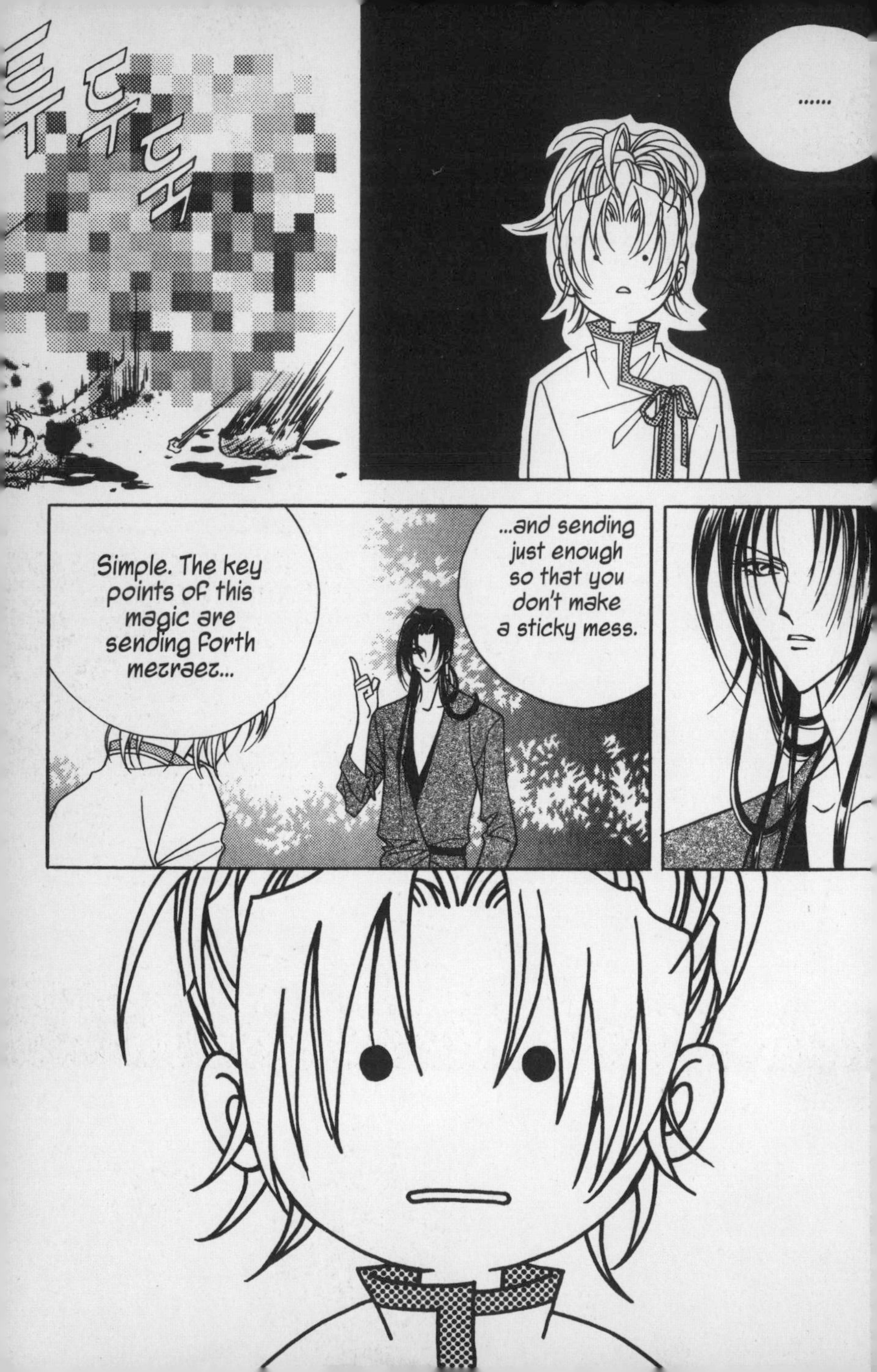
......
...and sending just enough so that you don't make a sticky mess.
Simple. The key points of this magic are sending forth metraet...

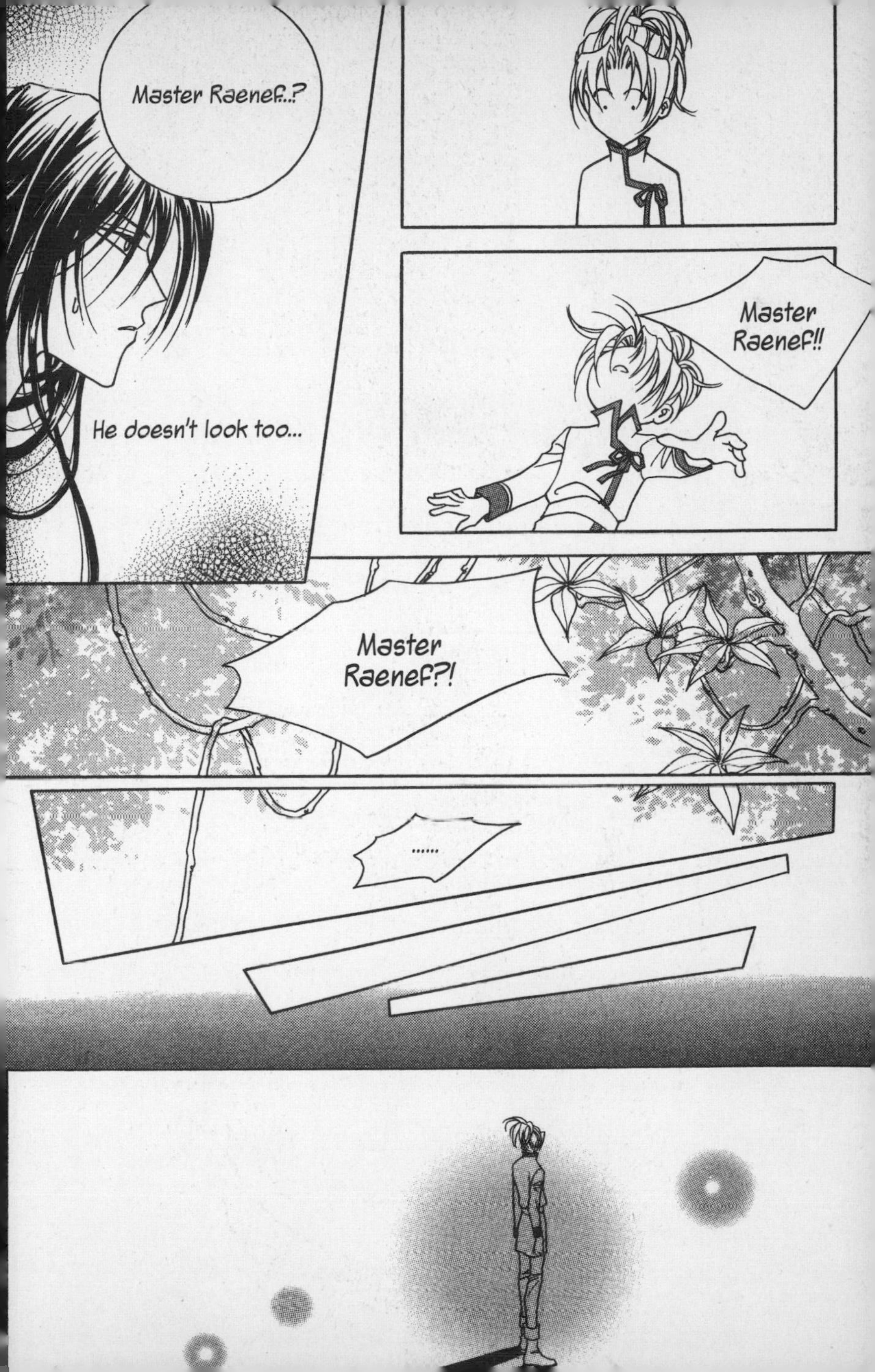
Master Raenef..?
He doesn't look too...
Master Raenef!!
Master Raenef?!
......

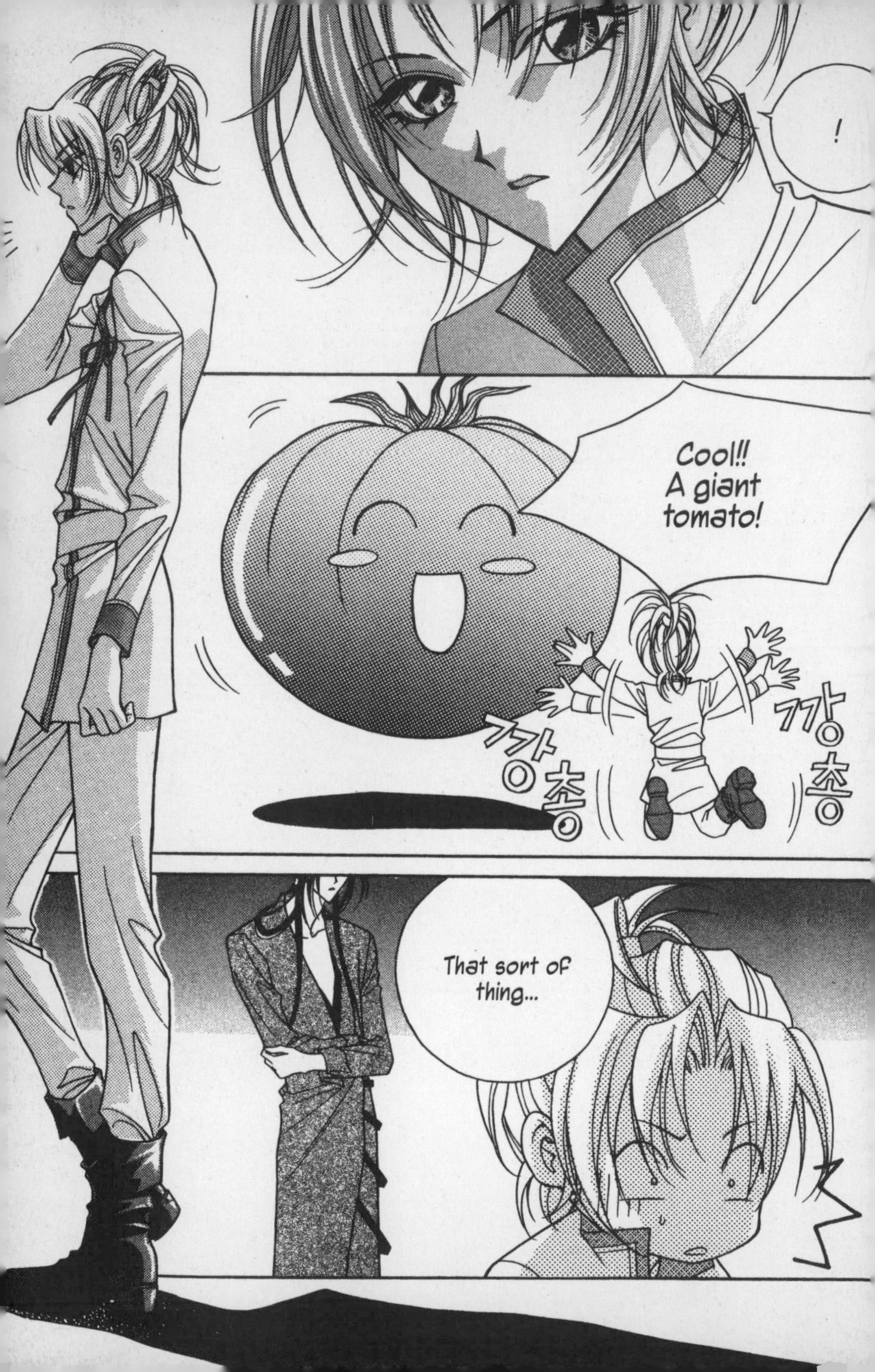
!
Cool!! A giant tomato!
깡총
깡총
That sort of thing...

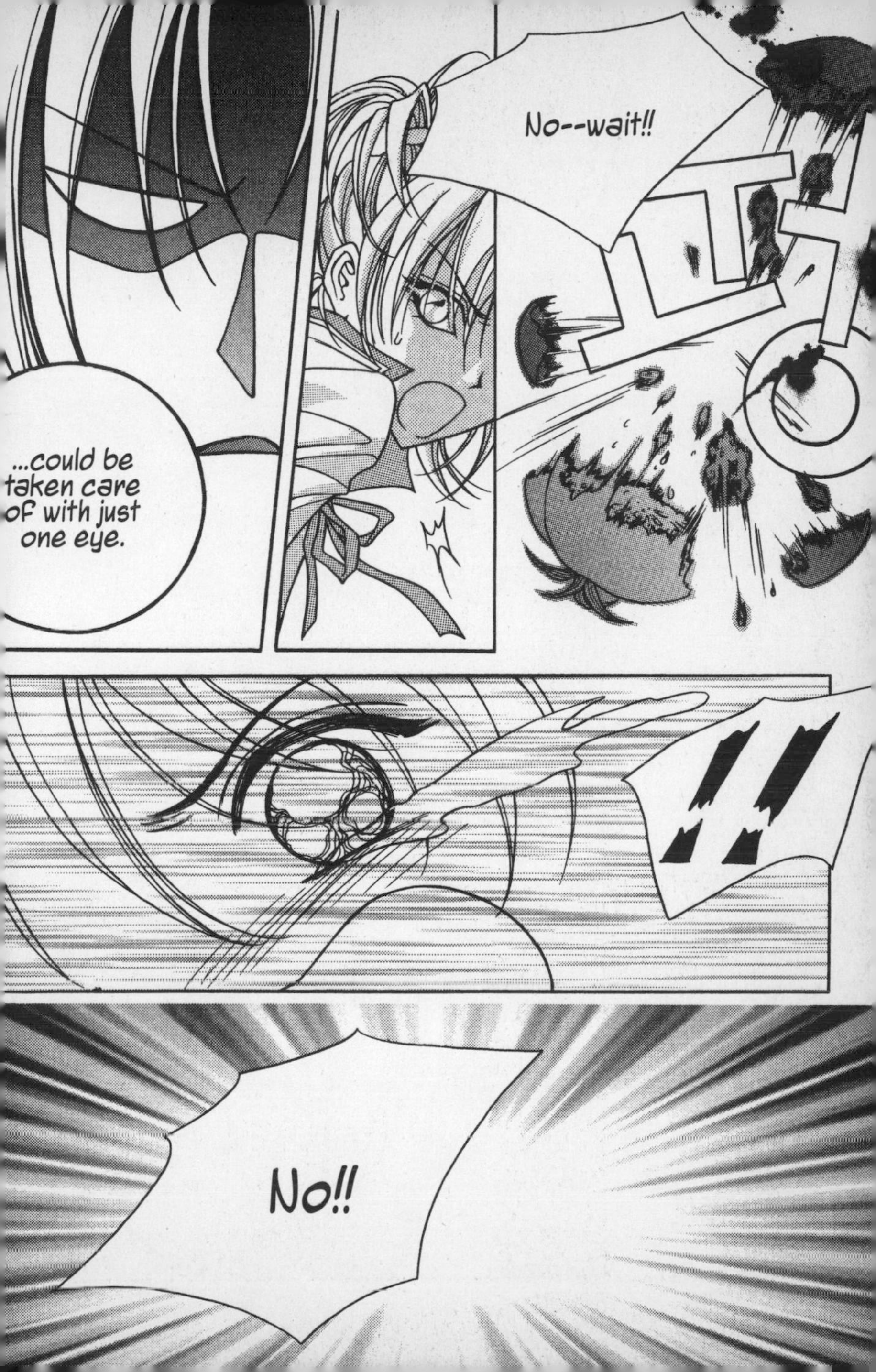
No--wait!!
...could be taken care of with just one eye.
!!
No!!

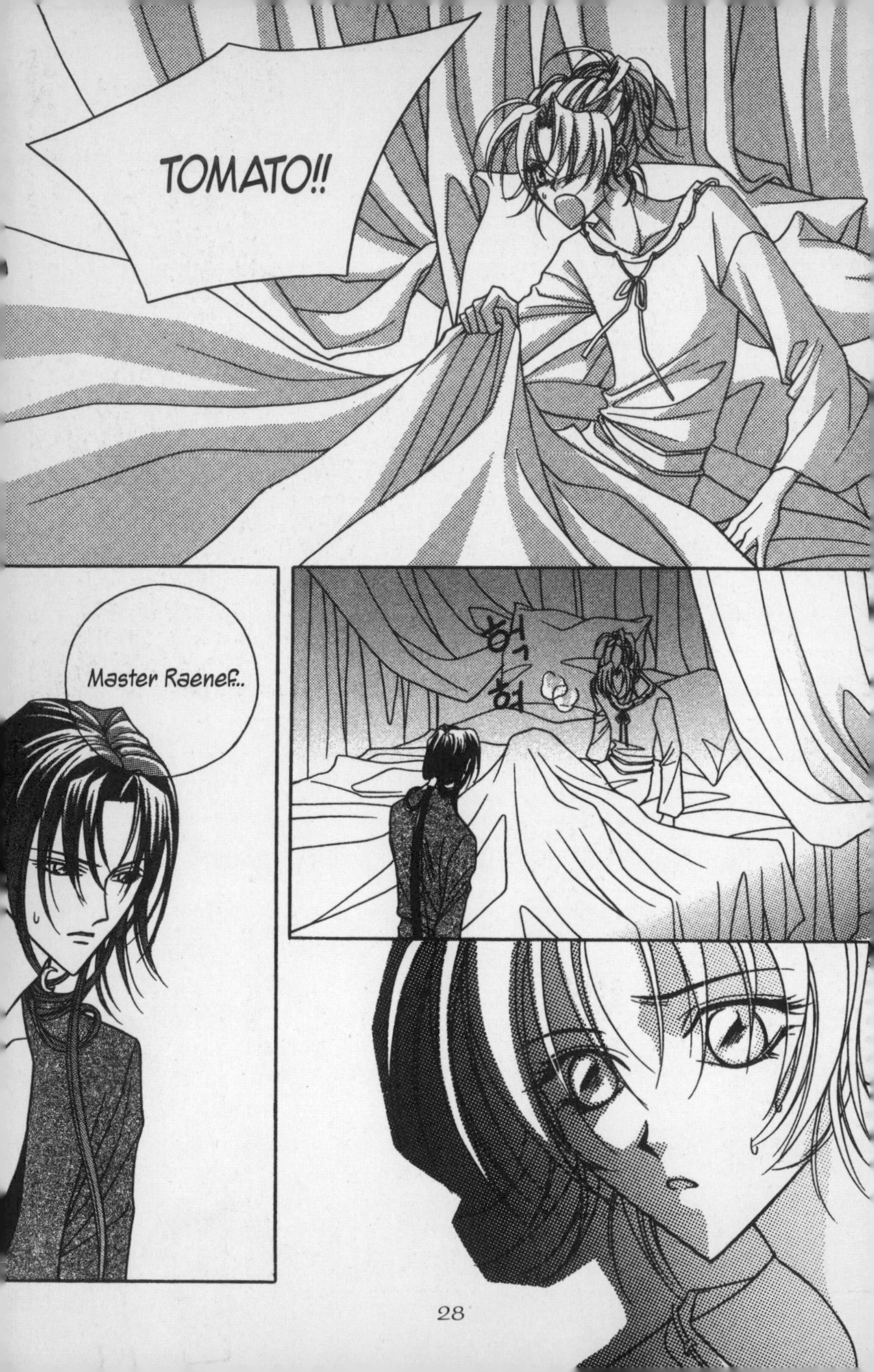
TOMATO!!
Master Raenef..

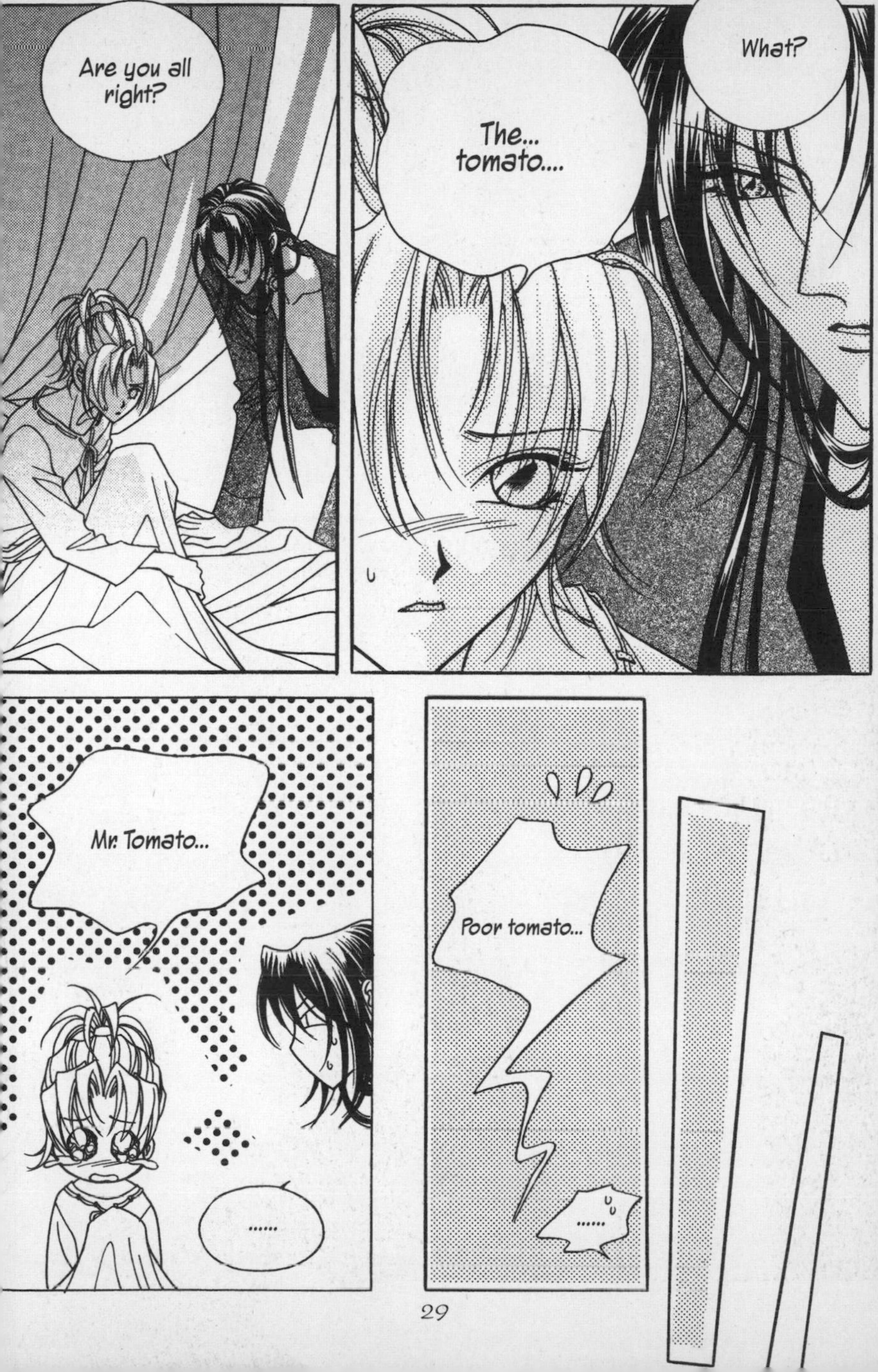

Are you all right?
The... tomato....
What?
Mr. Tomato...
......
Poor tomato...
......

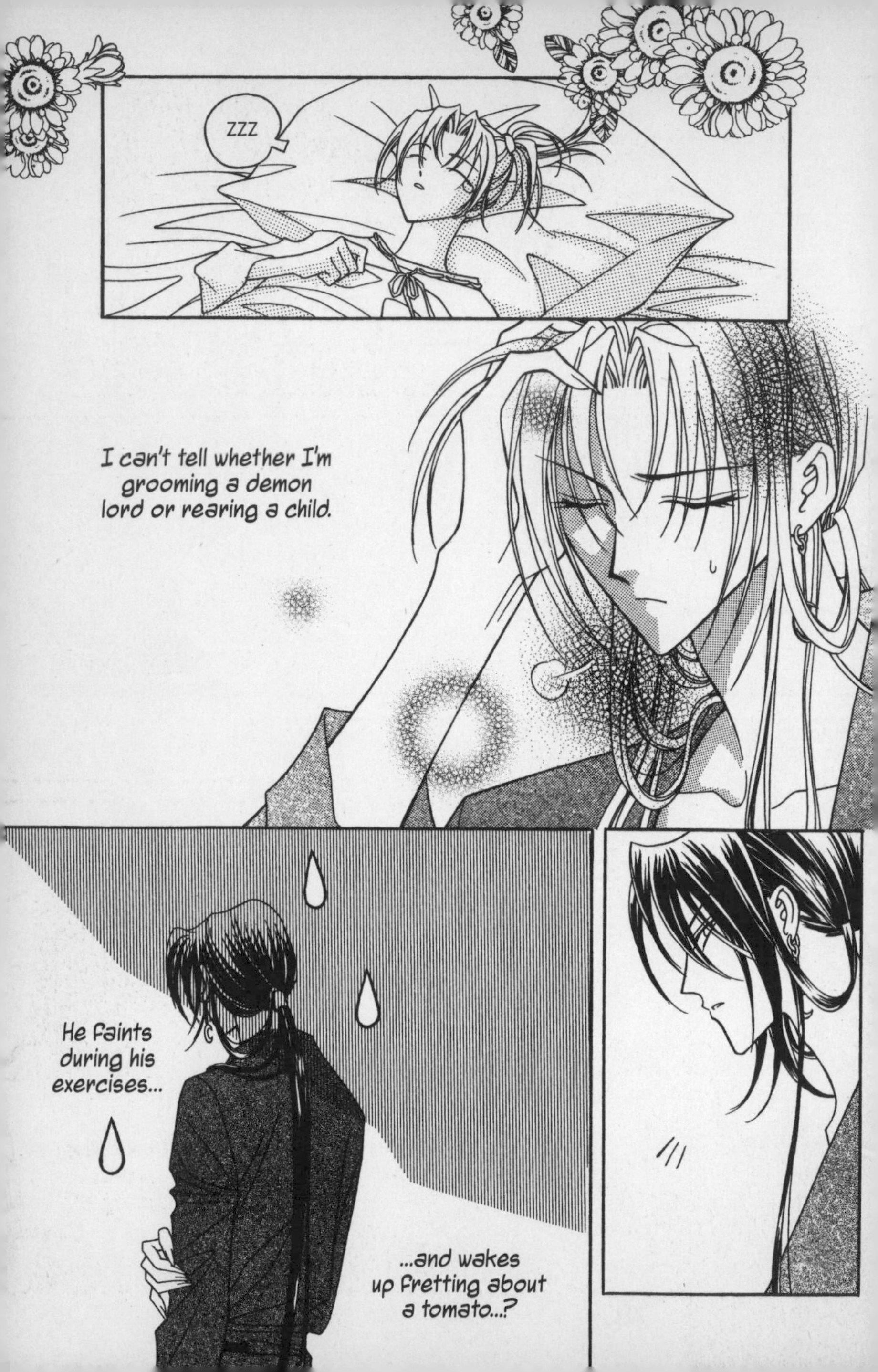
ZZZ
I can't tell whether I'm grooming a demon lord or rearing a child.
He faints during his exercises...
...and wakes up fretting about a tomato...?

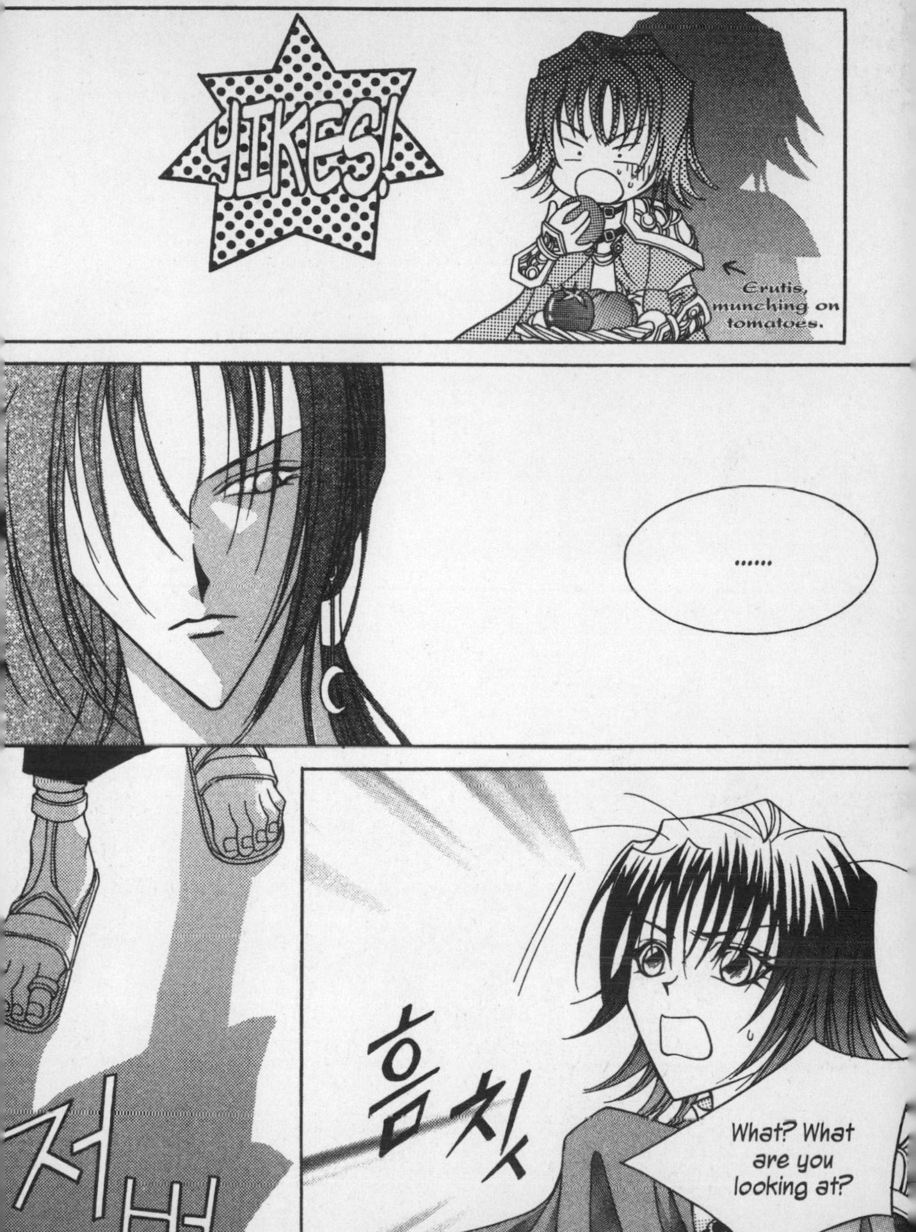
YIKES!
Erutis, munching on tomatoes.
......
저벅
흠칫
What? What are you looking at?

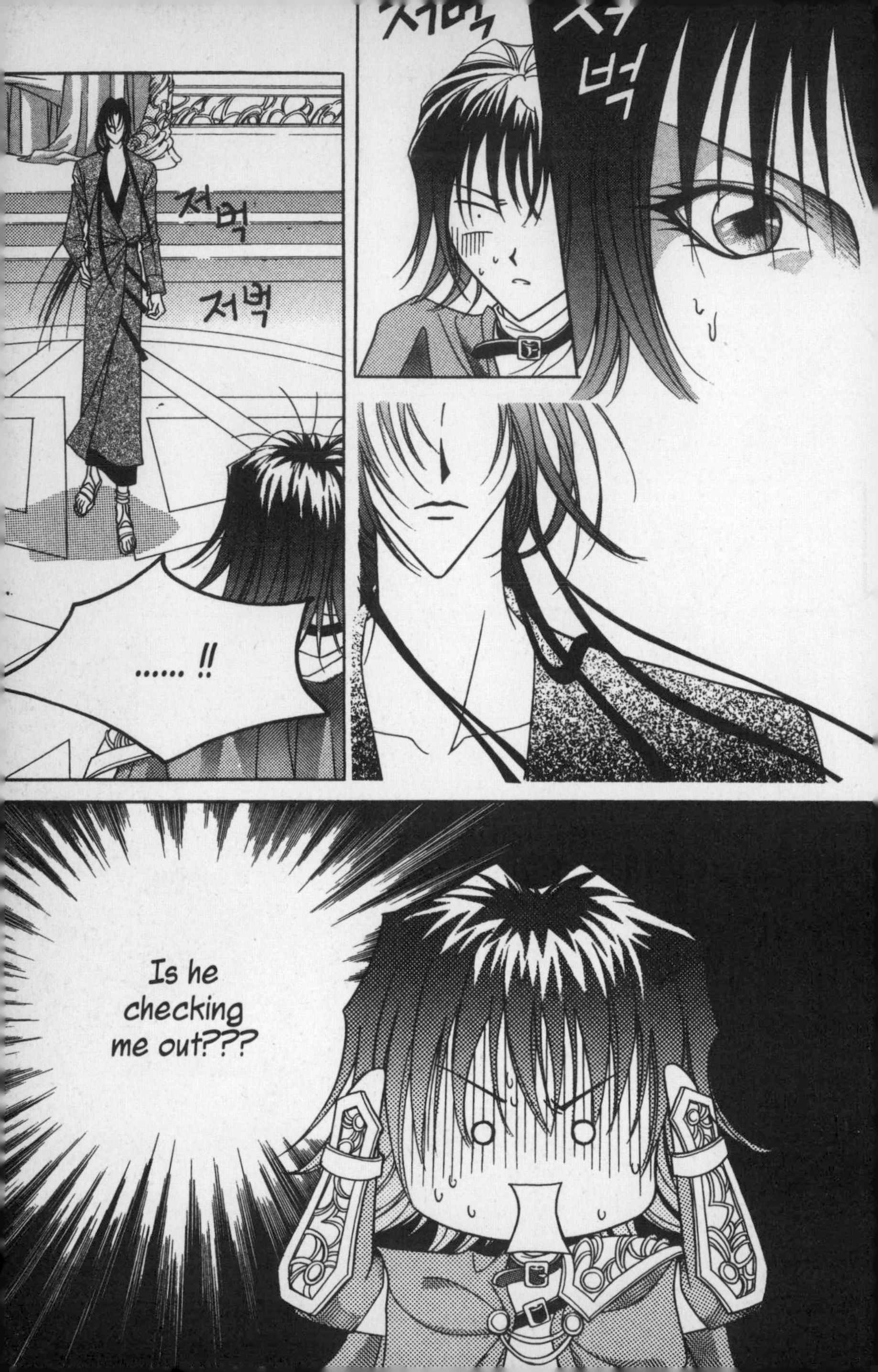
저벅
저벅
......!!
Is he checking me out???

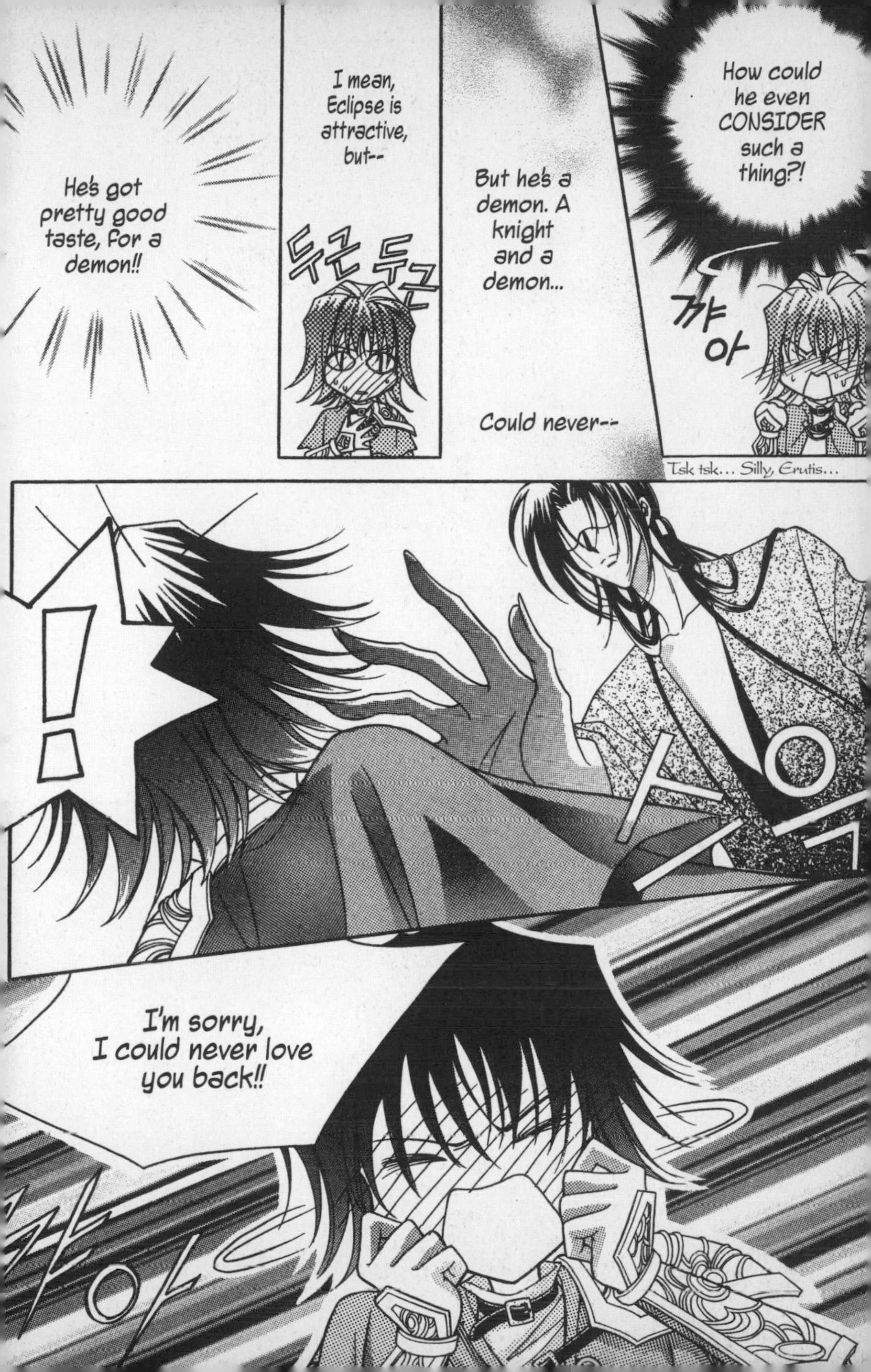
He's got pretty good taste, for a demon!!
I mean, Eclipse is attractive, but--
두근 두근
But he's a demon. A knight and a demon...
Could never--
How could he even CONSIDER such a thing?!
꺄아
Tsk tsk... Silly, Erutis...
!
I'm sorry, I could never love you back!!

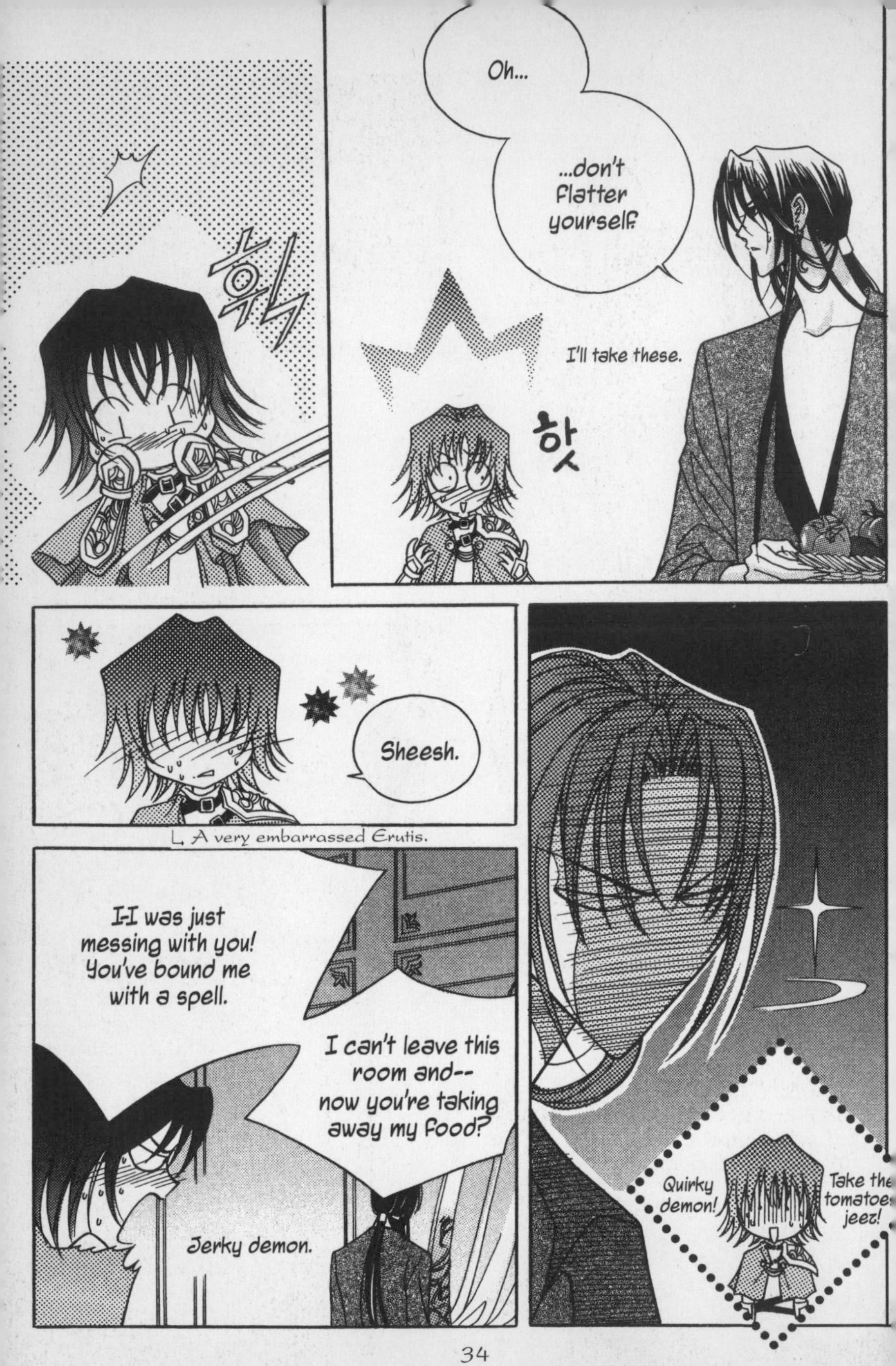
Oh...
...don't flatter yourself.
I'll take these.
핫
훅
Sheesh.
A very embarrassed Erutis.
I-I was just messing with you! You've bound me with a spell.
I can't leave this room and-- now you're taking away my food?
Jerky demon.
Take the tomatoes jeez!
Quirky demon!

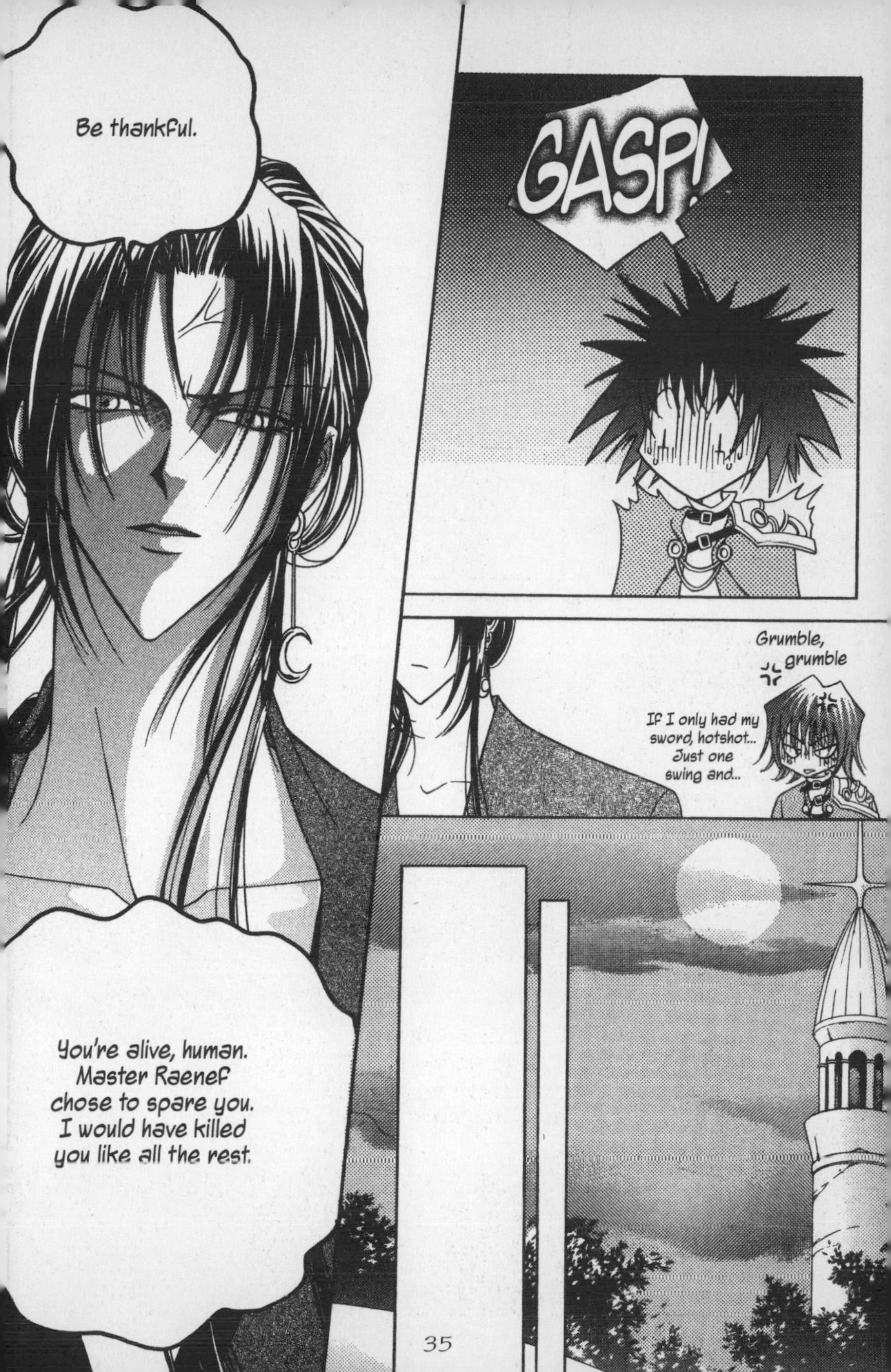

GASP!
Be thankful.
Grumble, grumble
If I only had my sword, hotshot... Just one swing and...
You're alive, human. Master Raenef chose to spare you. I would have killed you like all the rest.

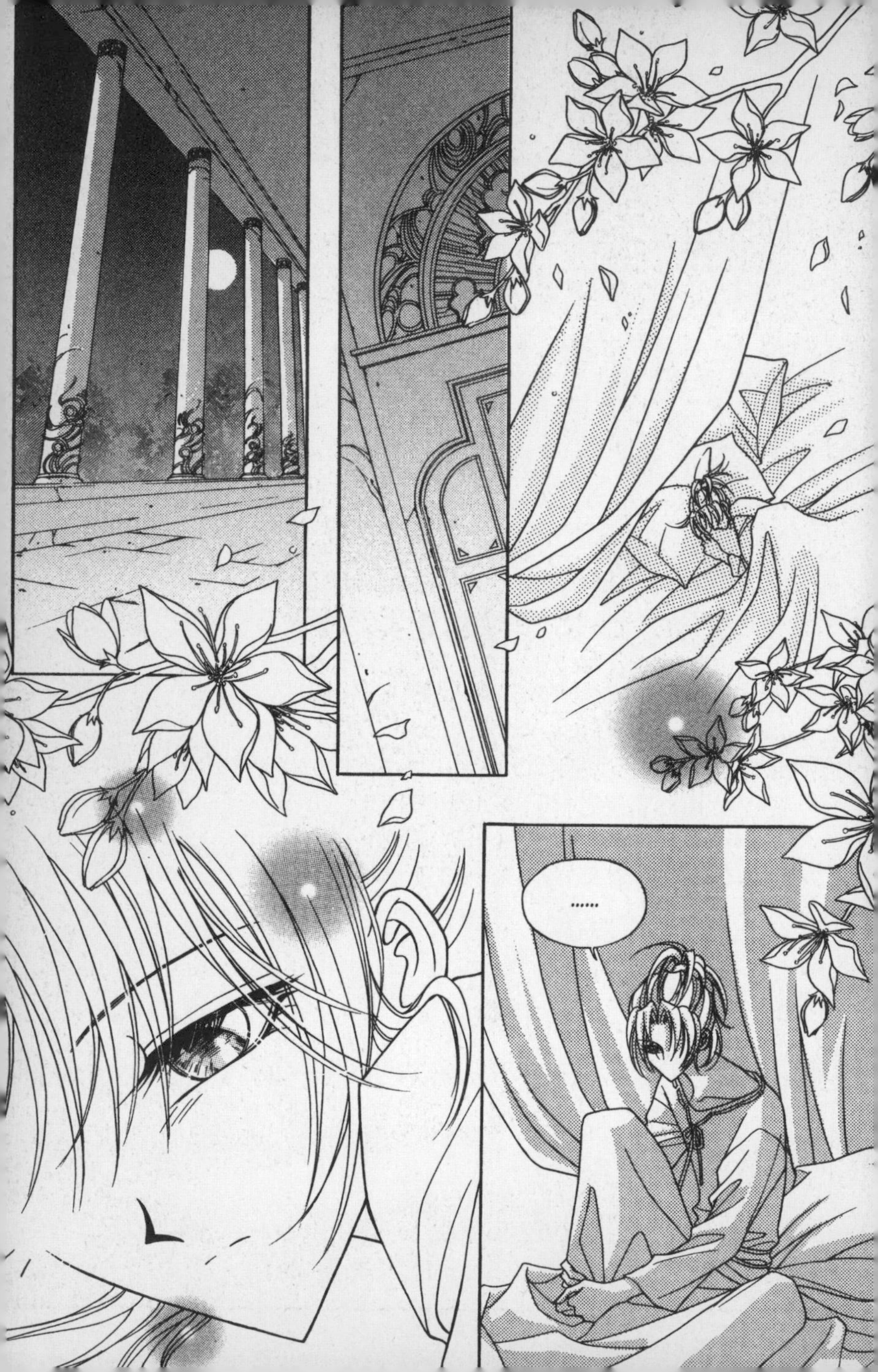
……

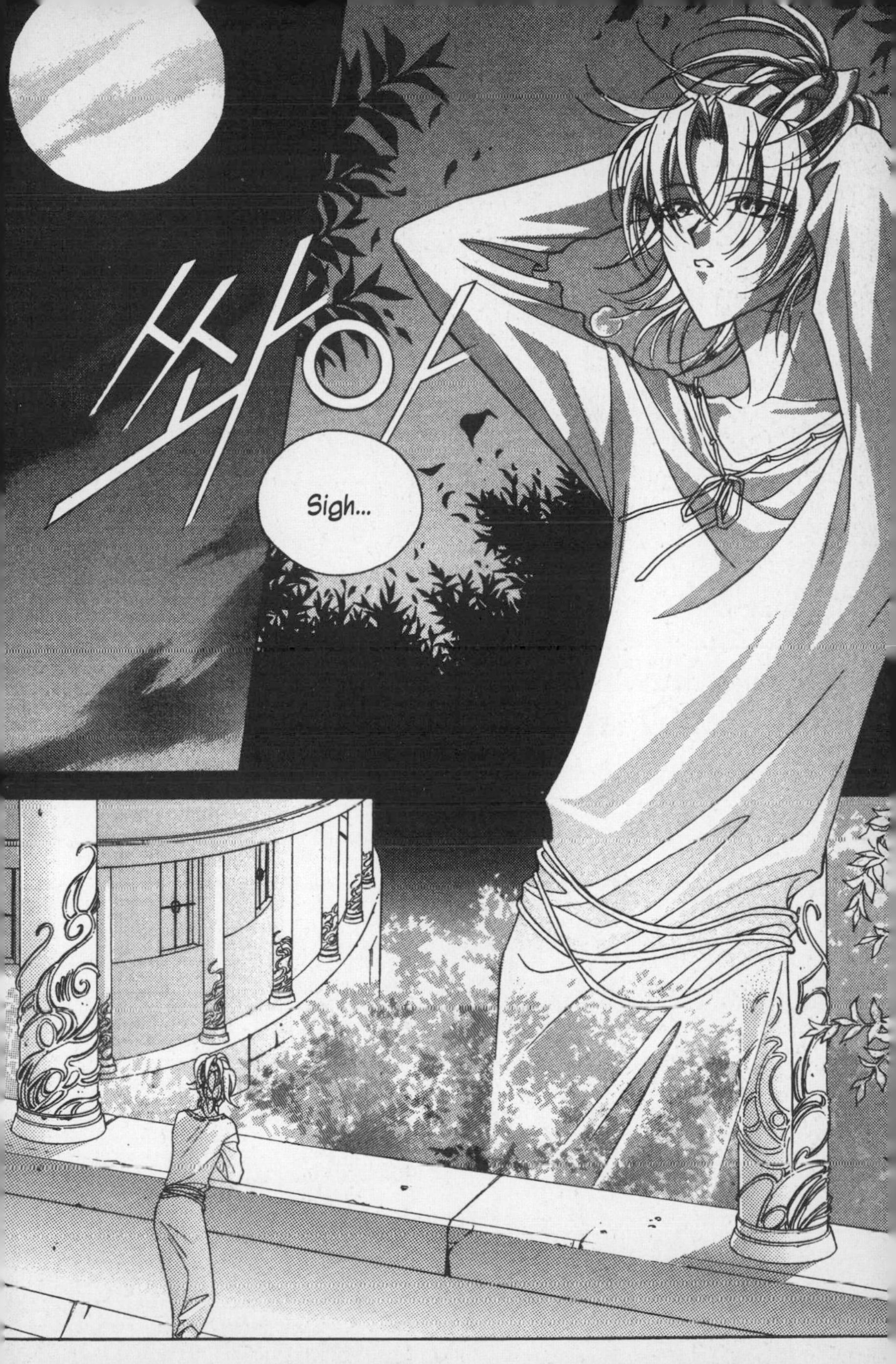
Sigh...

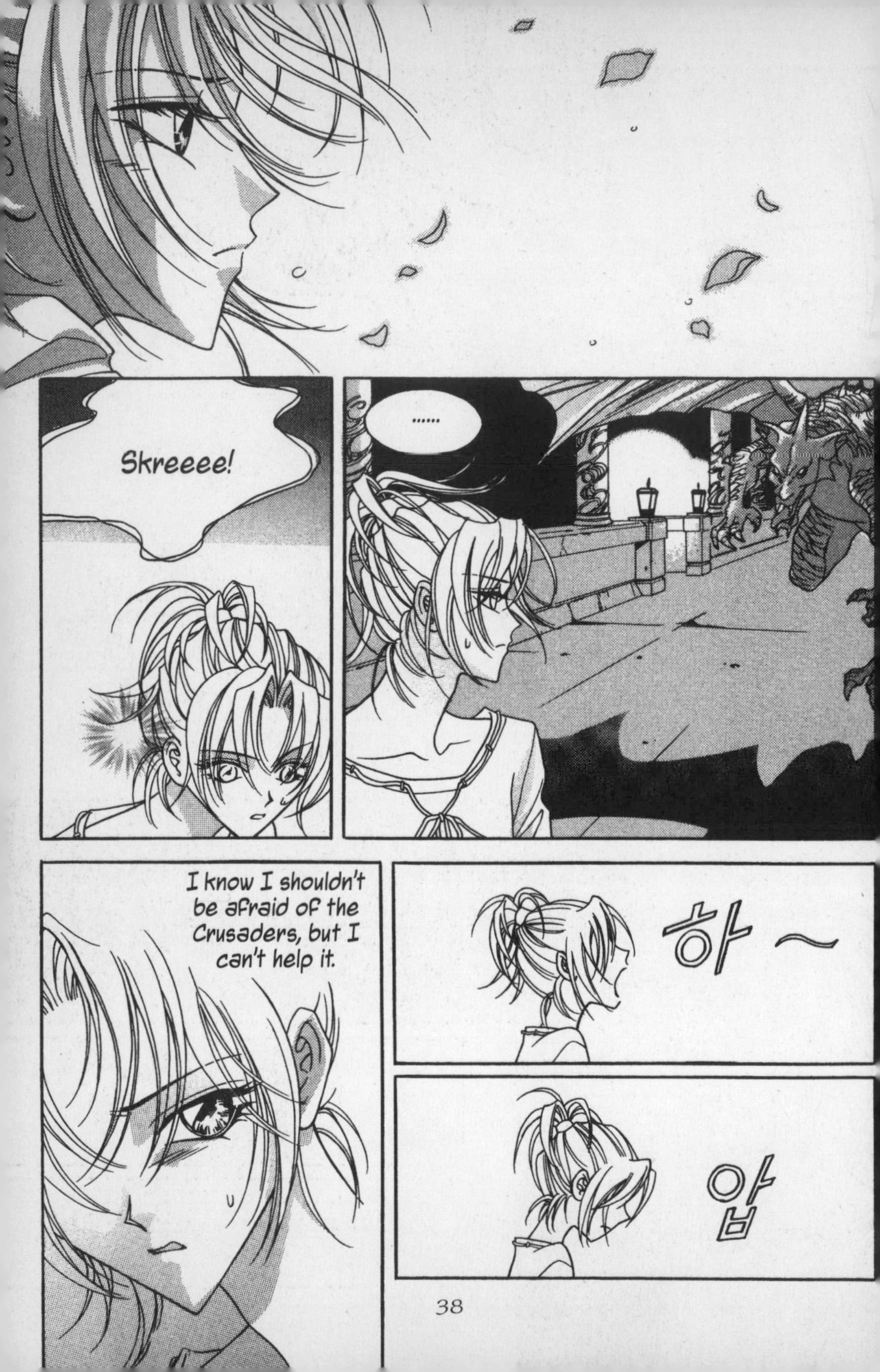
Skreeee!
......
I know I shouldn't be afraid of the Crusaders, but I can't help it.
하~
압

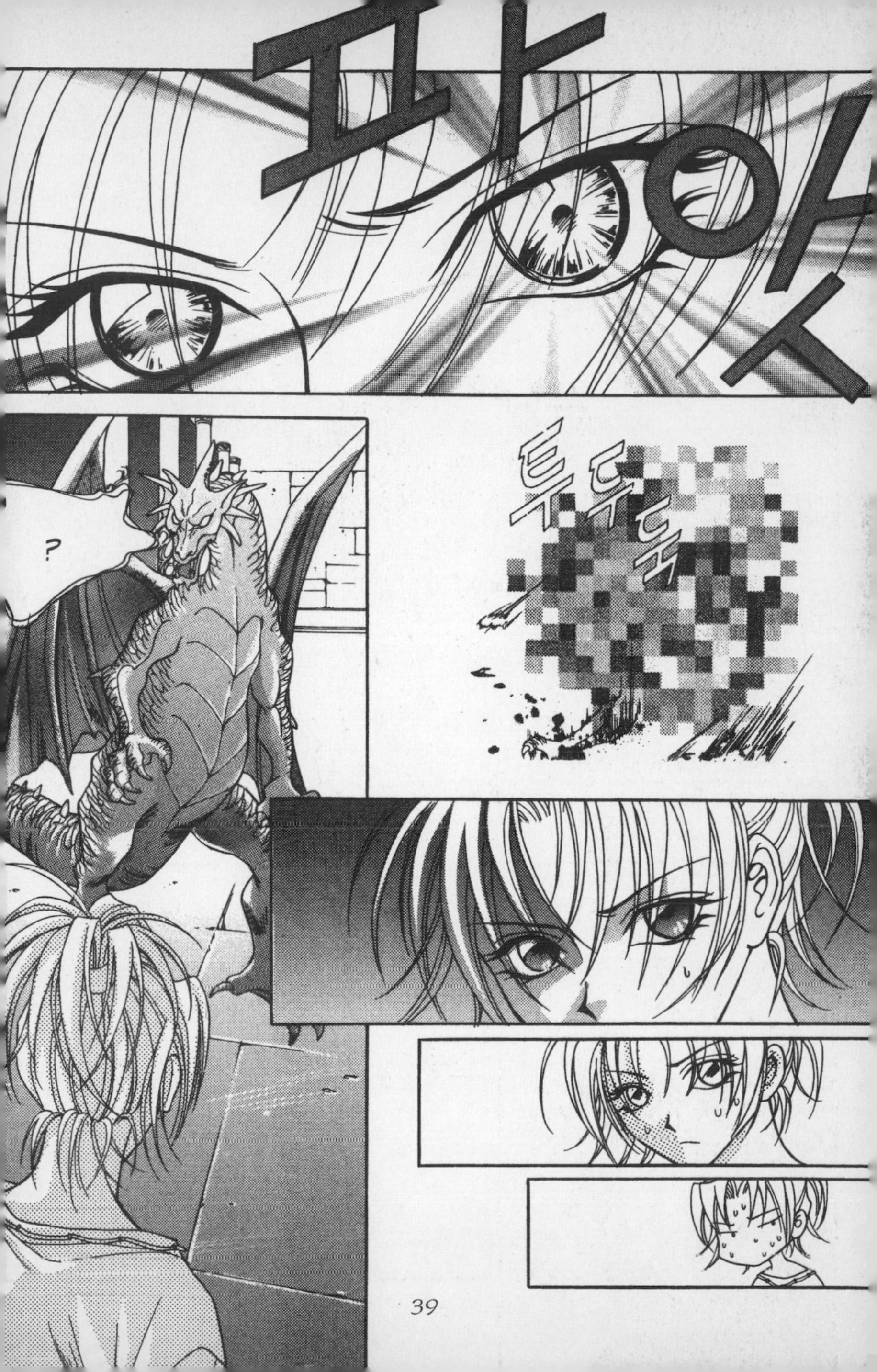
파앗
투두두
?

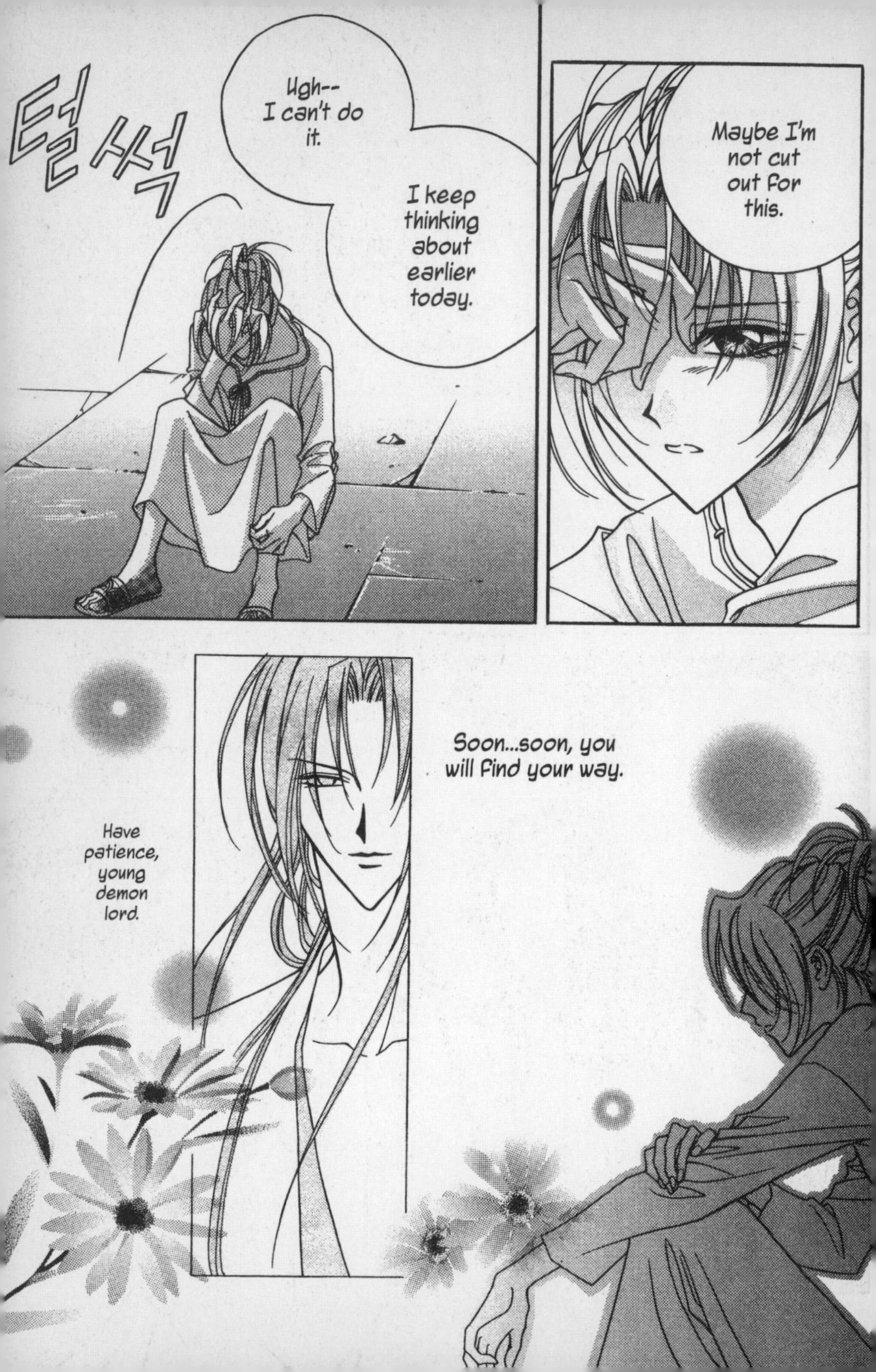
털썩
Ugh-- I can't do it.
I keep thinking about earlier today.
Maybe I'm not cut out for this.
Soon...soon, you will find your way.
Have patience, young demon lord.

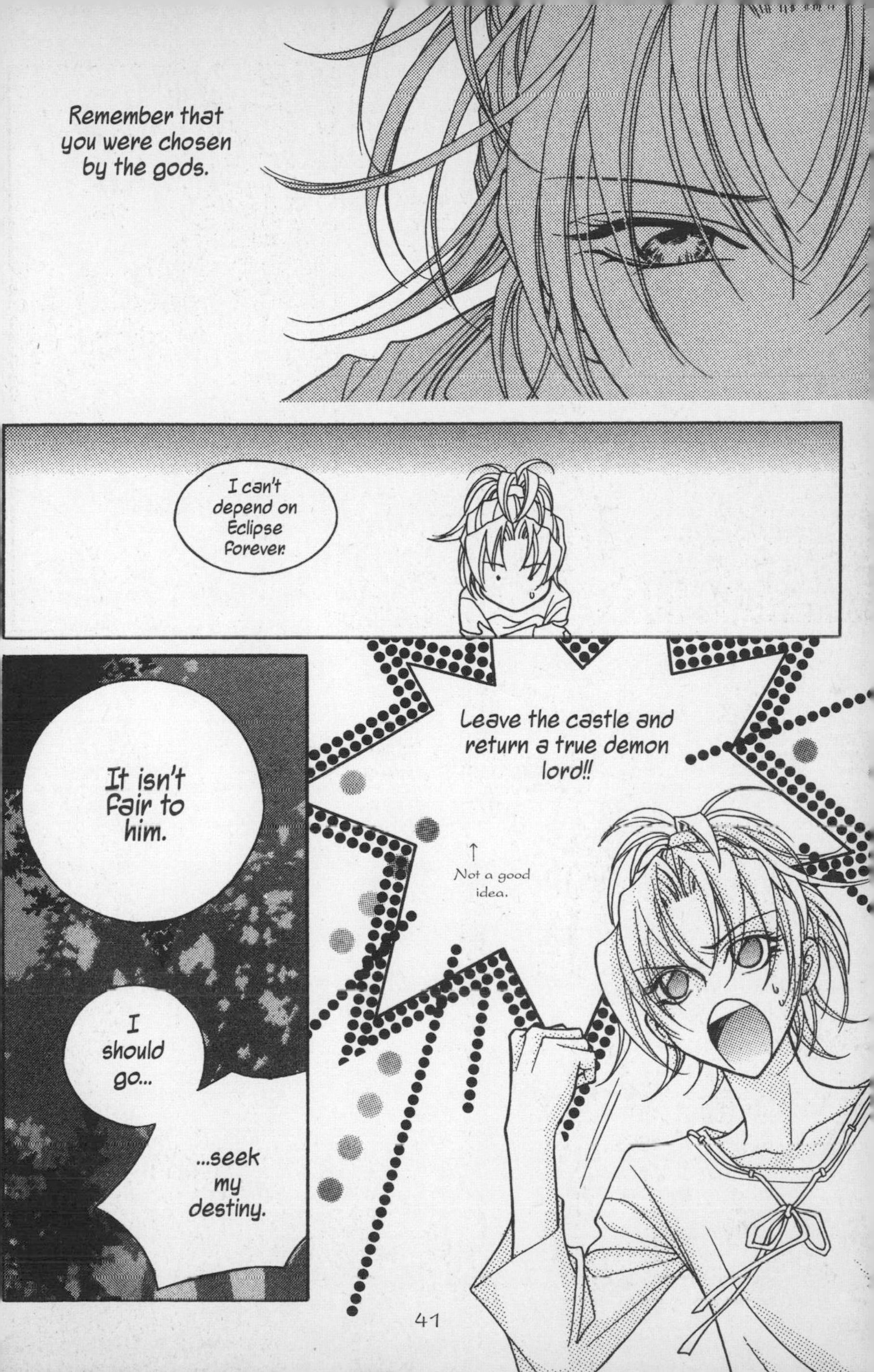
Remember that you were chosen by the gods.
I can't depend on Eclipse forever.
Leave the castle and return a true demon lord!!
↑ Not a good idea.
It isn't fair to him.
I should go...
...seek my destiny.

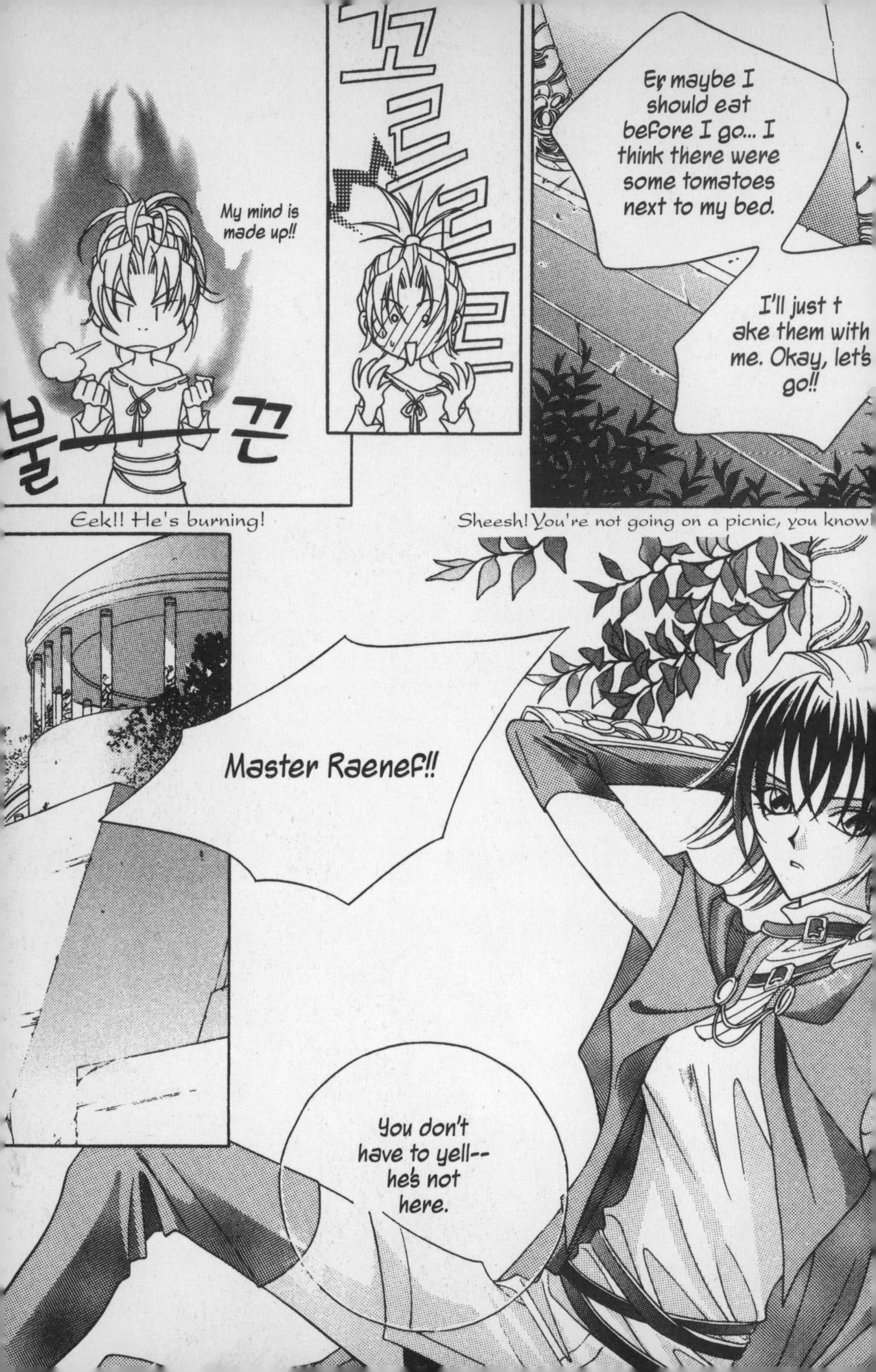
My mind is made up!!
불끈
Eek!! He's burning!
꼬르르르
Er, maybe I should eat before I go... I think there were some tomatoes next to my bed.
I'll just t ake them with me. Okay, let's go!!
Sheesh! You're not going on a picnic, you know!
Master Raenef!!
You don't have to yell--he's not here.

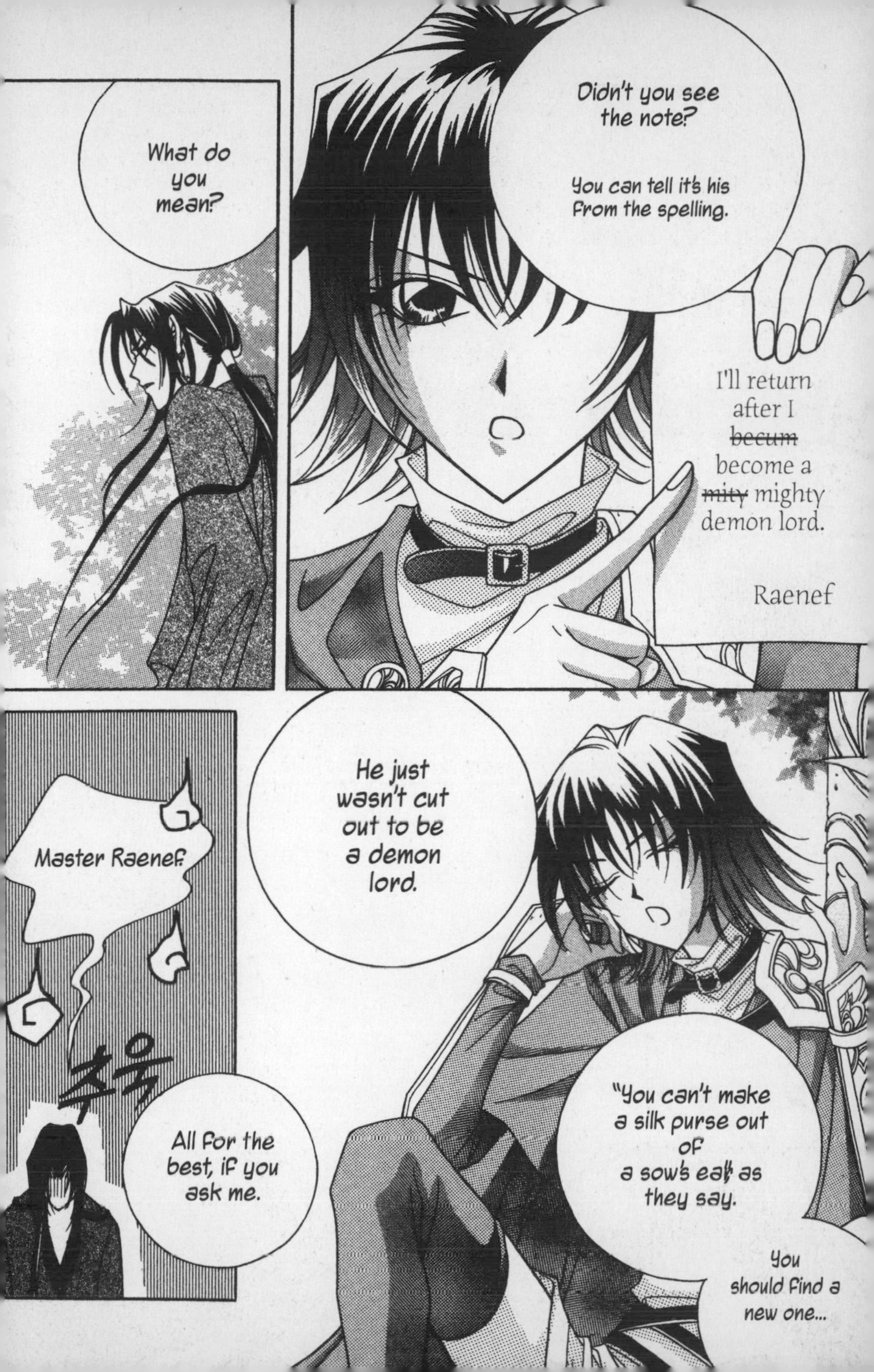

What do you mean?
Didn't you see the note?
You can tell it's his from the spelling.
I'll return after I ~~becum~~ become a ~~mity~~ mighty demon lord.
Raenef
He just wasn't cut out to be a demon lord.
"You can't make a silk purse out of a sow's ear," as they say.
You should find a new one...
Master Raenef.
추욱
All for the best, if you ask me.

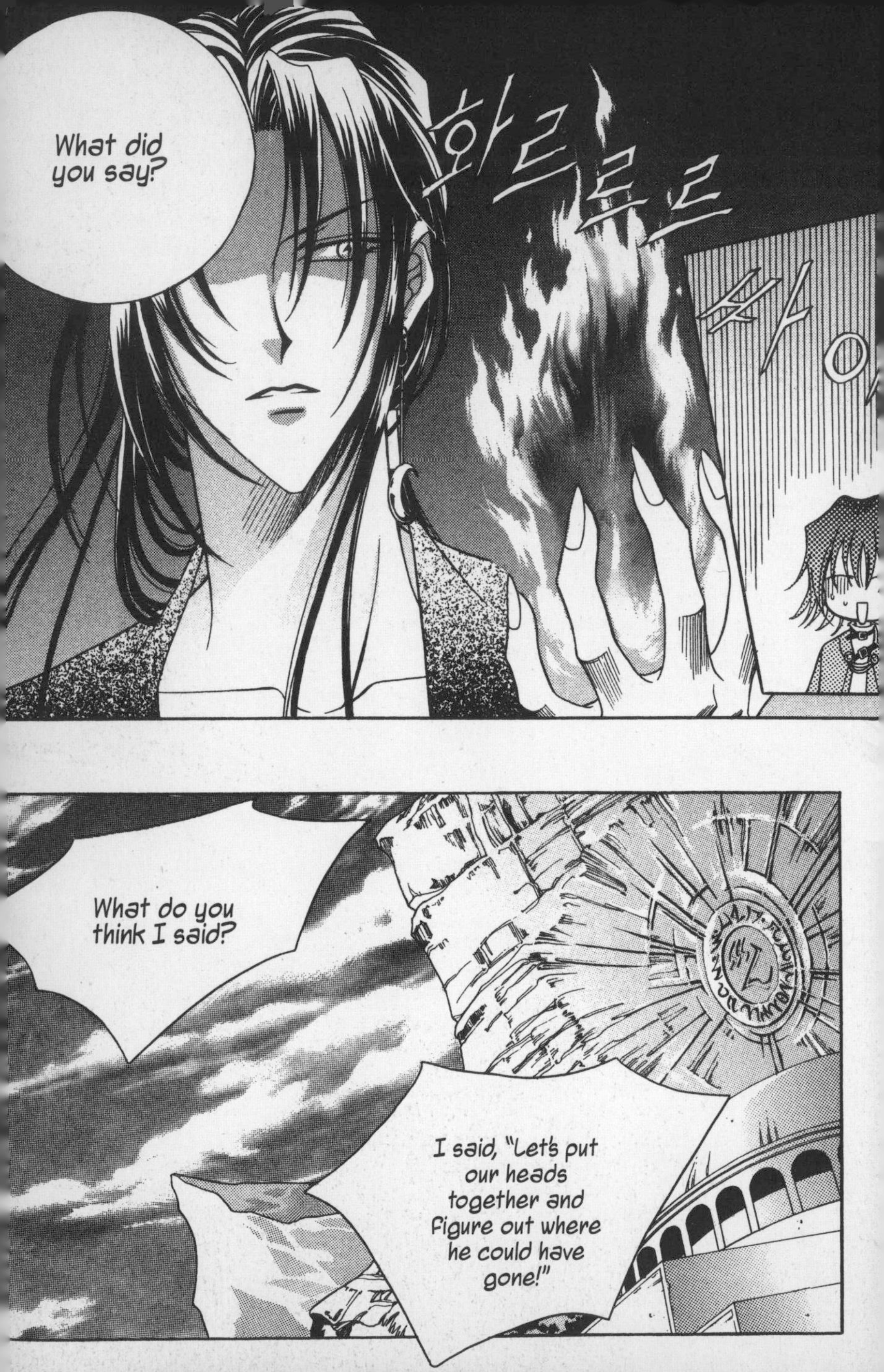
What did you say?
화르르르
What do you think I said?
I said, "Let's put our heads together and figure out where he could have gone!"

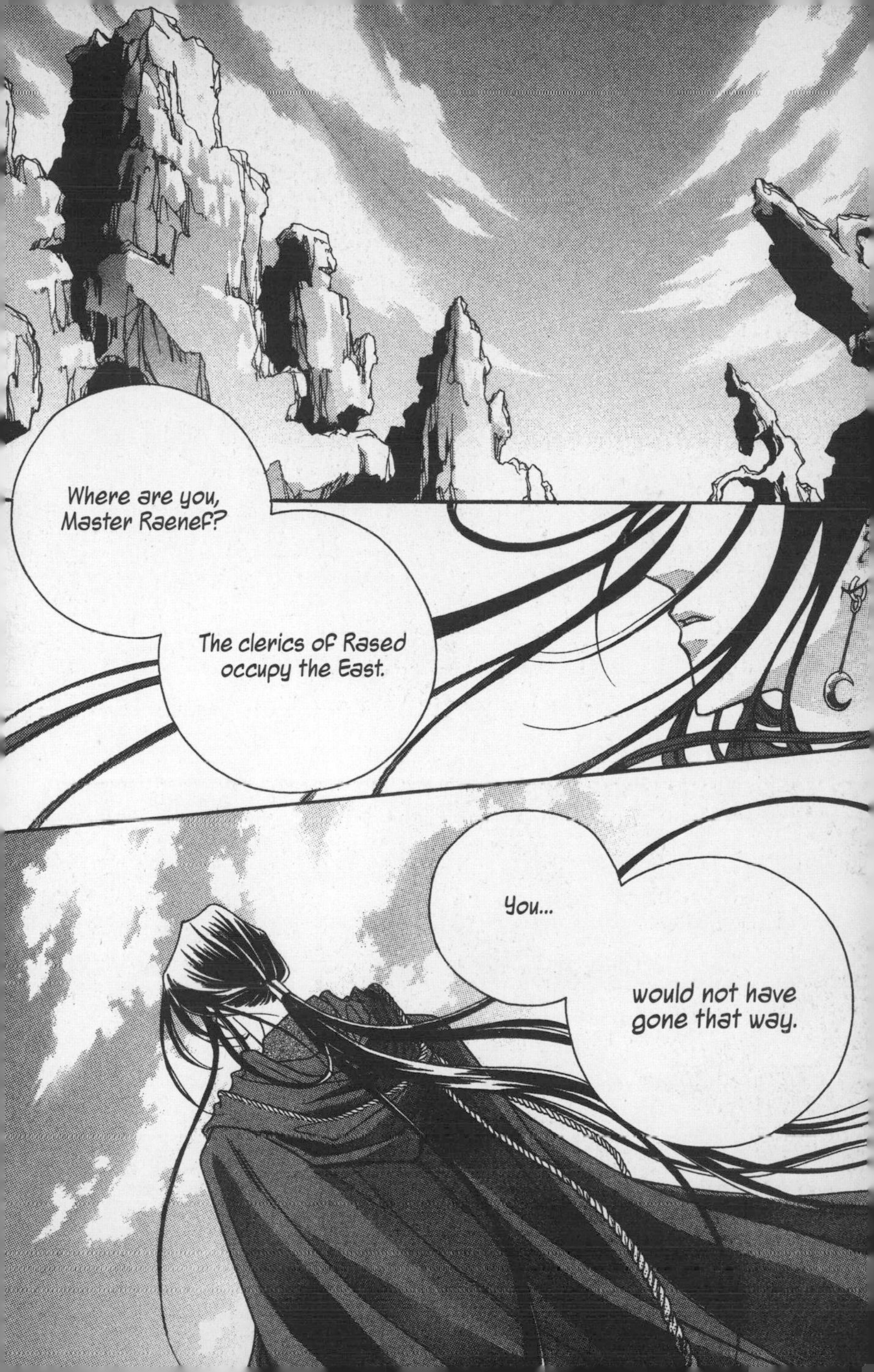
Where are you, Master Raenef?
The clerics of Rased occupy the East.
You...
would not have gone that way.

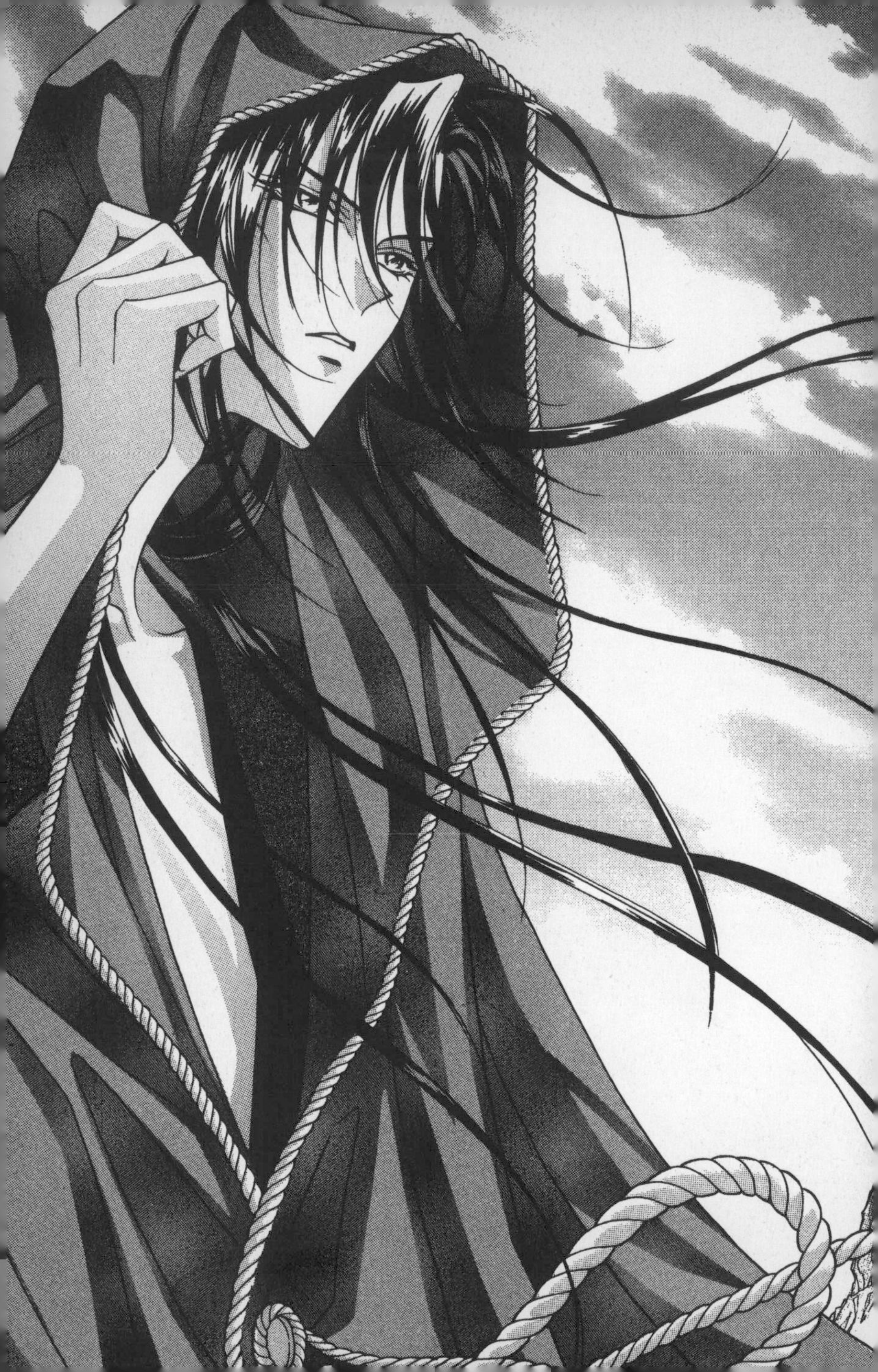

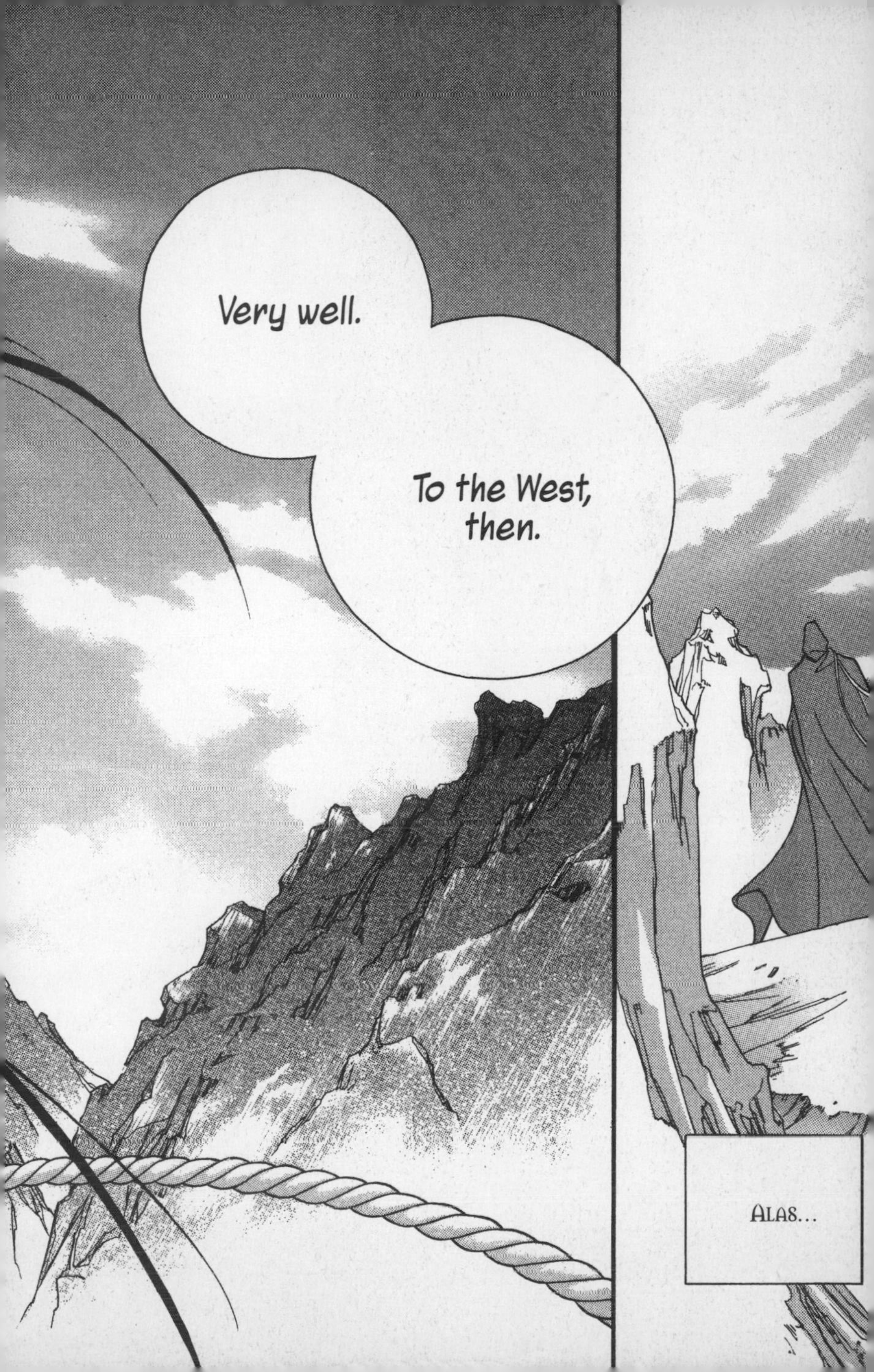
Very well.
To the West, then.
Alas...

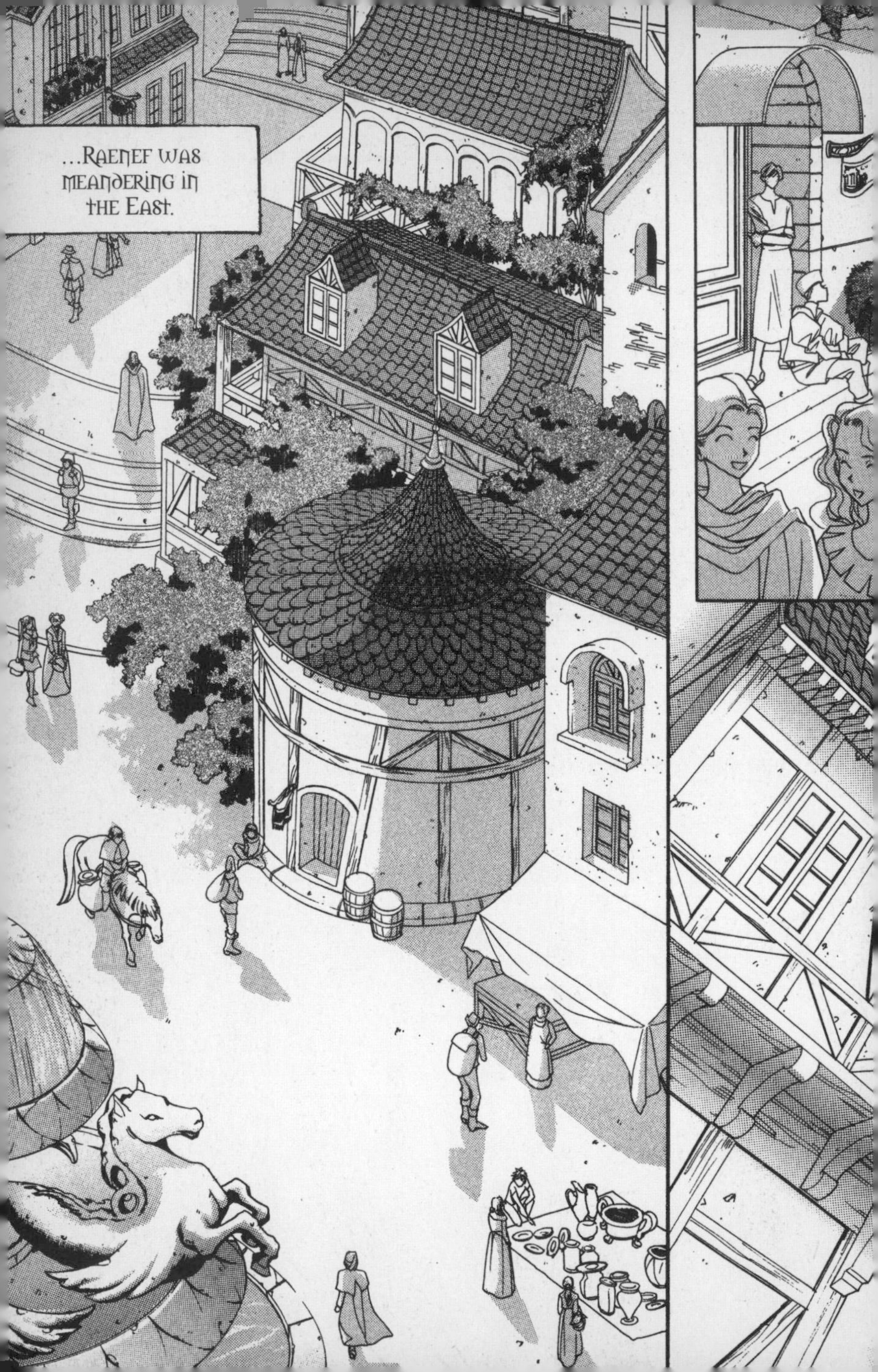
...Raenef was meandering in the East.

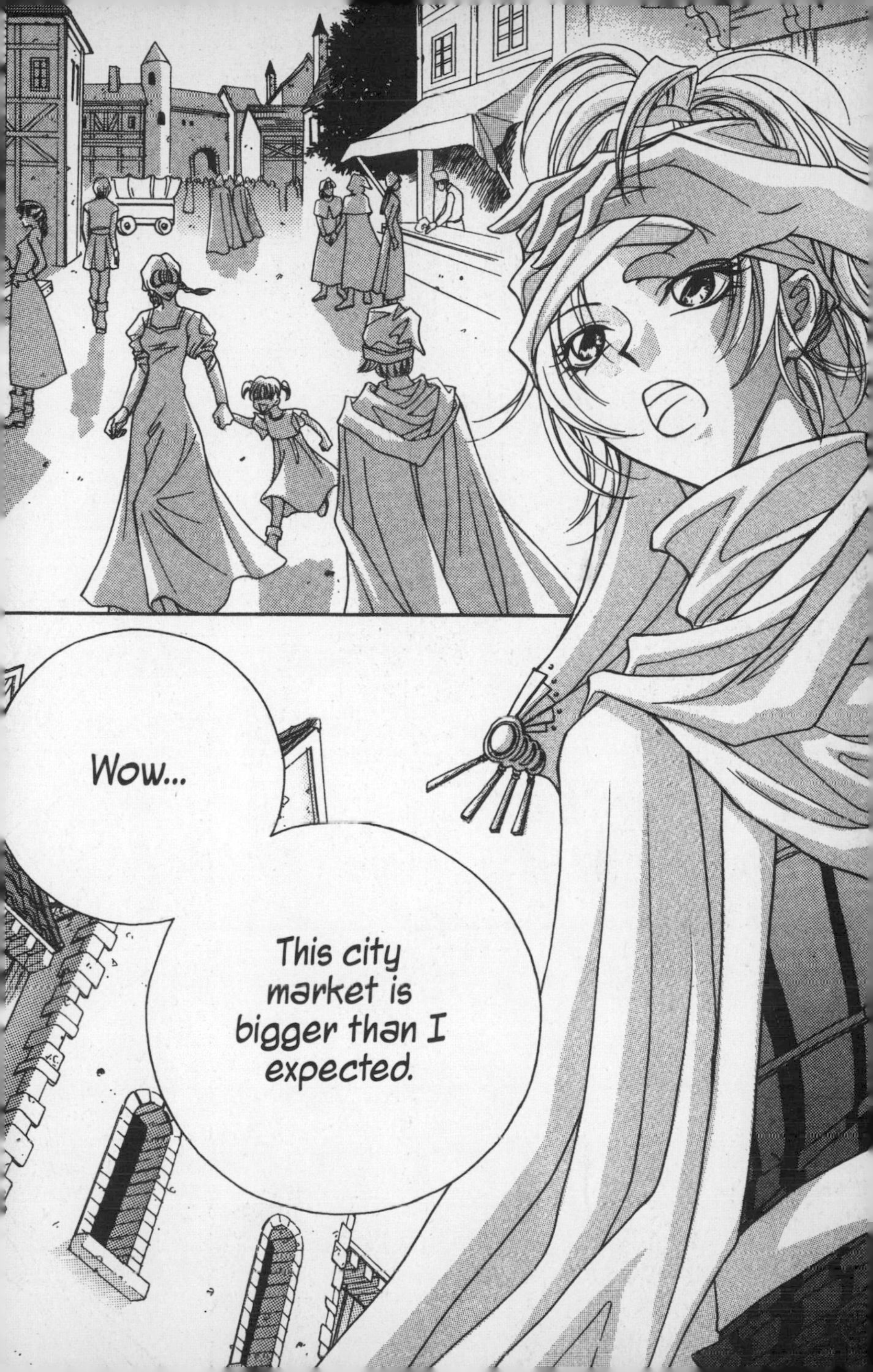
Wow...
This city market is bigger than I expected.

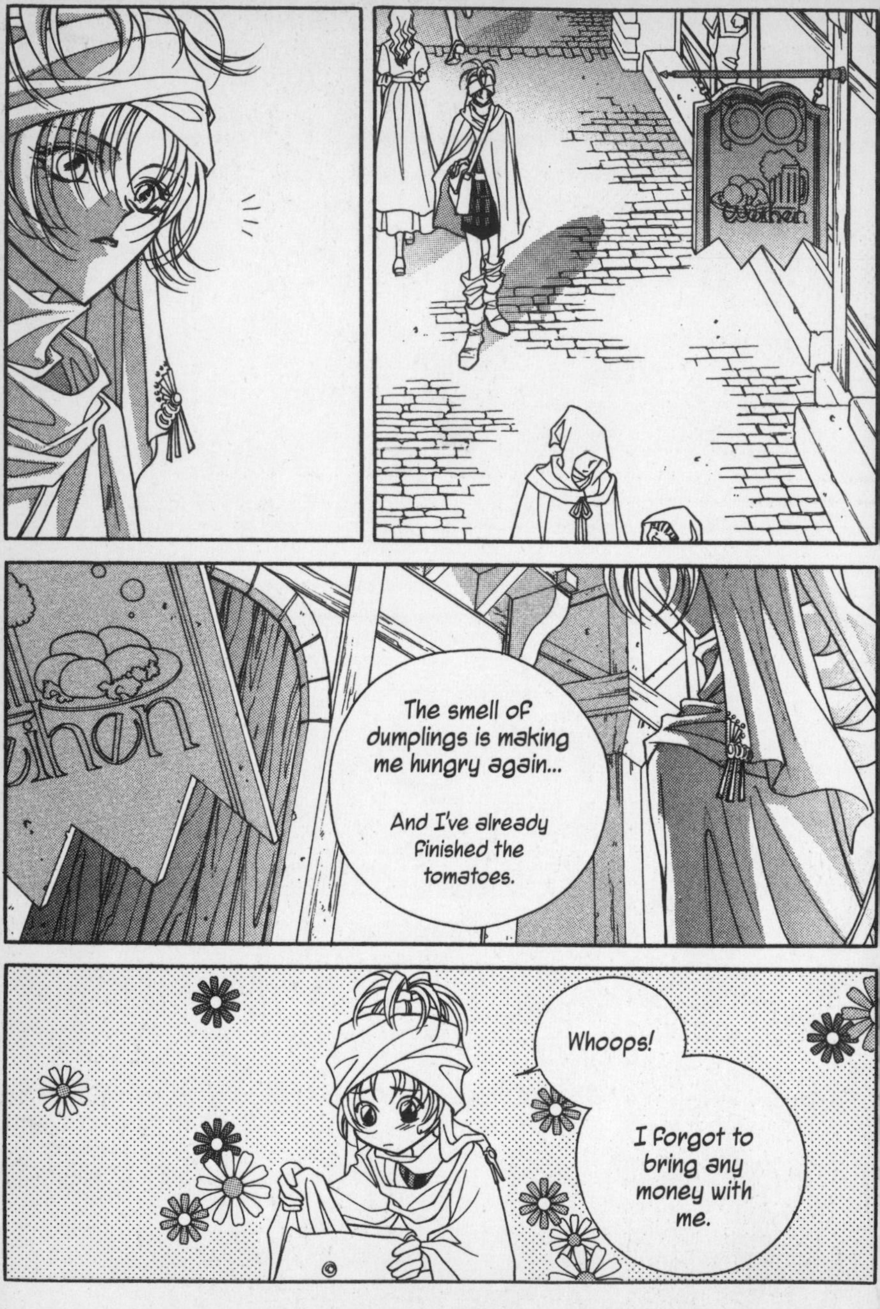
The smell of dumplings is making me hungry again...
And I've already finished the tomatoes.
Whoops!
I forgot to bring any money with me.

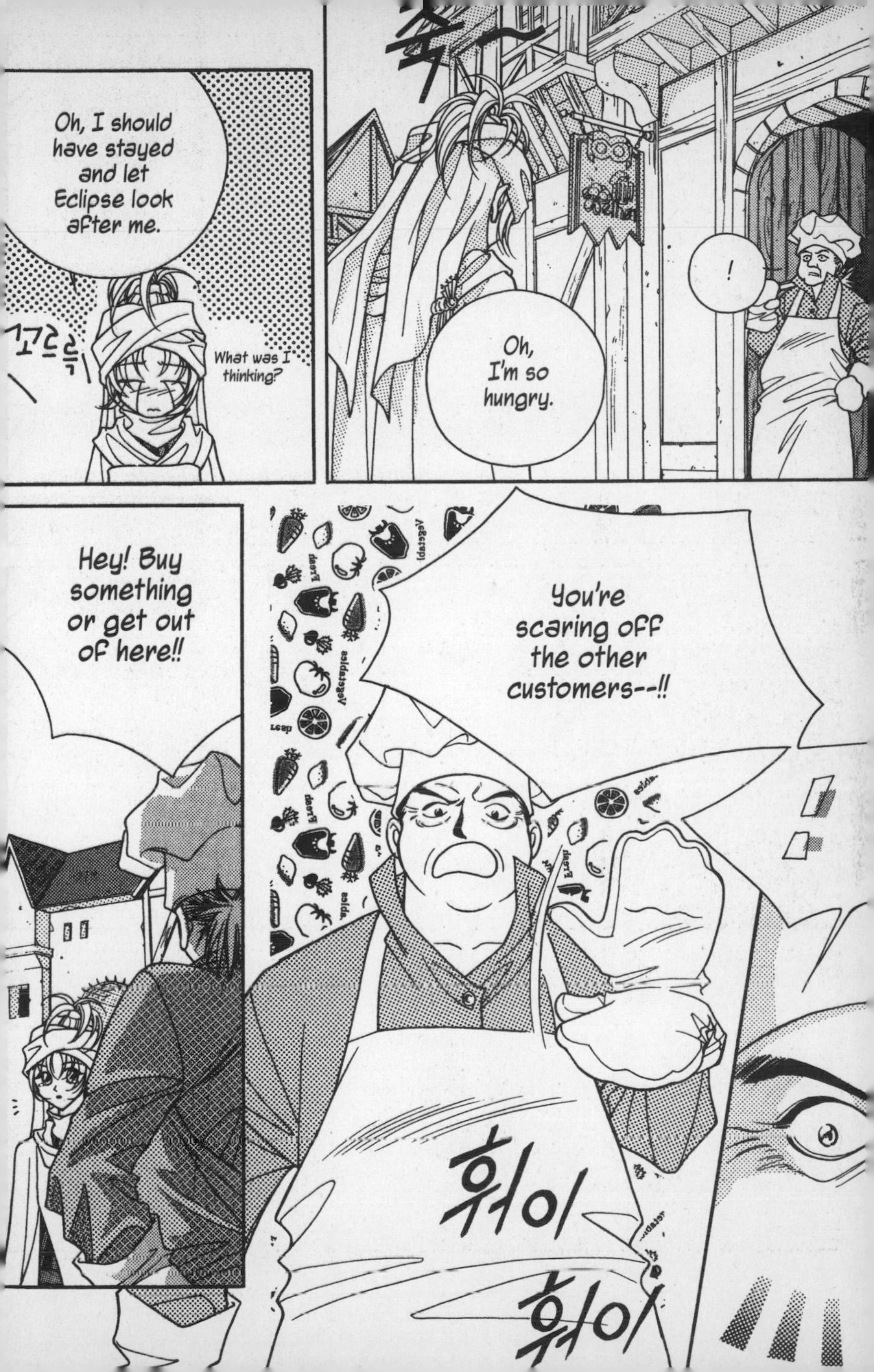

Oh, I should have stayed and let Eclipse look after me.
What was I thinking?
Oh, I'm so hungry.
!
Hey! Buy something or get out of here!!
You're scaring off the other customers--!!
훠이 훠이

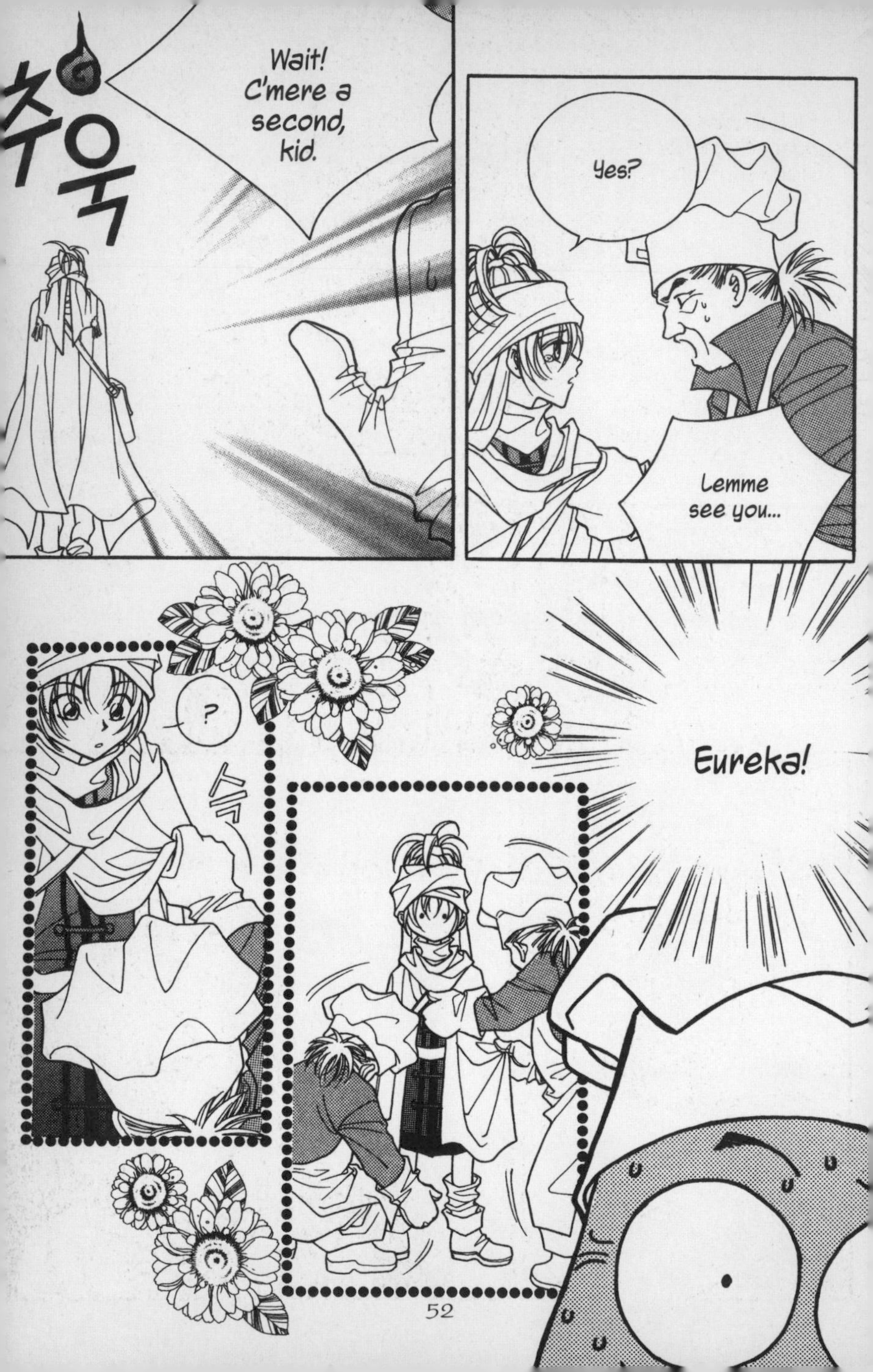
Wait! C'mere a second, kid.
Yes?
Lemme see you...
?
Eureka!

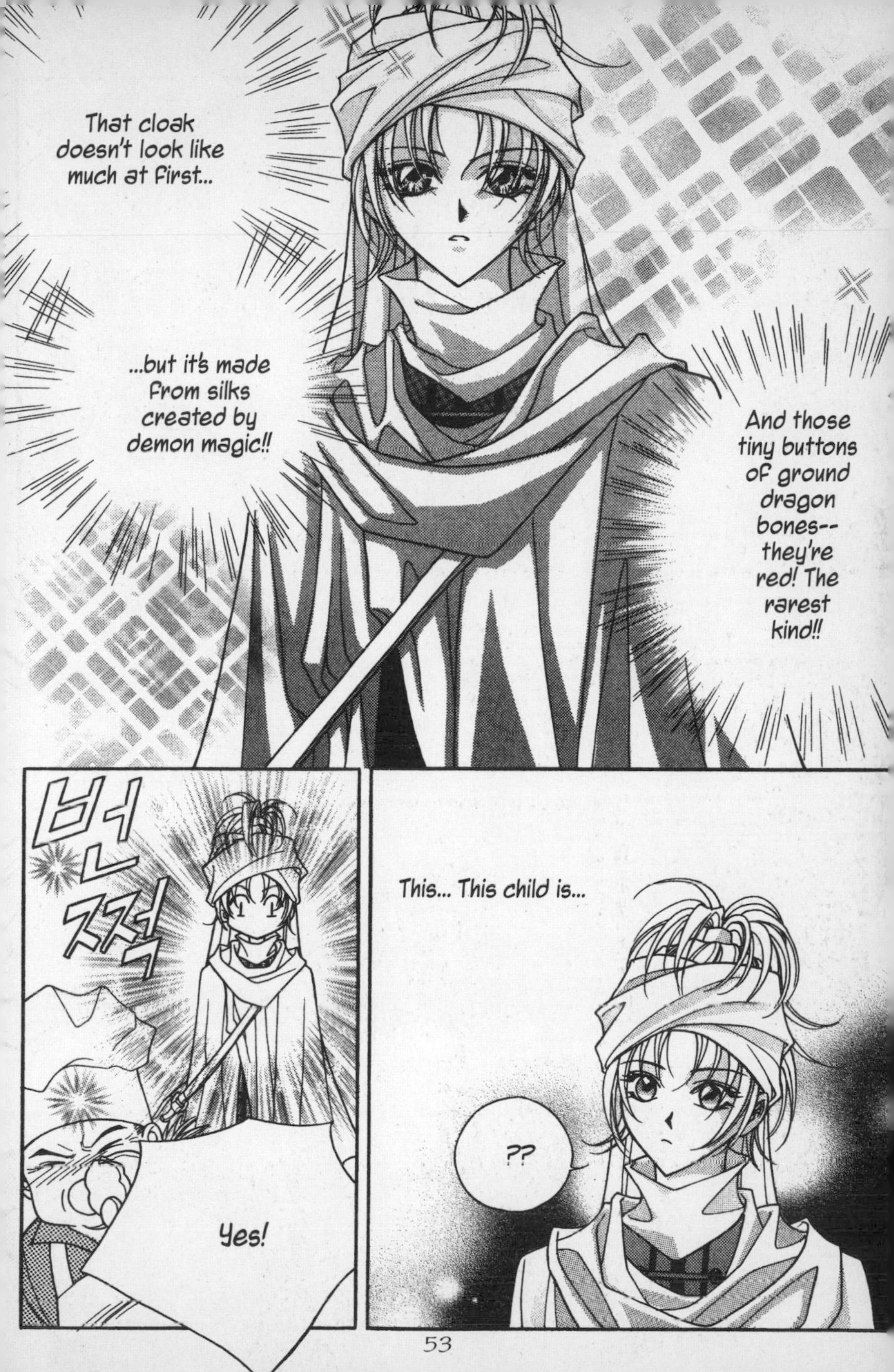
That cloak doesn't look like much at first...
...but it's made from silks created by demon magic!!
And those tiny buttons of ground dragon bones-- they're red! The rarest kind!!
This... This child is...
??
번쩍
Yes!

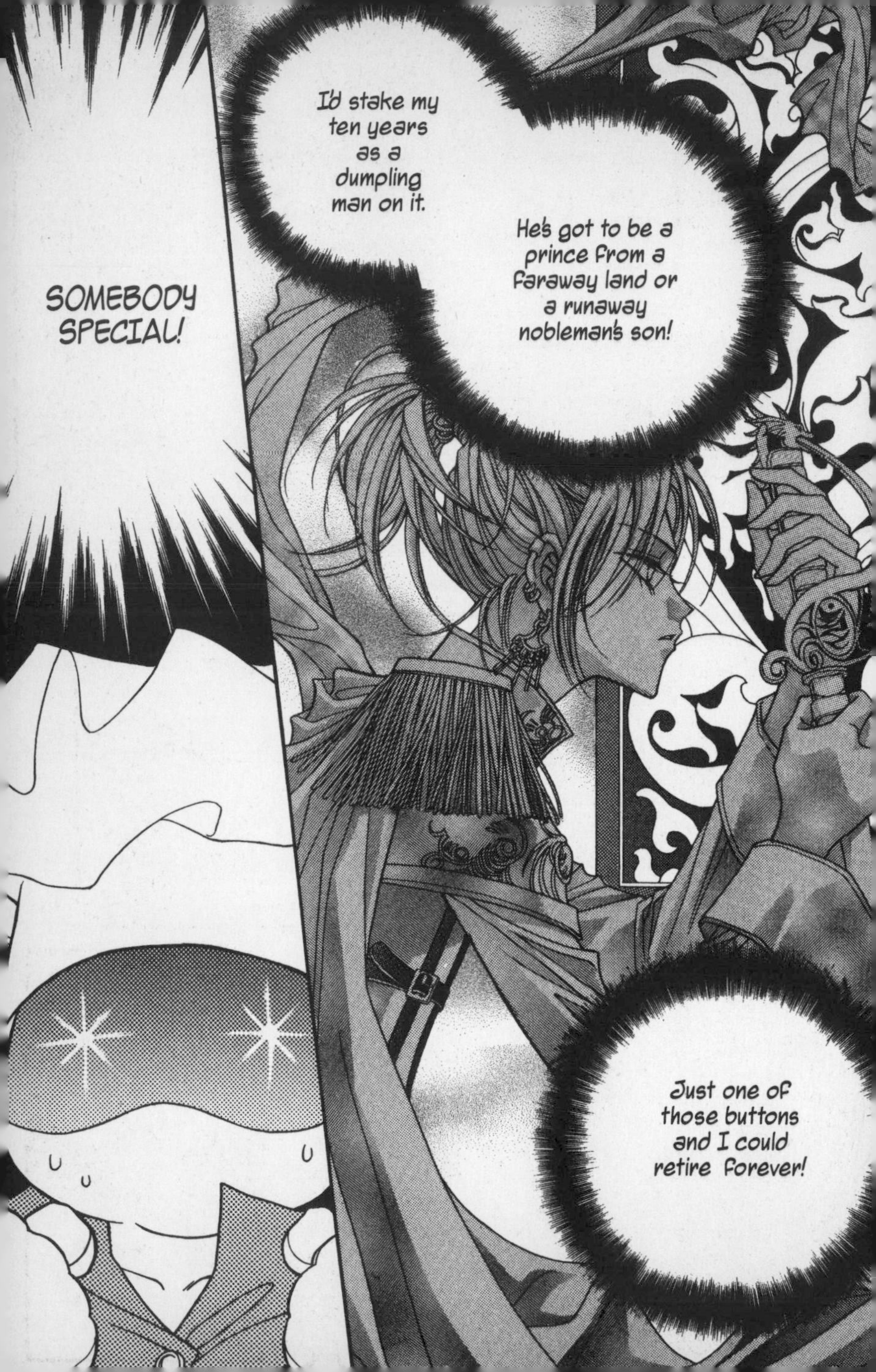
I'd stake my ten years as a dumpling man on it.
He's got to be a prince from a faraway land or a runaway nobleman's son!
Just one of those buttons and I could retire forever!
SOMEBODY SPECIAL!

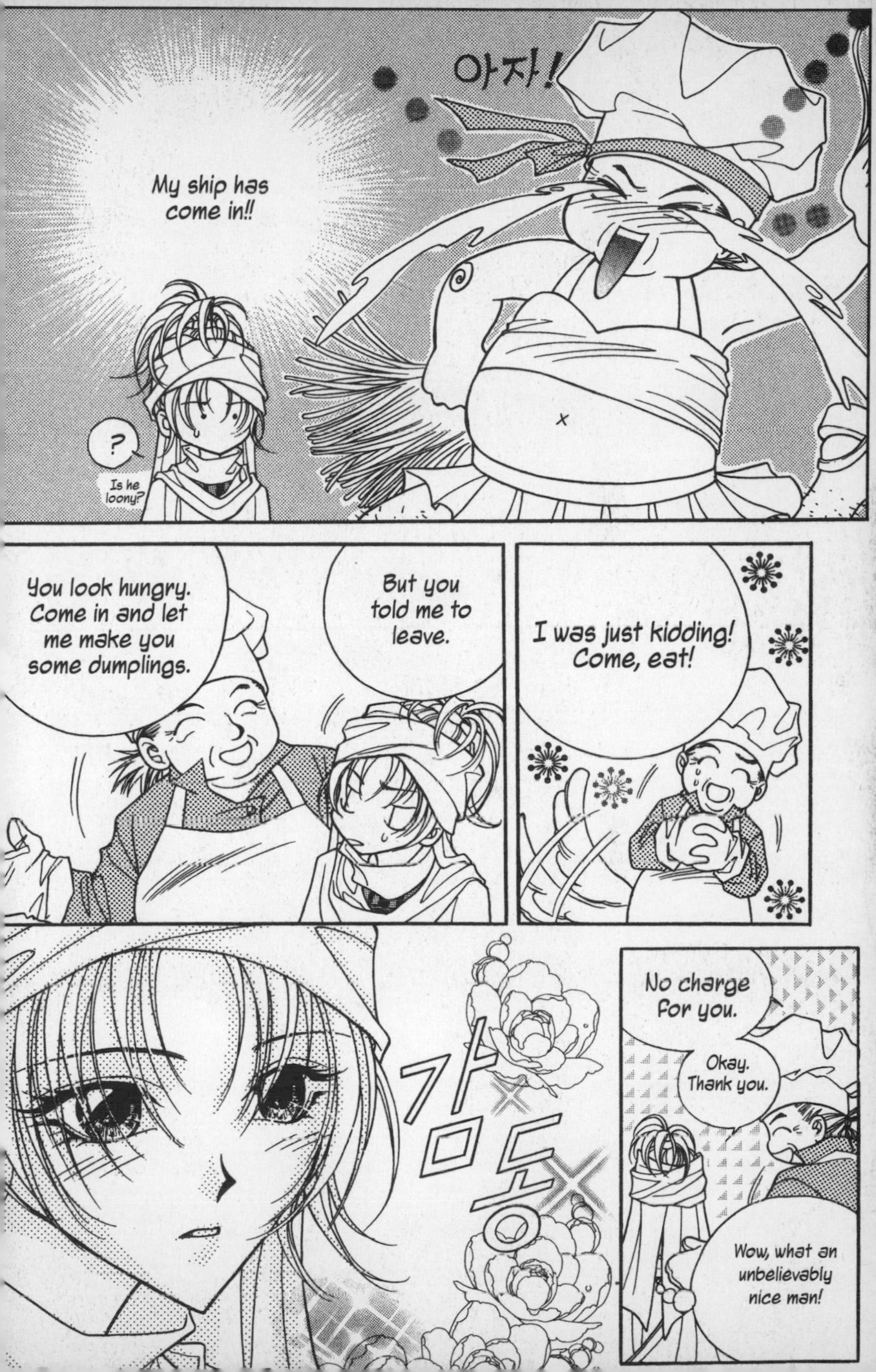
아자!
My ship has come in!!
?
Is he loony?
You look hungry. Come in and let me make you some dumplings.
But you told me to leave.
I was just kidding! Come, eat!
가
모
동
No charge for you.
Okay. Thank you.
Wow, what an unbelievably nice man!

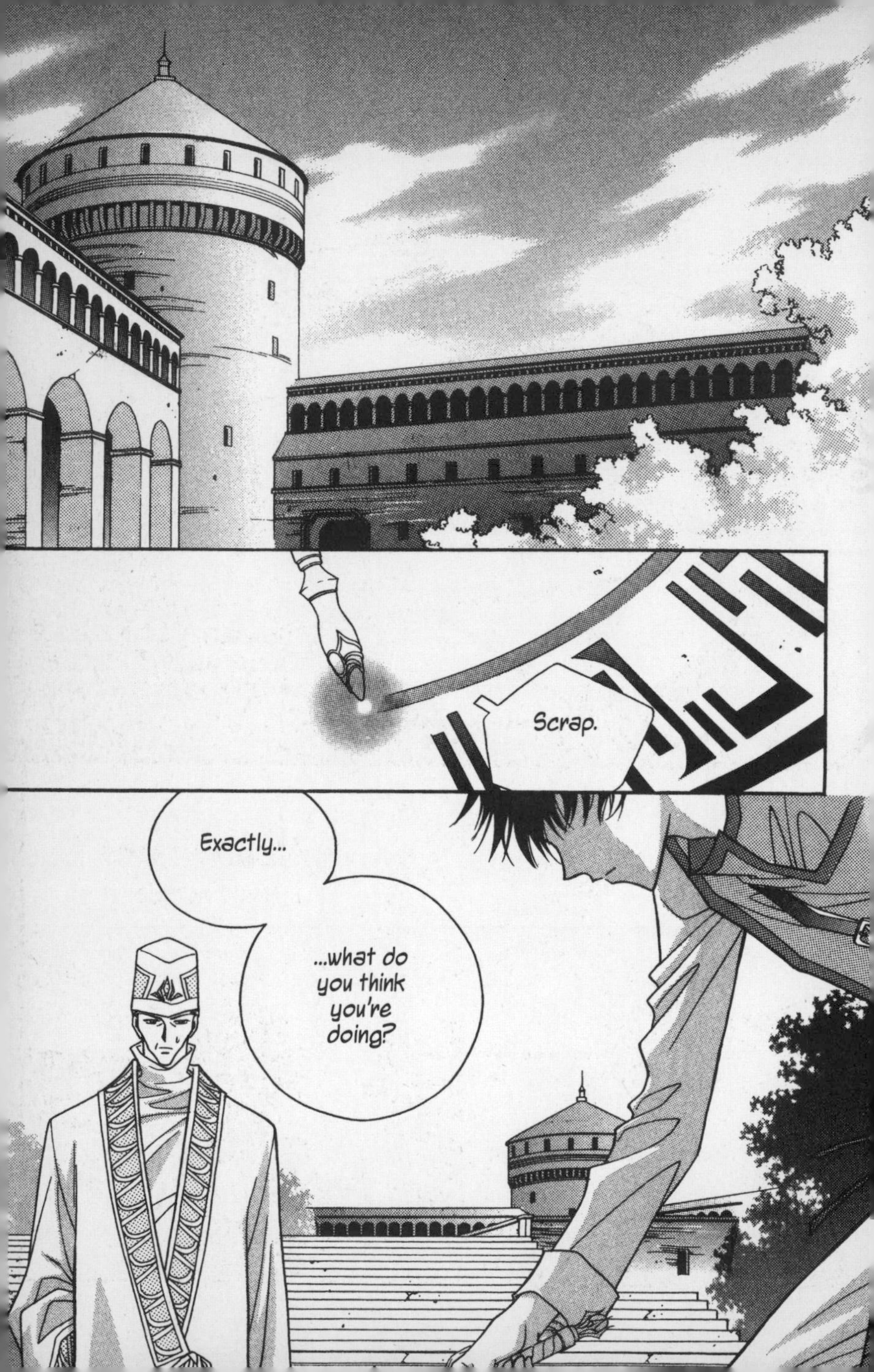
Scrap.
Exactly...
...what do you think you're doing?

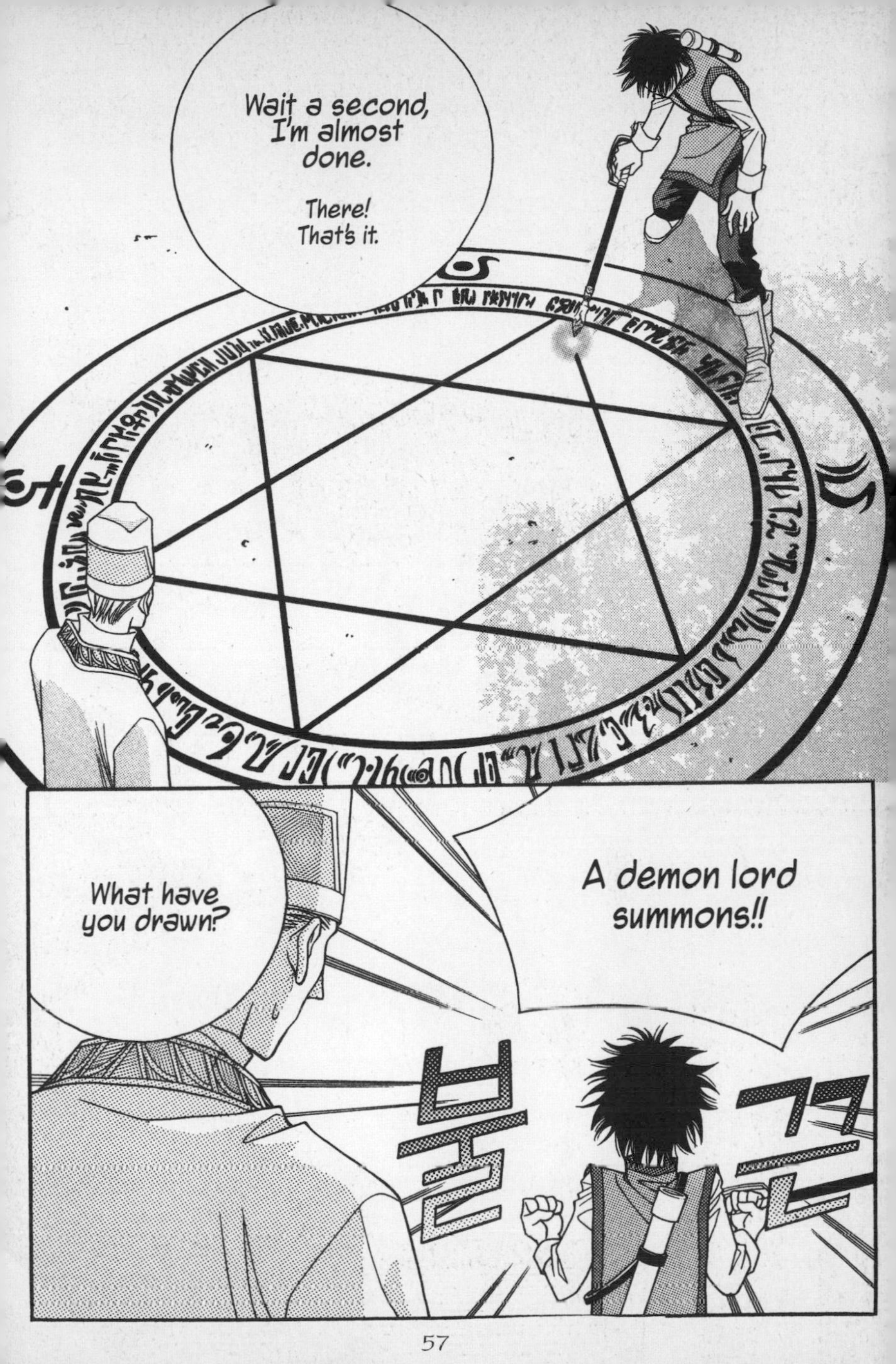
Wait a second, I'm almost done.
There! That's it.
What have you drawn?
A demon lord summons!!

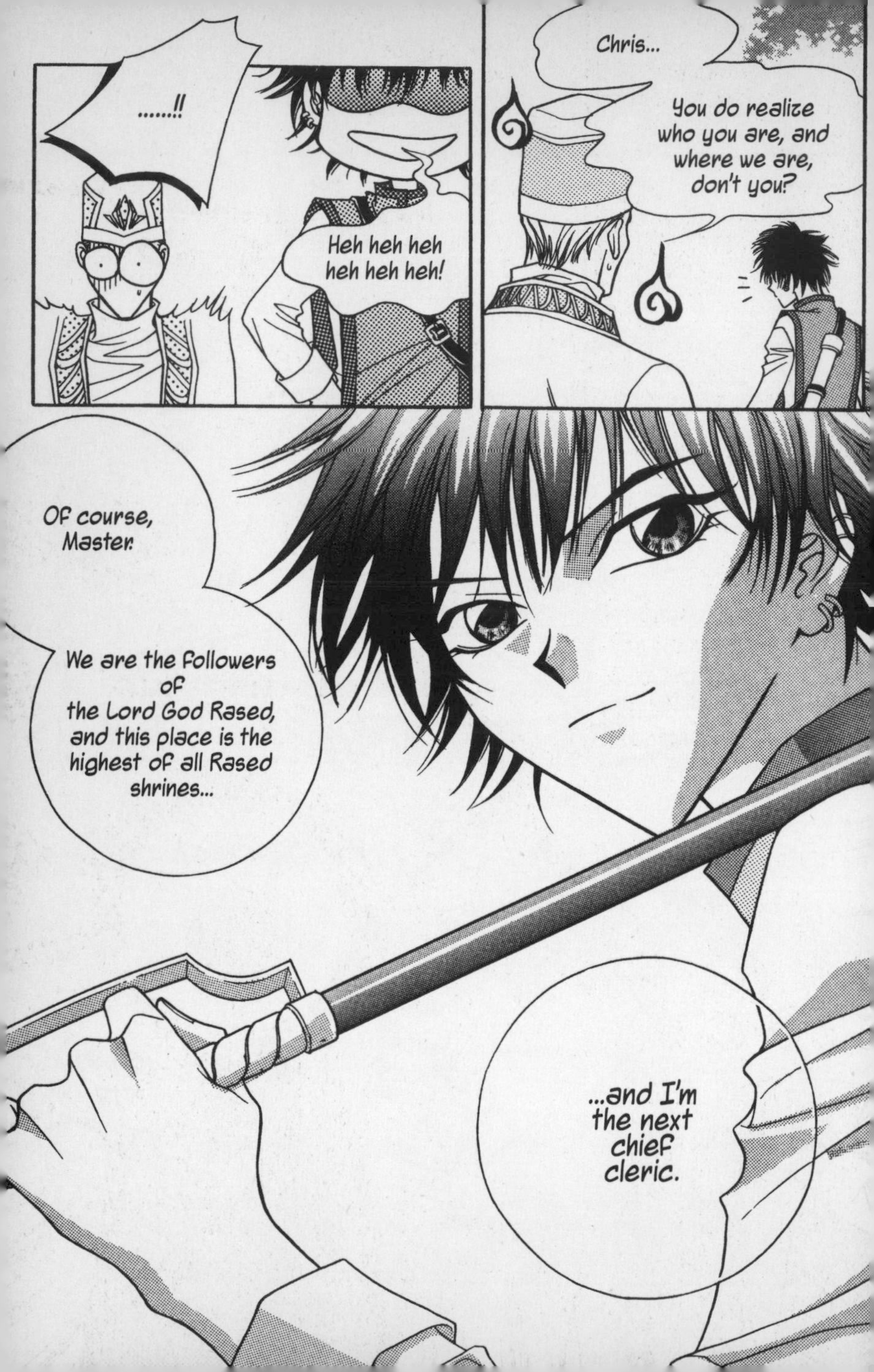
Chris...
You do realize who you are, and where we are, don't you?
Heh heh heh heh heh heh!
......!!
Of course, Master.
We are the followers of the Lord God Rased, and this place is the highest of all Rased shrines...
...and I'm the next chief cleric.

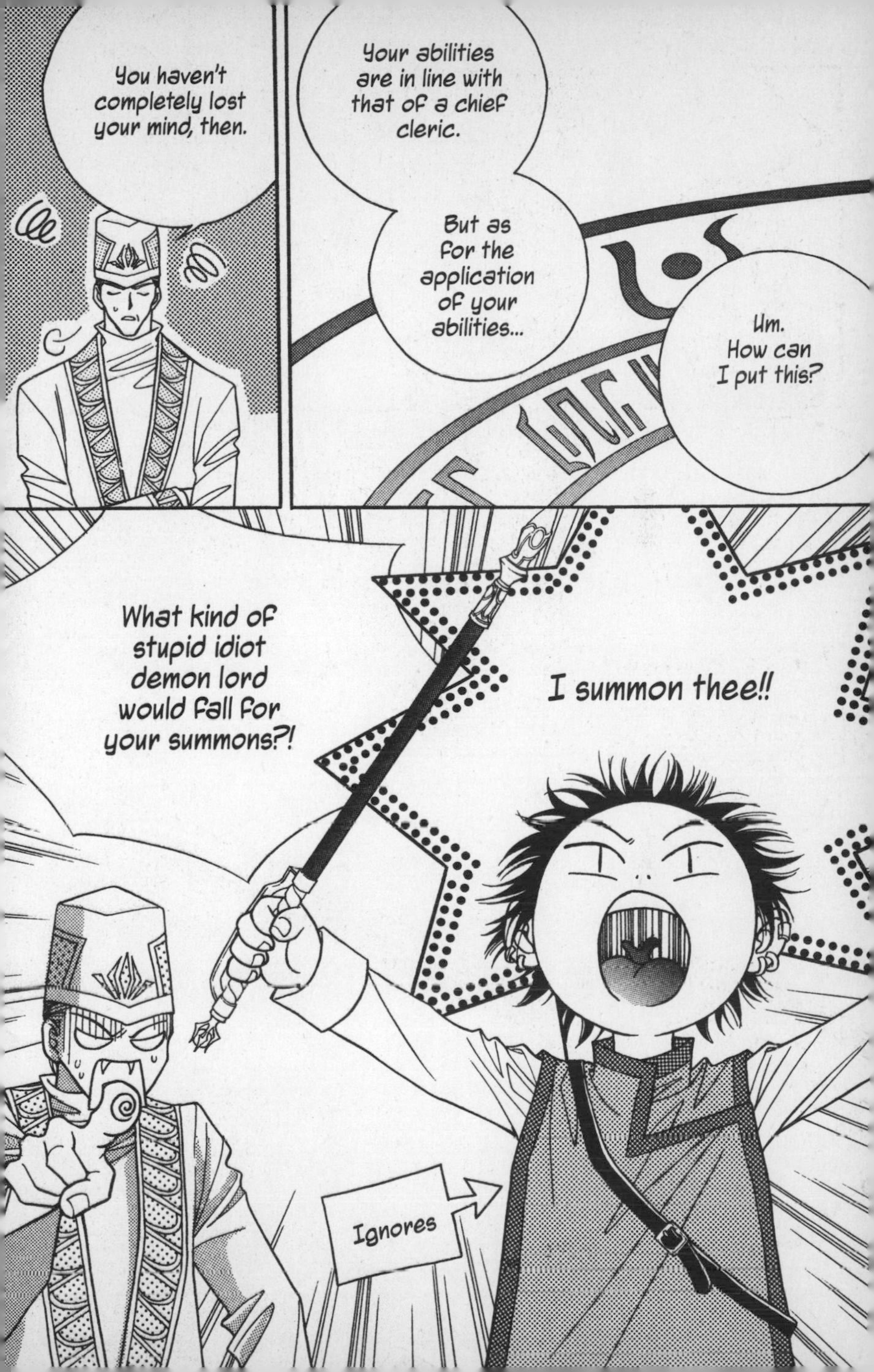

You haven't completely lost your mind, then.
Your abilities are in line with that of a chief cleric.
But as for the application of your abilities...
Um. How can I put this?
What kind of stupid idiot demon lord would fall for your summons?!
I summon thee!!
Ignores

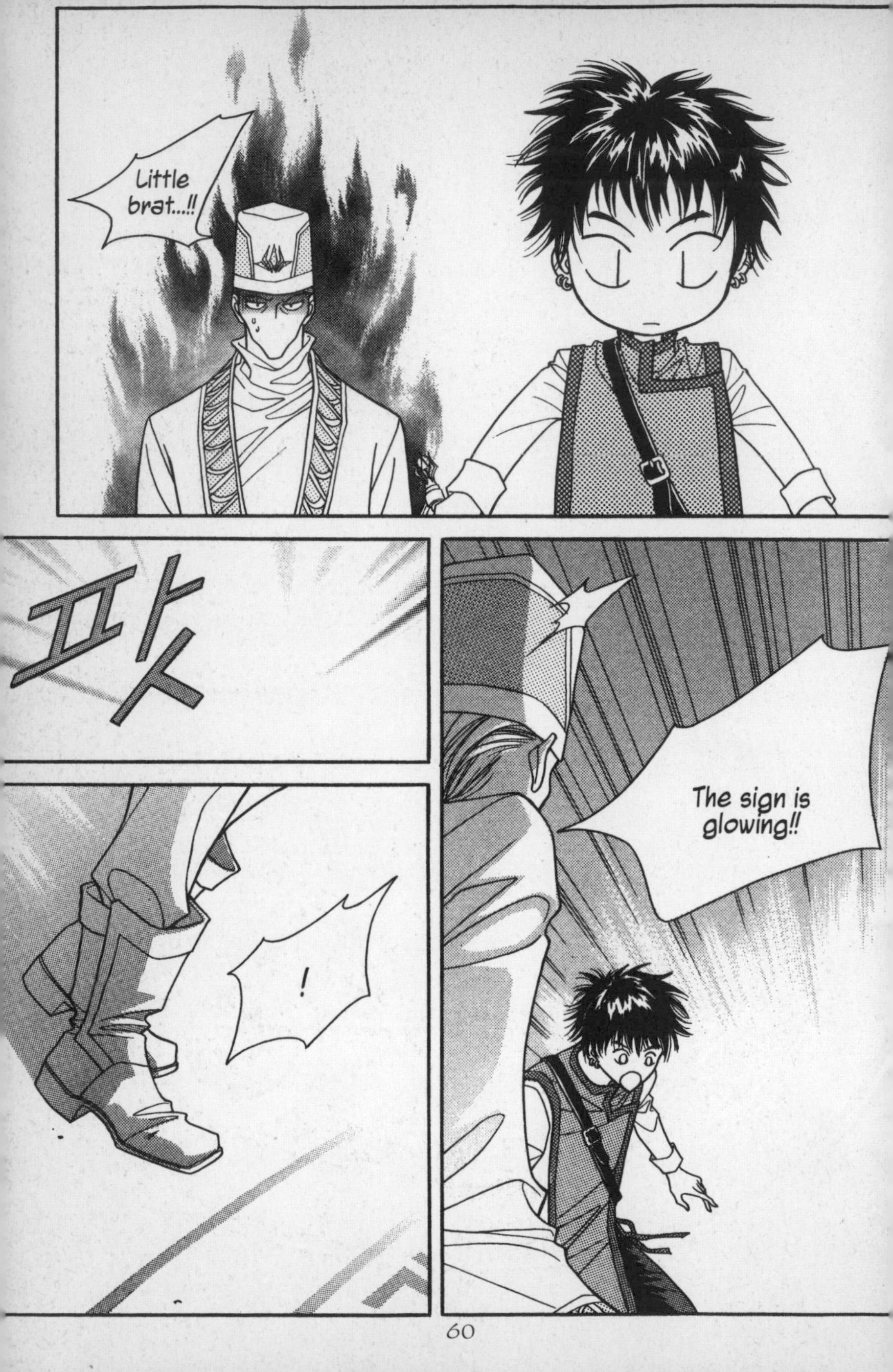

Little brat...!!
The sign is glowing!!
!

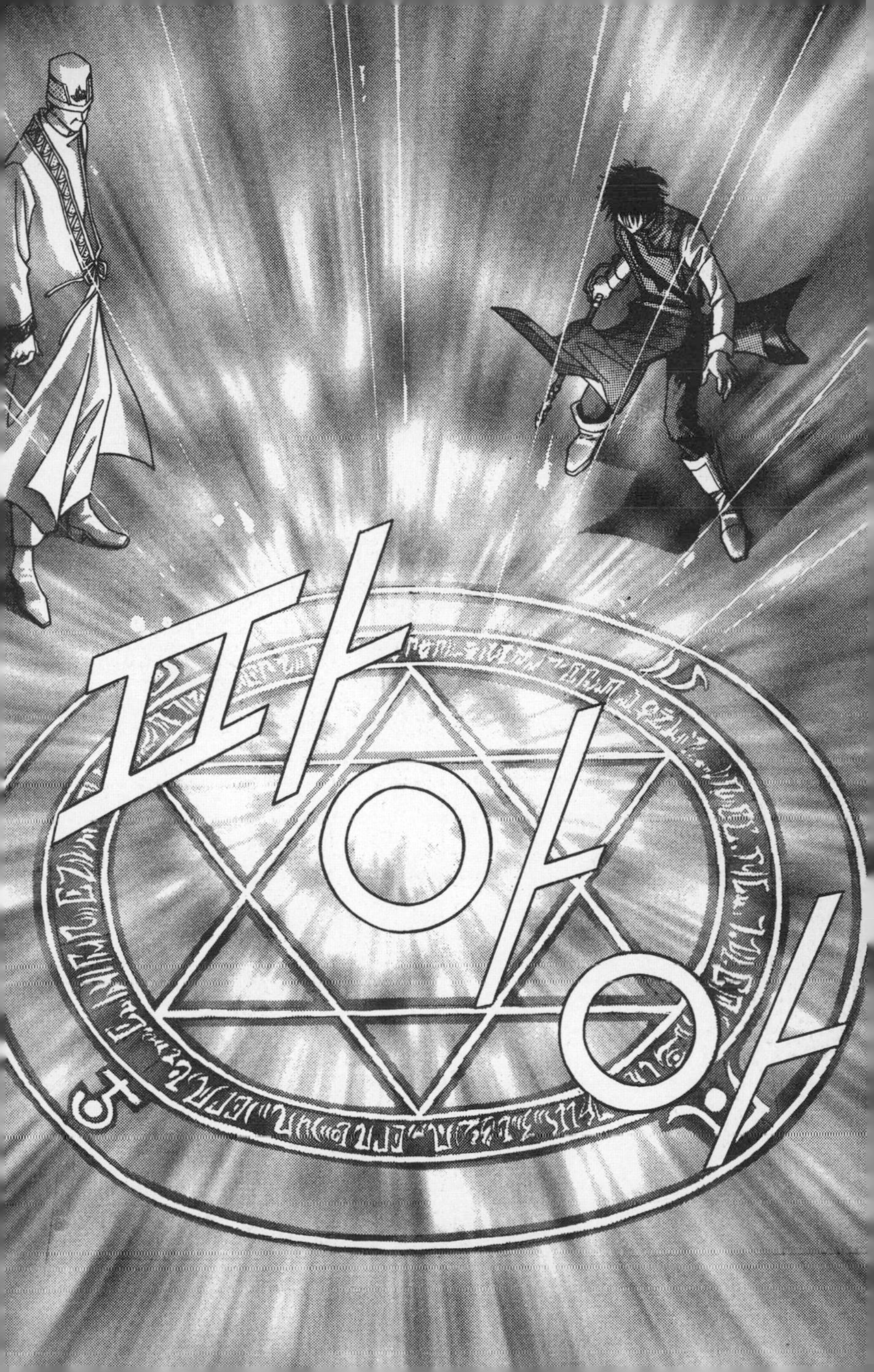
파아아

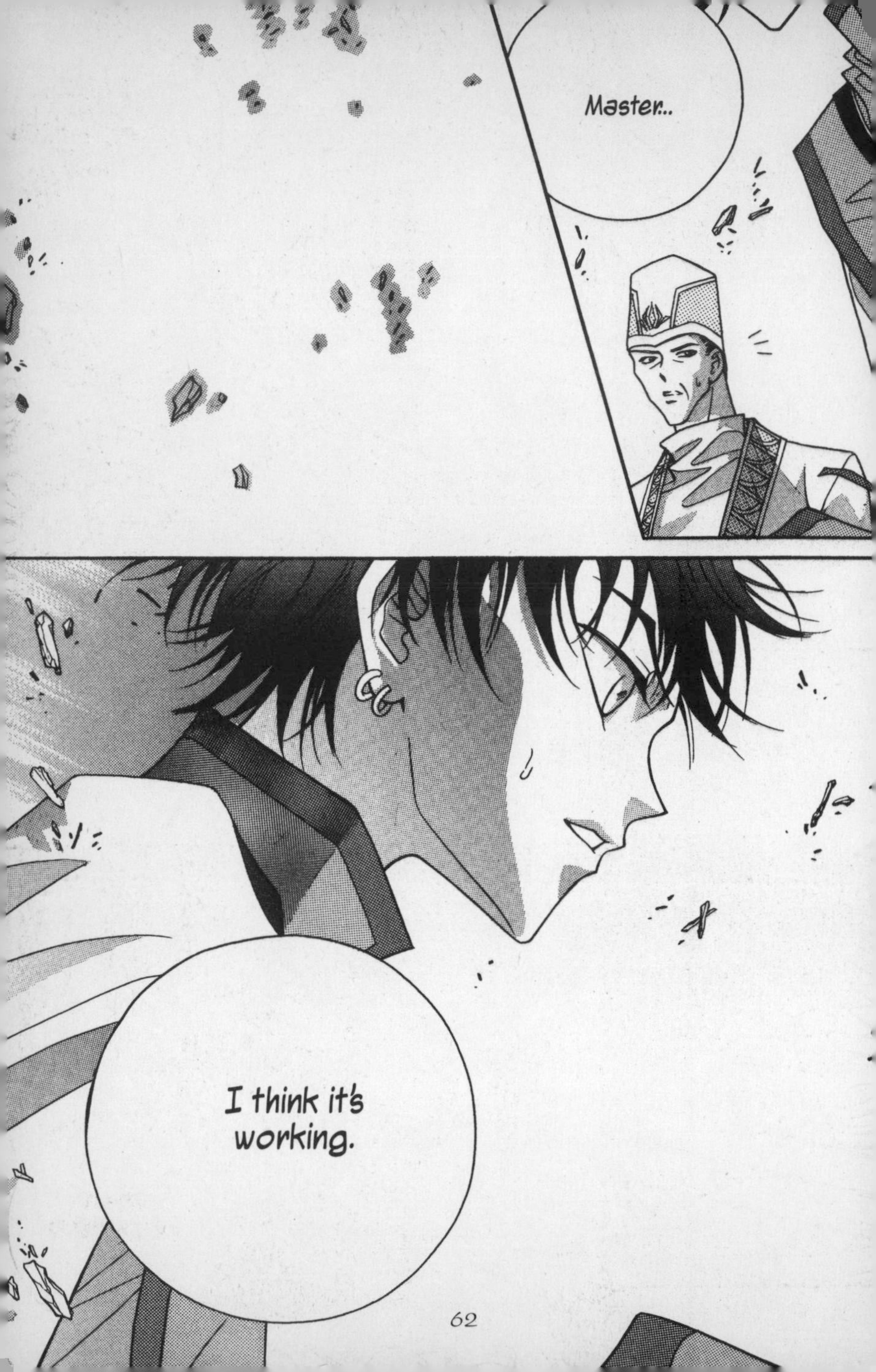
Master...
I think it's working.

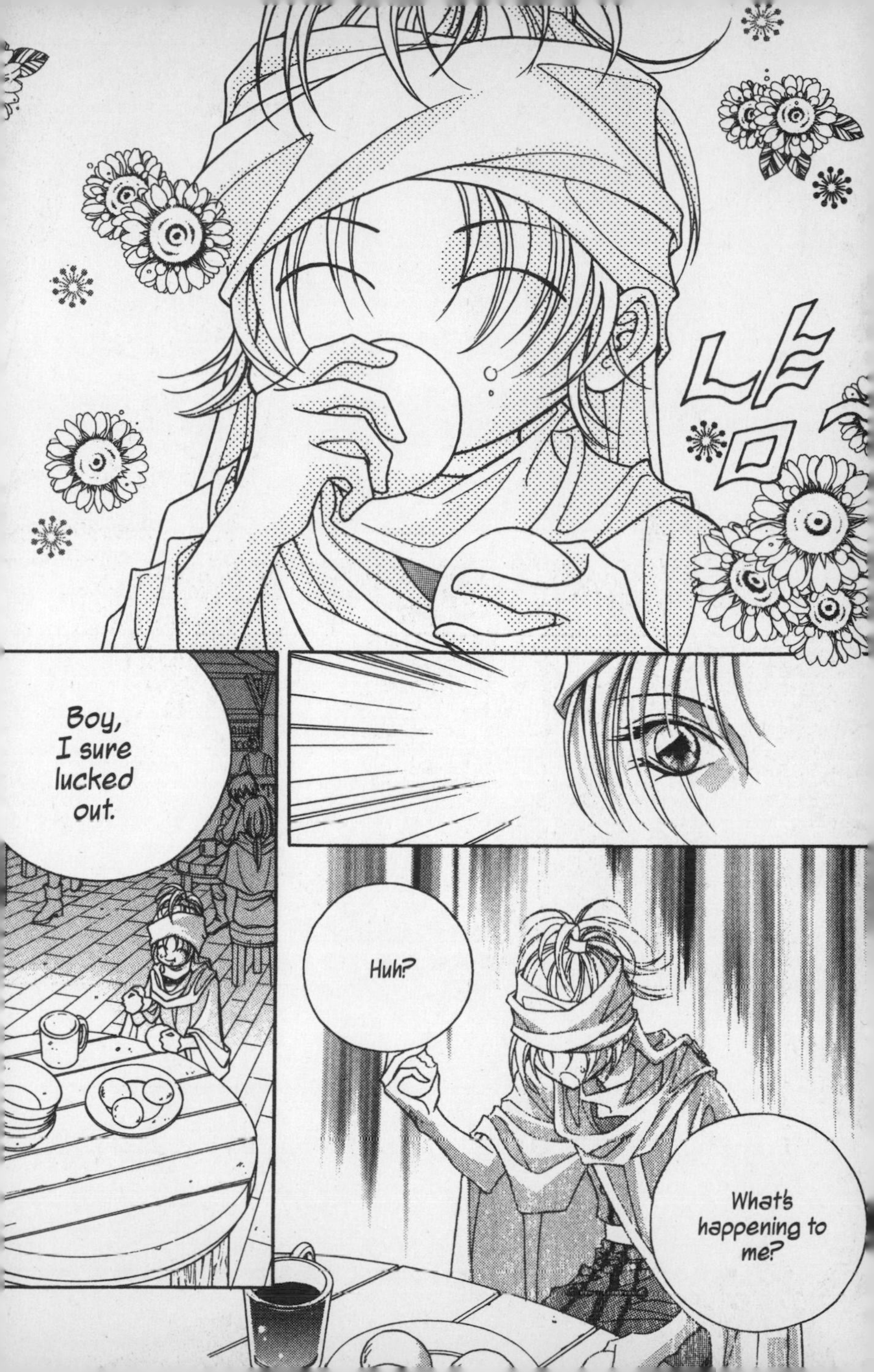
Boy, I sure lucked out.
Huh?
What's happening to me?

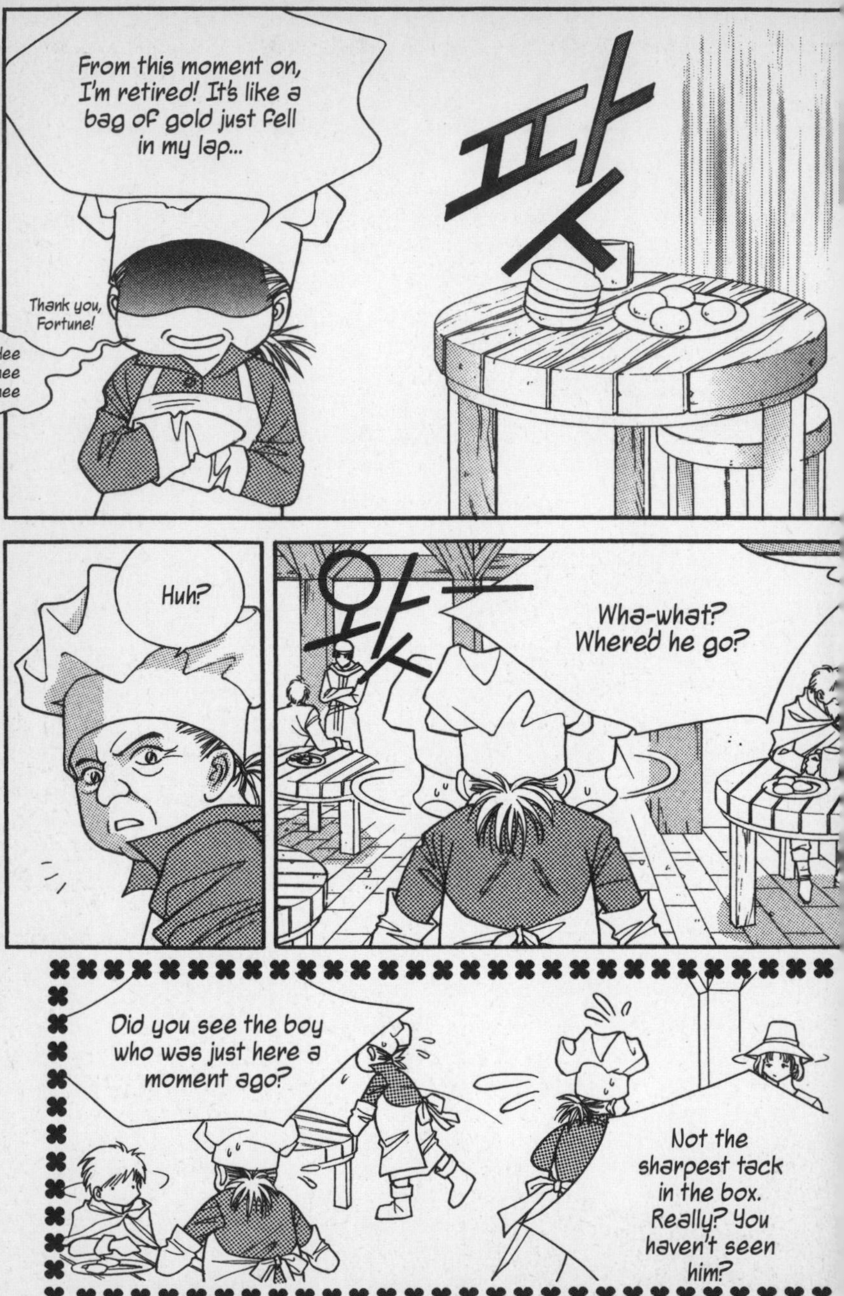

From this moment on, I'm retired! It's like a bag of gold just fell in my lap...
Thank you, Fortune!
Hee hee hee
Huh?
Wha-what? Where'd he go?
Did you see the boy who was just here a moment ago?
Not the sharpest tack in the box.
Really? You haven't seen him?

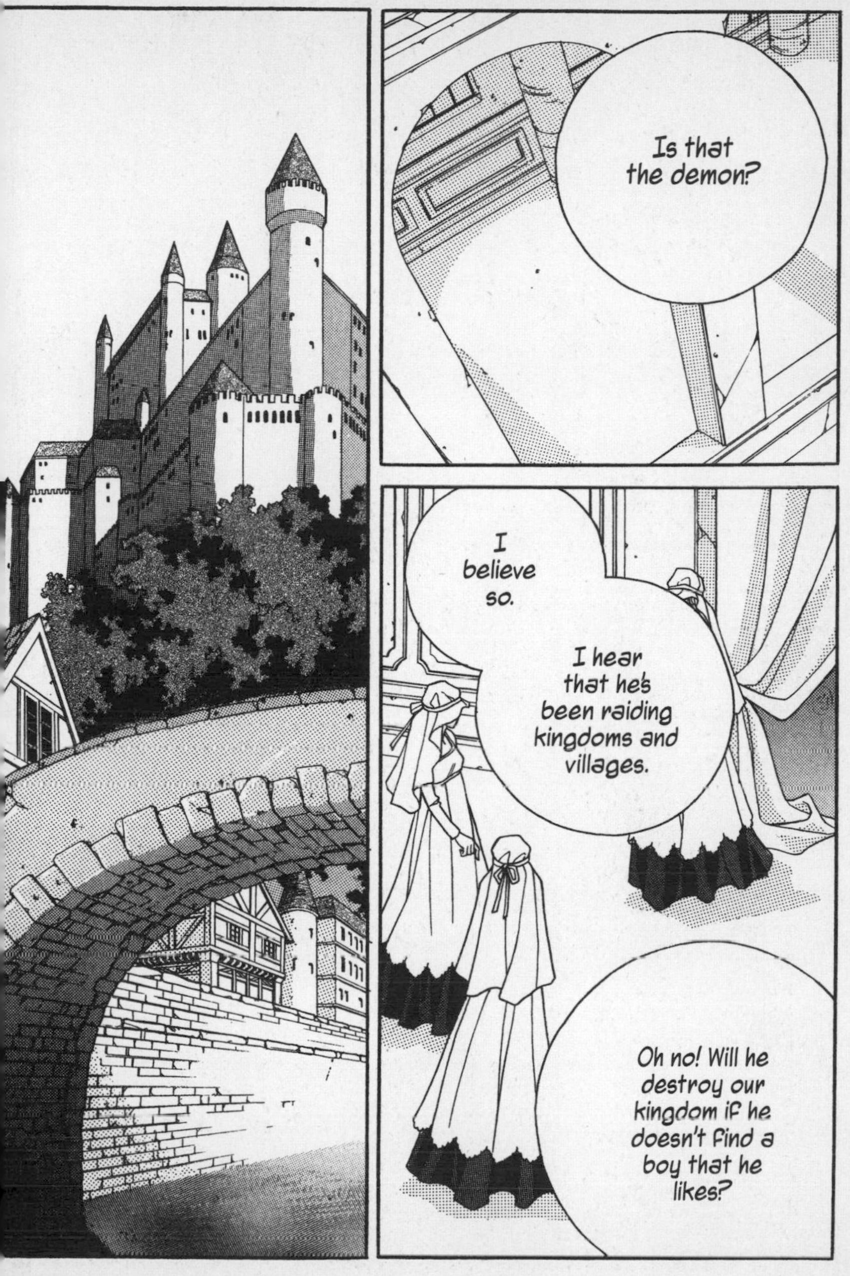
Is that the demon?
I believe so.
I hear that he's been raiding kingdoms and villages.
Oh no! Will he destroy our kingdom if he doesn't find a boy that he likes?

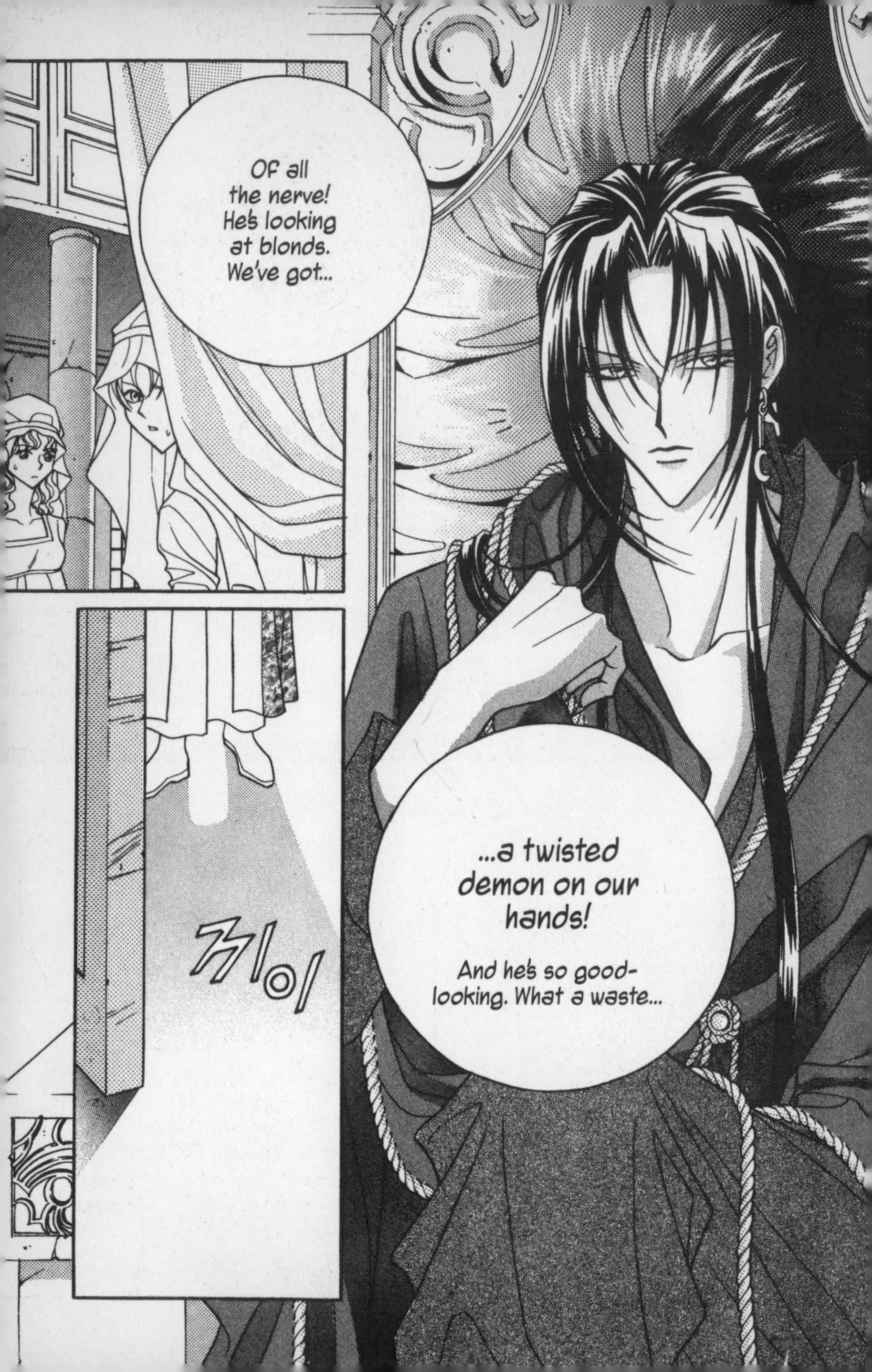

Of all the nerve! He's looking at blonds. We've got...
끼이
...a twisted demon on our hands!
And he's so good-looking. What a waste...

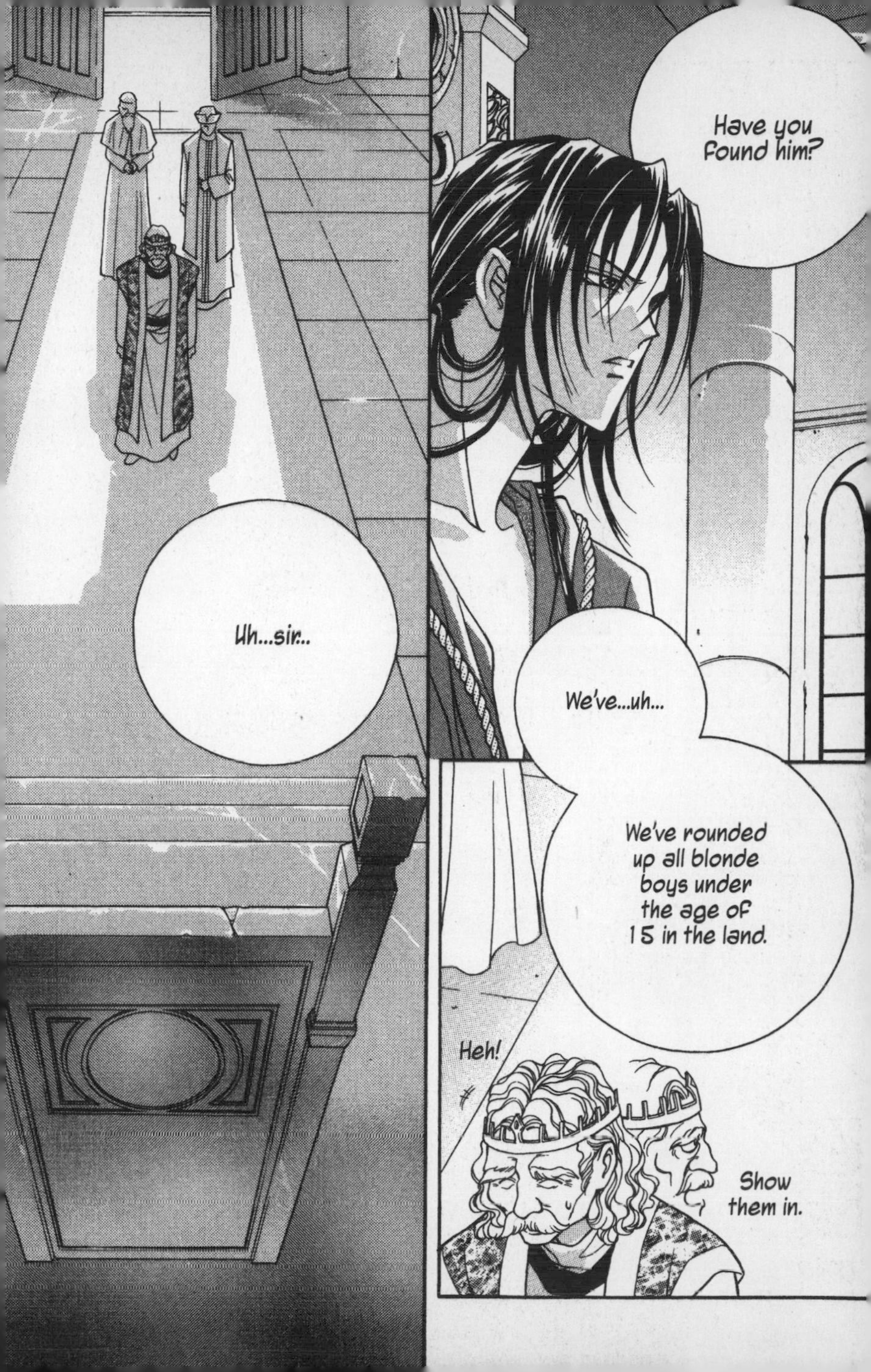
Have you found him?
Uh...sir..
We've...uh...
We've rounded up all blonde boys under the age of 15 in the land.
Heh!
Show them in.

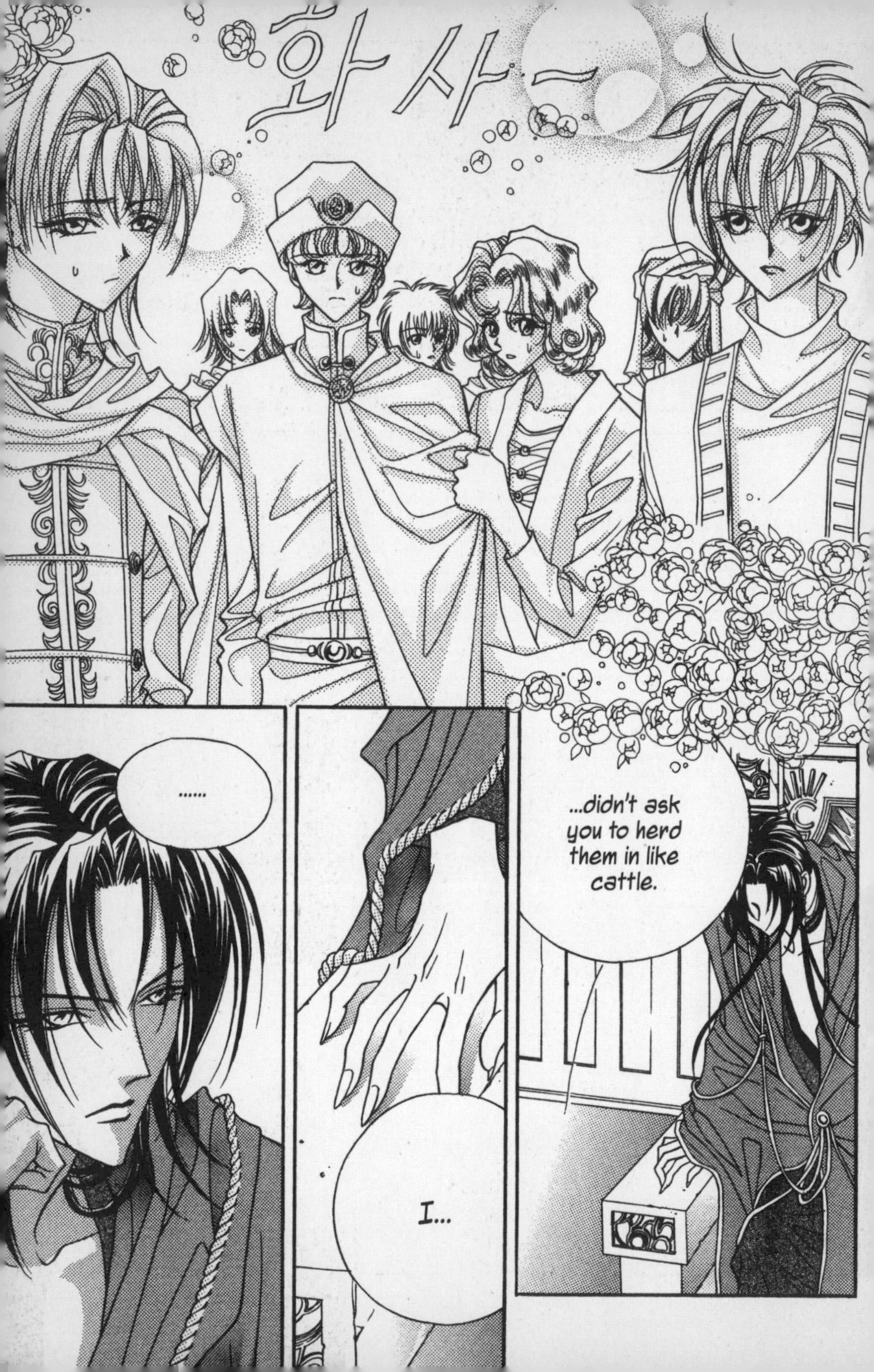
화사—
...didn't ask you to herd them in like cattle.
I...
......

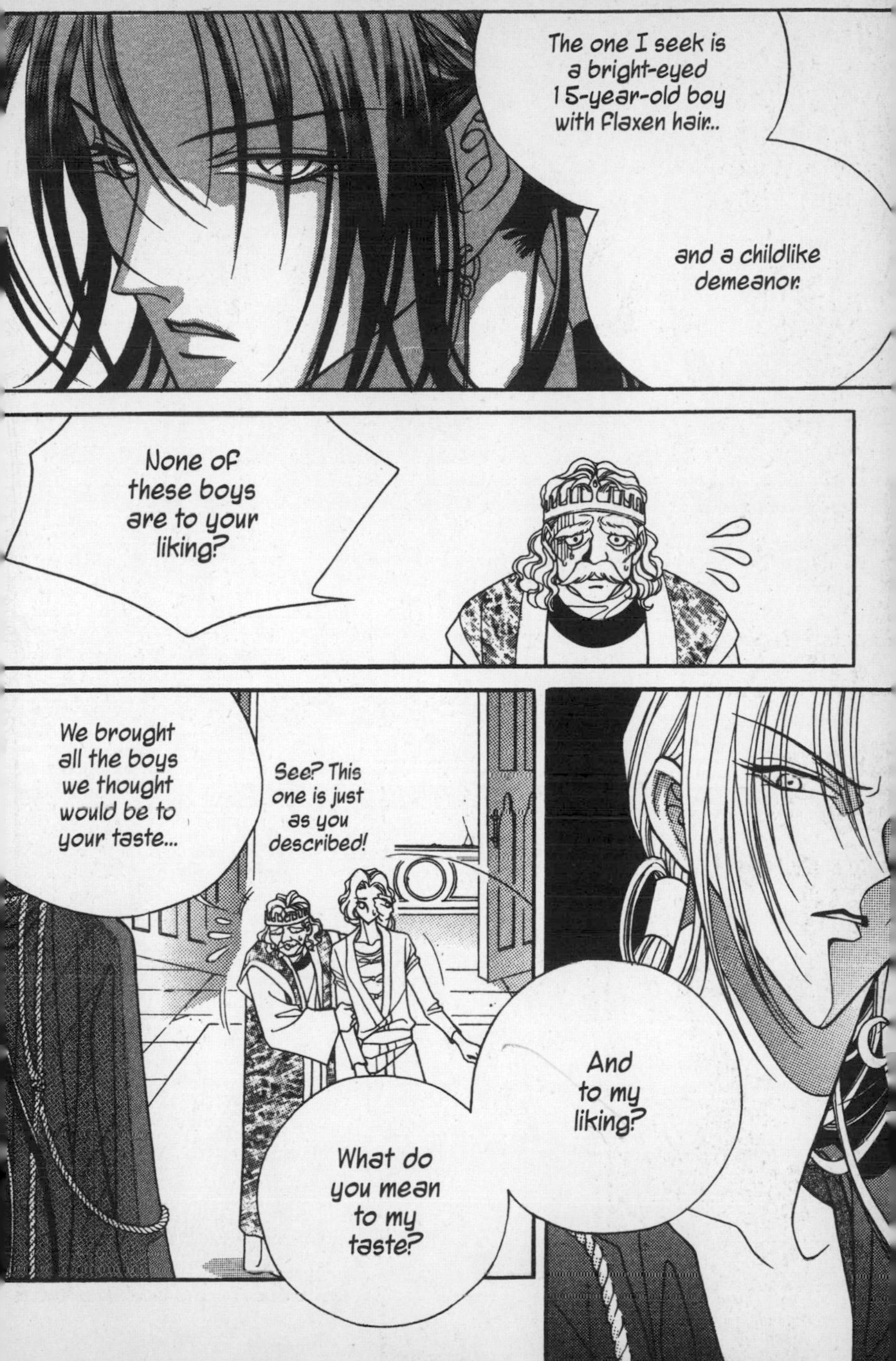
The one I seek is a bright-eyed 15-year-old boy with flaxen hair..
and a childlike demeanor.
None of these boys are to your liking?
We brought all the boys we thought would be to your taste...
See? This one is just as you described!
And to my liking?
What do you mean to my taste?

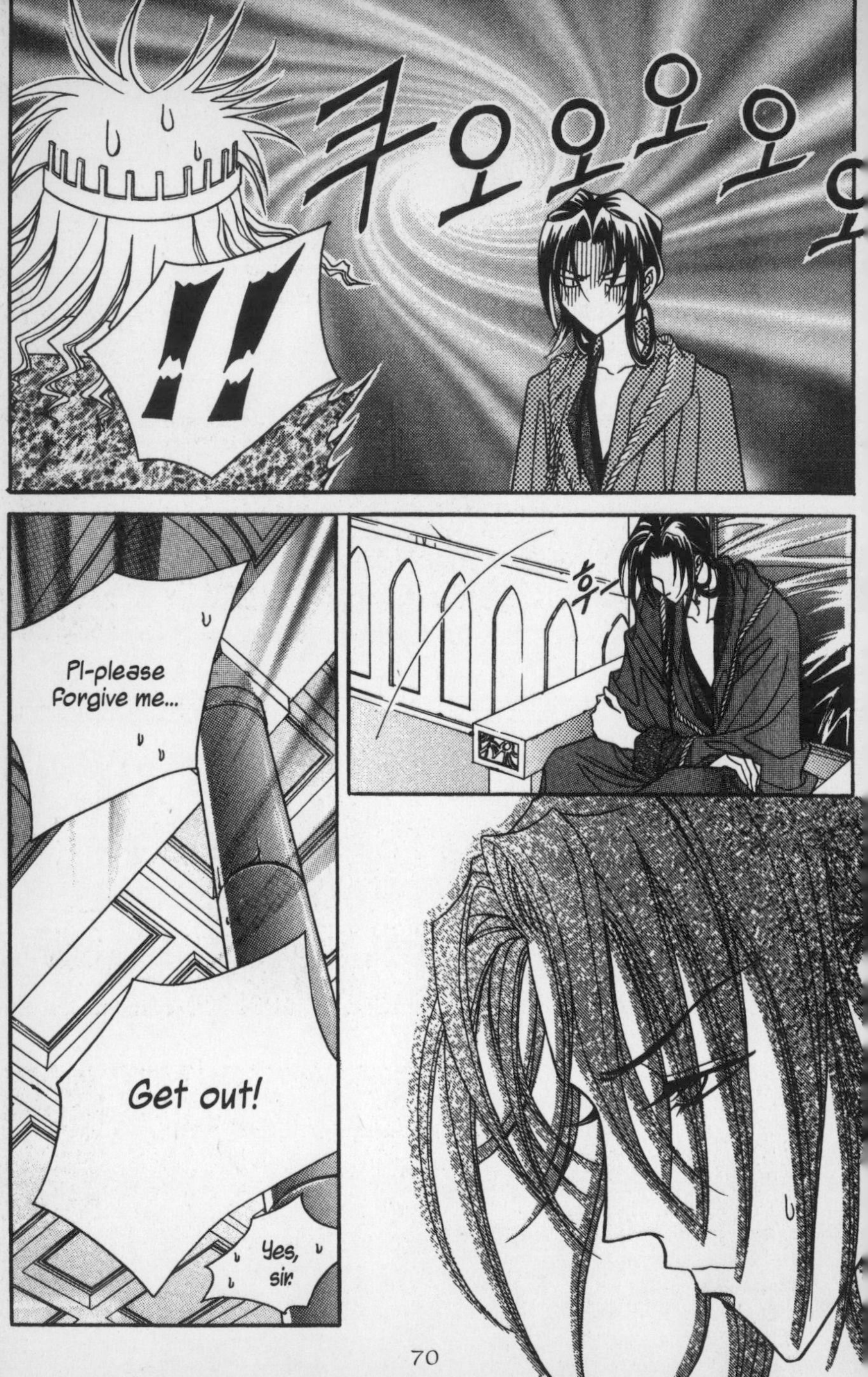
!!
Pl-please forgive me...
Get out!
Yes, sir.

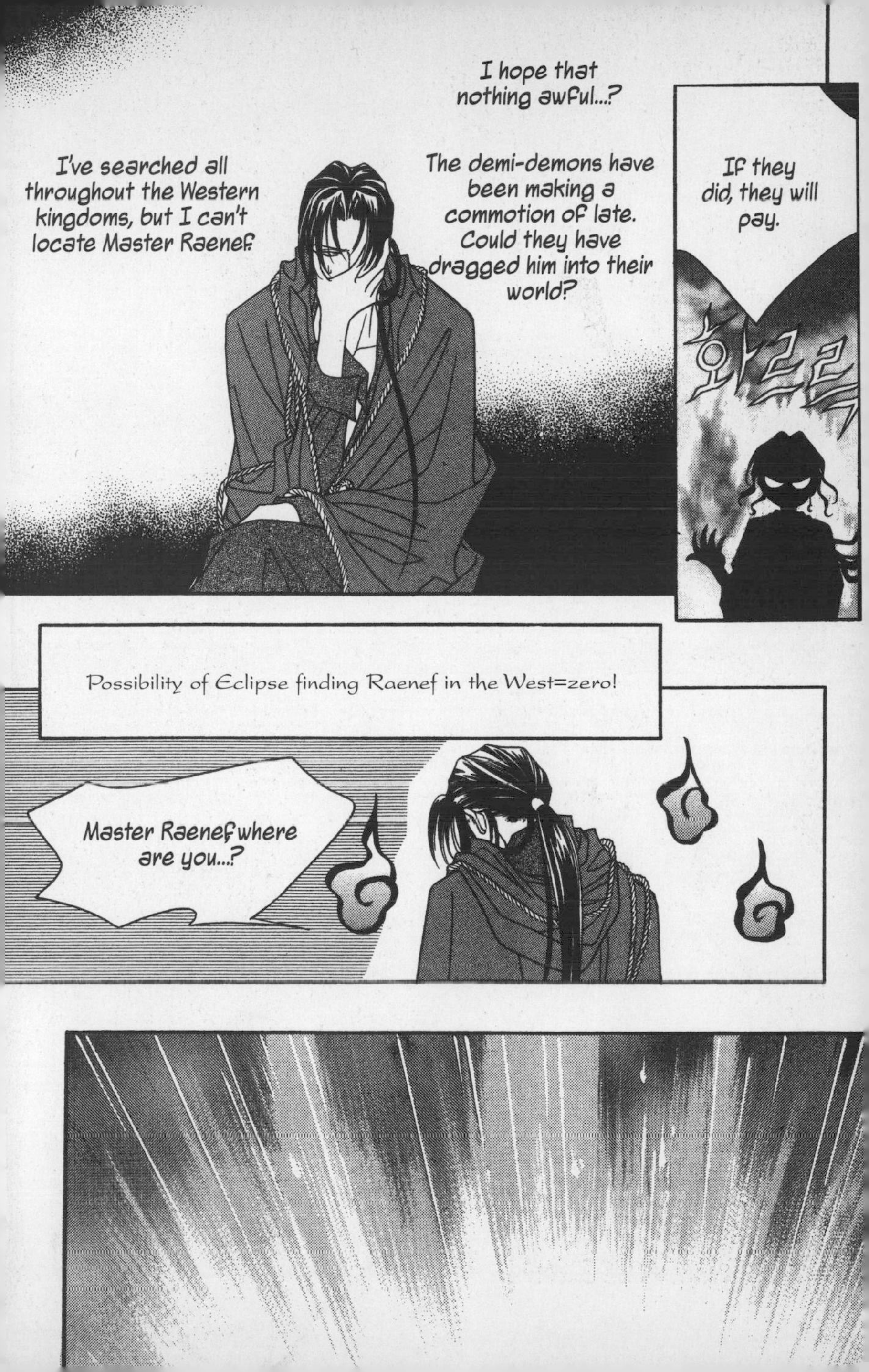
I hope that nothing awful...?
If they did, they will pay.
The demi-demons have been making a commotion of late. Could they have dragged him into their world?
I've searched all throughout the Western kingdoms, but I can't locate Master Raenef.
Possibility of Eclipse finding Raenef in the West=zero!
Master Raenef, where are you...?

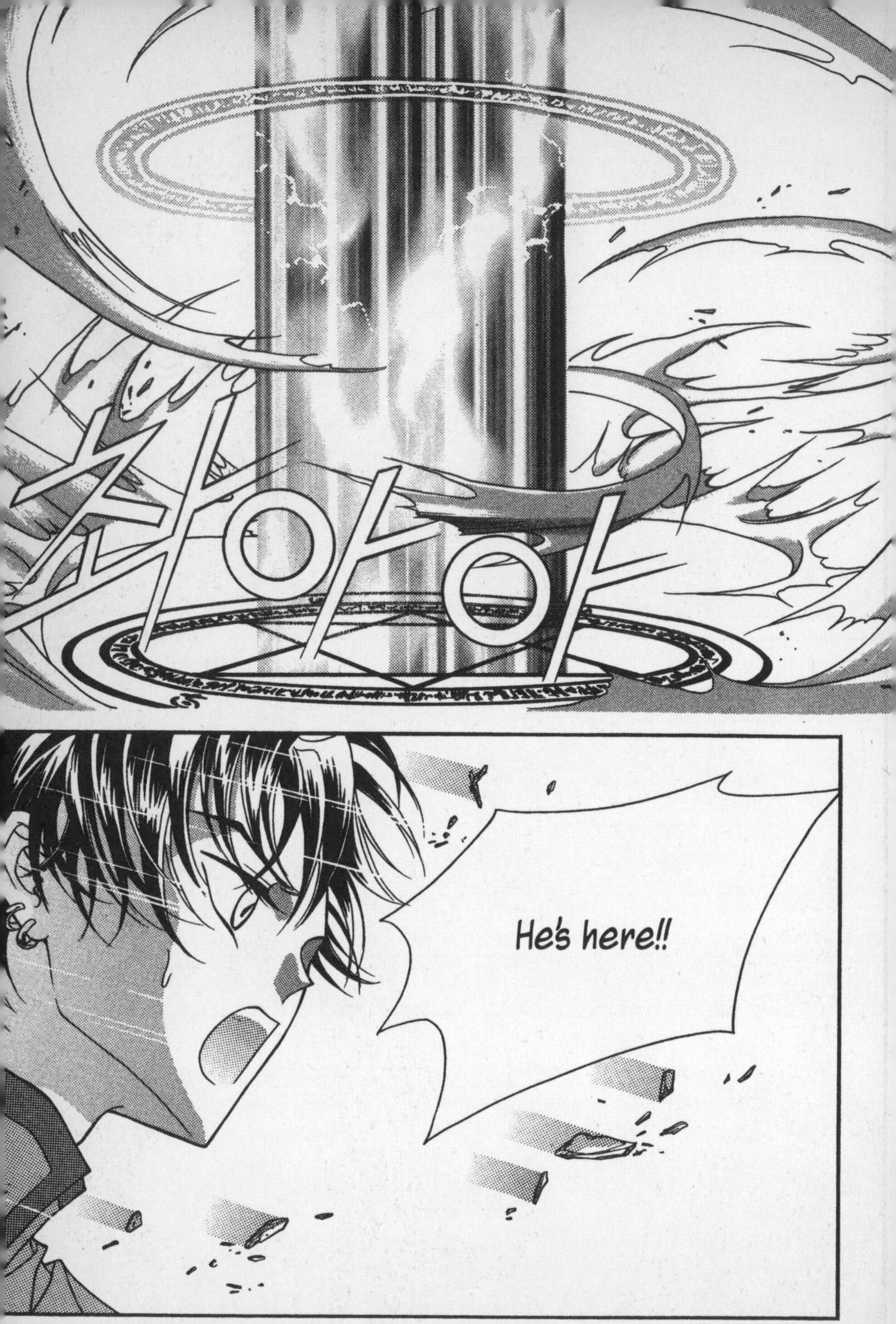
He's here!!

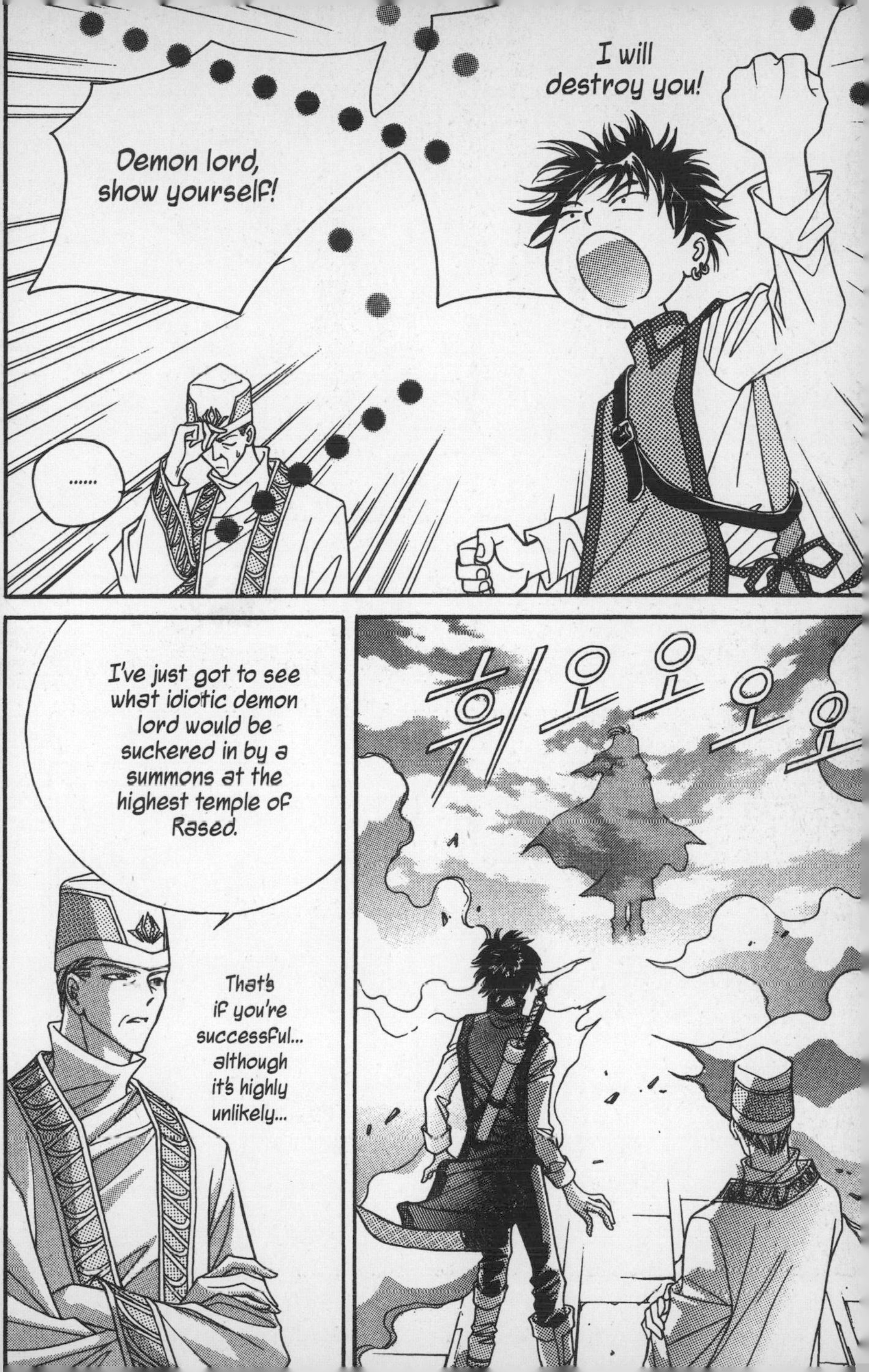
Demon lord, show yourself!
I will destroy you!
......
I've just got to see what idiotic demon lord would be suckered in by a summons at the highest temple of Rased.
That's if you're successful... although it's highly unlikely...
휘오오오오

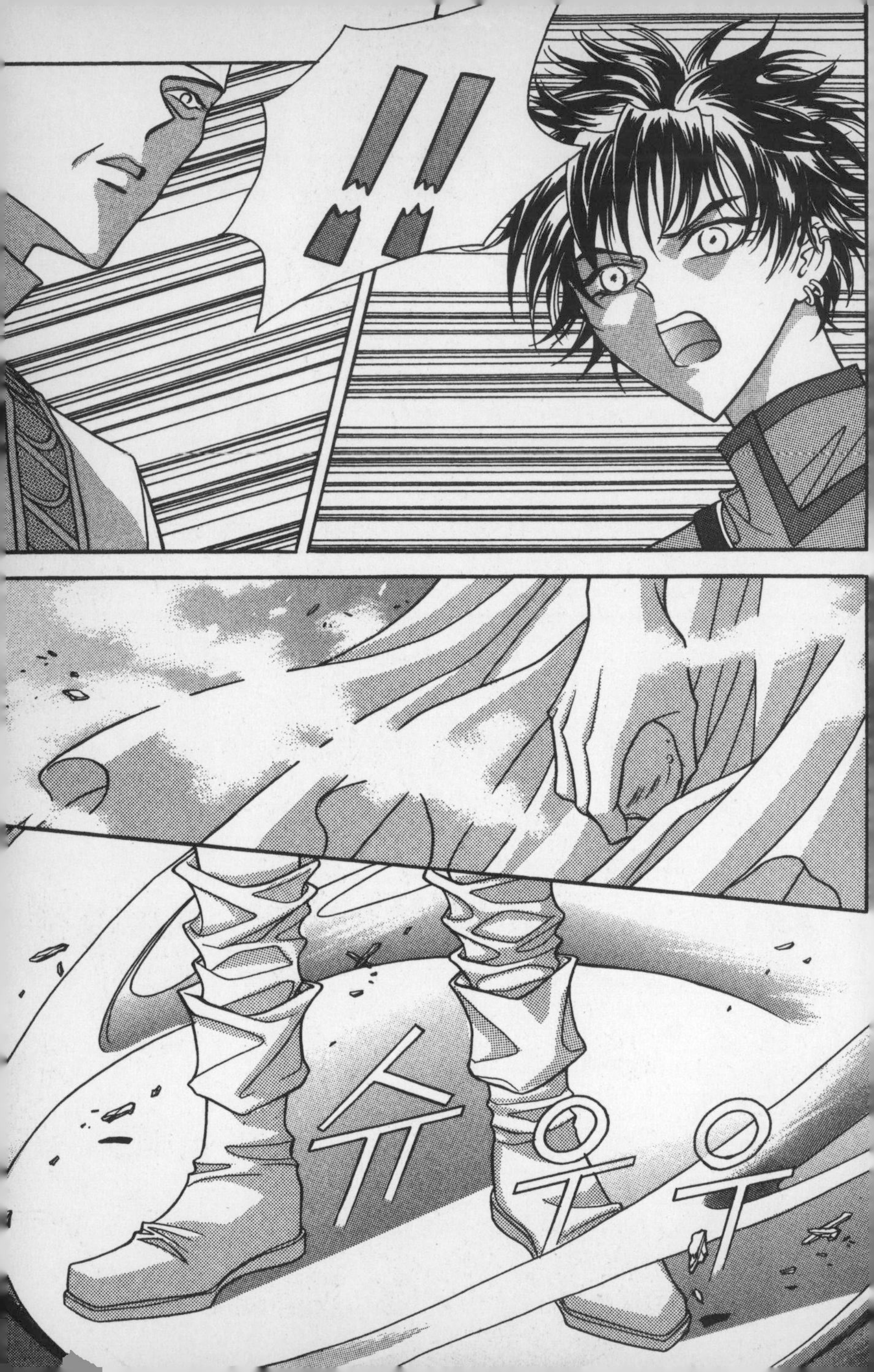
!!

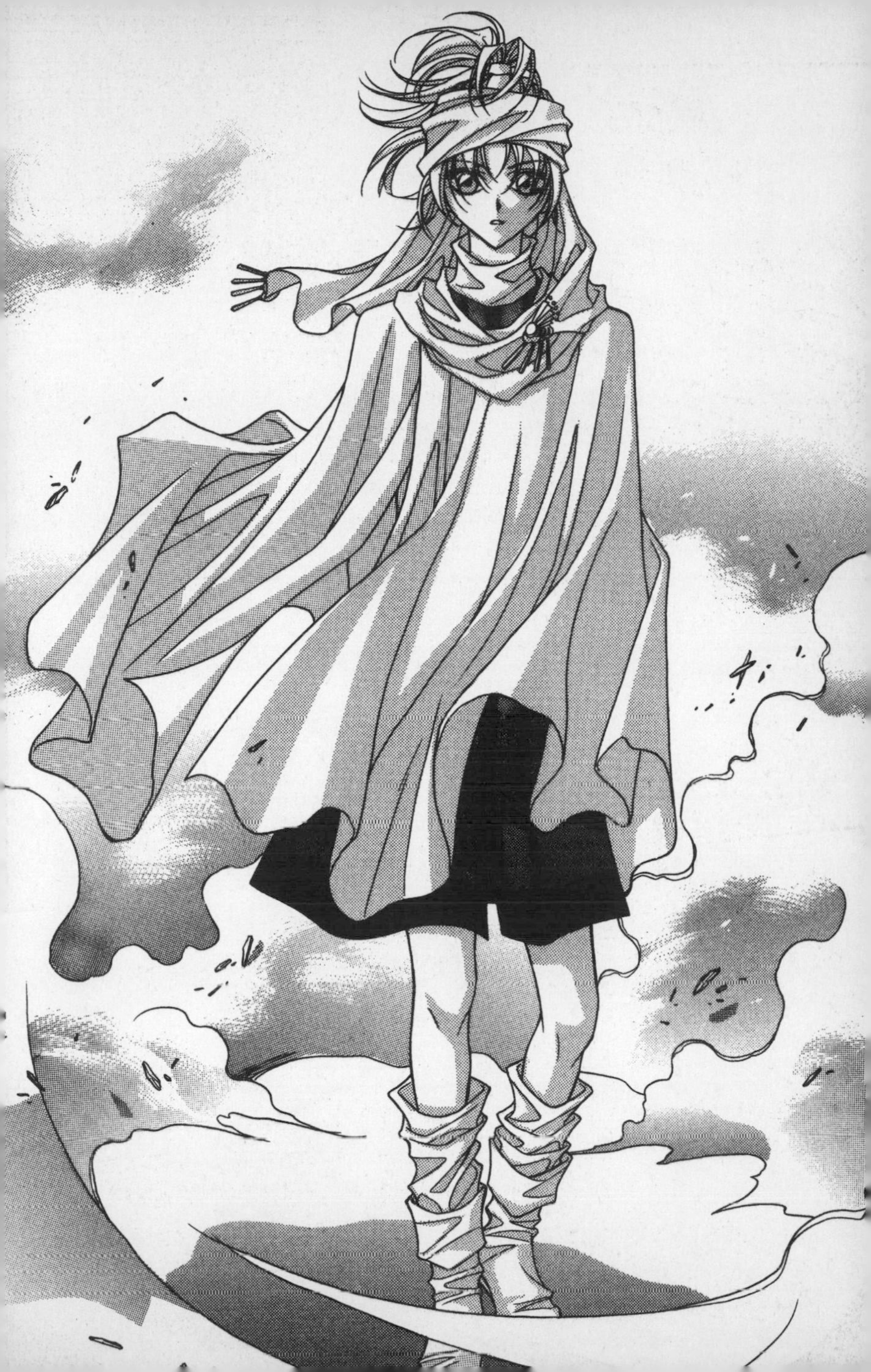

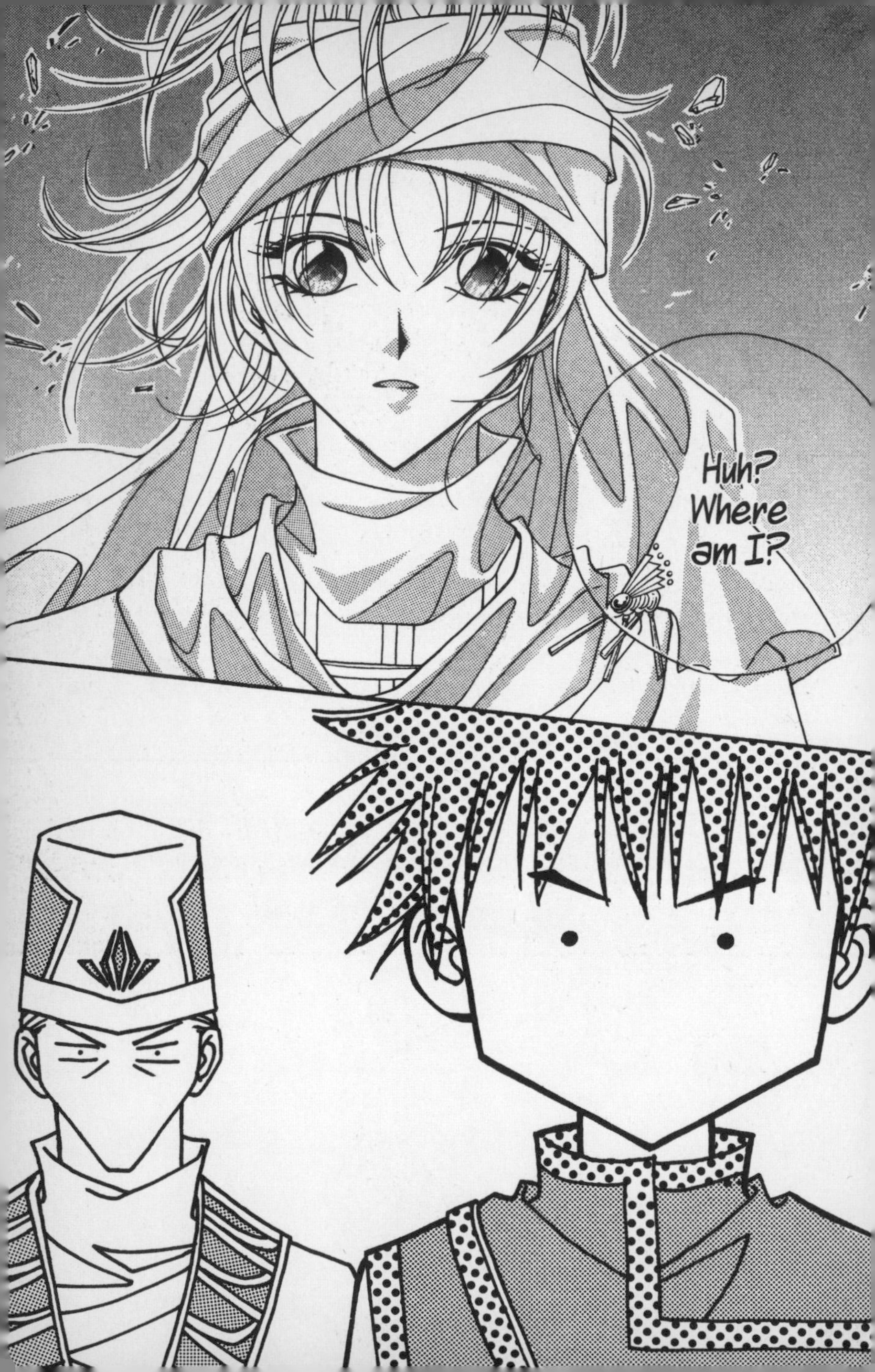
Huh? Where am I?

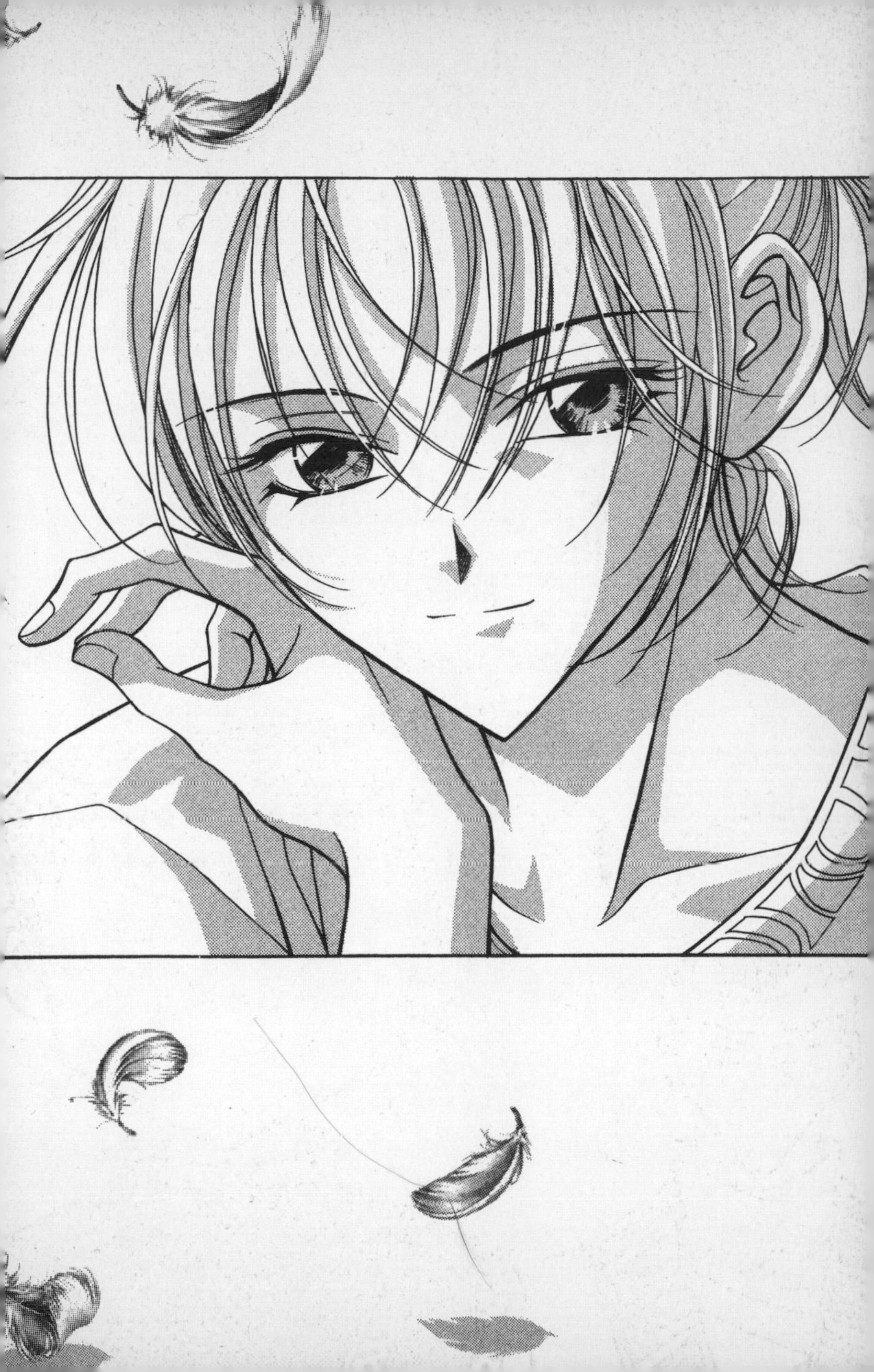

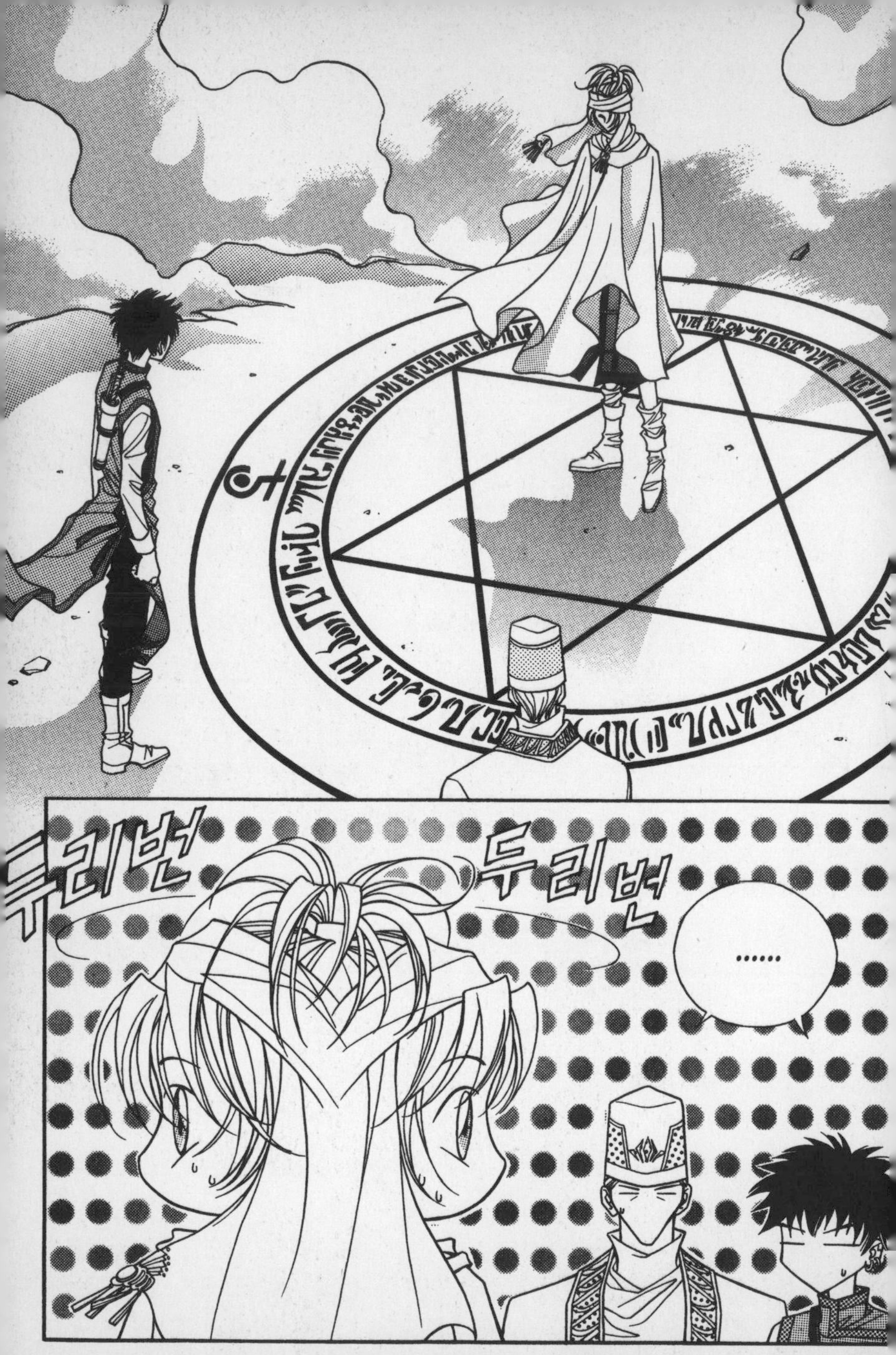
두리번
두리번
......

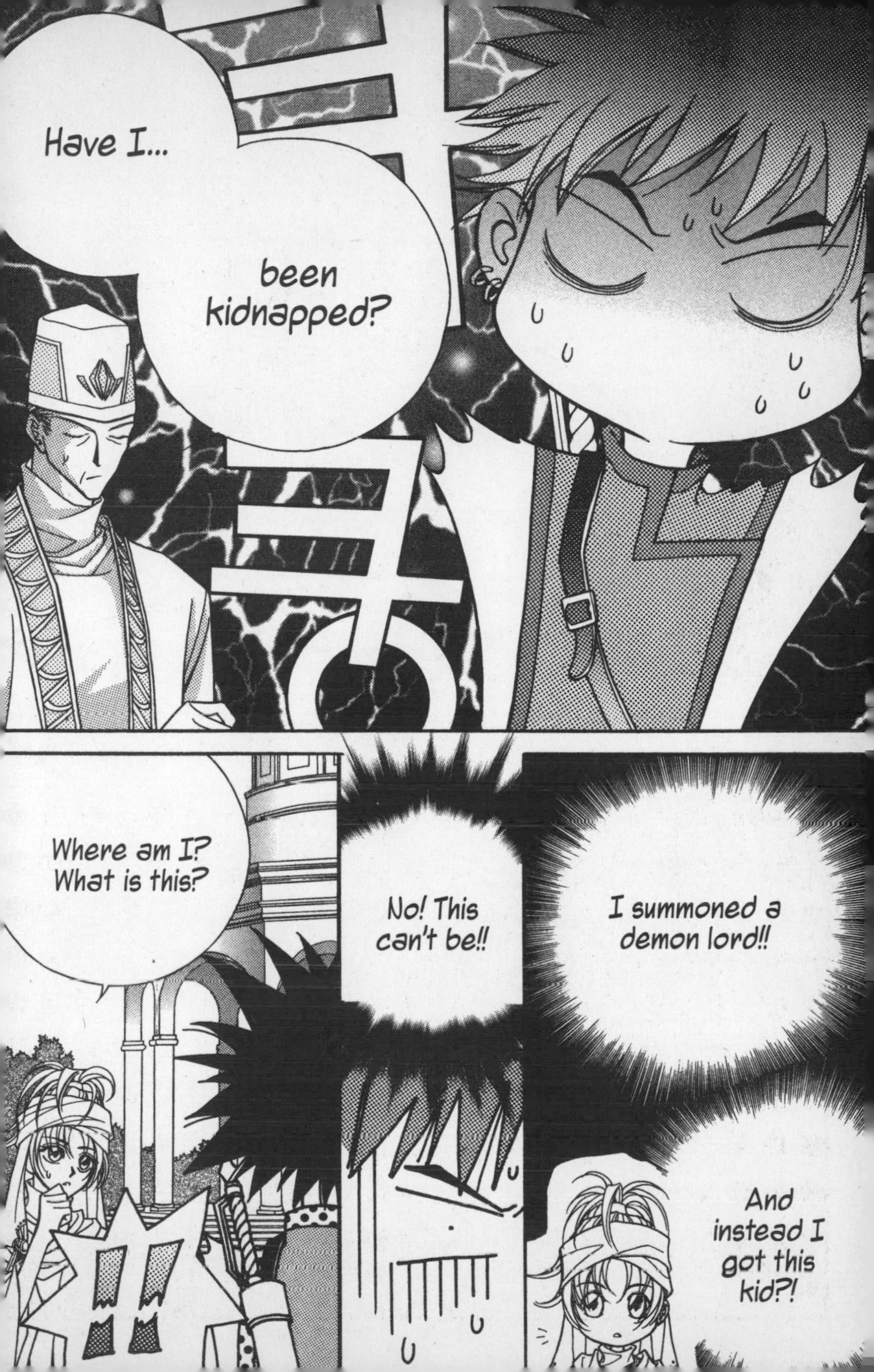
Have I...
been kidnapped?
No! This can't be!!
I summoned a demon lord!!
Where am I? What is this?
And instead I got this kid?!

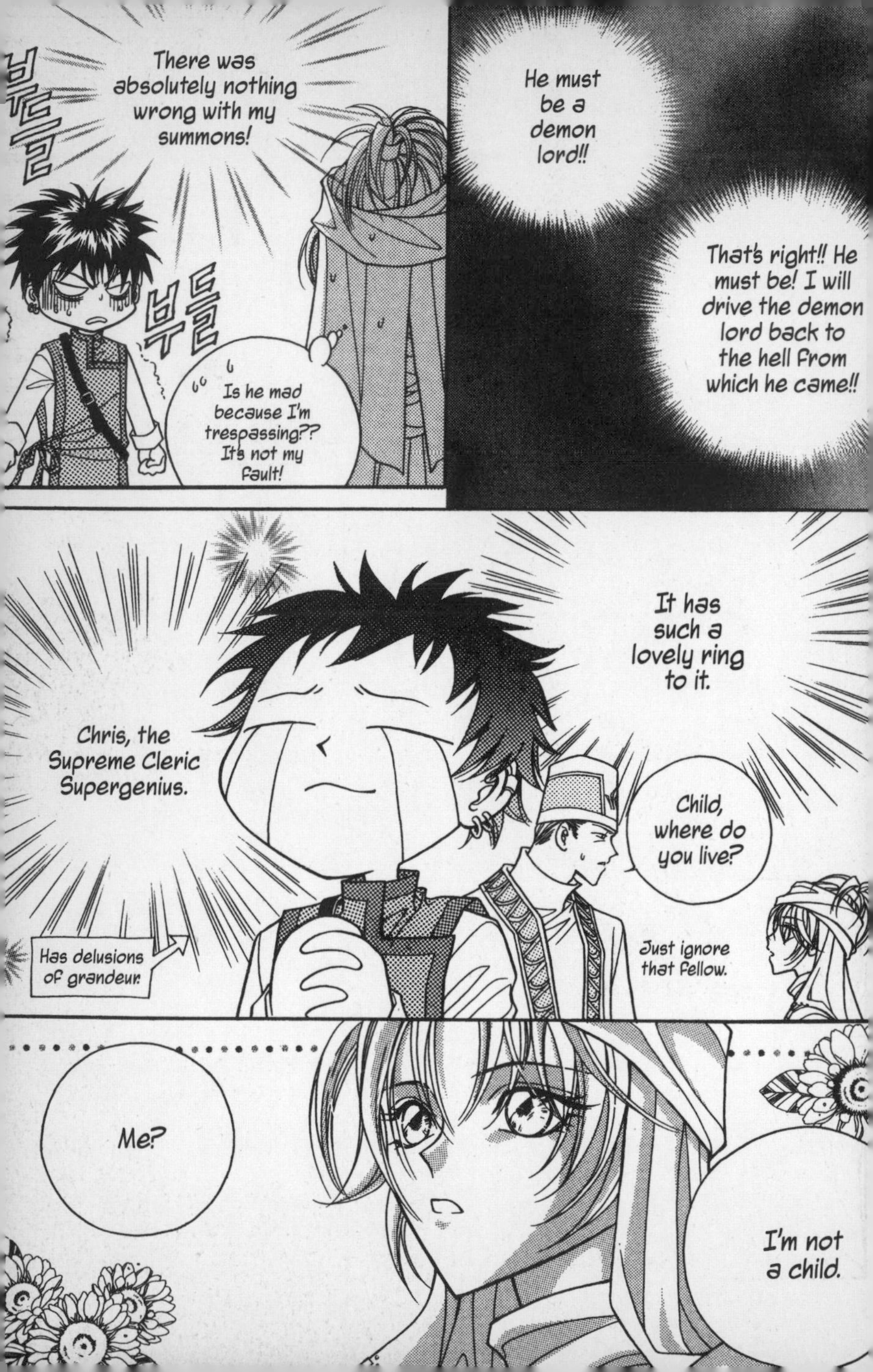

There was absolutely nothing wrong with my summons!
Is he mad because I'm trespassing?? It's not my fault!
He must be a demon lord!!
That's right!! He must be! I will drive the demon lord back to the hell from which he came!!
Chris, the Supreme Cleric Supergenius.
Has delusions of grandeur.
It has such a lovely ring to it.
Child, where do you live?
Just ignore that fellow.
Me?
I'm not a child.

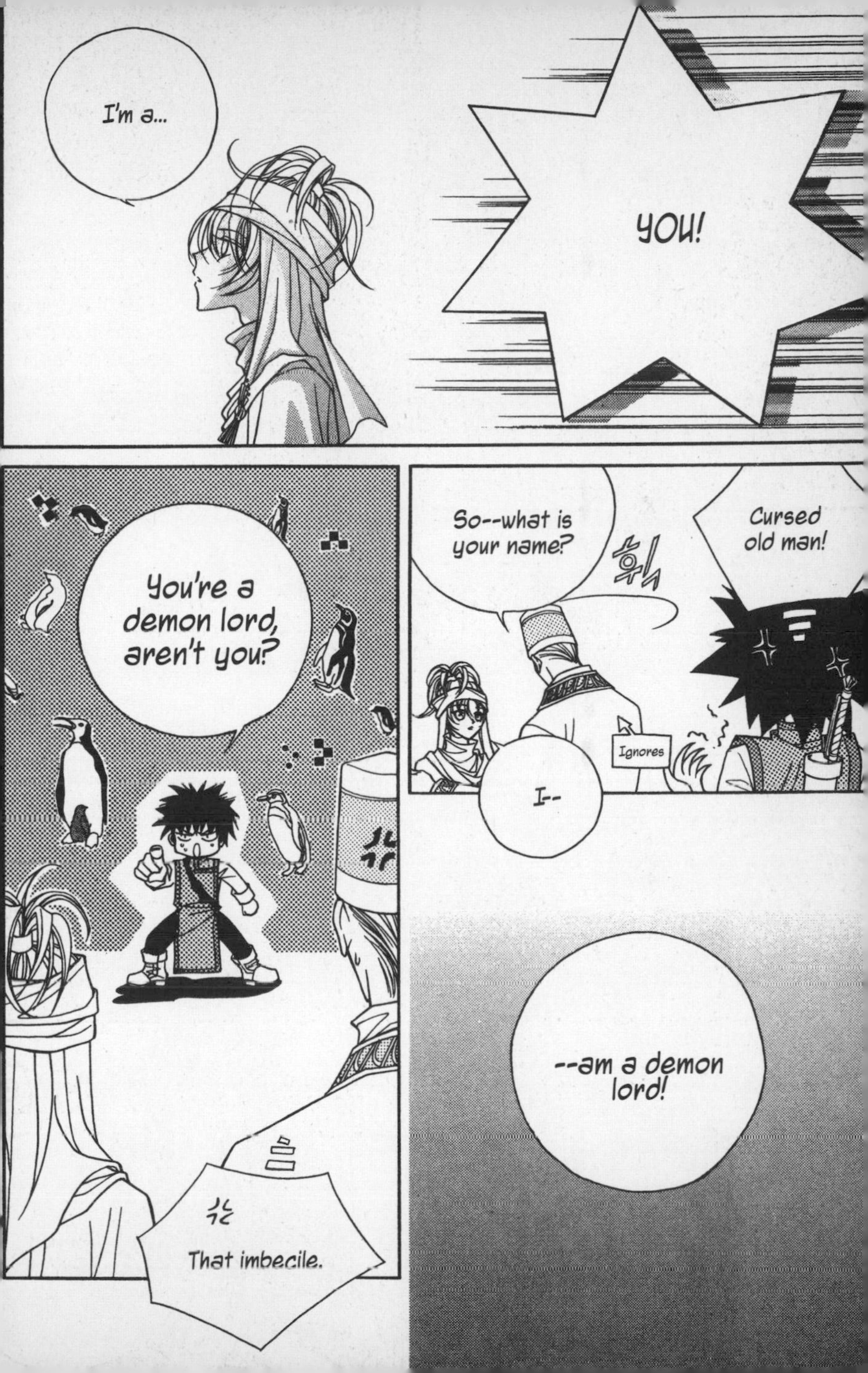
I'm a...
YOU!
You're a demon lord, aren't you?
That imbecile.
So--what is your name?
Cursed old man!
Ignores
I--
--am a demon lord!

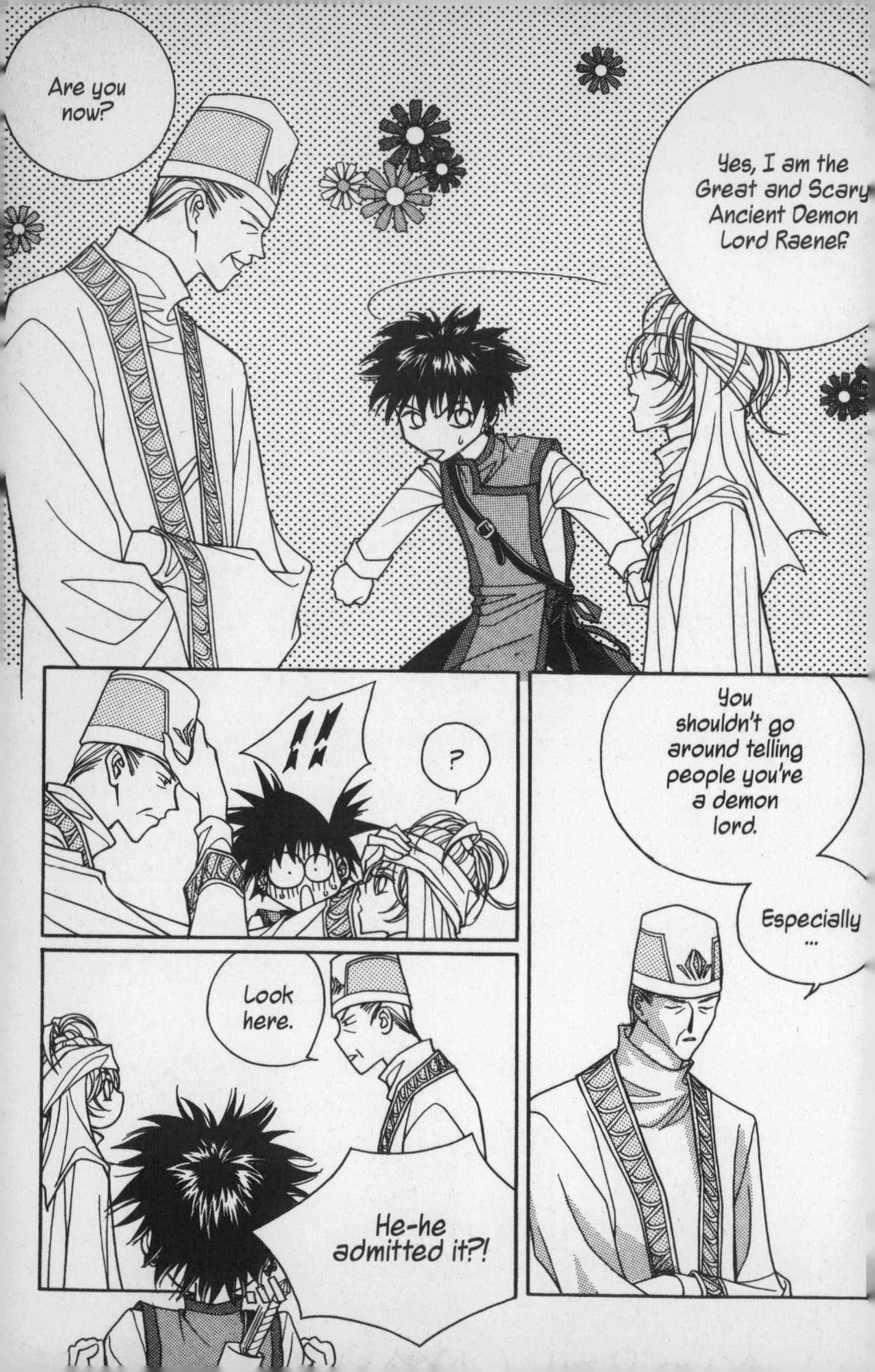
Yes, I am the Great and Scary Ancient Demon Lord Raenef.
Are you now?
You shouldn't go around telling people you're a demon lord.
Especially ...
!!
?
Look here.
He-he admitted it?!

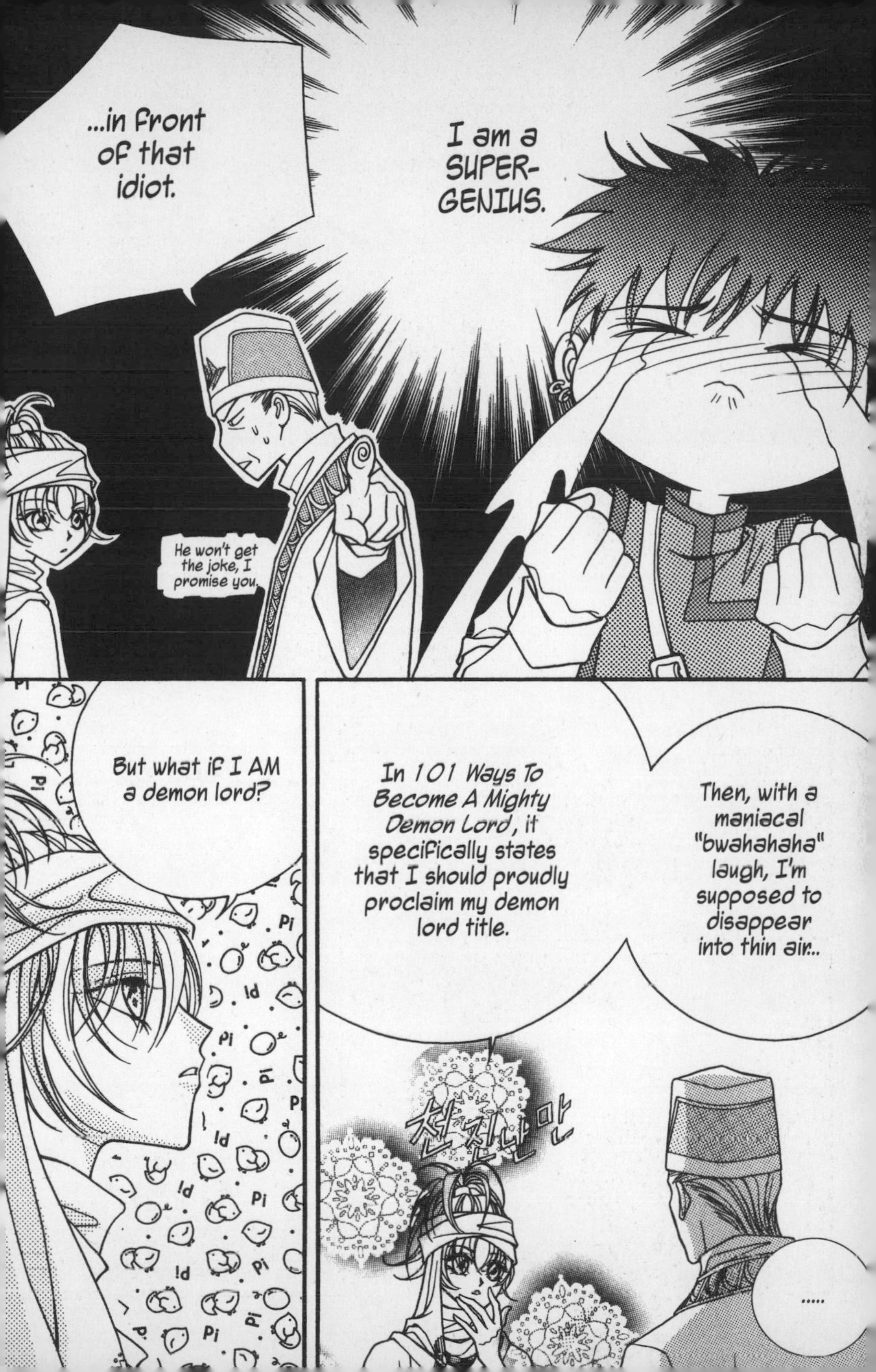

...in front of that idiot.
I am a SUPER-GENIUS.
He won't get the joke, I promise you.
But what if I AM a demon lord?
In 101 Ways To Become A Mighty Demon Lord, it specifically states that I should proudly proclaim my demon lord title.
Then, with a maniacal "bwahahaha" laugh, I'm supposed to disappear into thin air..
천진난만
.....

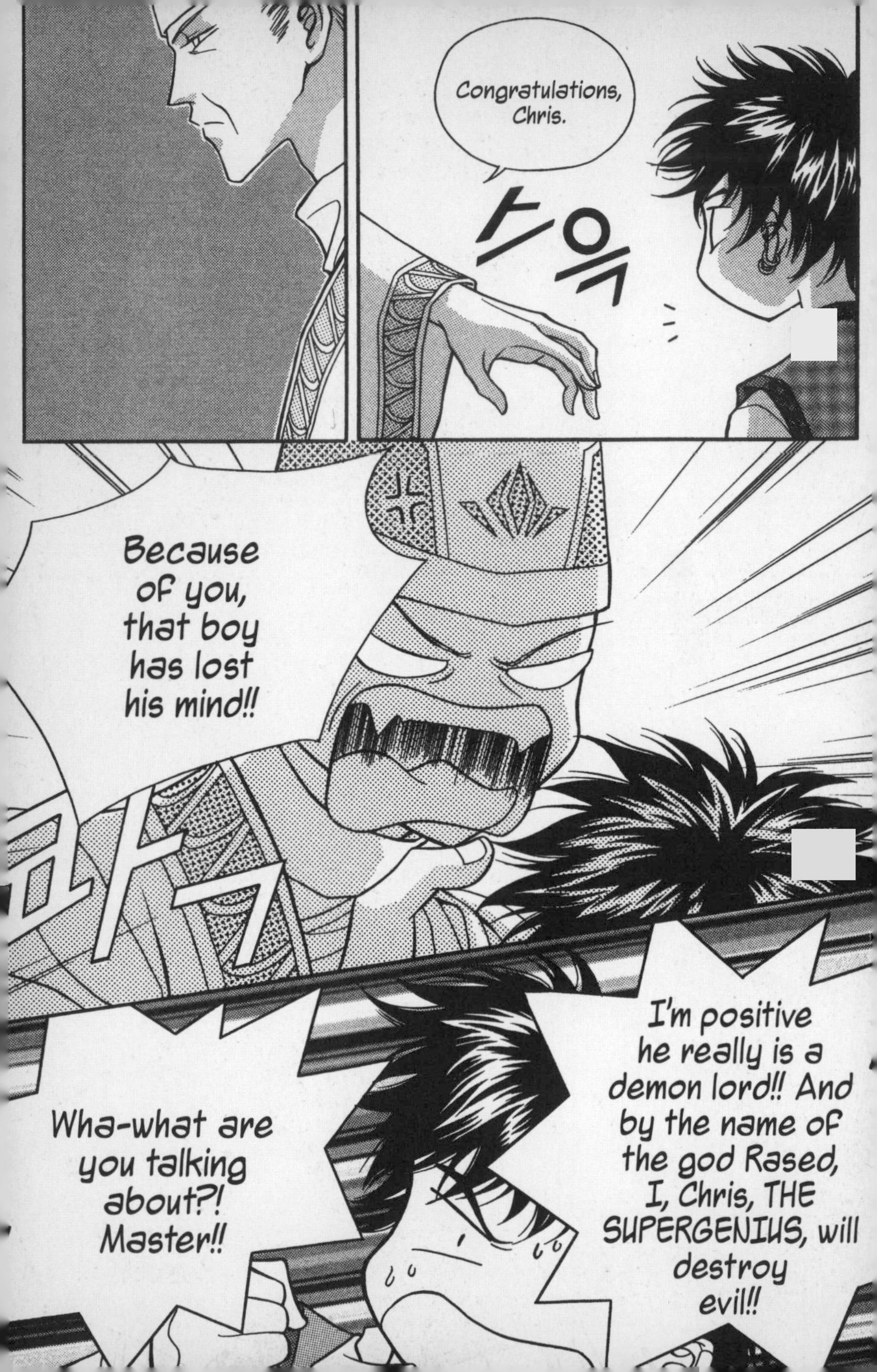

Congratulations, Chris.
Because of you, that boy has lost his mind!!
I'm positive he really is a demon lord!! And by the name of the god Rased, I, Chris, THE SUPERGENIUS, will destroy evil!!
Wha-what are you talking about?! Master!!

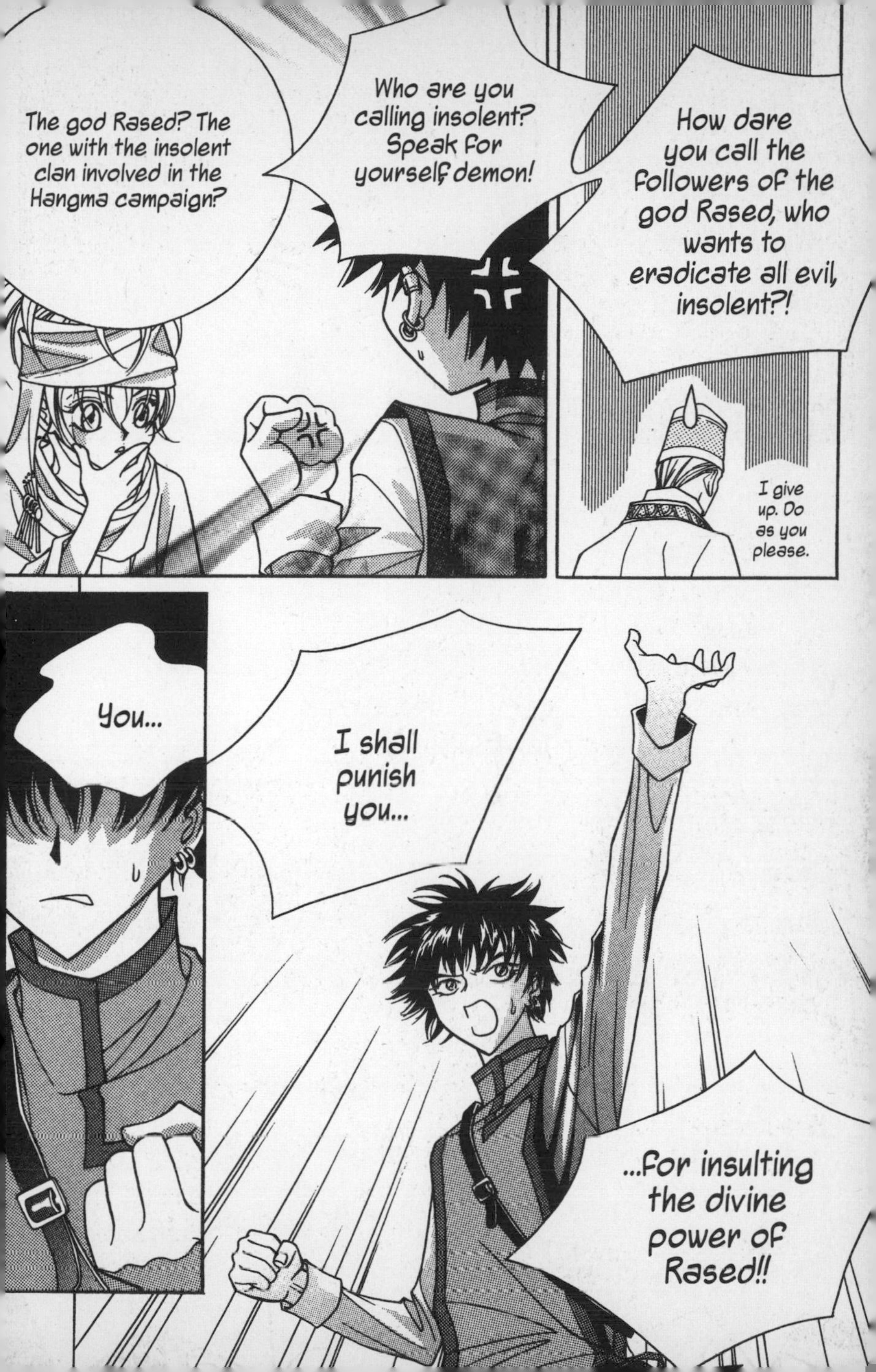

The god Rased? The one with the insolent clan involved in the Hangma campaign?
Who are you calling insolent? Speak for yourself, demon!
How dare you call the followers of the god Rased, who wants to eradicate all evil, insolent?!
I give up. Do as you please.
You...
I shall punish you...
...for insulting the divine power of Rased!!

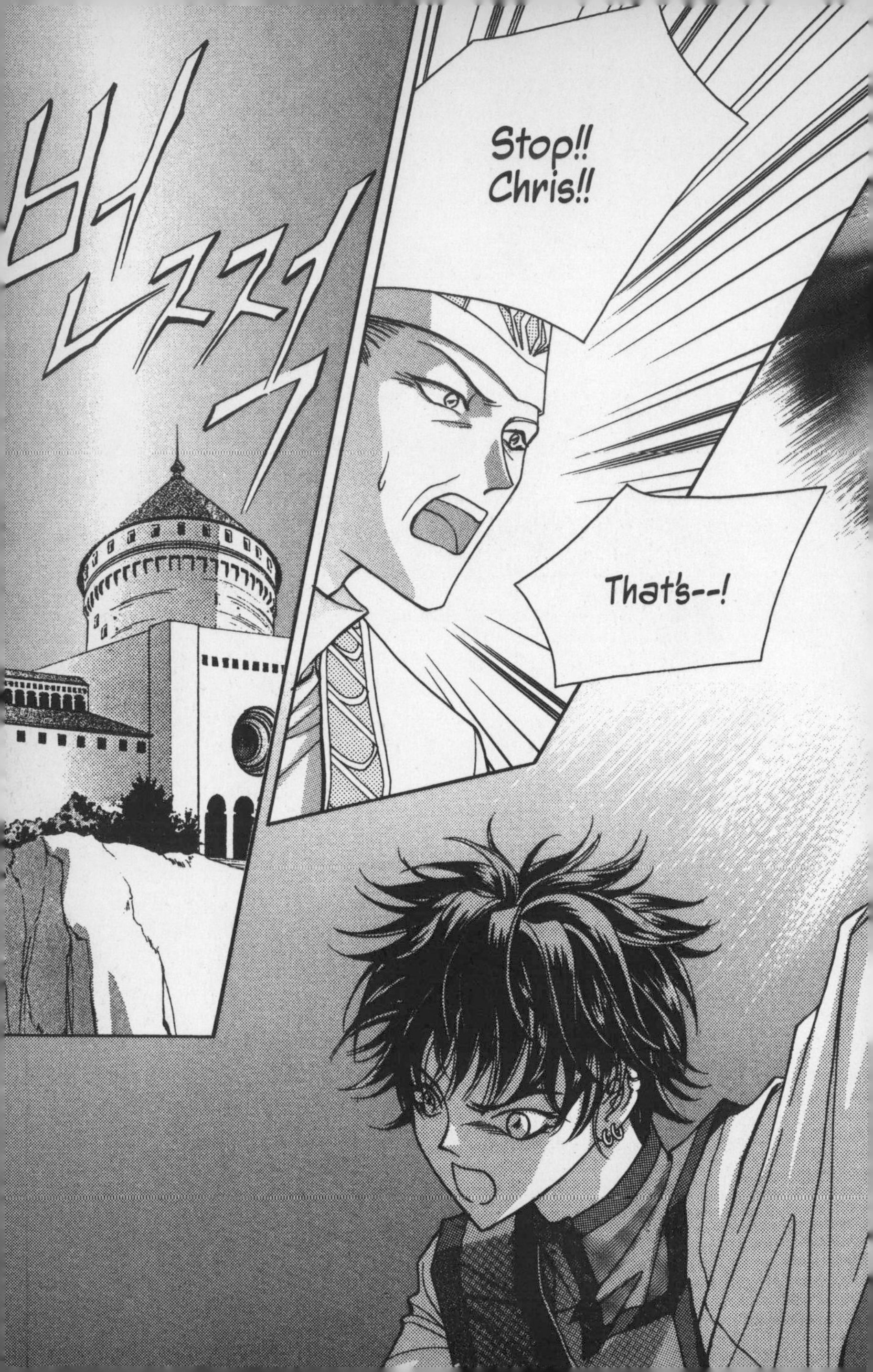
Stop!!
Chris!!
That's--!

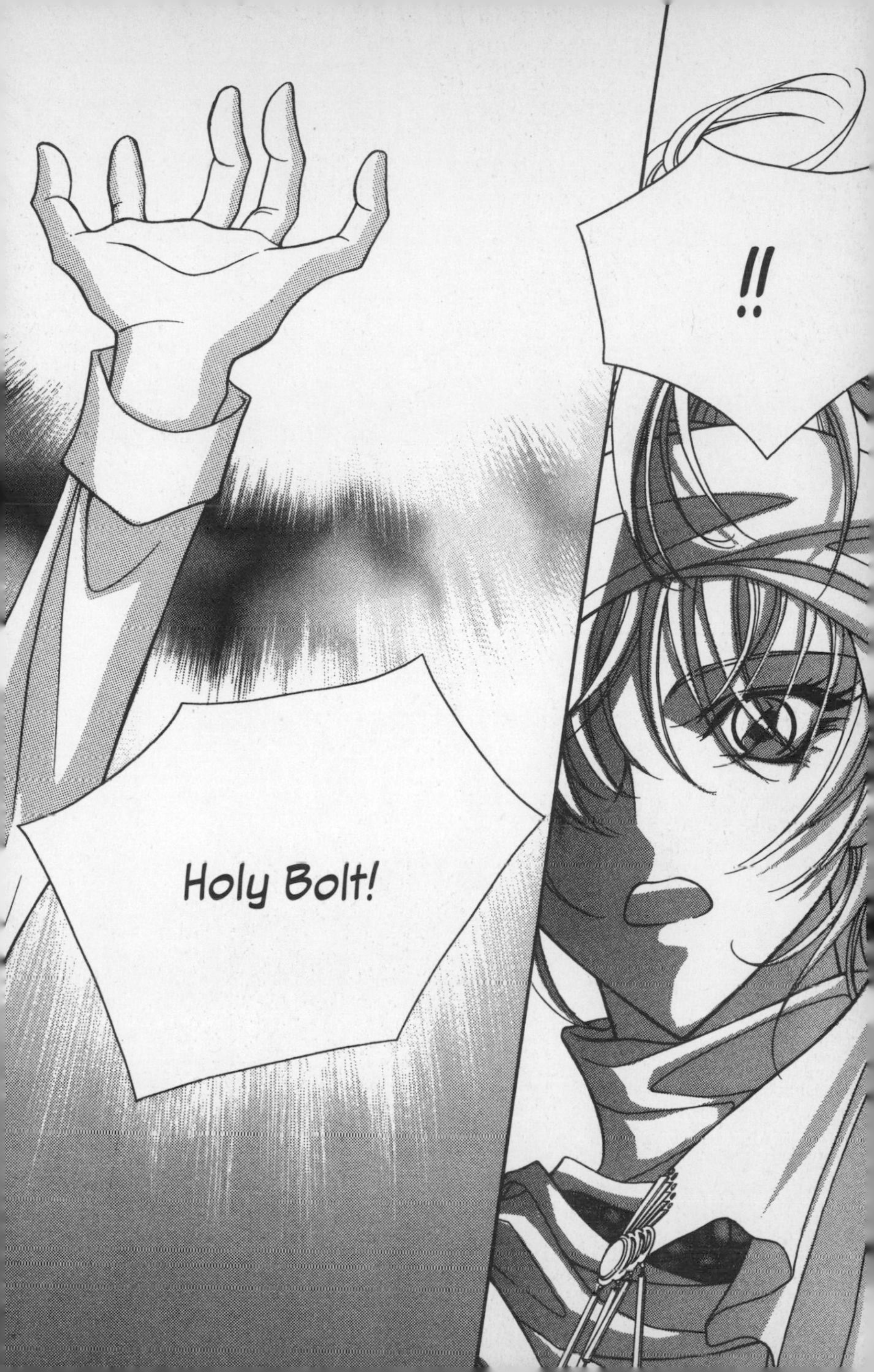
!!
Holy Bolt!

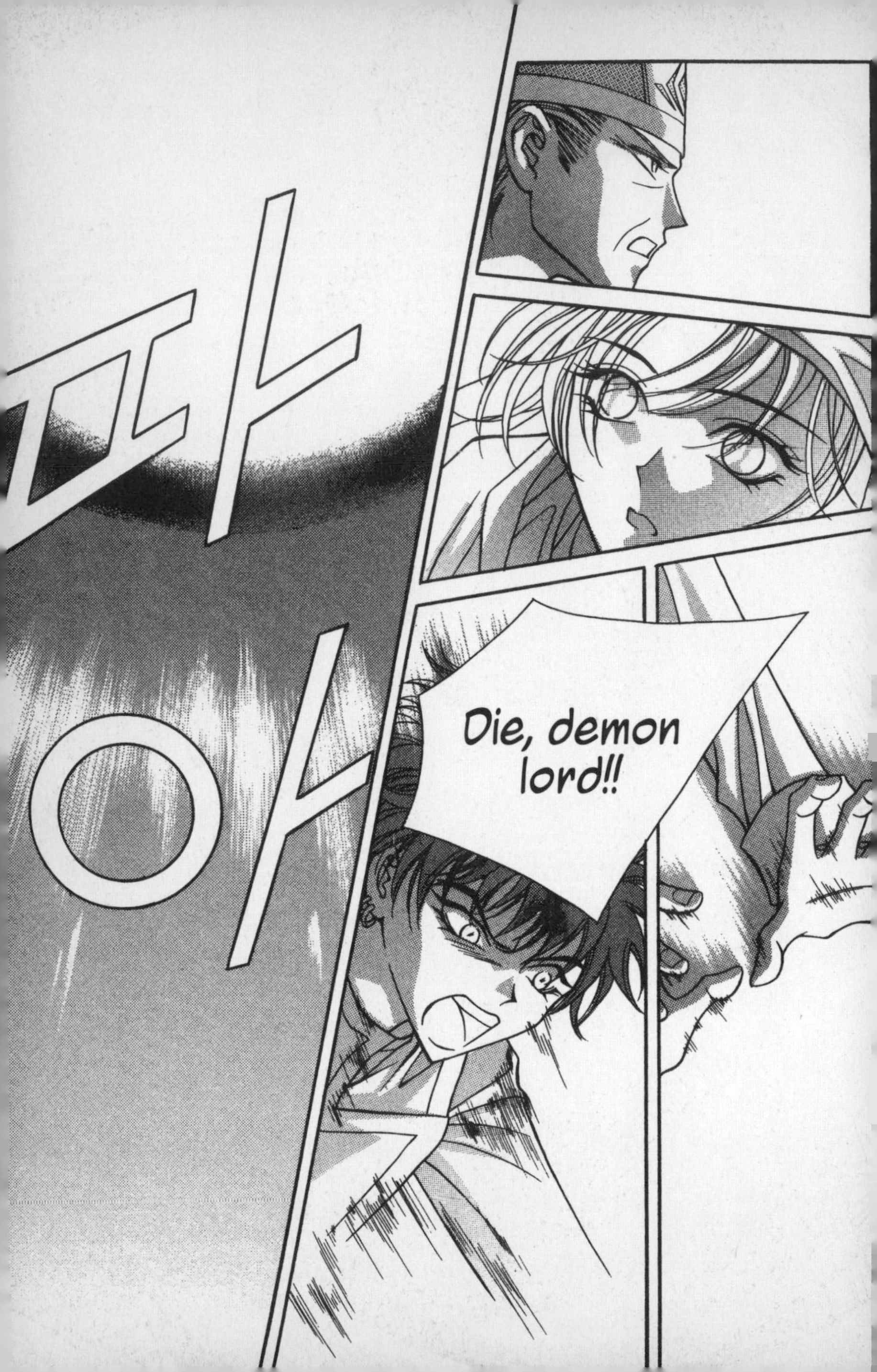
Die, demon lord!!

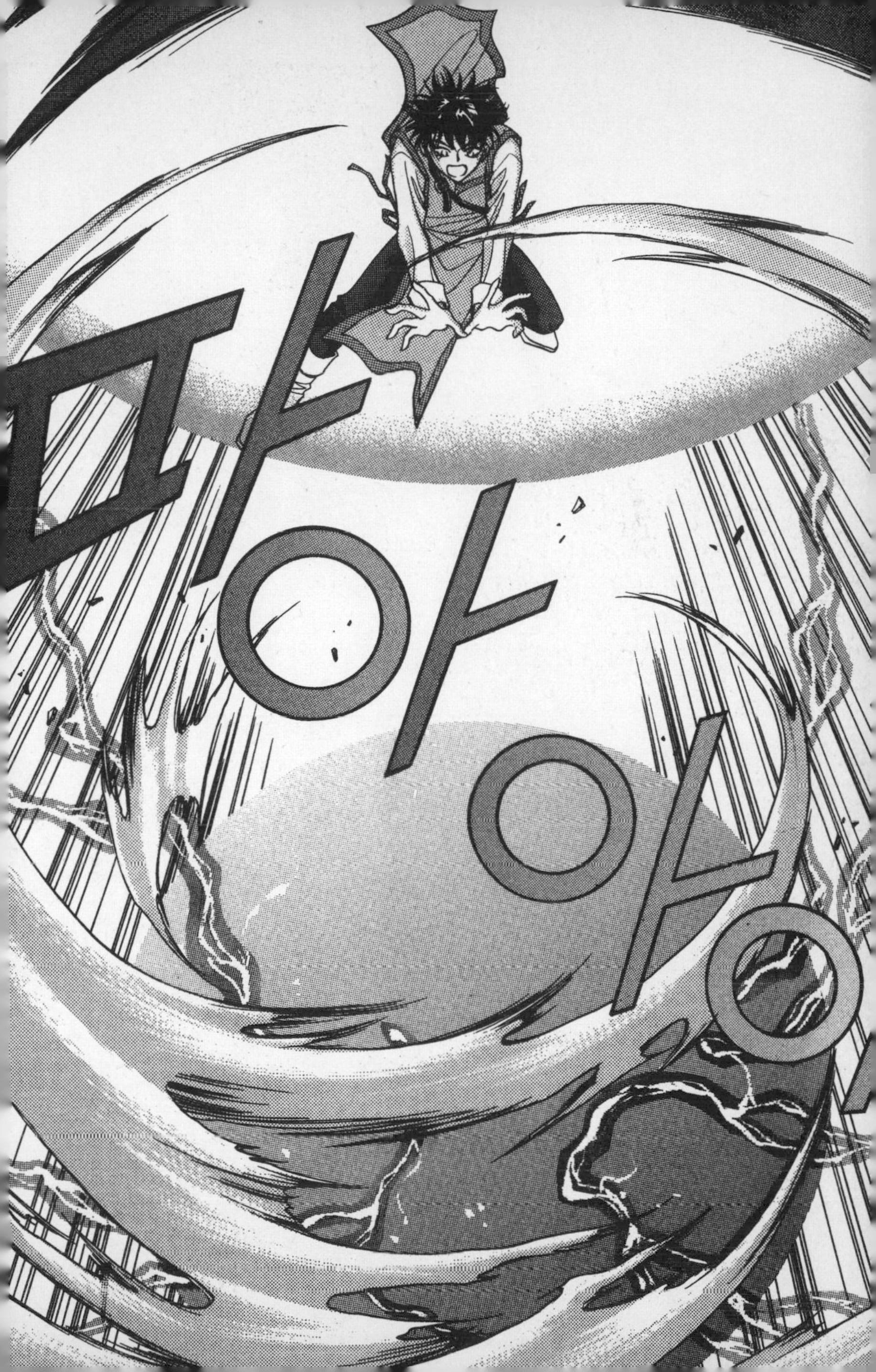
파아아아

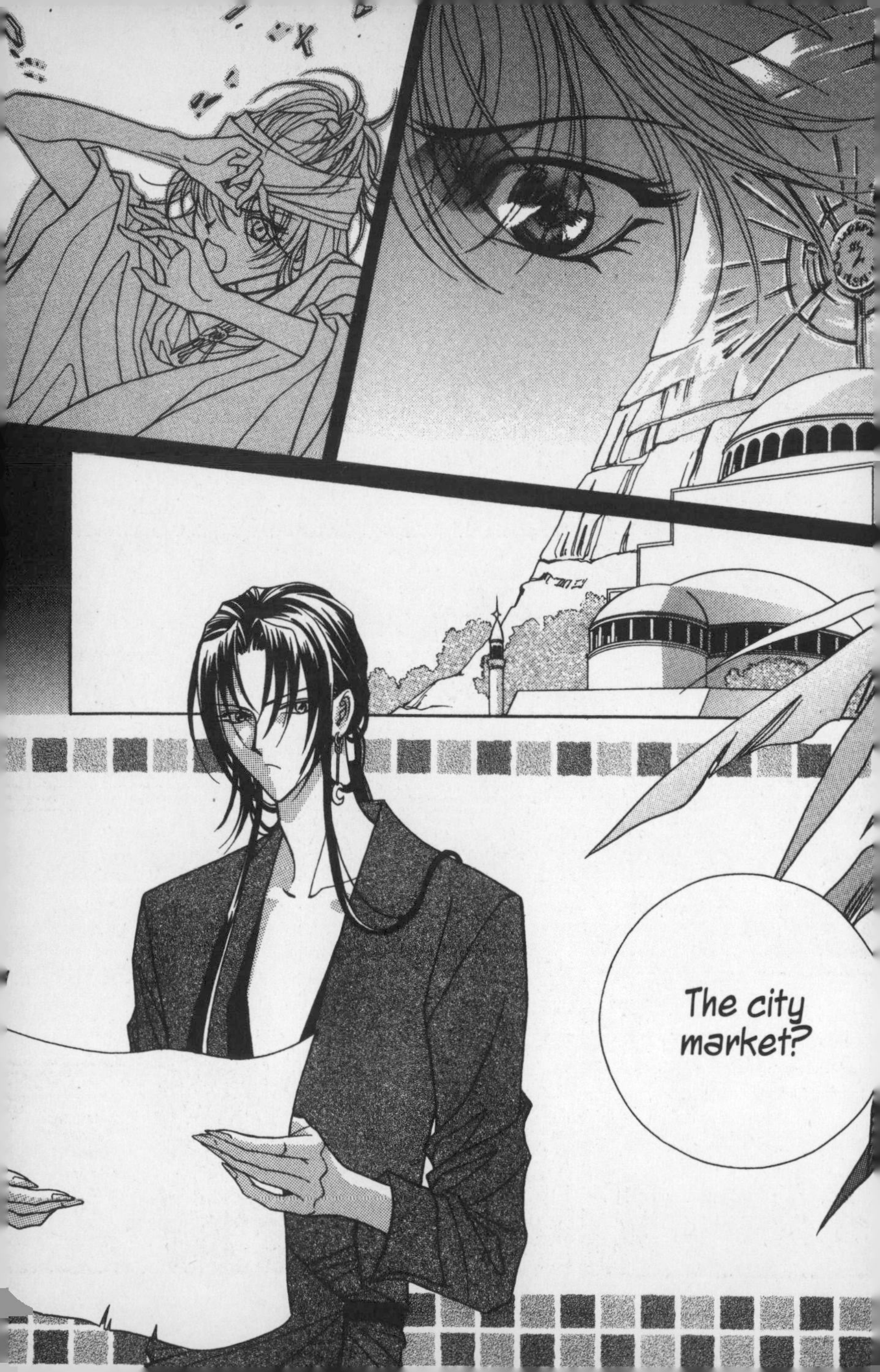
The city market?

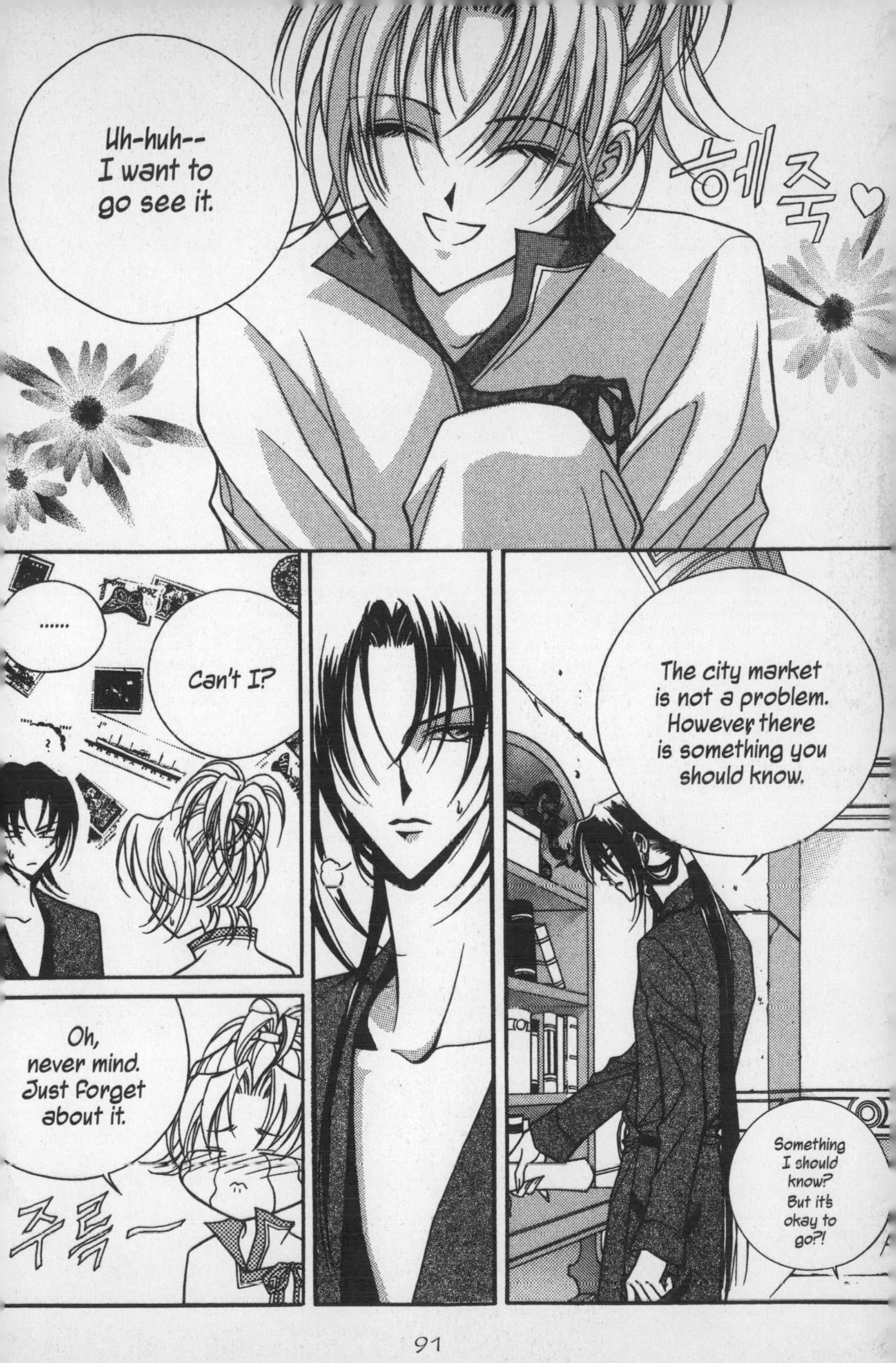
Uh-huh--
I want to go see it.
헤죽♥
......
Can't I?
Oh, never mind. Just forget about it.
주륵—
The city market is not a problem. However, there is something you should know.
Something I should know? But it's okay to go?!

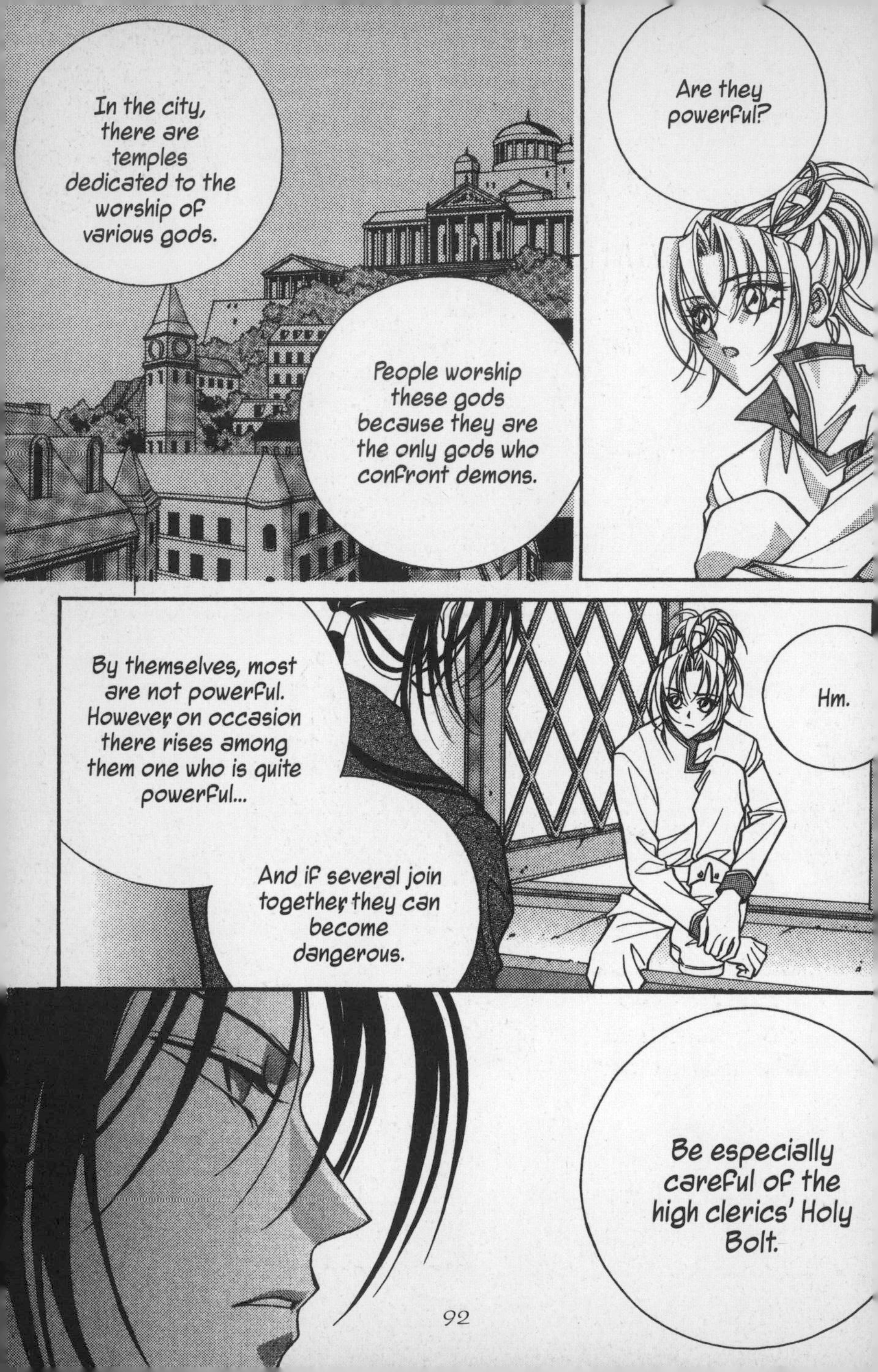

In the city, there are temples dedicated to the worship of various gods.
People worship these gods because they are the only gods who confront demons.
Are they powerful?
By themselves, most are not powerful. However, on occasion there rises among them one who is quite powerful...
And if several join together, they can become dangerous.
Hm.
Be especially careful of the high clerics' Holy Bolt.

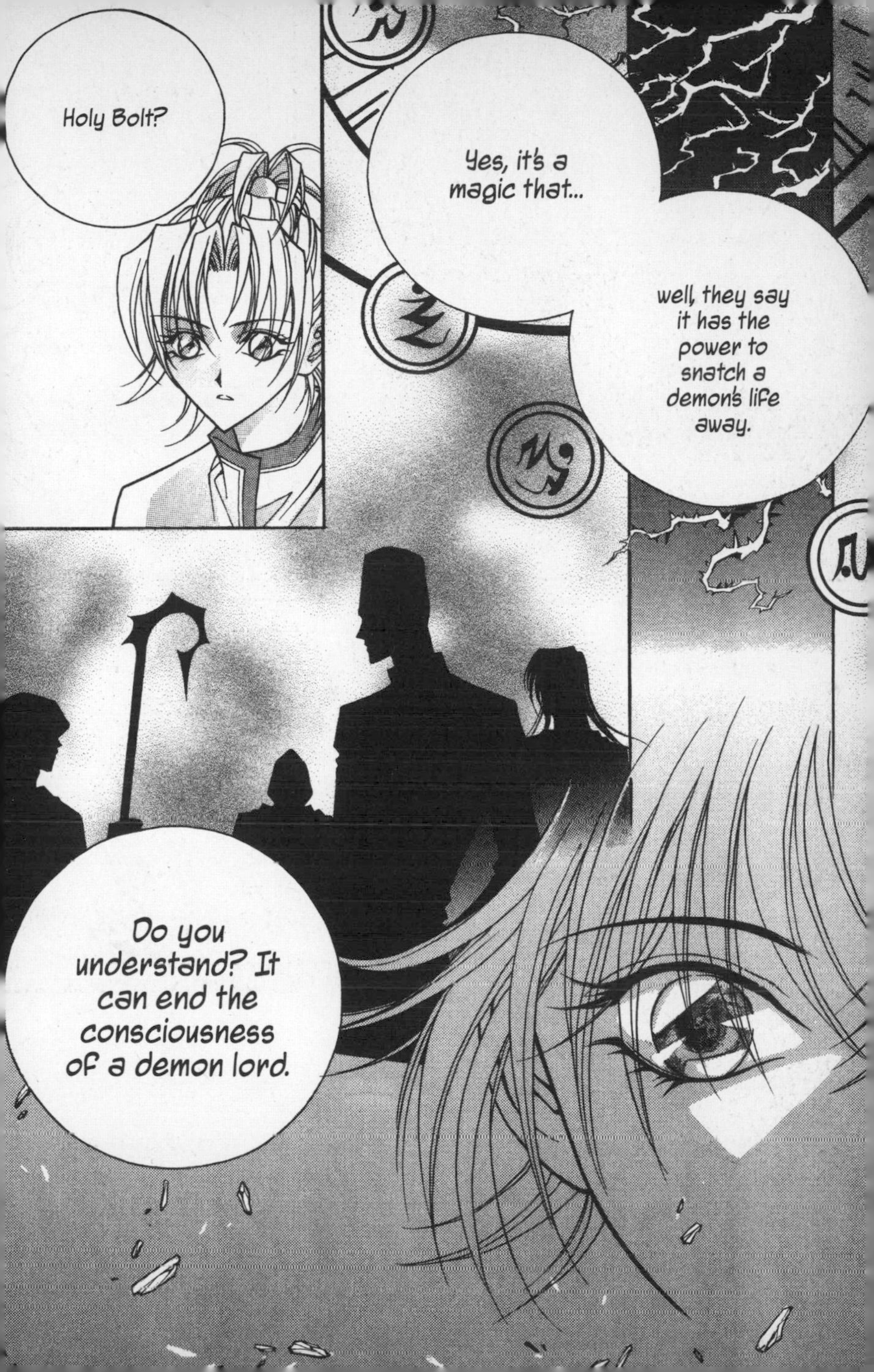
Holy Bolt?
Yes, it's a magic that...
well, they say it has the power to snatch a demon's life away.
Do you understand? It can end the consciousness of a demon lord.

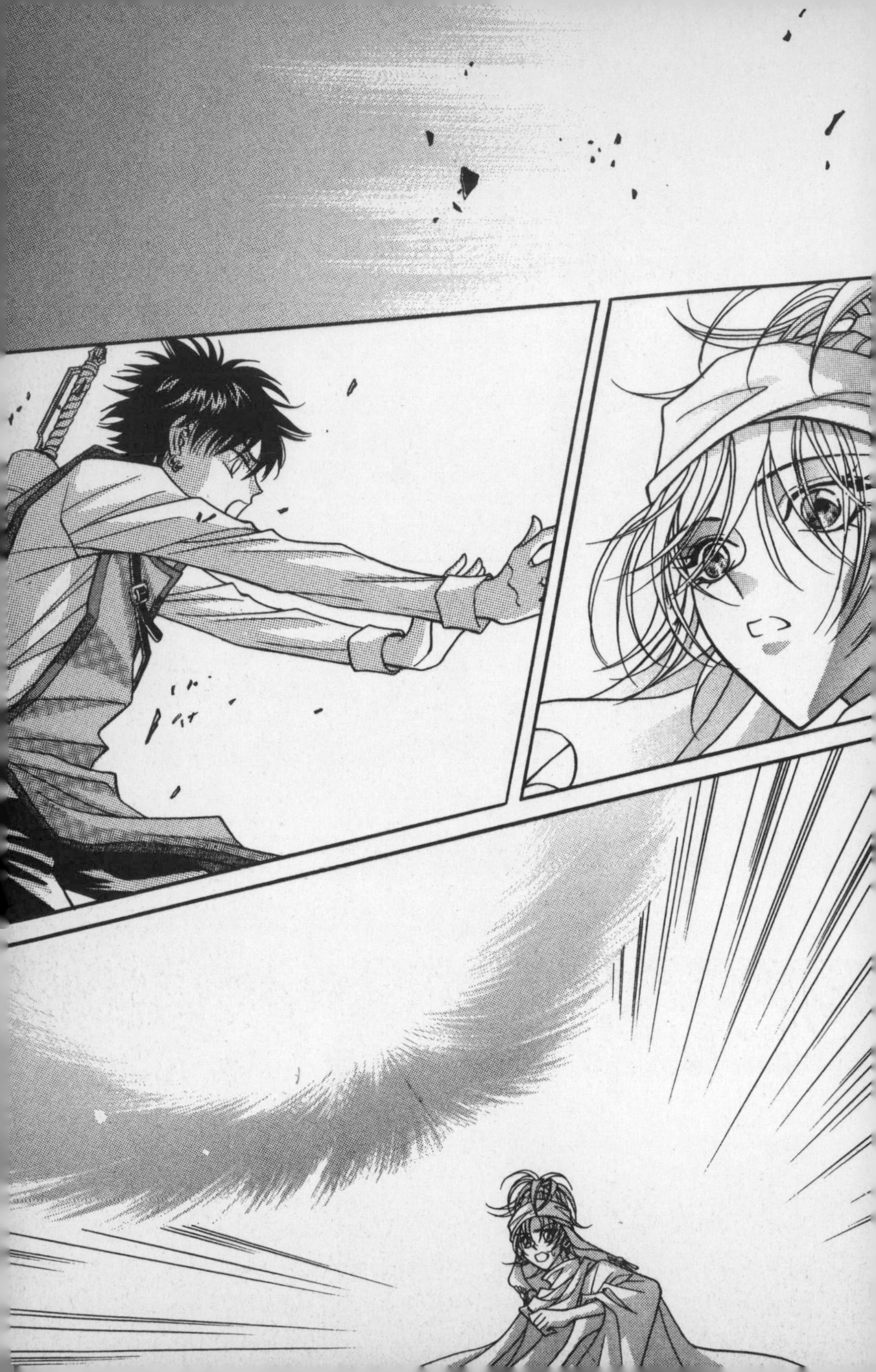

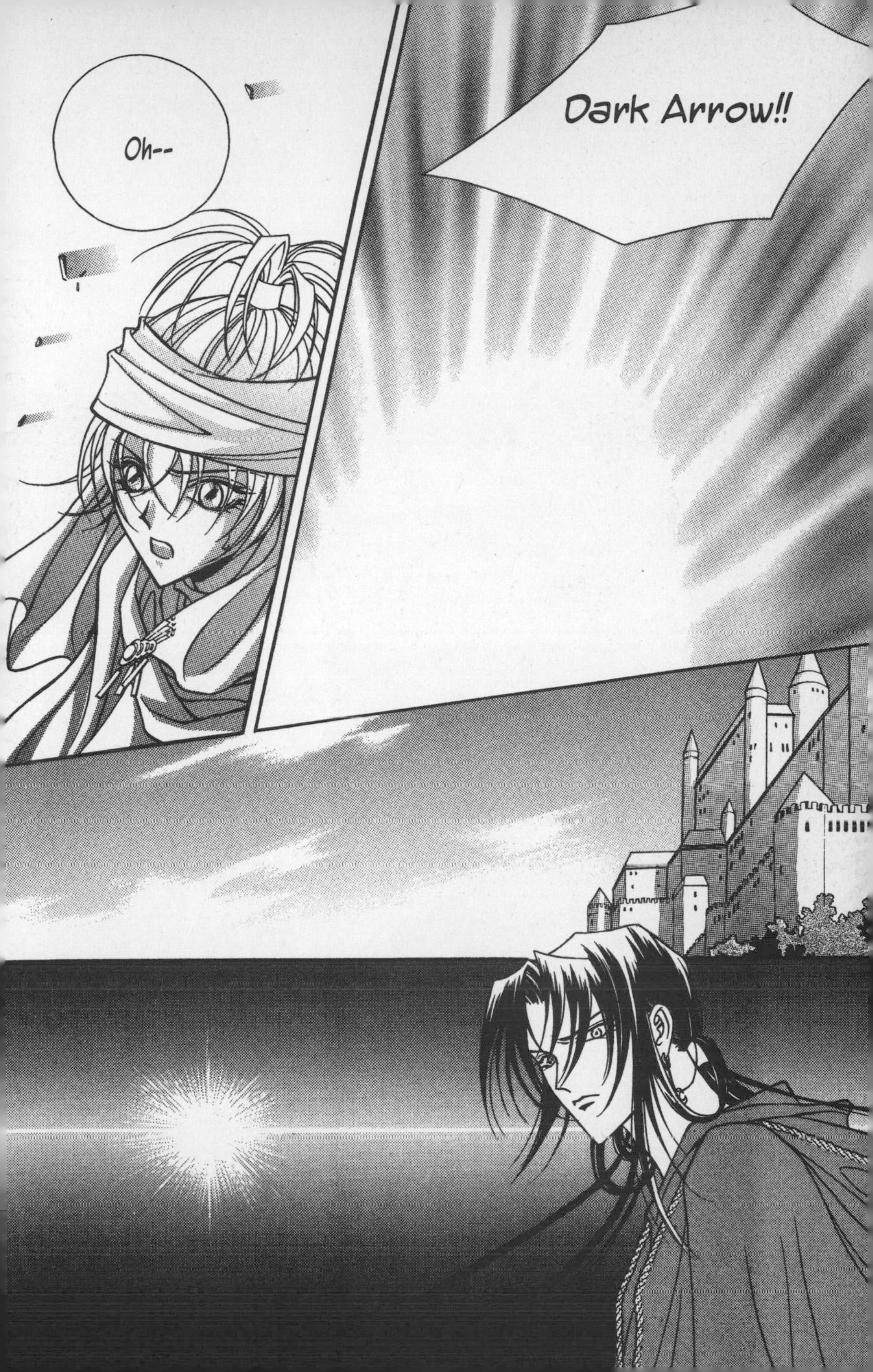
Dark Arrow!!
Oh--

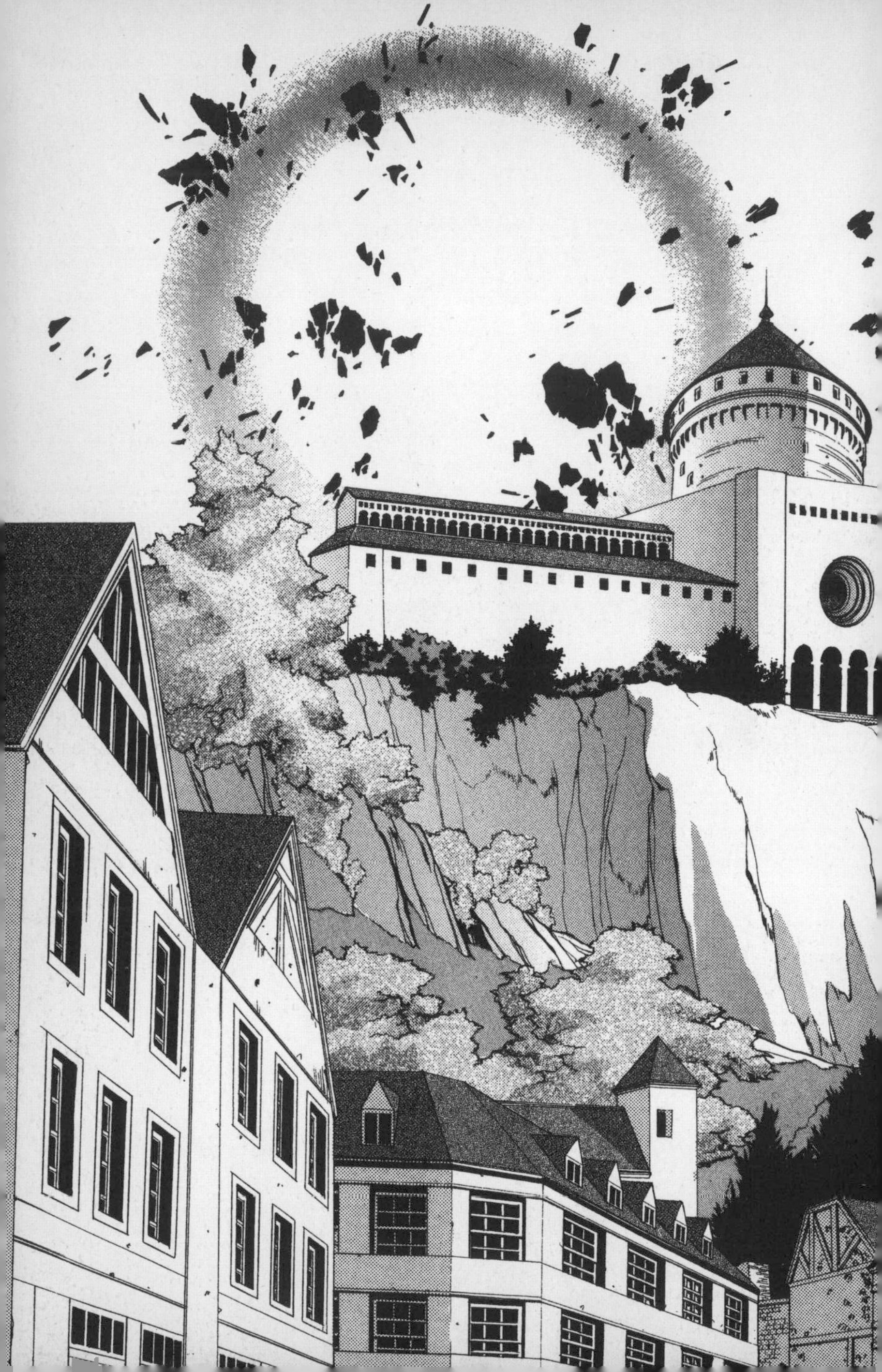

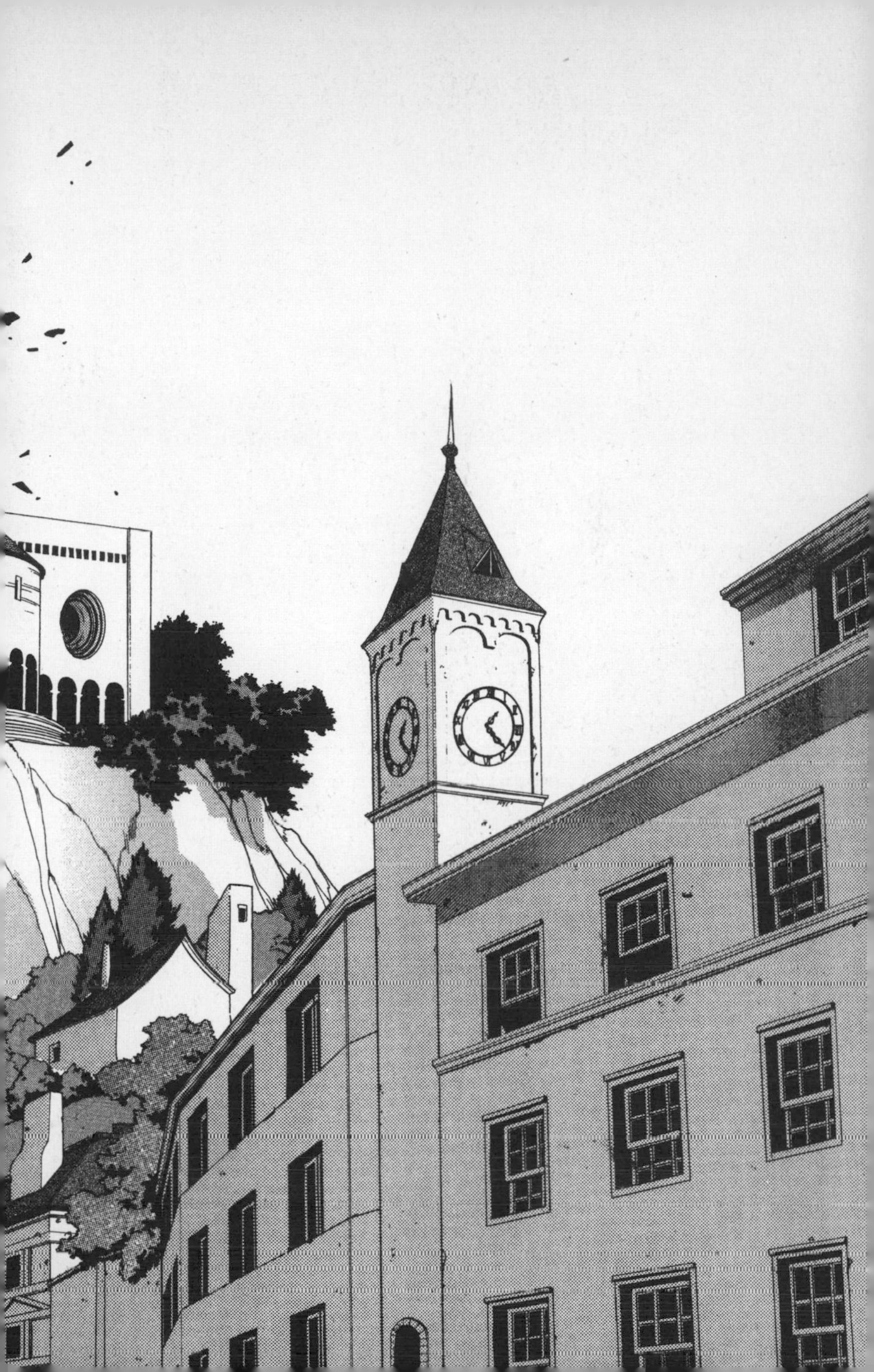

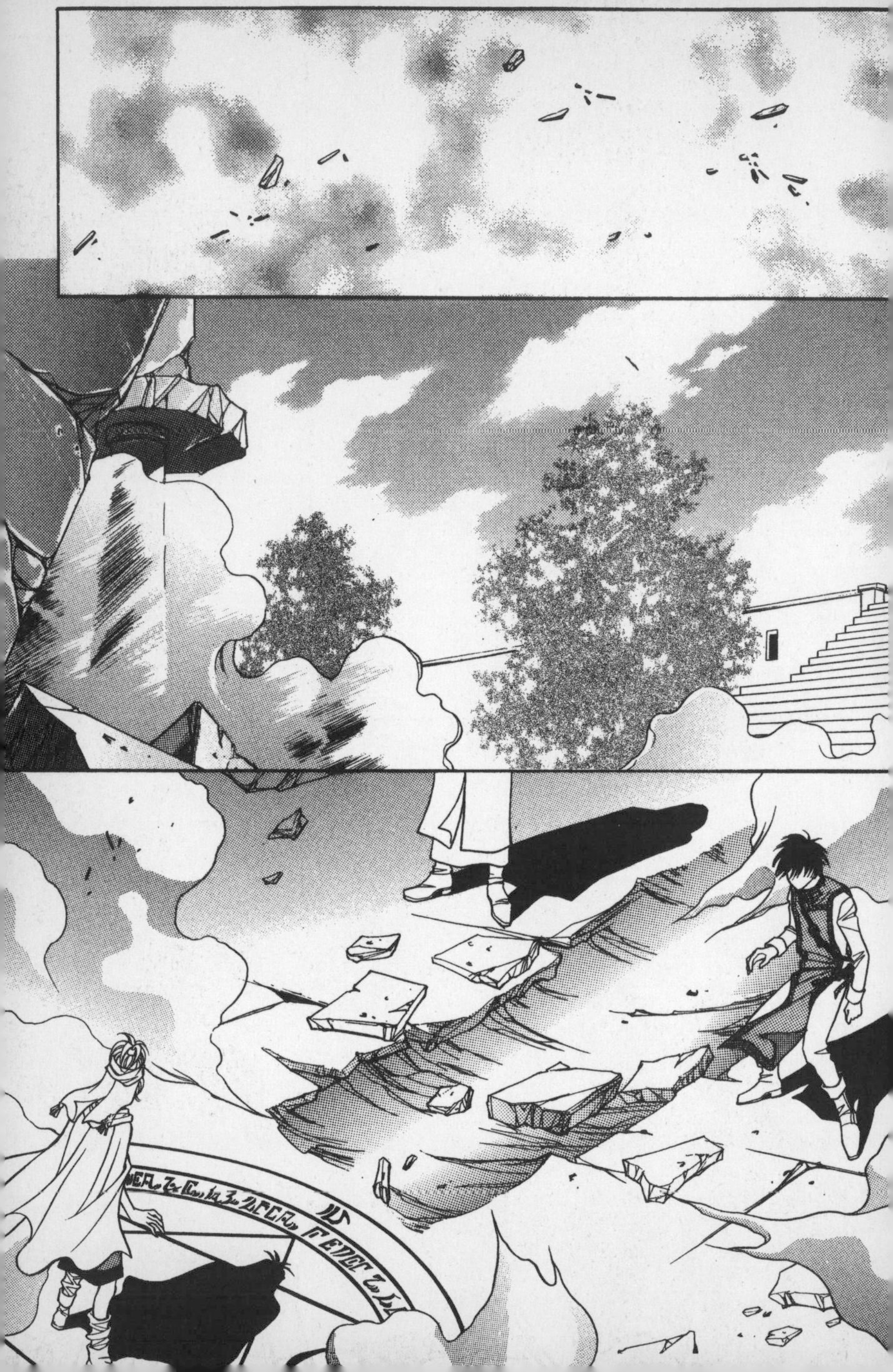

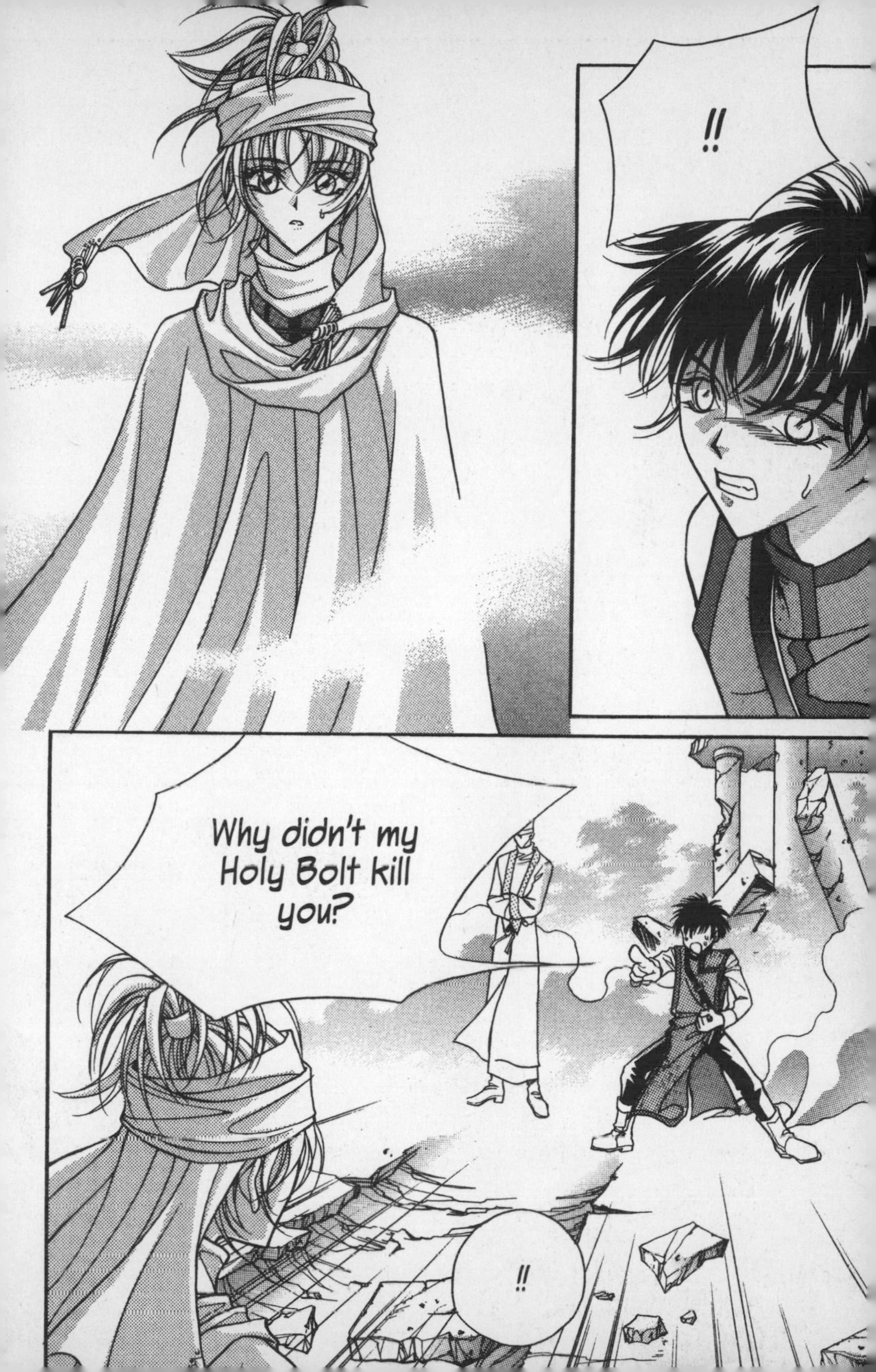
!!
Why didn't my Holy Bolt kill you?
!!

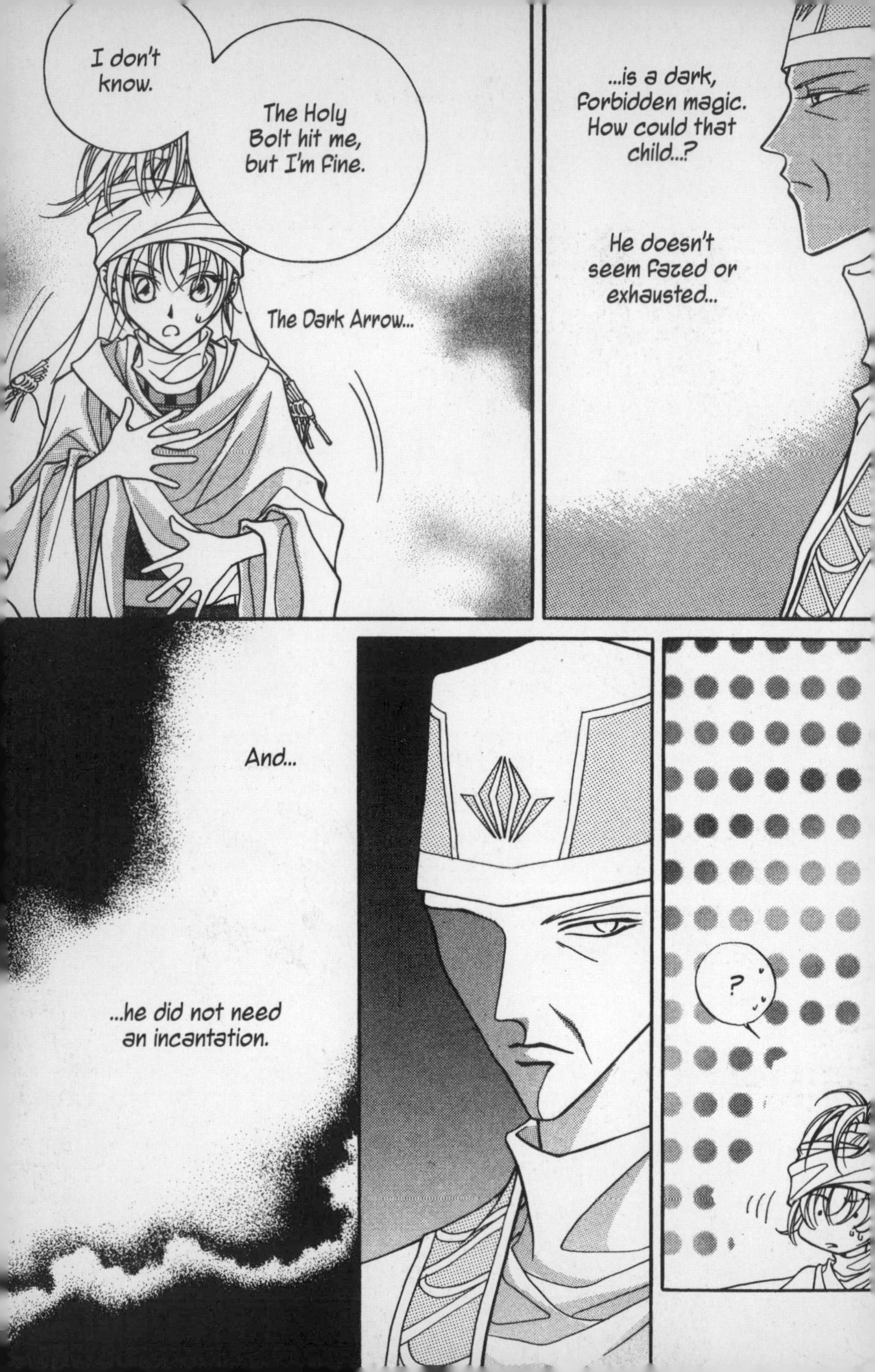
I don't know.
The Holy Bolt hit me, but I'm fine.
The Dark Arrow...
...is a dark, forbidden magic. How could that child...?
He doesn't seem fazed or exhausted...
And...
...he did not need an incantation.
?

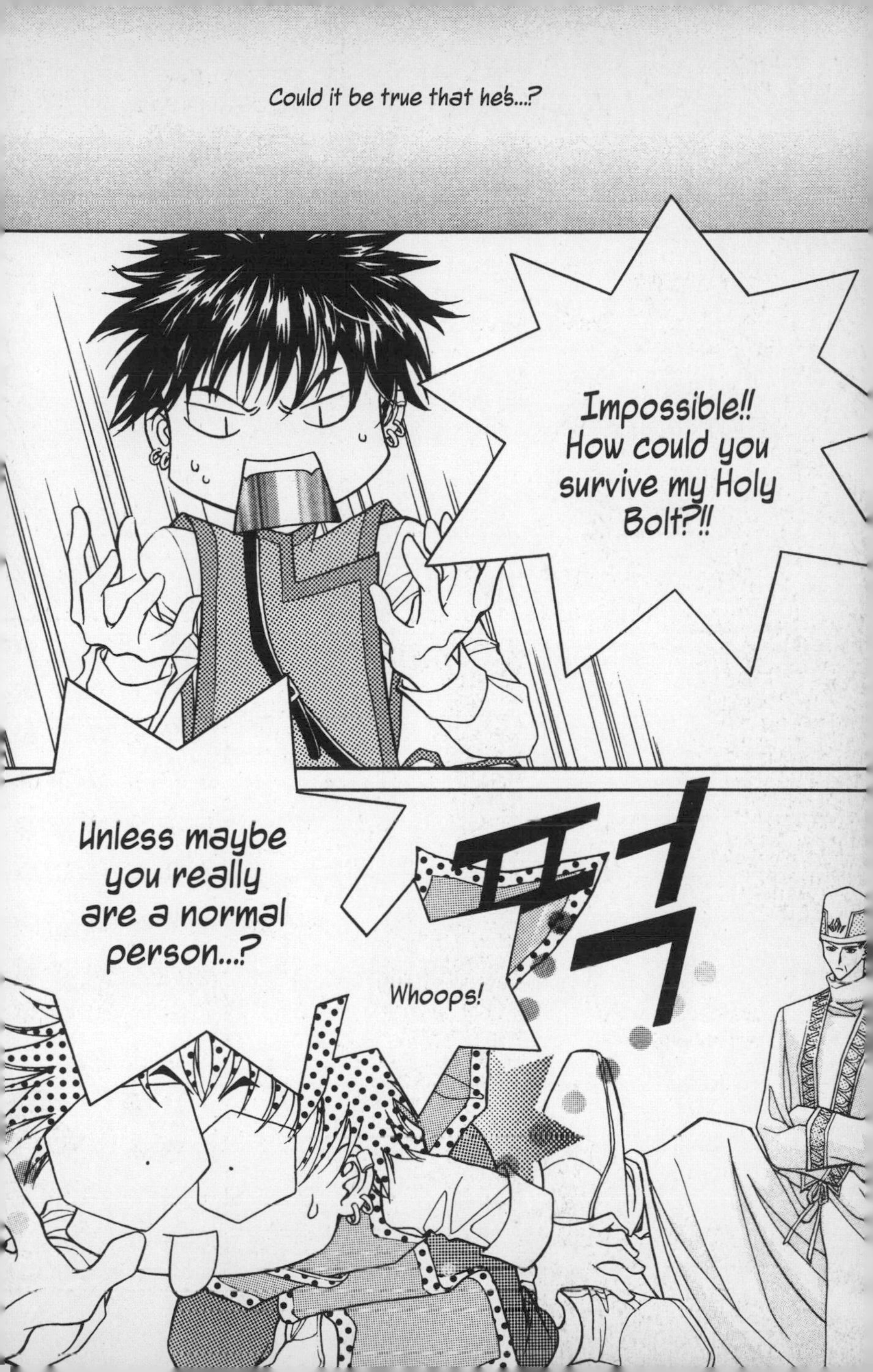
Could it be true that he's...?
Impossible!! How could you survive my Holy Bolt?!!
Unless maybe you really are a normal person...?
Whoops!

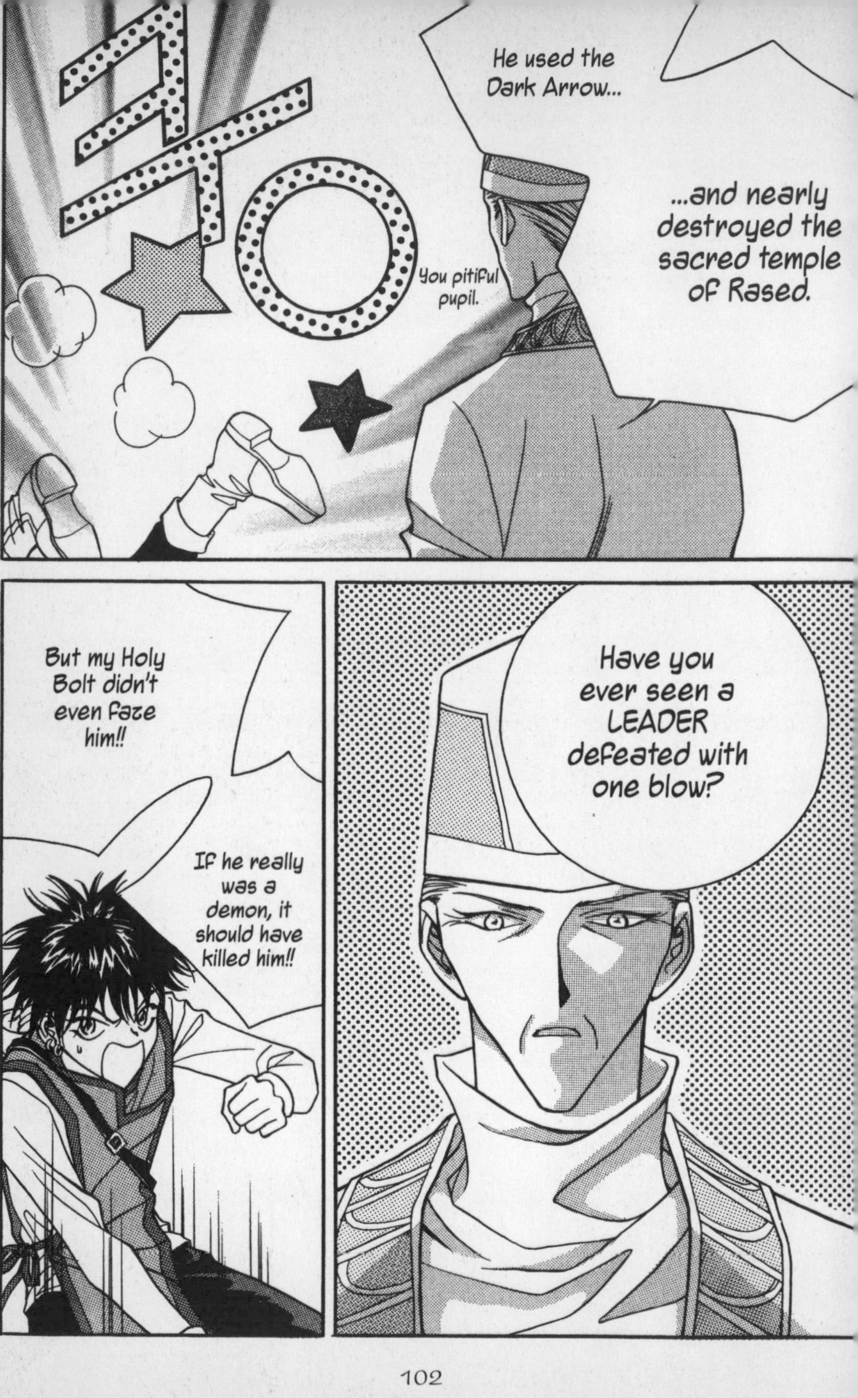
He used the Dark Arrow...
...and nearly destroyed the sacred temple of Rased.
You pitiful pupil.
Have you ever seen a LEADER defeated with one blow?
But my Holy Bolt didn't even faze him!!
If he really was a demon, it should have killed him!!

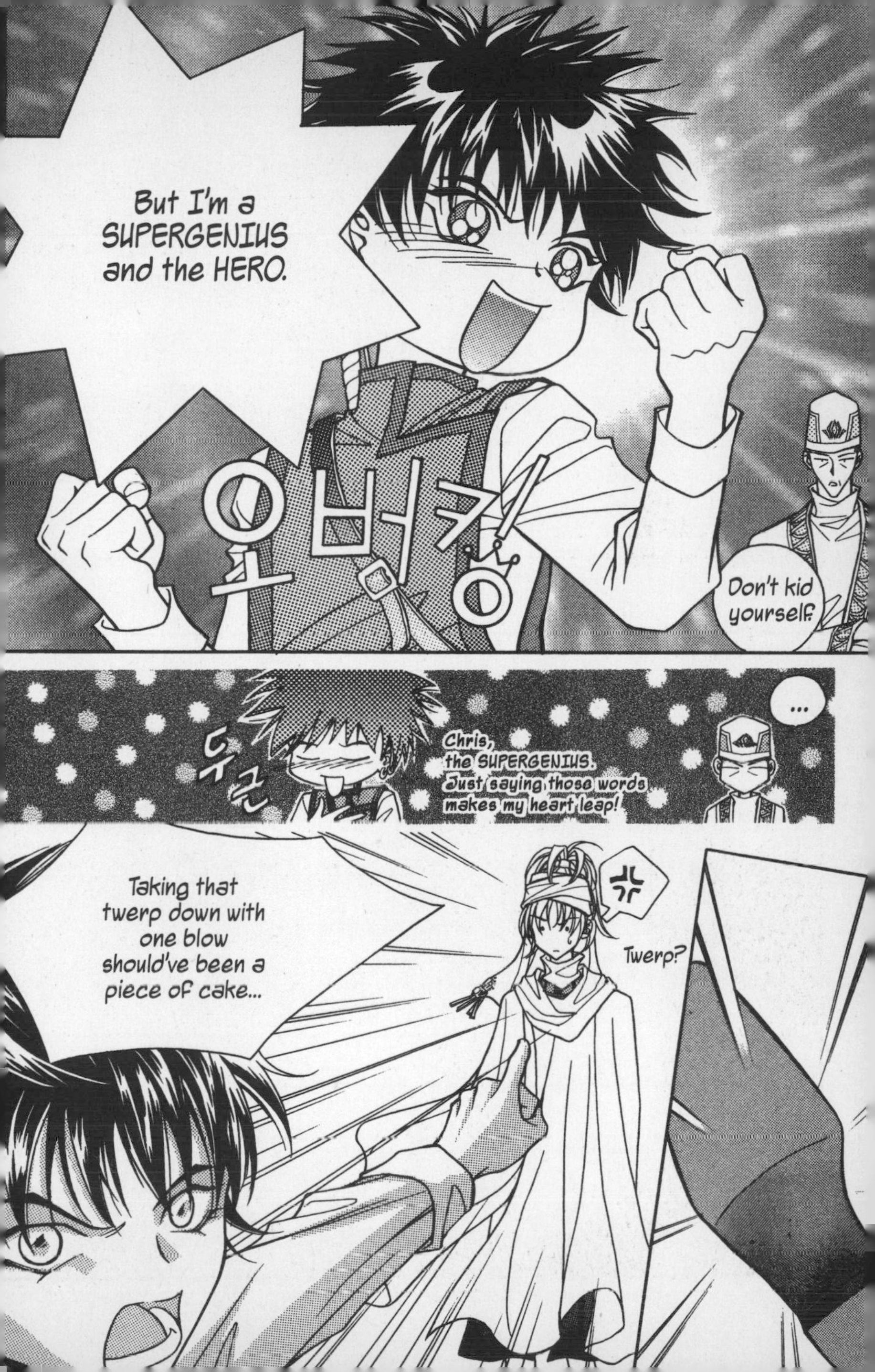

But I'm a SUPERGENIUS and the HERO.
Don't kid yourself.
Chris, the SUPERGENIUS. Just saying those words makes my heart leap!
...
Twerp?
Taking that twerp down with one blow should've been a piece of cake...

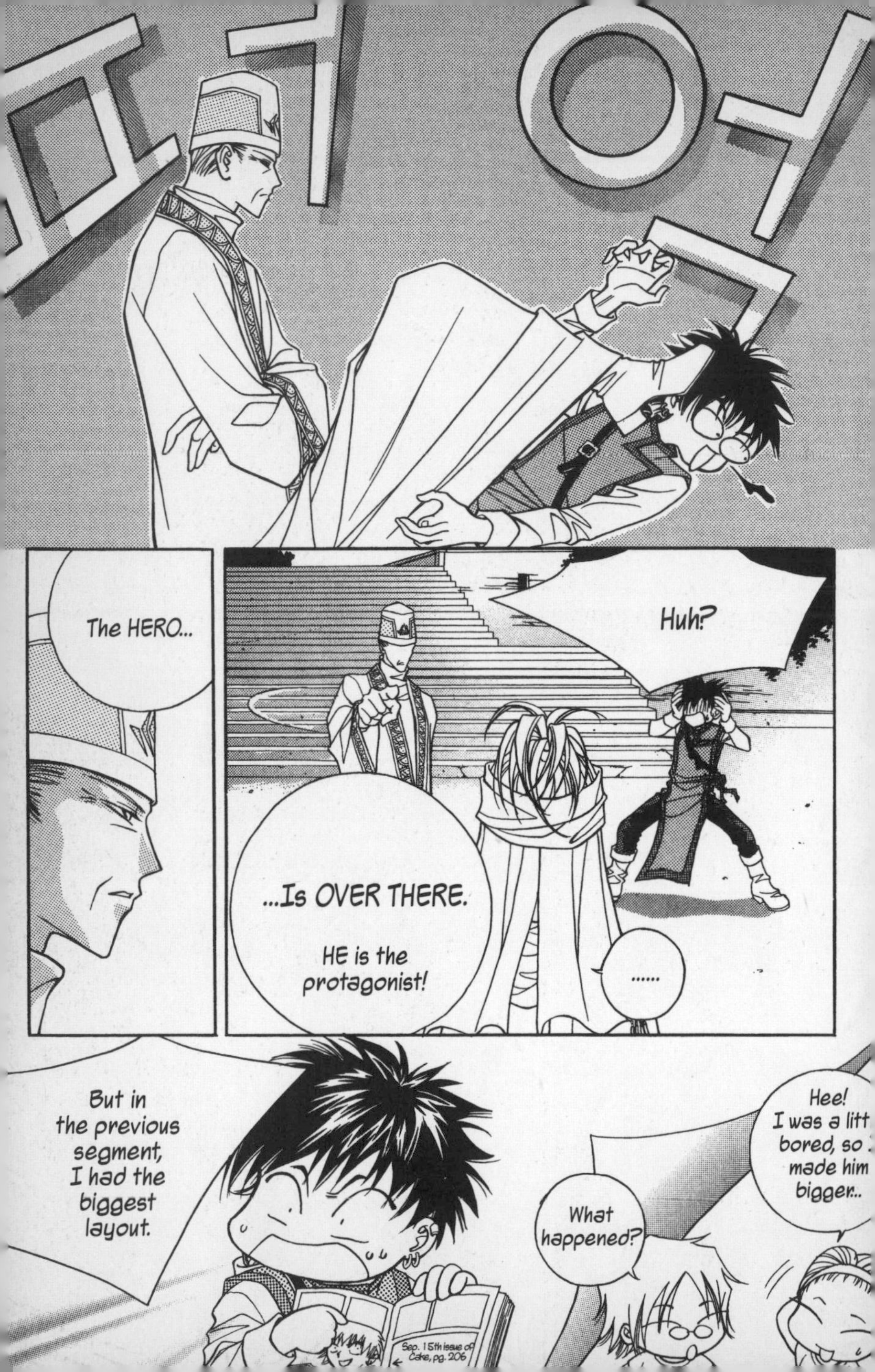

Huh?
The HERO...
...Is OVER THERE.
HE is the protagonist!
......
Hee! I was a litt bored, so made him bigger...
What happened?
But in the previous segment, I had the biggest layout.
Sep. 15th issue of Cake, pg. 206

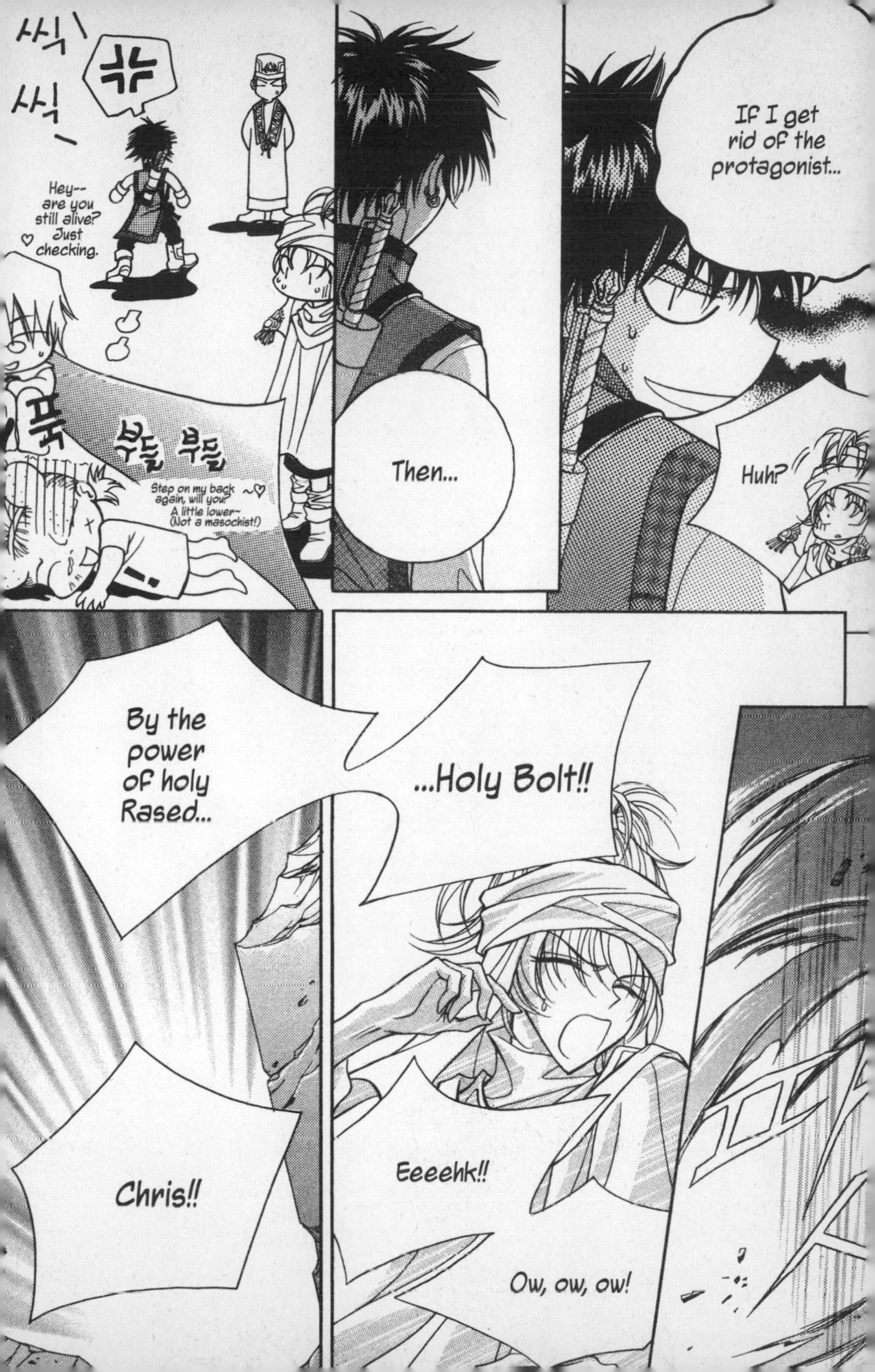
Hey-- are you still alive? Just checking. ♡
푹
부들 부들
Step on my back again, will you? ~♡ A little lower~ (Not a masochist!)
Then...
If I get rid of the protagonist...
Huh?
By the power of holy Rased...
...Holy Bolt!!
Chris!!
Eeeehk!!
Ow, ow, ow!

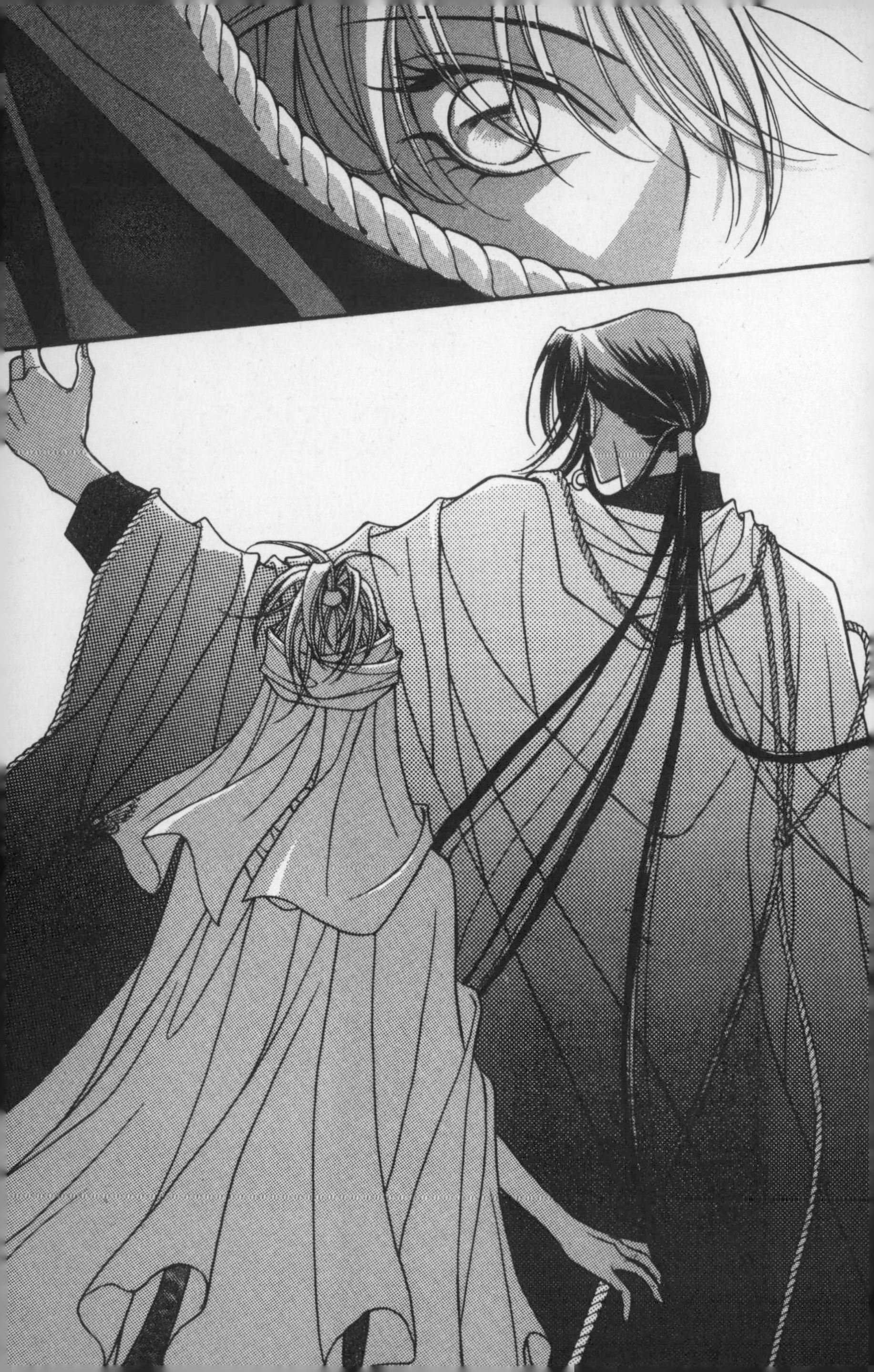

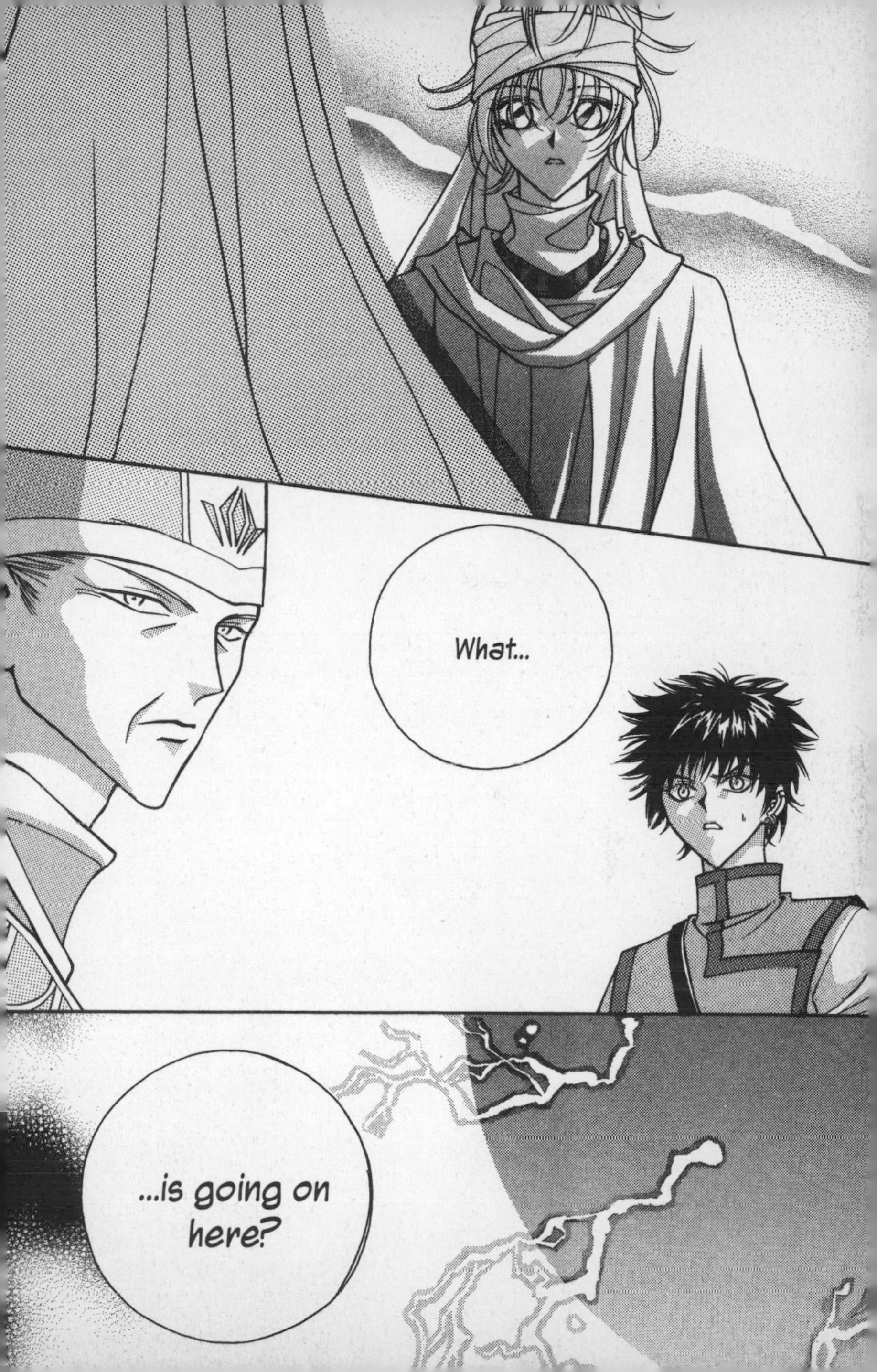
What...
...is going on here?

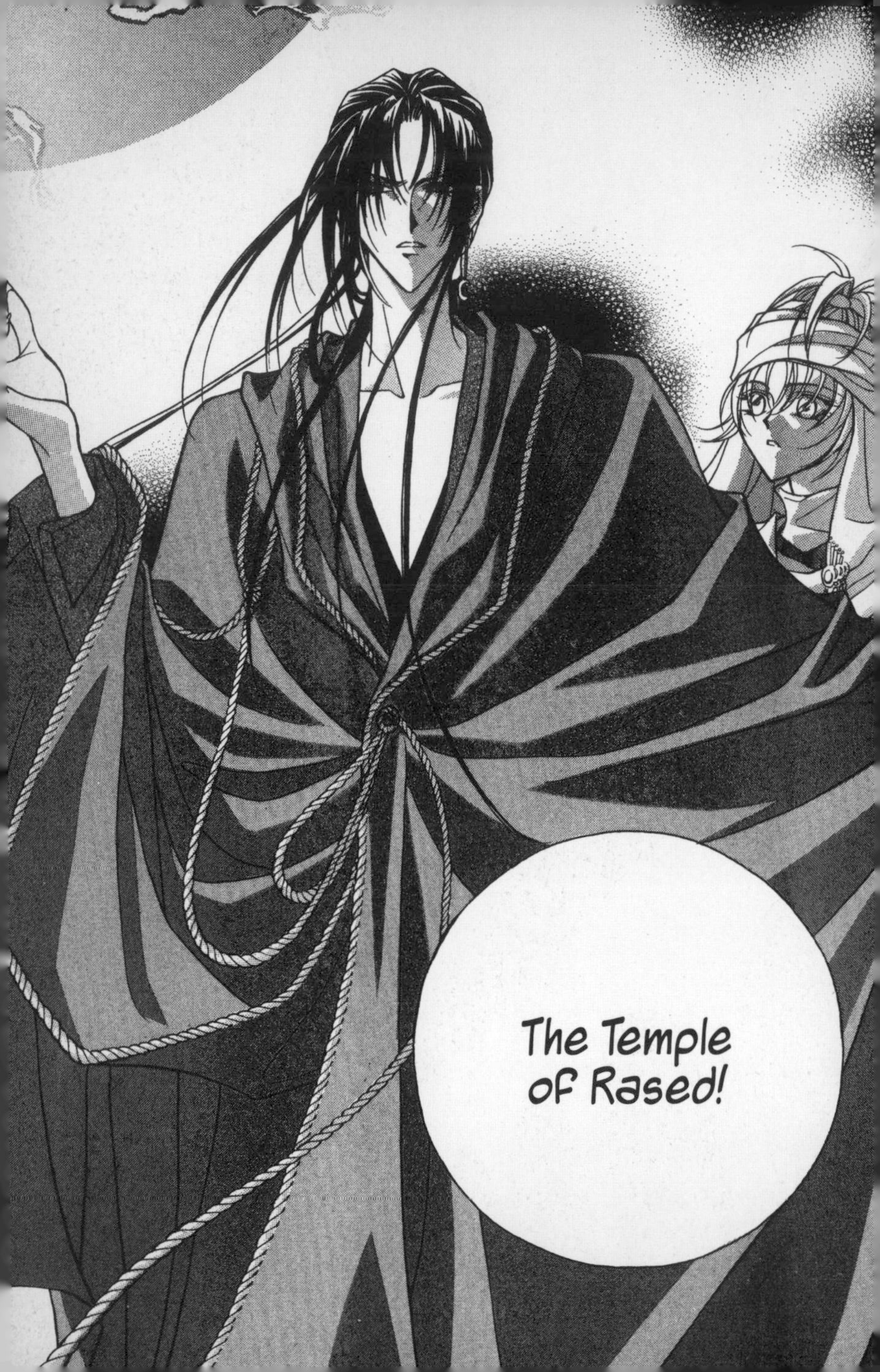
The Temple of Rased!

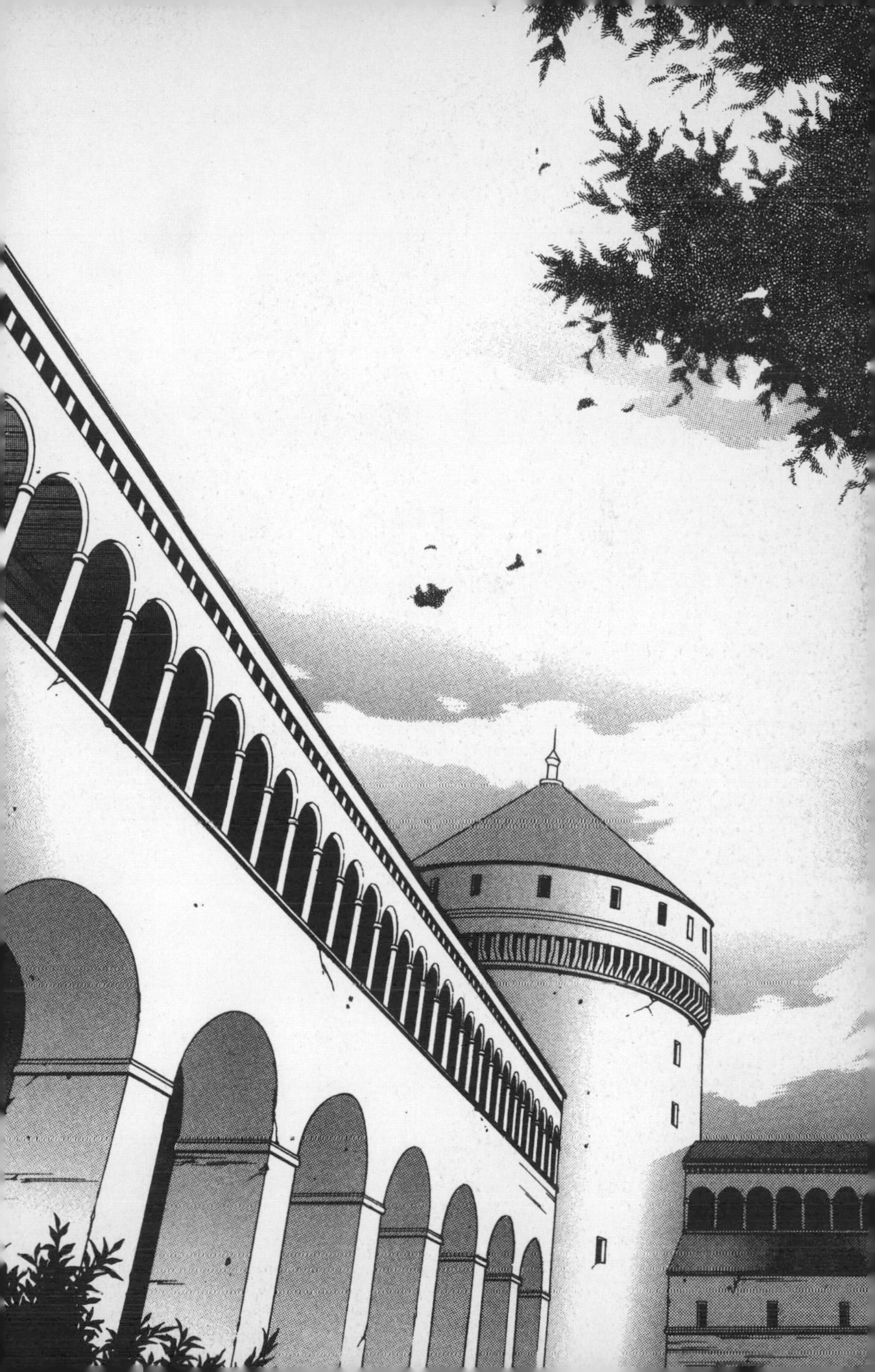

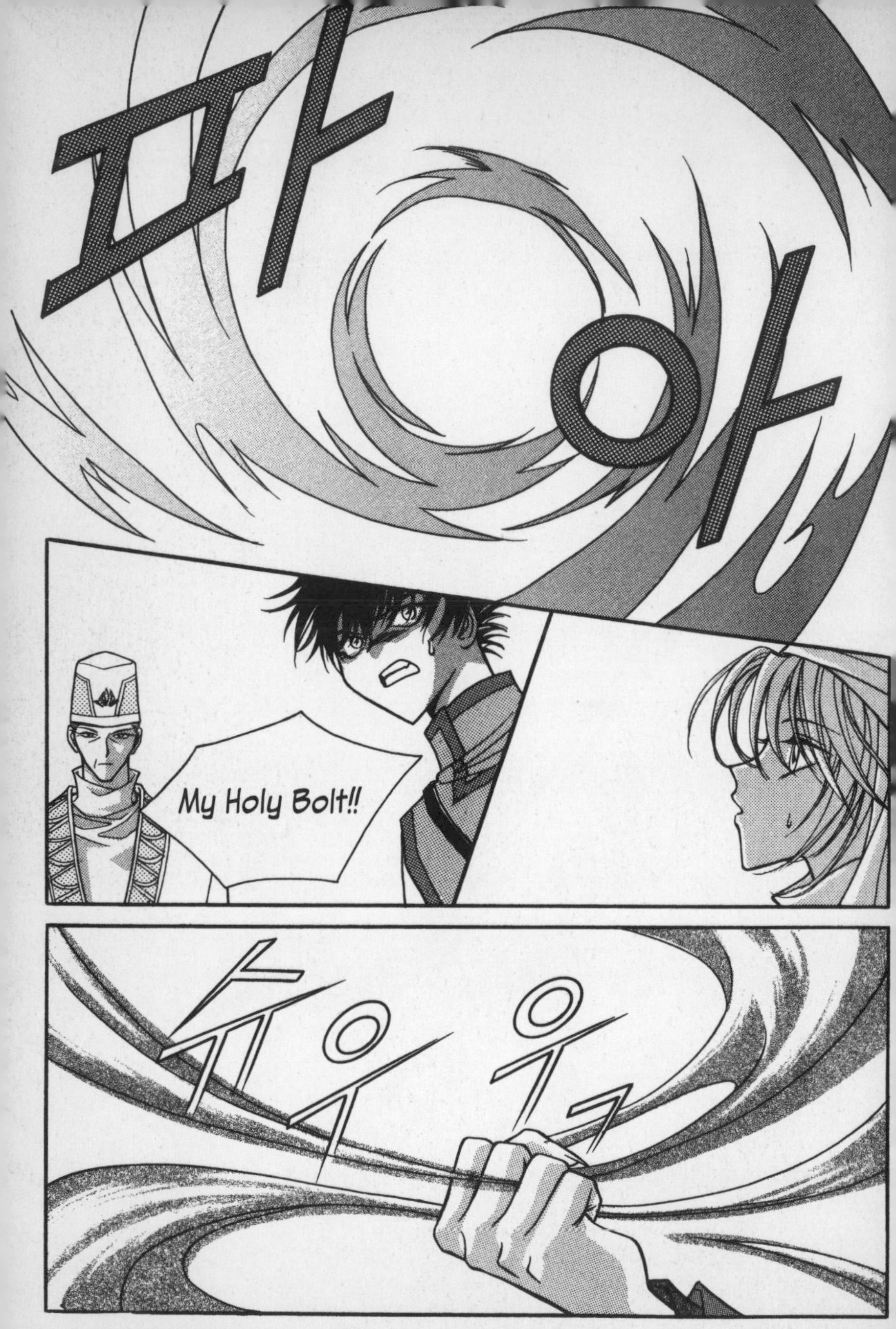
파아
My Holy Bolt!!

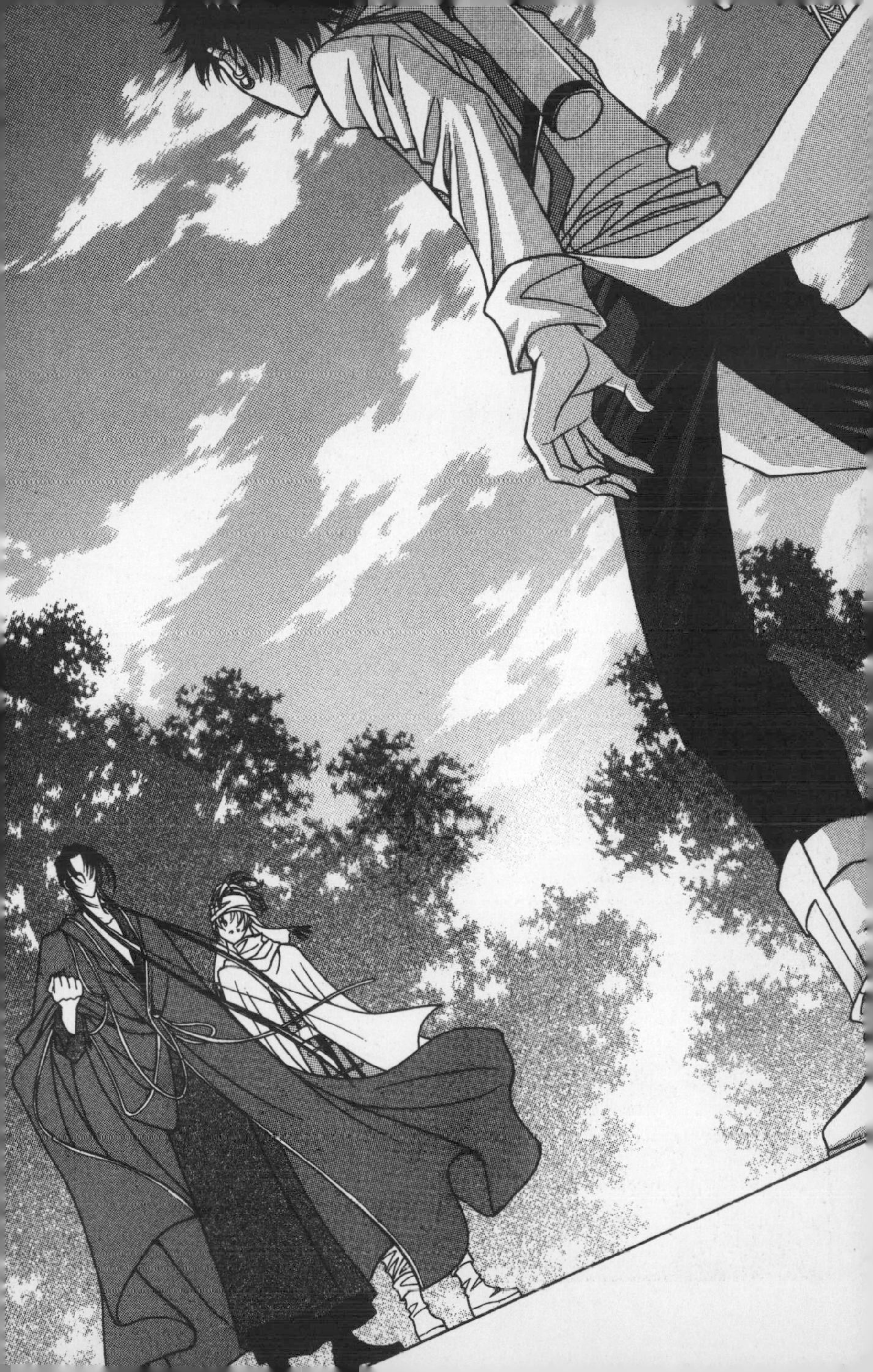

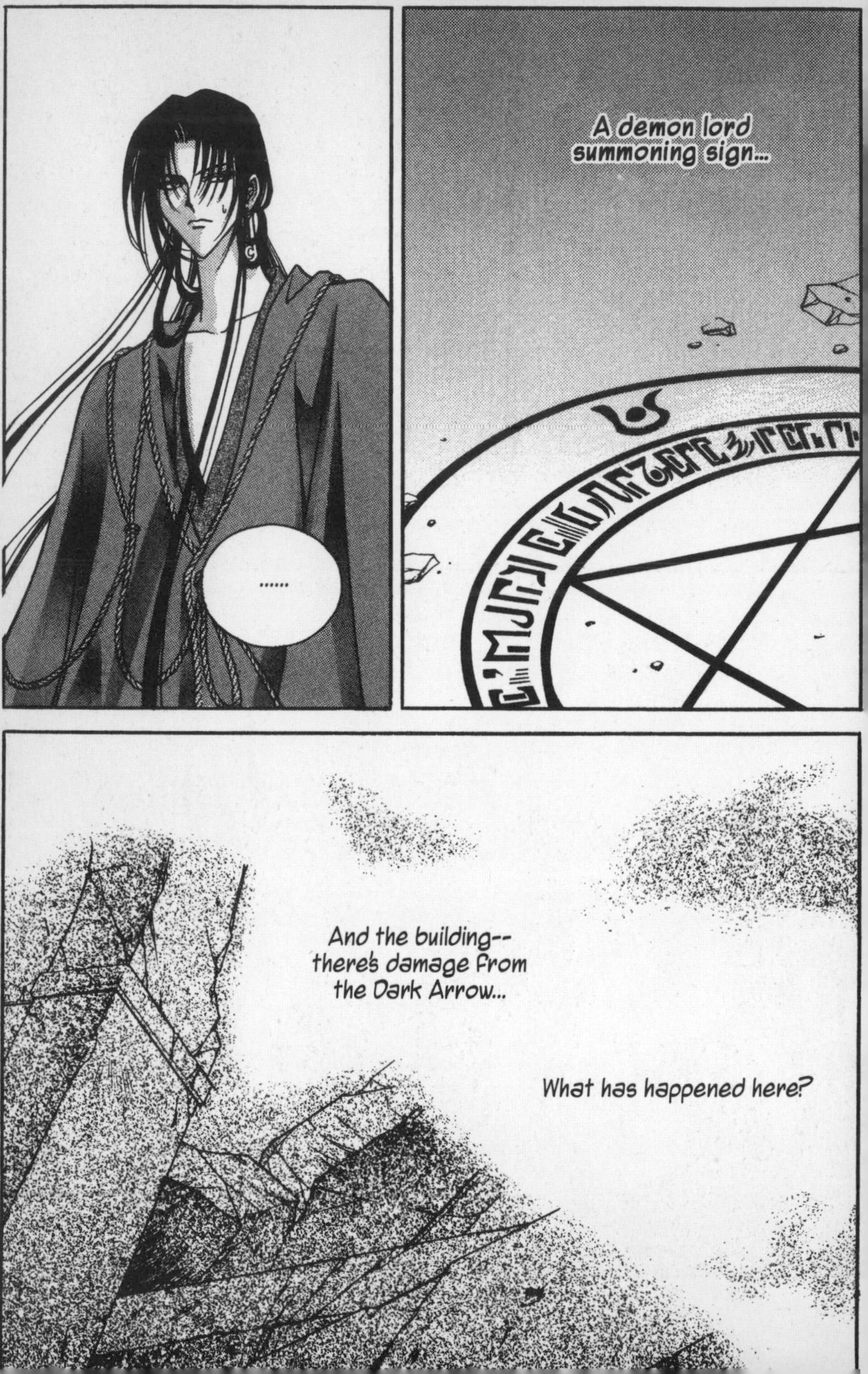
A demon lord summoning sign...
......
And the building--there's damage from the Dark Arrow...
What has happened here?

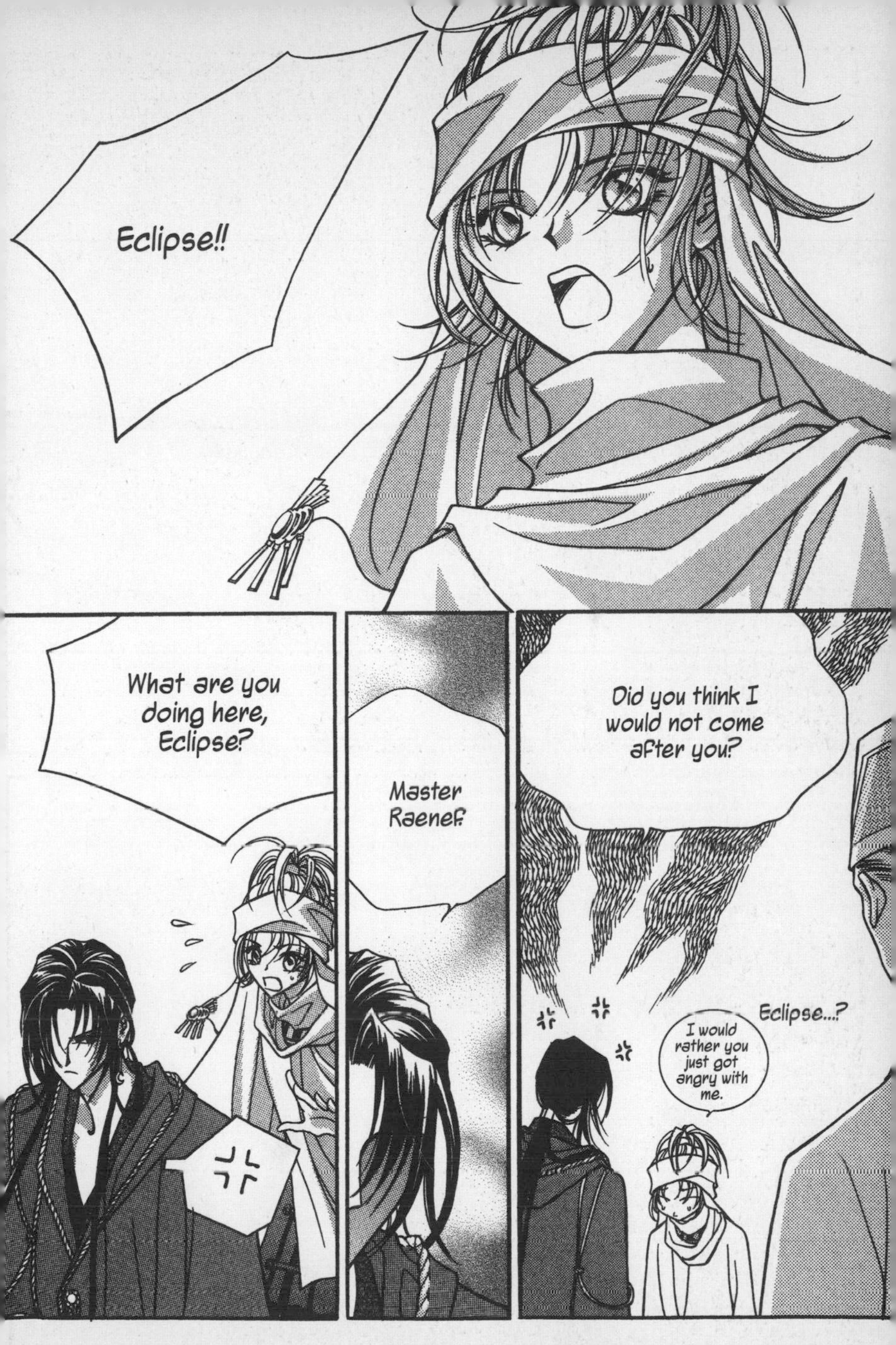
Eclipse!!
Did you think I would not come after you?
Eclipse...?
I would rather you just got angry with me.
Master Raenef.
What are you doing here, Eclipse?

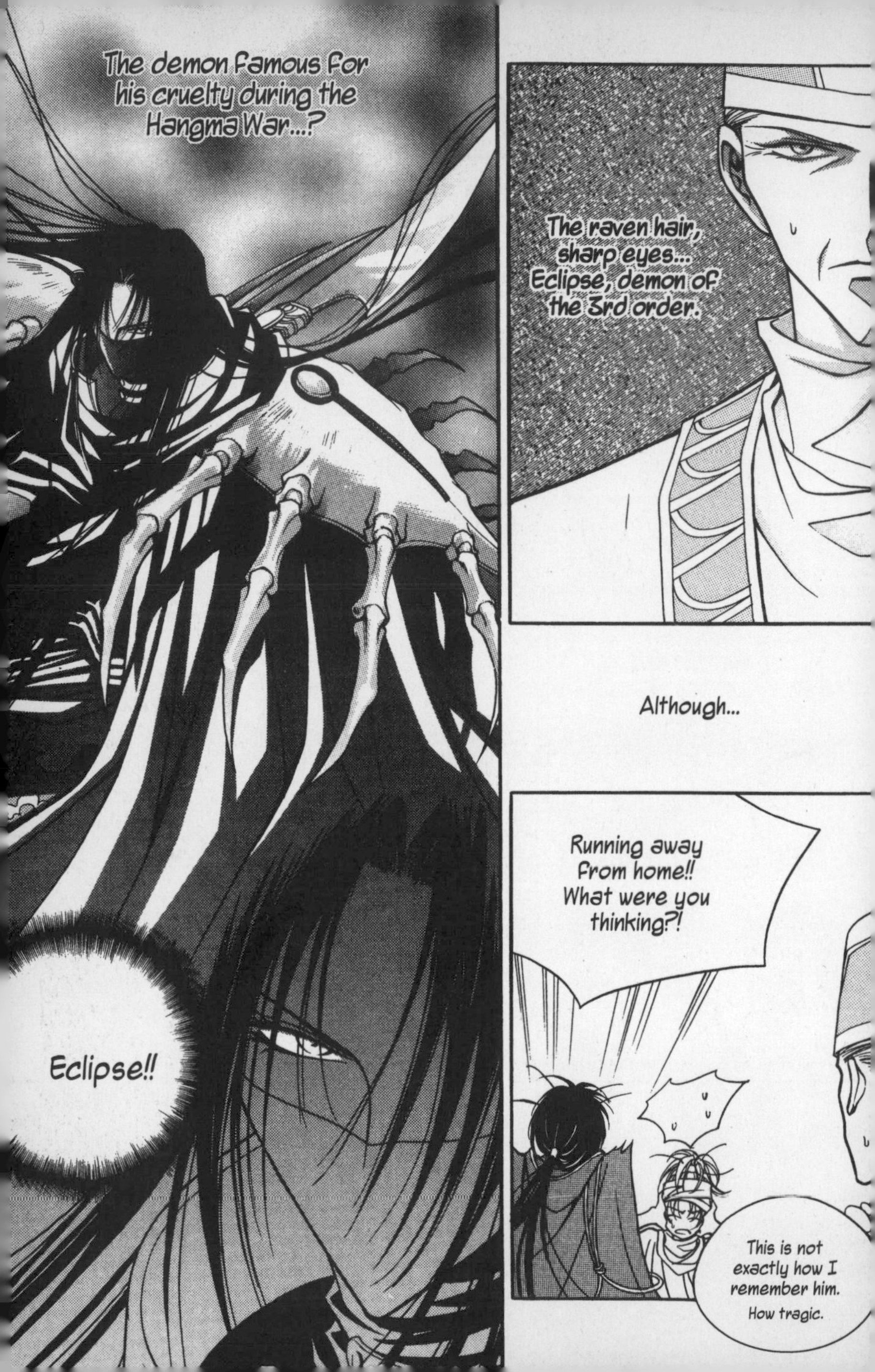
The raven hair, sharp eyes... Eclipse, demon of the 3rd order.
The demon famous for his cruelty during the Hangma War...?
Eclipse!!
Although...
Running away from home!! What were you thinking?!
This is not exactly how I remember him.
How tragic.

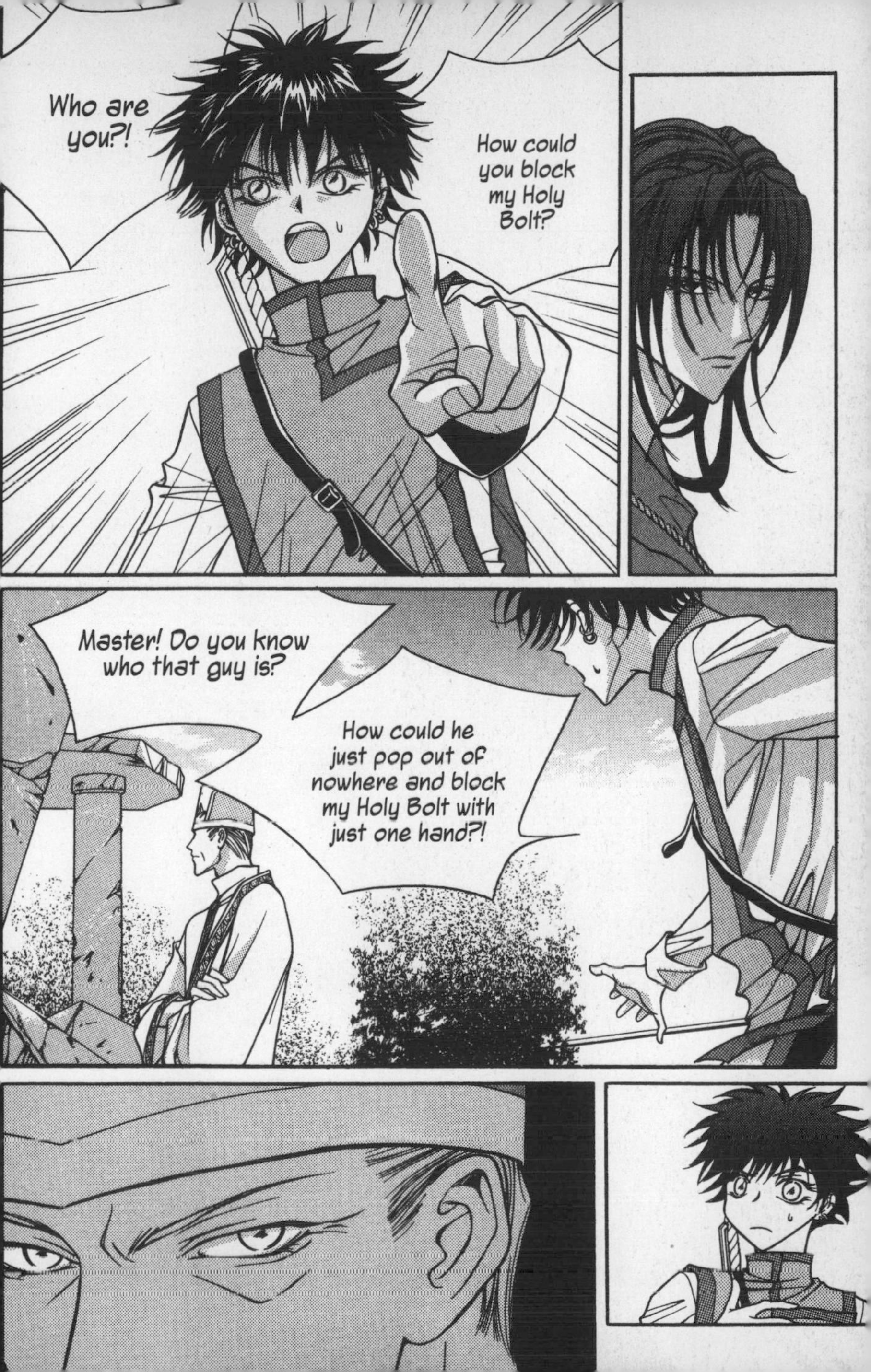
Who are you?!
How could you block my Holy Bolt?
Master! Do you know who that guy is?
How could he just pop out of nowhere and block my Holy Bolt with just one hand?!

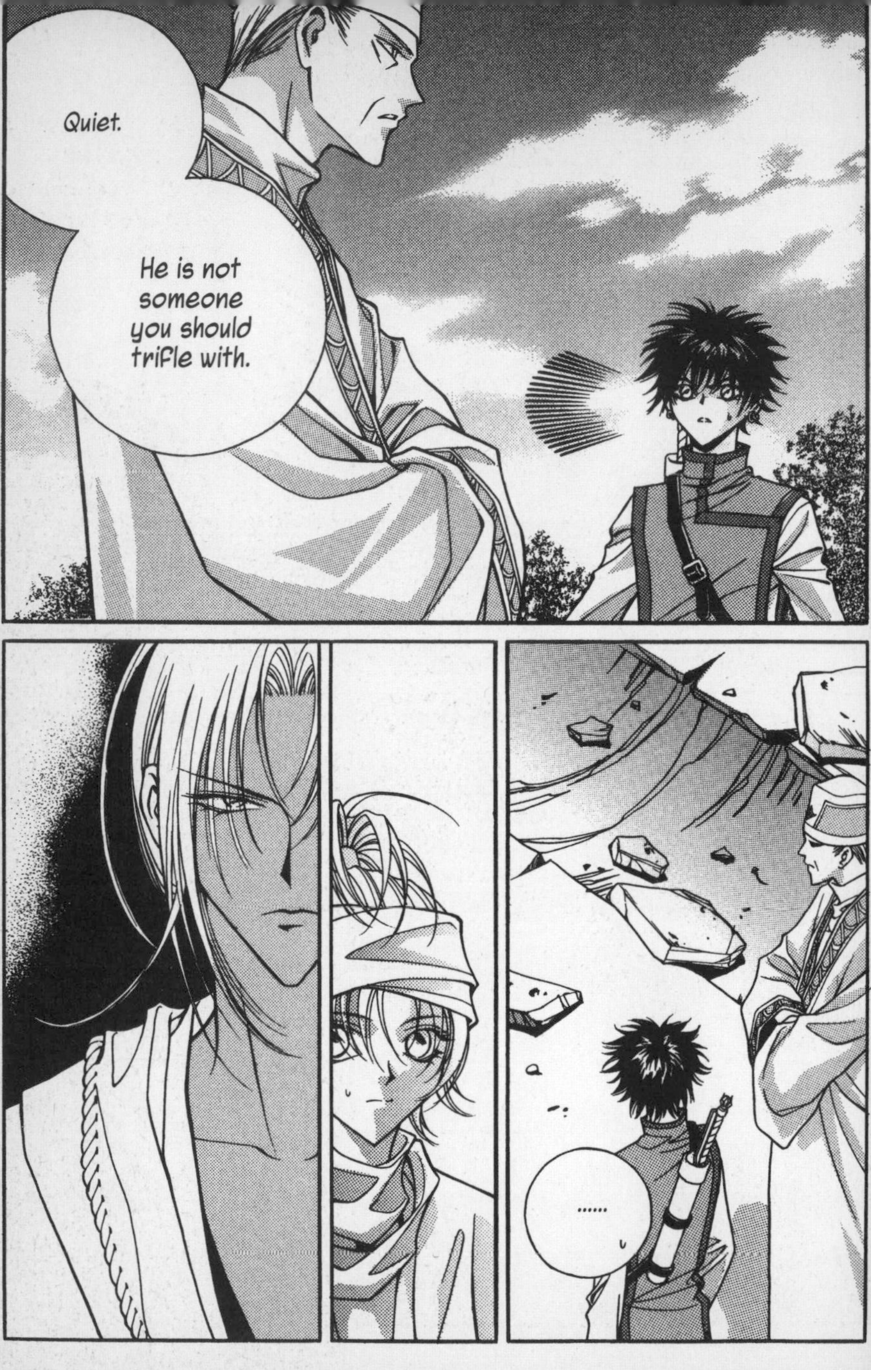
Quiet.
He is not someone you should trifle with.
......

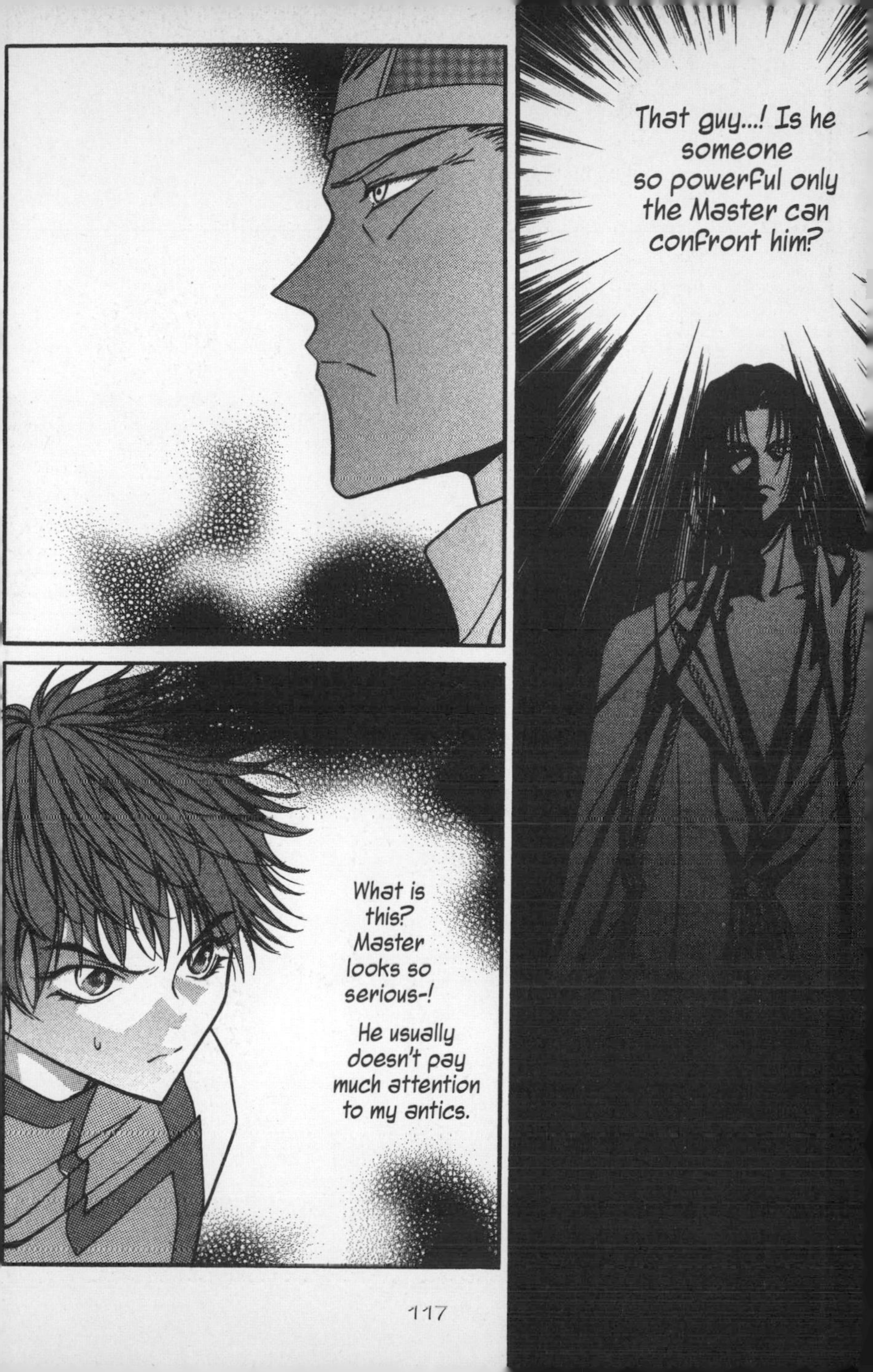
That guy...! Is he someone so powerful only the Master can confront him?
What is this? Master looks so serious-!
He usually doesn't pay much attention to my antics.

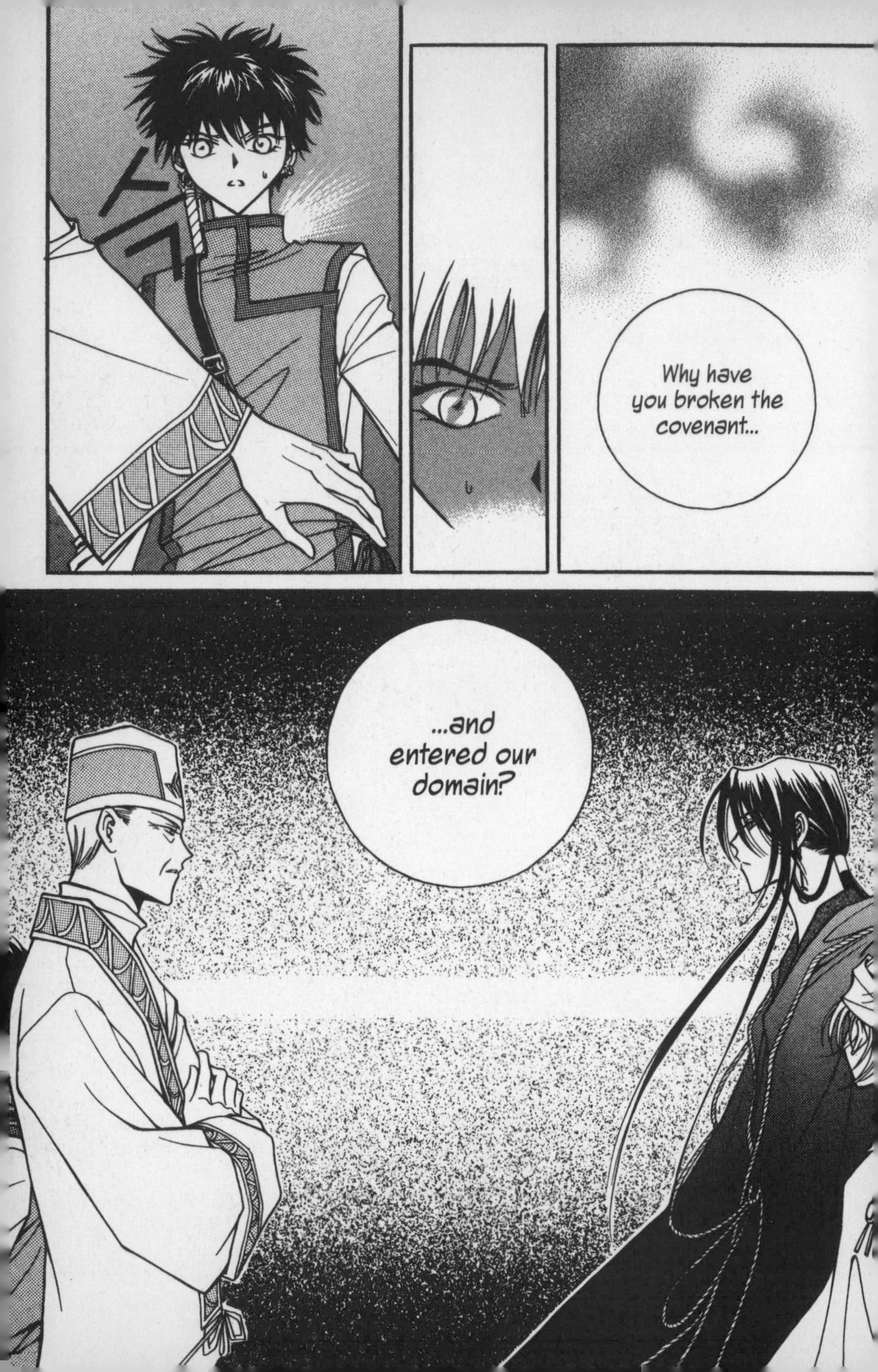
Why have you broken the covenant...
...and entered our domain?

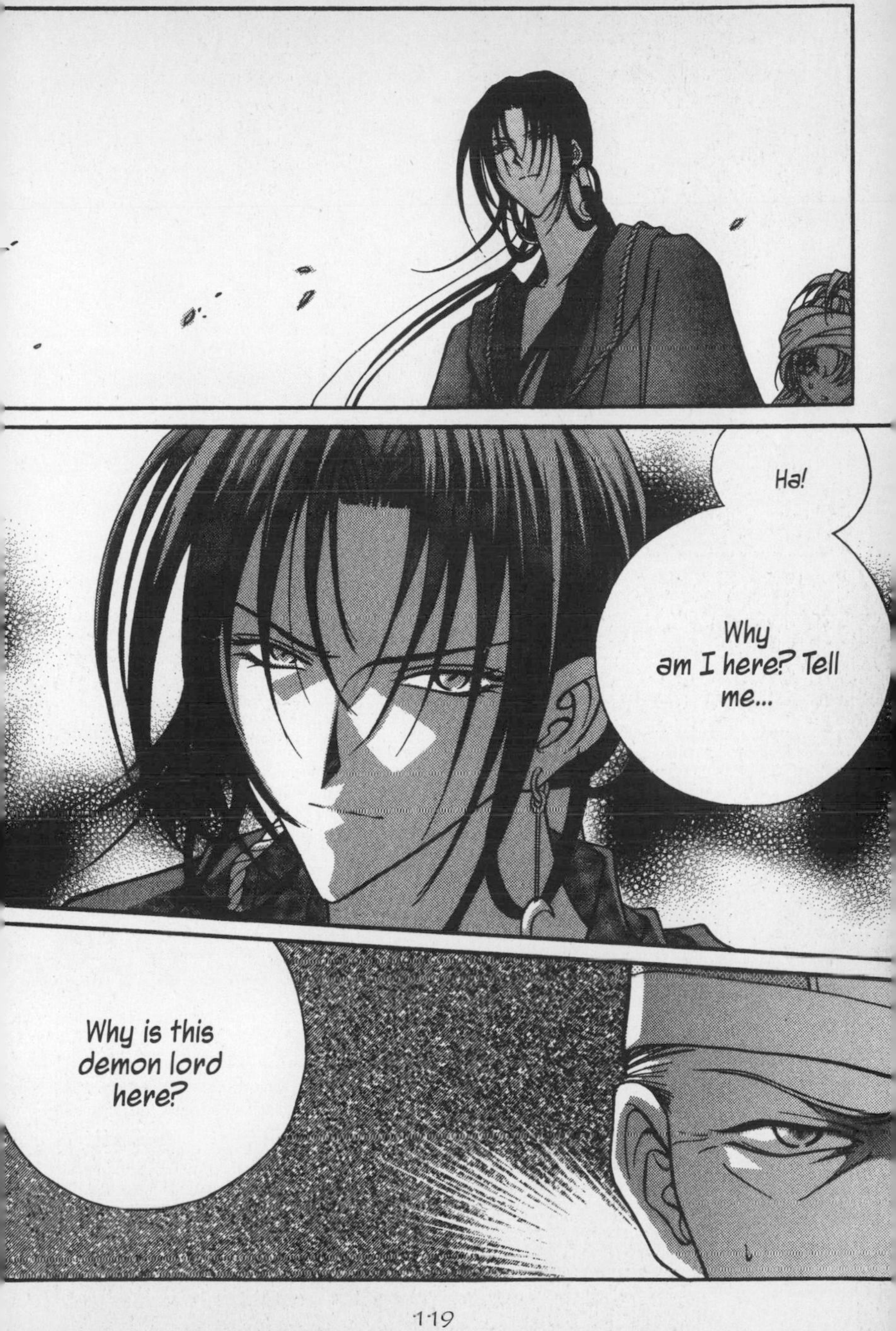
Ha!
Why am I here? Tell me...
Why is this demon lord here?

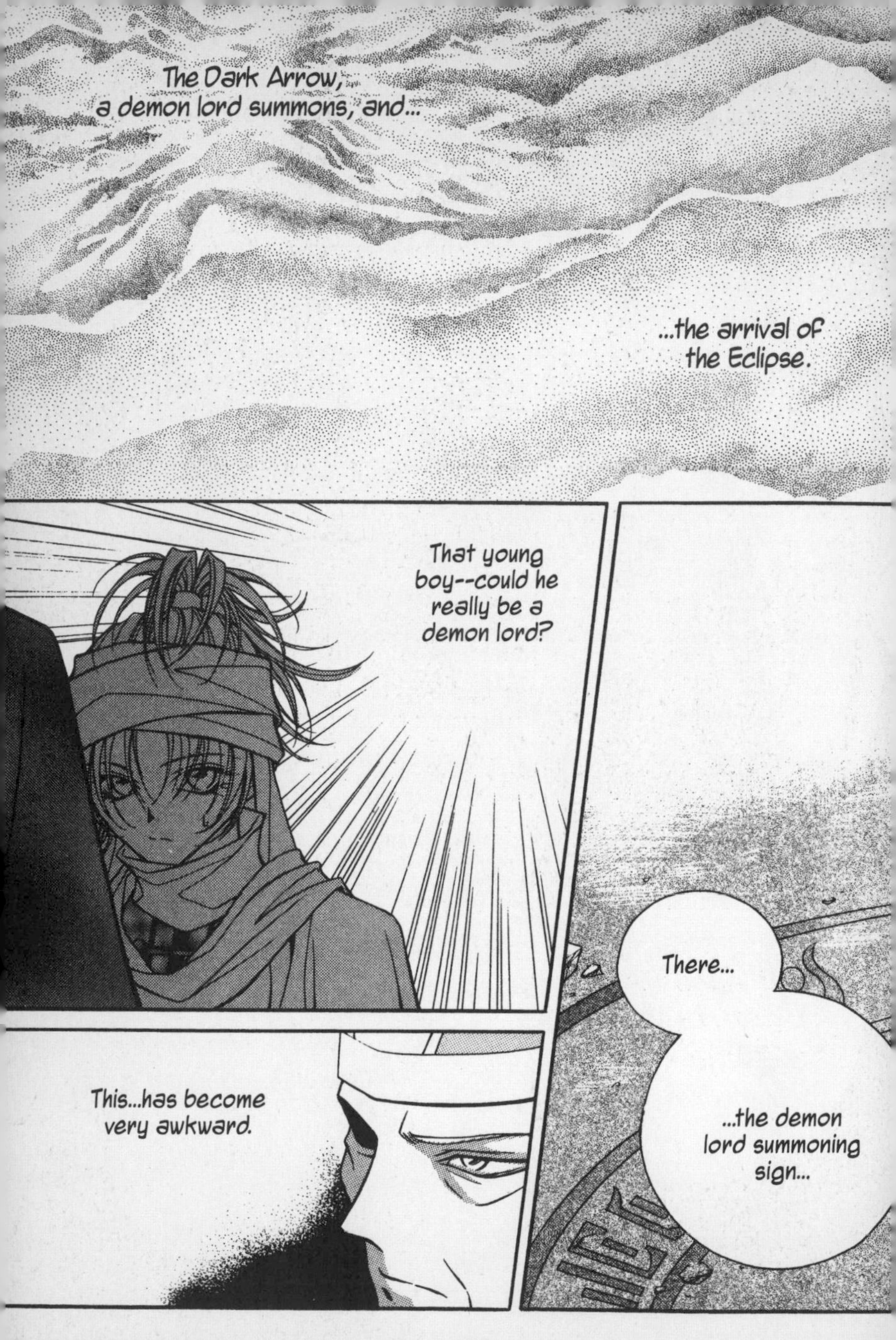
The Dark Arrow, a demon lord summons, and...
...the arrival of the Eclipse.
There...
...the demon lord summoning sign...
That young boy--could he really be a demon lord?
This...has become very awkward.

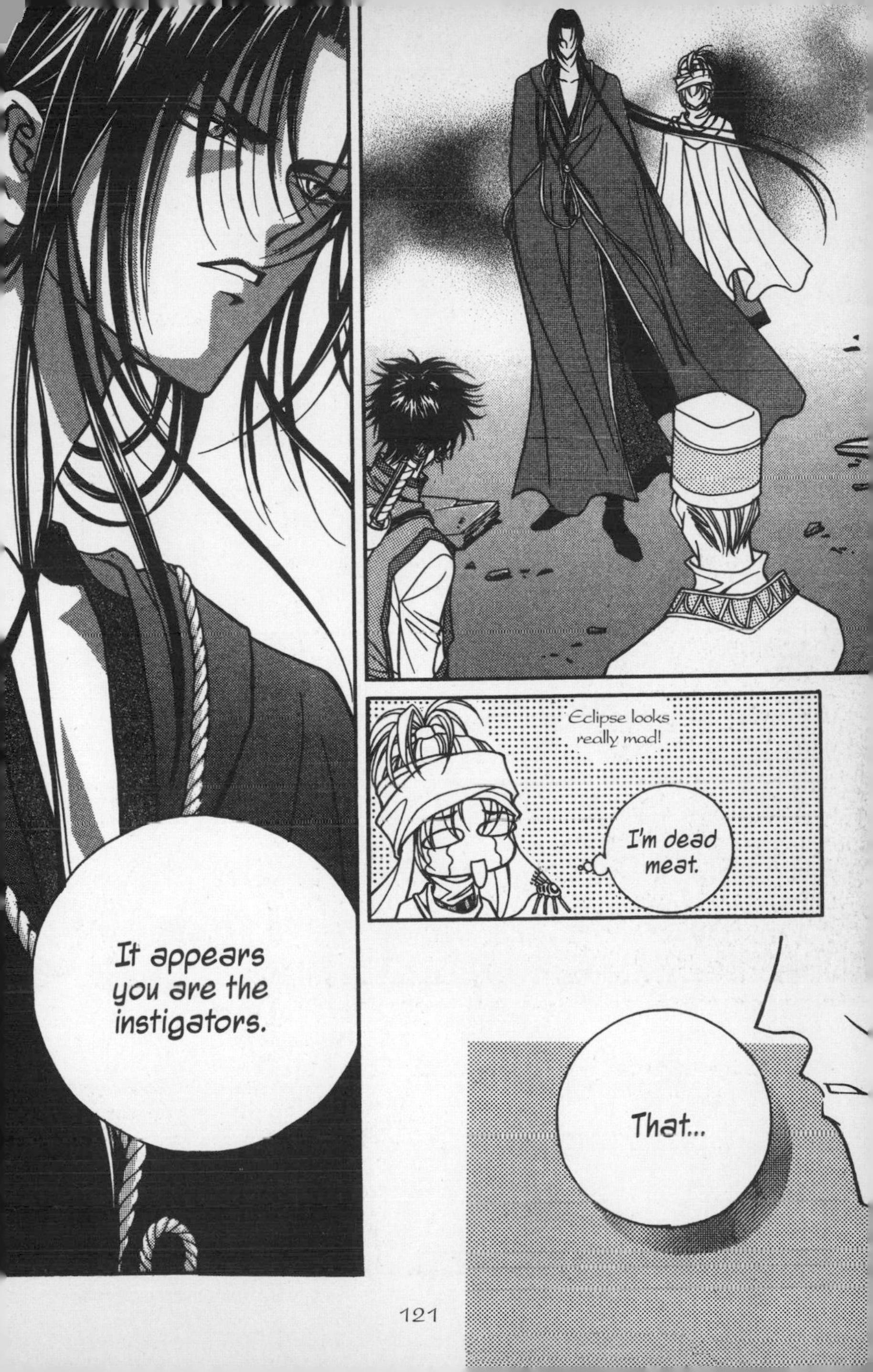
Eclipse looks really mad!
I'm dead meat.
It appears you are the instigators.
That...

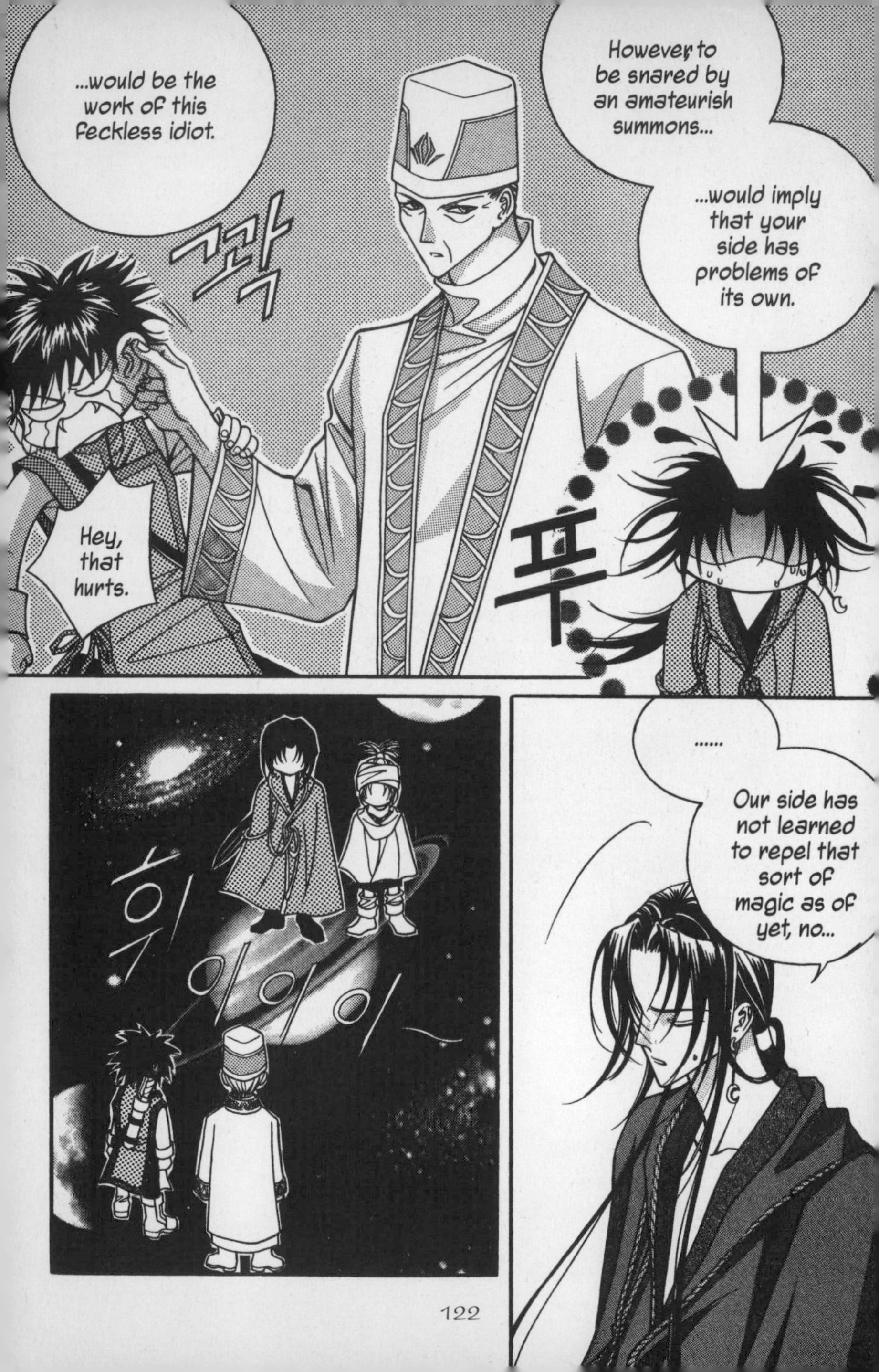
...would be the work of this feckless idiot.
Hey, that hurts.
However, to be snared by an amateurish summons...
...would imply that your side has problems of its own.
푸
......
Our side has not learned to repel that sort of magic as of yet, no...

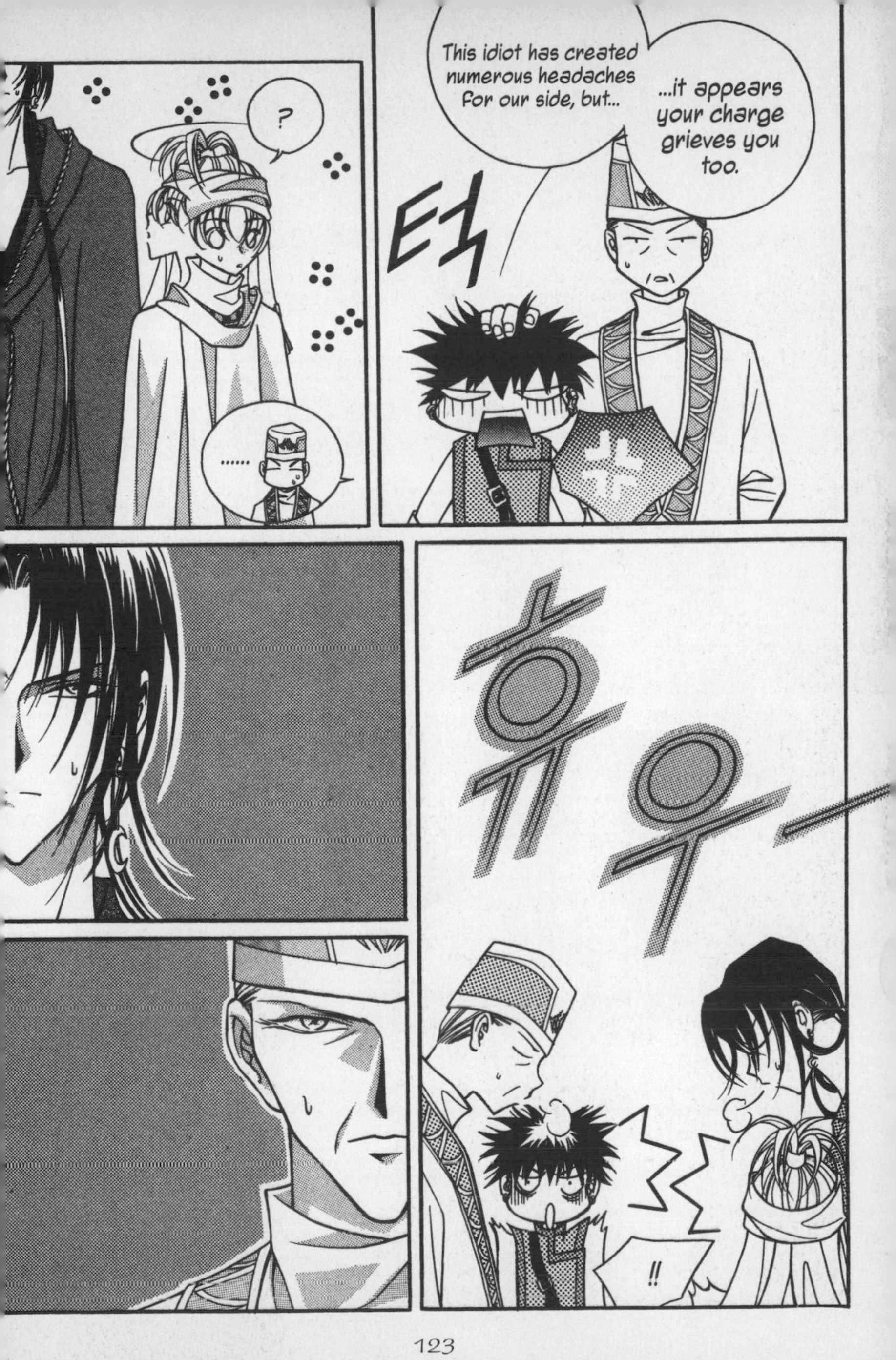
This idiot has created numerous headaches for our side, but...
...it appears your charge grieves you too.
?
......
!!

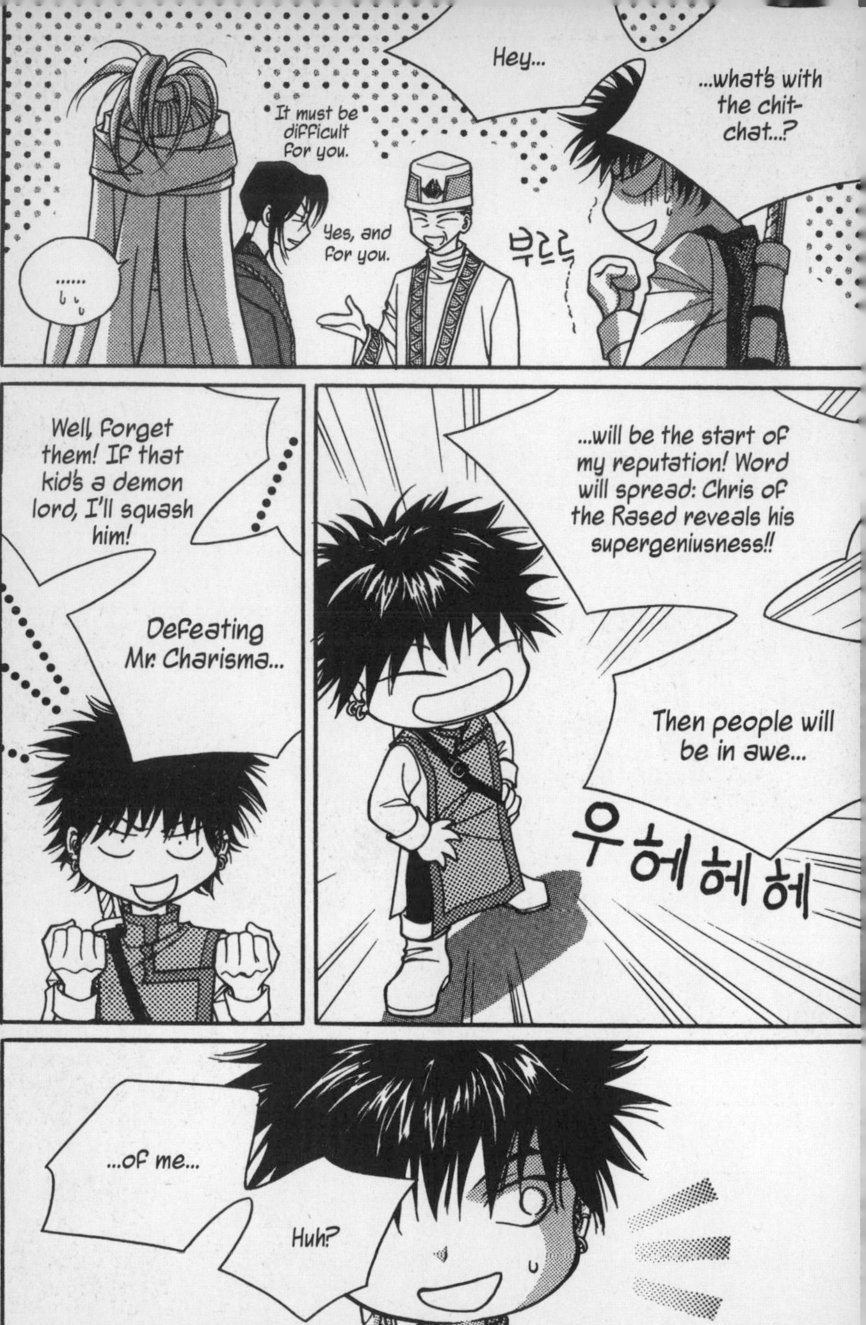
It must be difficult for you.
Yes, and for you.
......
Hey...
...what's with the chit-chat...?
부르륵
Well, forget them! If that kid's a demon lord, I'll squash him!
Defeating Mr. Charisma...
...will be the start of my reputation! Word will spread: Chris of the Rased reveals his supergeniusness!!
Then people will be in awe...
우헤헤헤
...of me...
Huh?

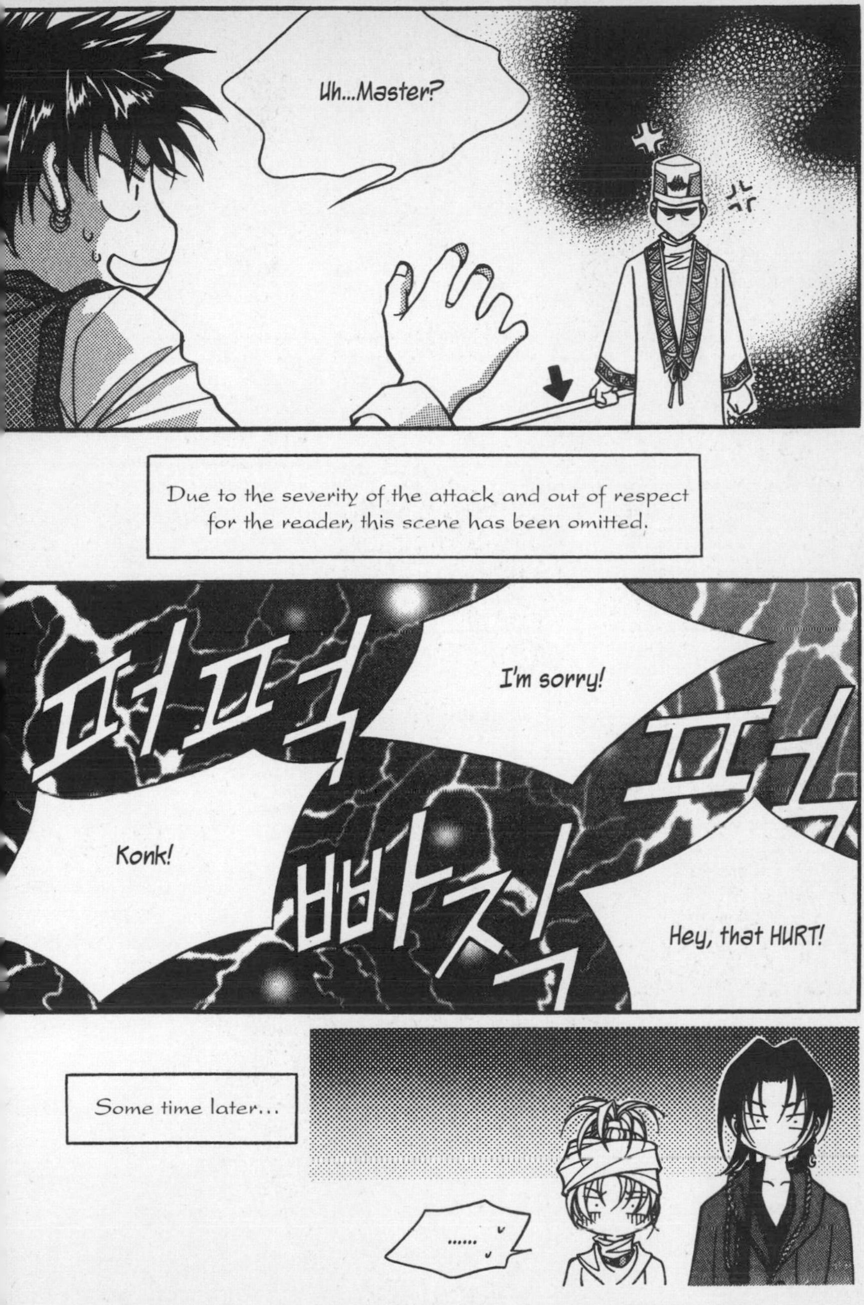
Uh...Master?
Due to the severity of the attack and out of respect for the reader, this scene has been omitted.
퍼퍽
I'm sorry!
퍽
Konk!
빠직
Hey, that HURT!
Some time later...
......

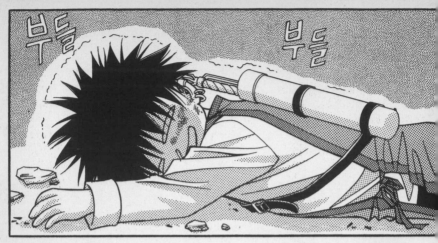

Harumph...

I'm sorry you had to see that.

......

Admin style

Yes, well...

I'm sure you remember the nonaggression pact between the clerics and the demons.

126

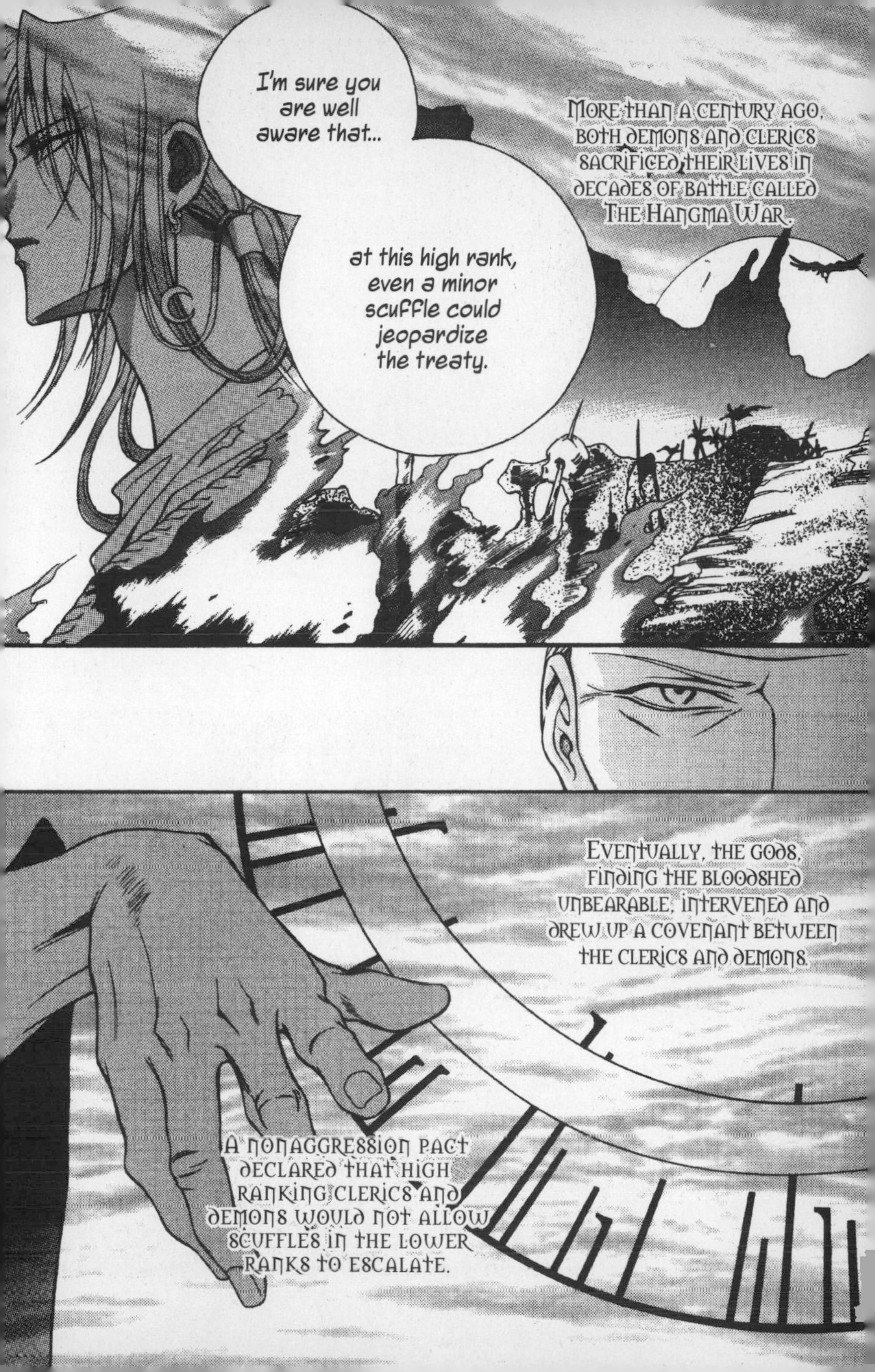

I'm sure you are well aware that...
at this high rank, even a minor scuffle could jeopardize the treaty.
More than a century ago, both demons and clerics sacrificed their lives in decades of battle called The Hangma War.
Eventually, the gods, finding the bloodshed unbearable, intervened and drew up a covenant between the clerics and demons.
A nonaggression pact declared that high ranking clerics and demons would not allow scuffles in the lower ranks to escalate.

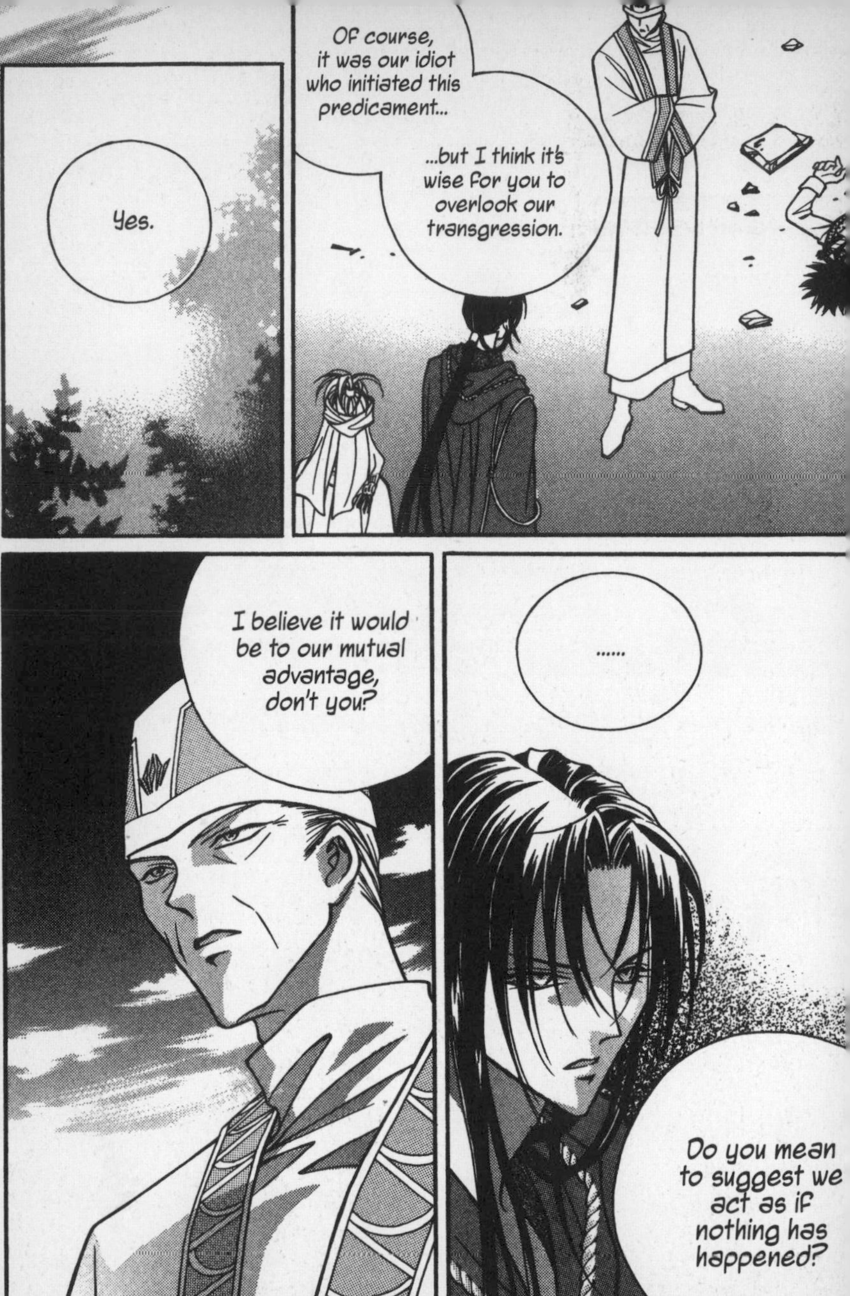
Of course, it was our idiot who initiated this predicament...
...but I think it's wise for you to overlook our transgression.
Yes.
......
Do you mean to suggest we act as if nothing has happened?
I believe it would be to our mutual advantage, don't you?

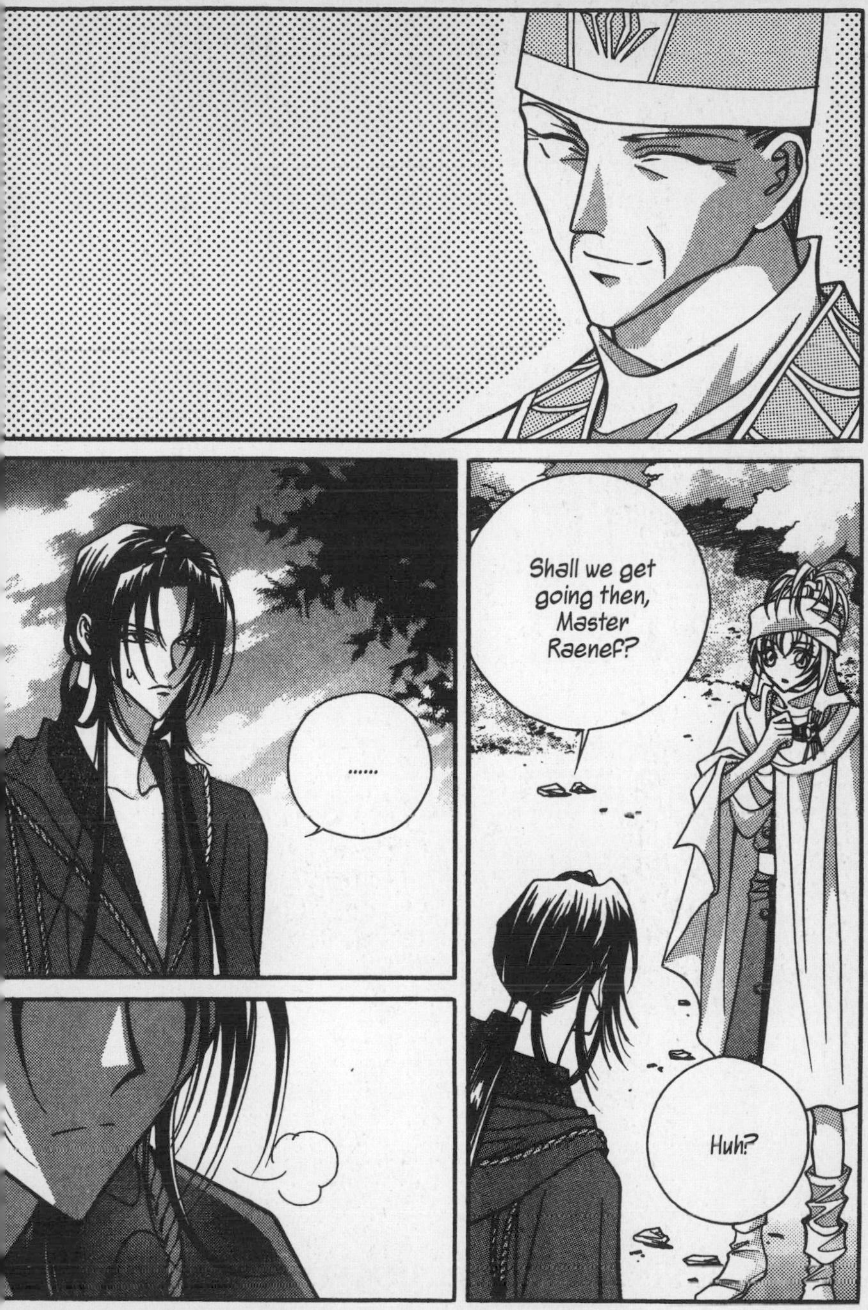
Shall we get going then, Master Raenef?
......
Huh?

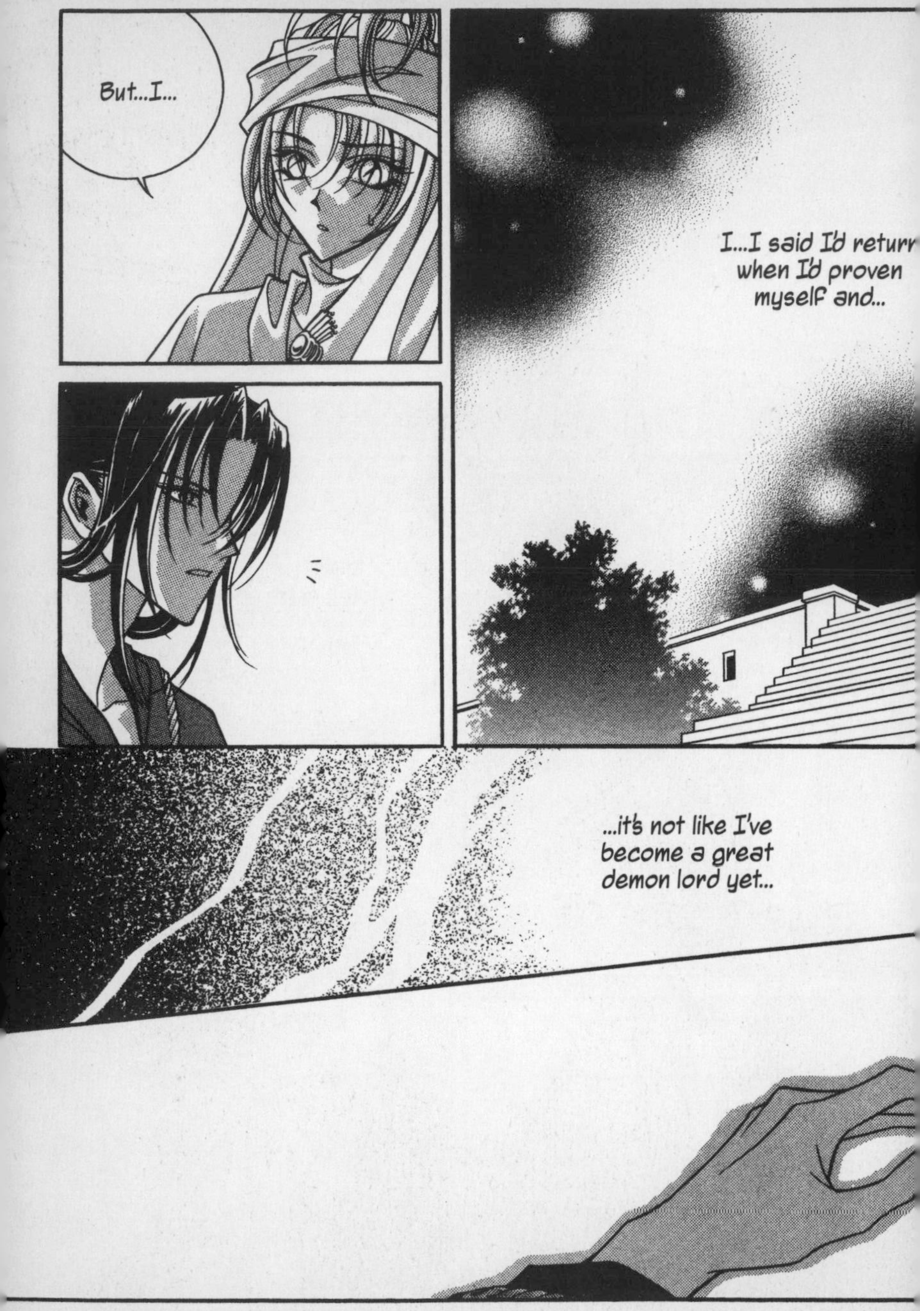
I...I said I'd return when I'd proven myself and...
But...I...
...it's not like I've become a great demon lord yet...

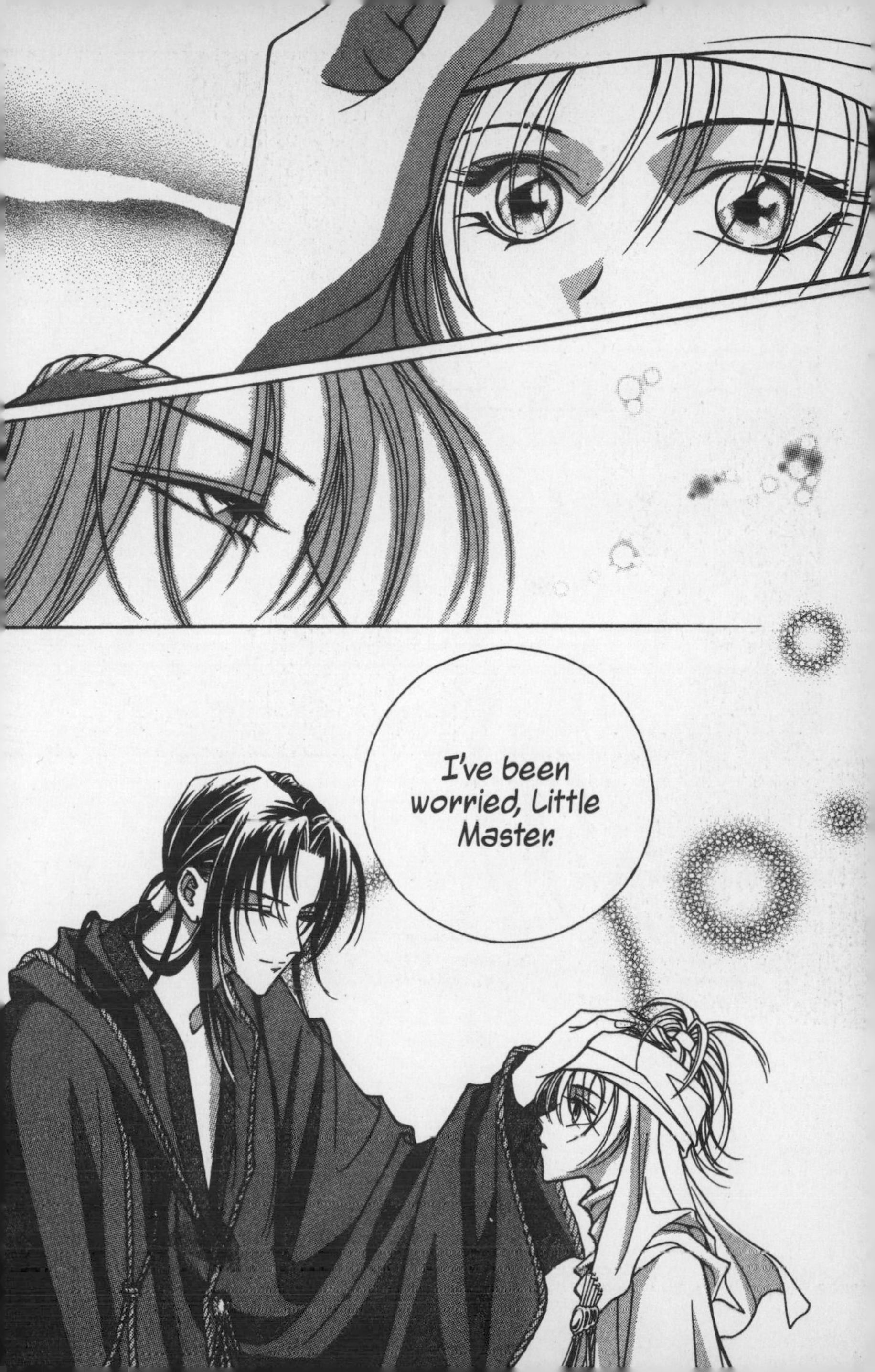
I've been worried, Little Master.

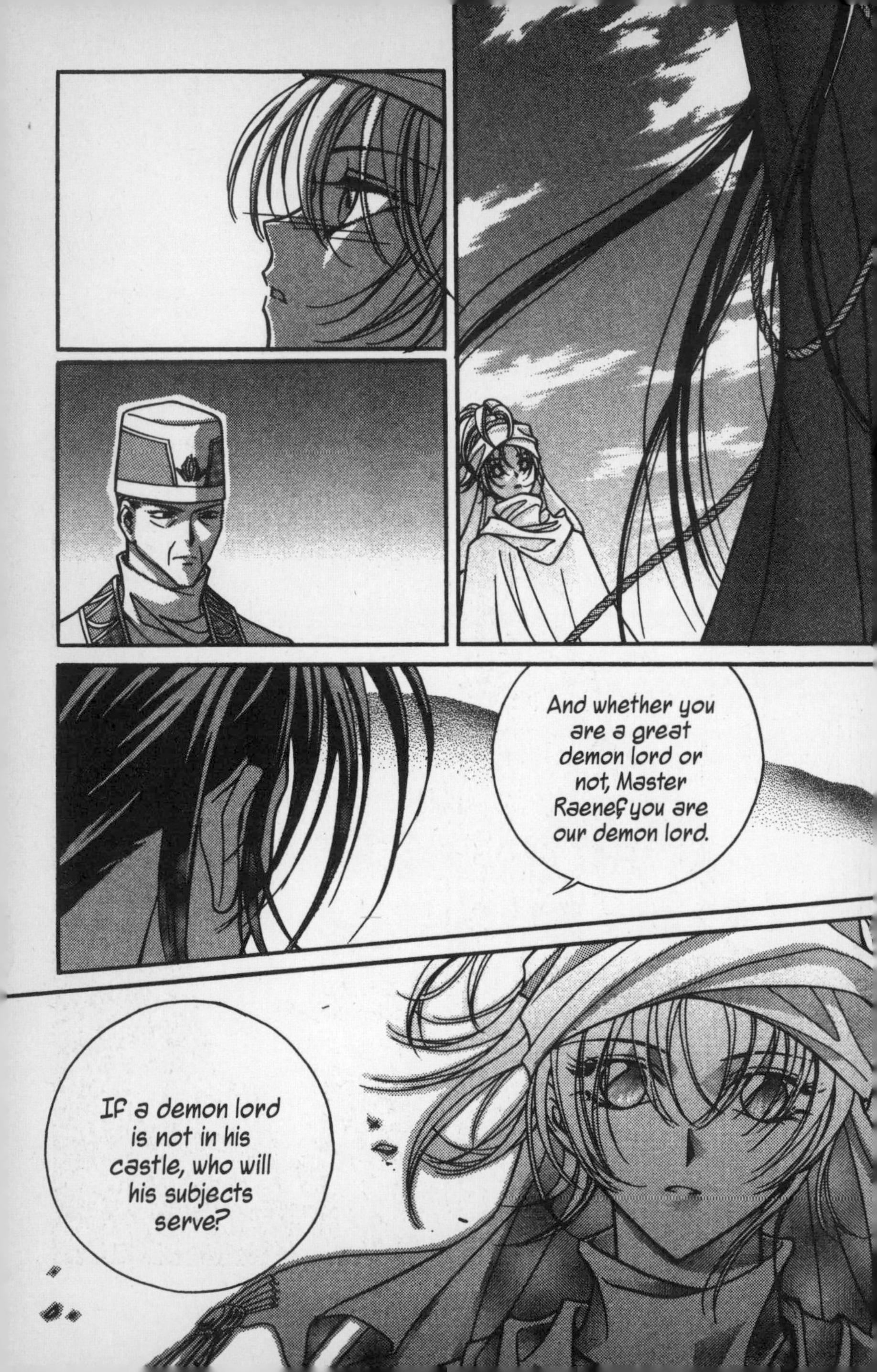
And whether you are a great demon lord or not, Master Raenef, you are our demon lord.
If a demon lord is not in his castle, who will his subjects serve?

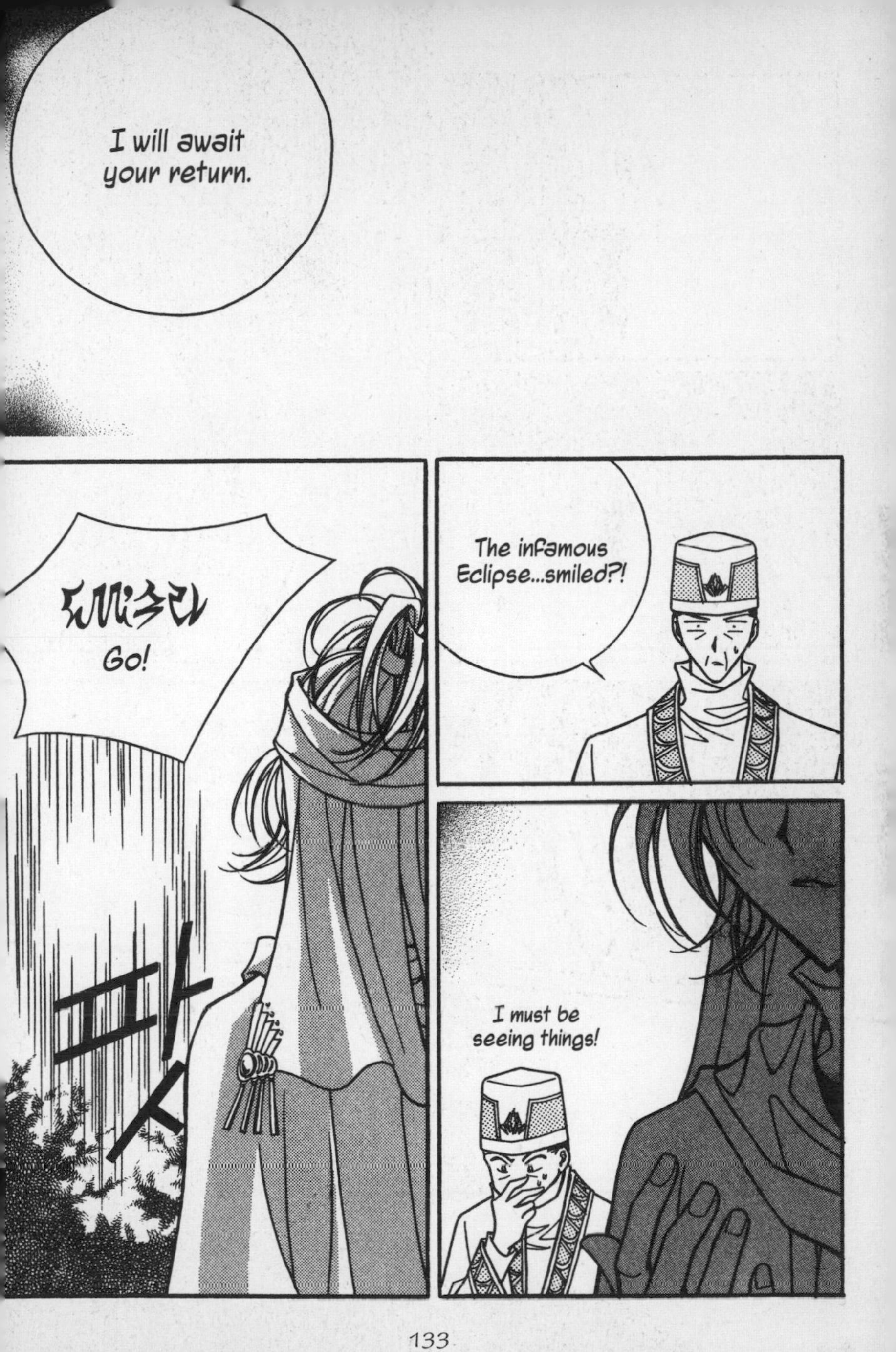
I will await your return.
Go!
The infamous Eclipse...smiled?!
I must be seeing things!

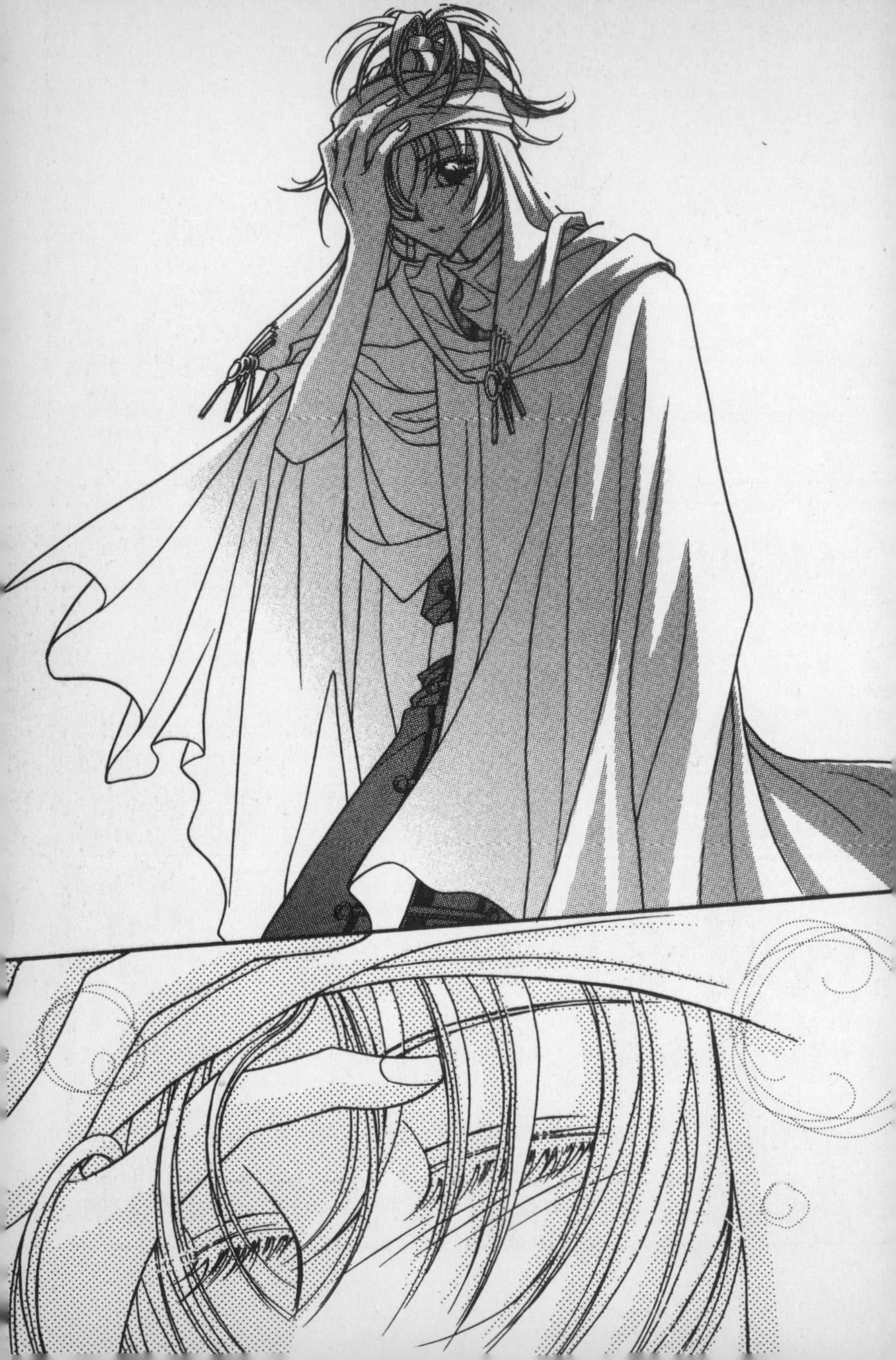

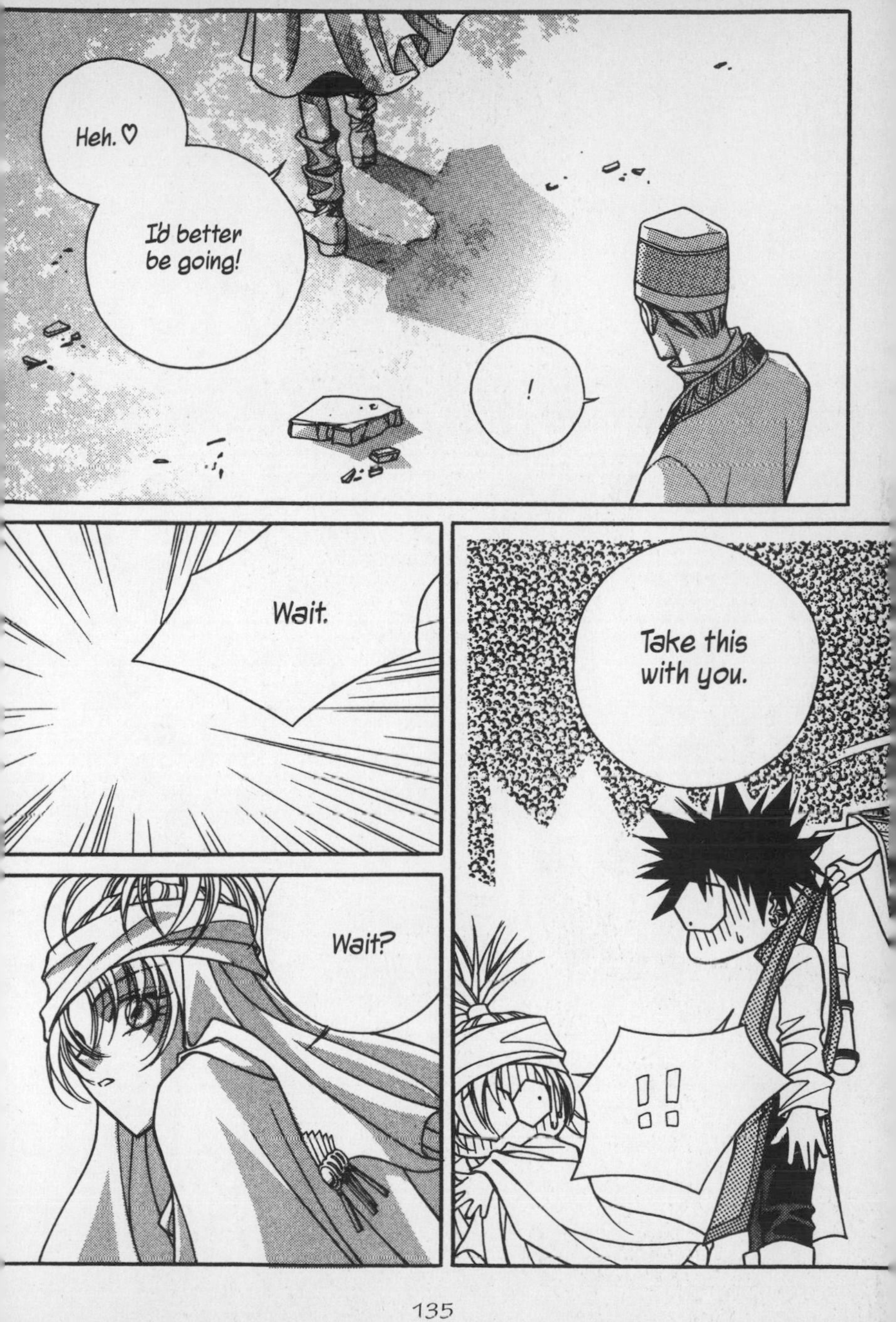
Heh. ♡
I'd better be going!
!
Take this with you.
Wait.
!!
Wait?

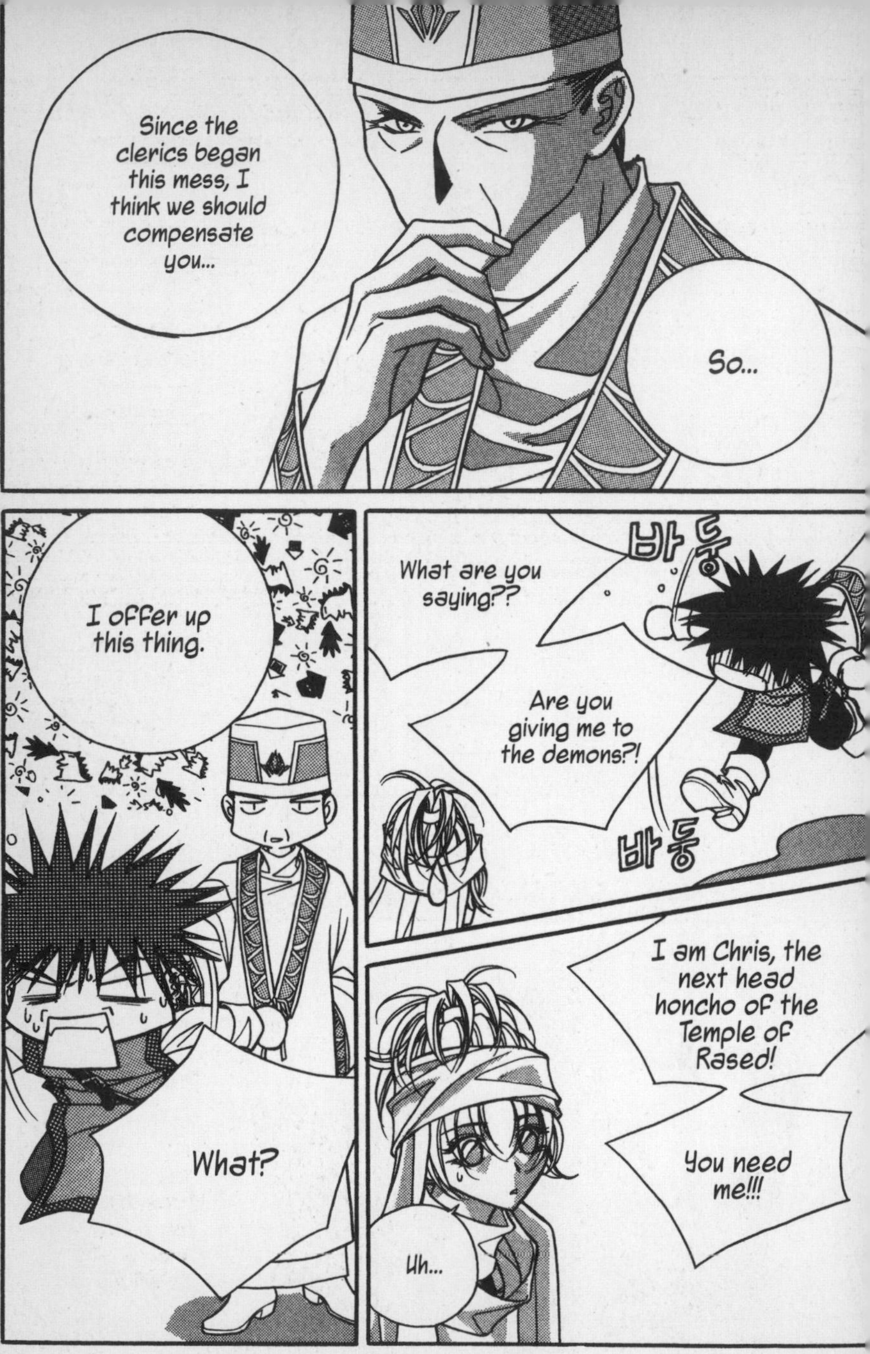
Since the clerics began this mess, I think we should compensate you...
So...
I offer up this thing.
What?
What are you saying??
Are you giving me to the demons?!
바둥
바둥
I am Chris, the next head honcho of the Temple of Rased!
You need me!!!
Uh...

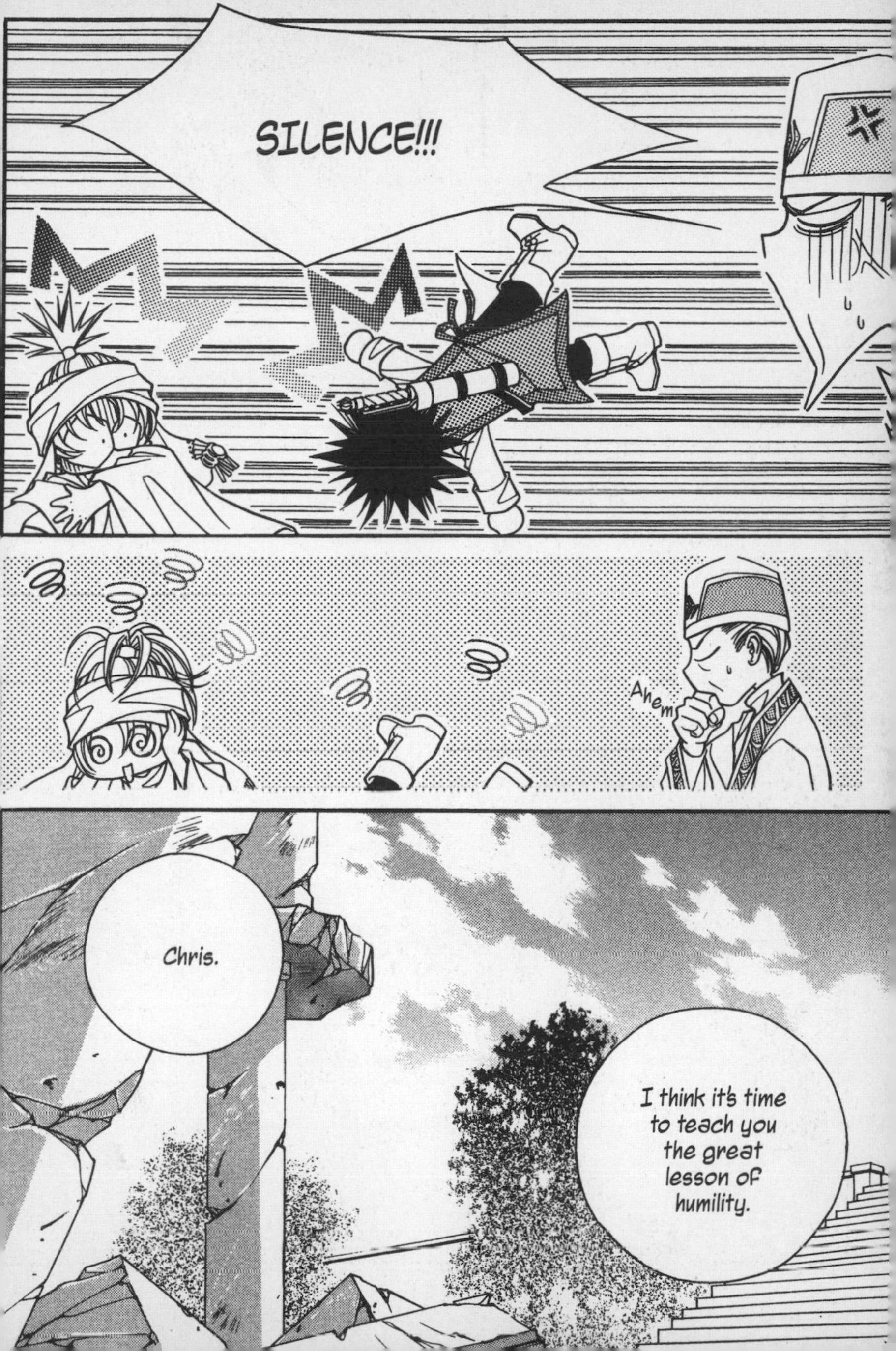
SILENCE!!!
Ahem
Chris.
I think it's time to teach you the great lesson of humility.

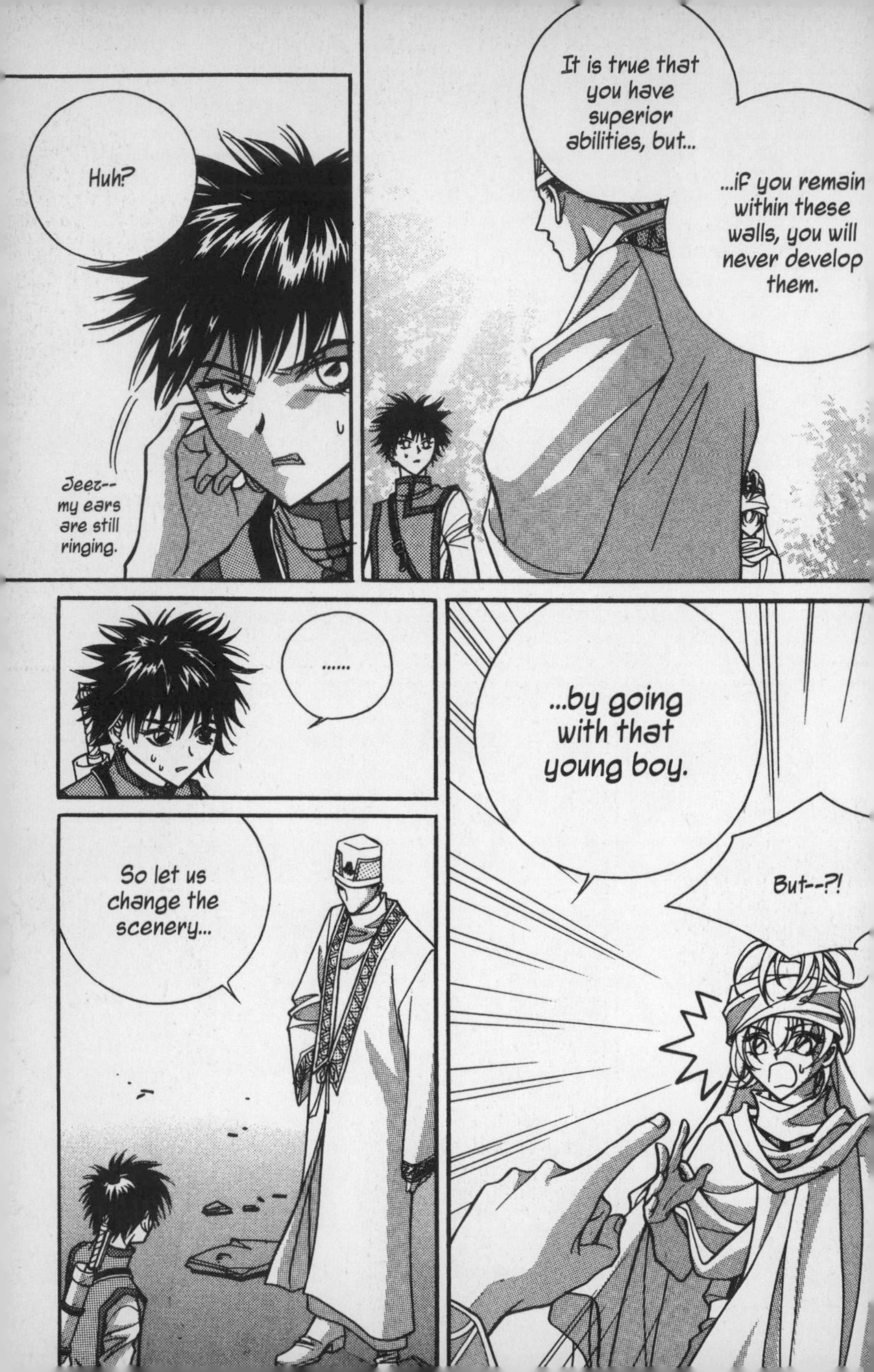
Huh?
Jeez-- my ears are still ringing.
It is true that you have superior abilities, but...
...if you remain within these walls, you will never develop them.
......
So let us change the scenery...
...by going with that young boy.
But--?!

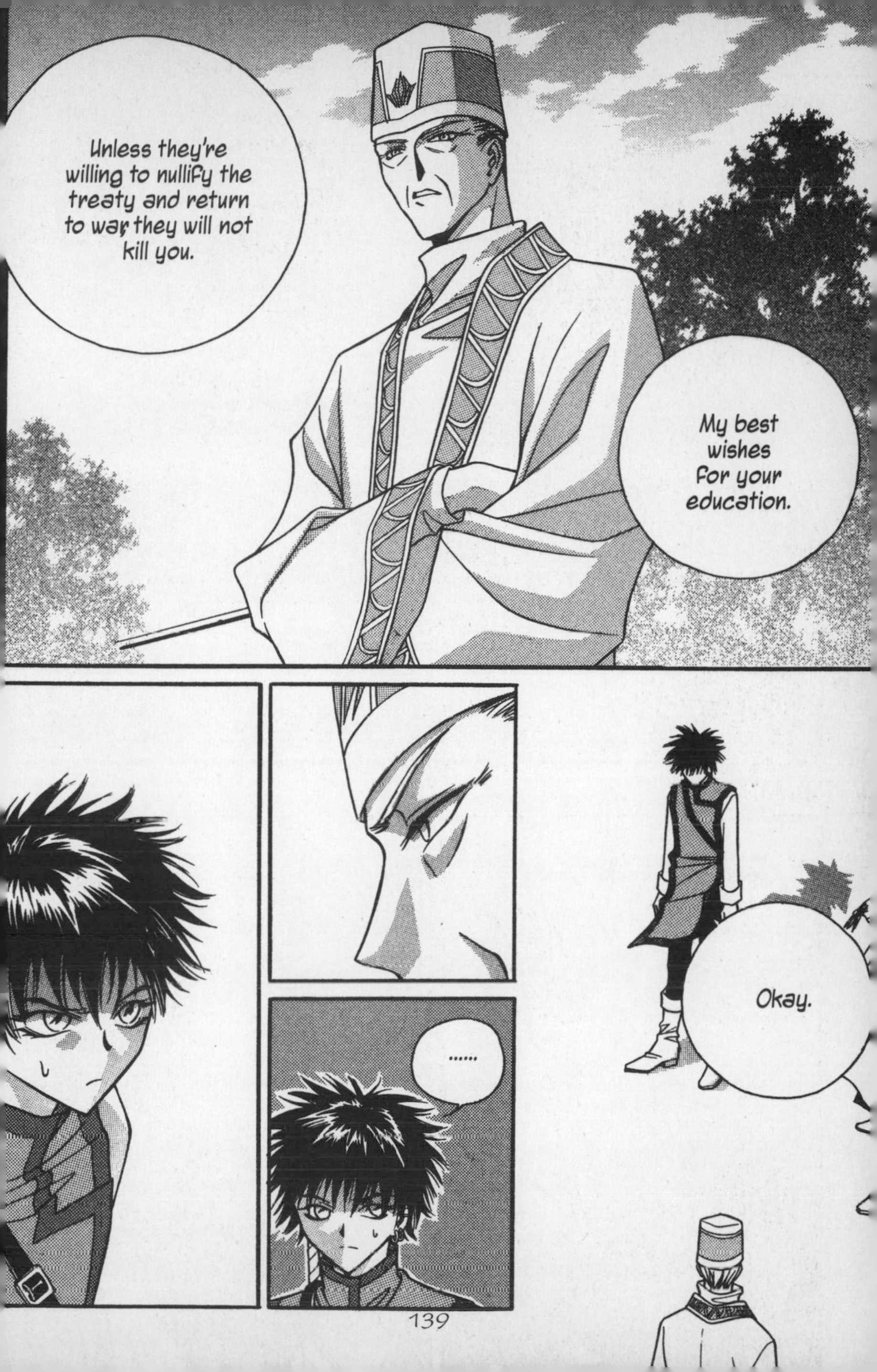
Unless they're willing to nullify the treaty and return to war, they will not kill you.
My best wishes for your education.
......
Okay.

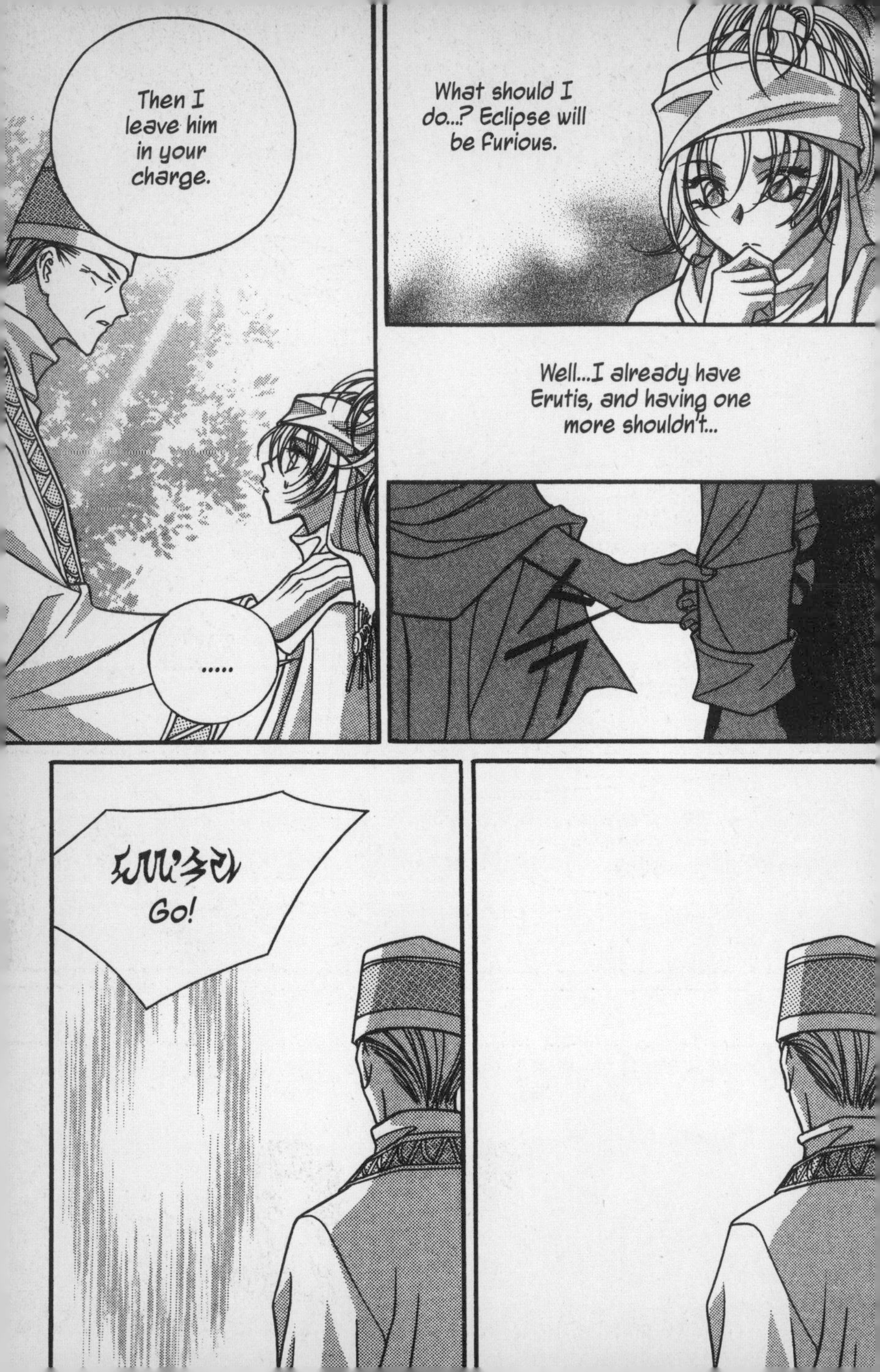
Then I leave him in your charge.
.....
What should I do...? Eclipse will be furious.
Well...I already have Erutis, and having one more shouldn't...
Go!

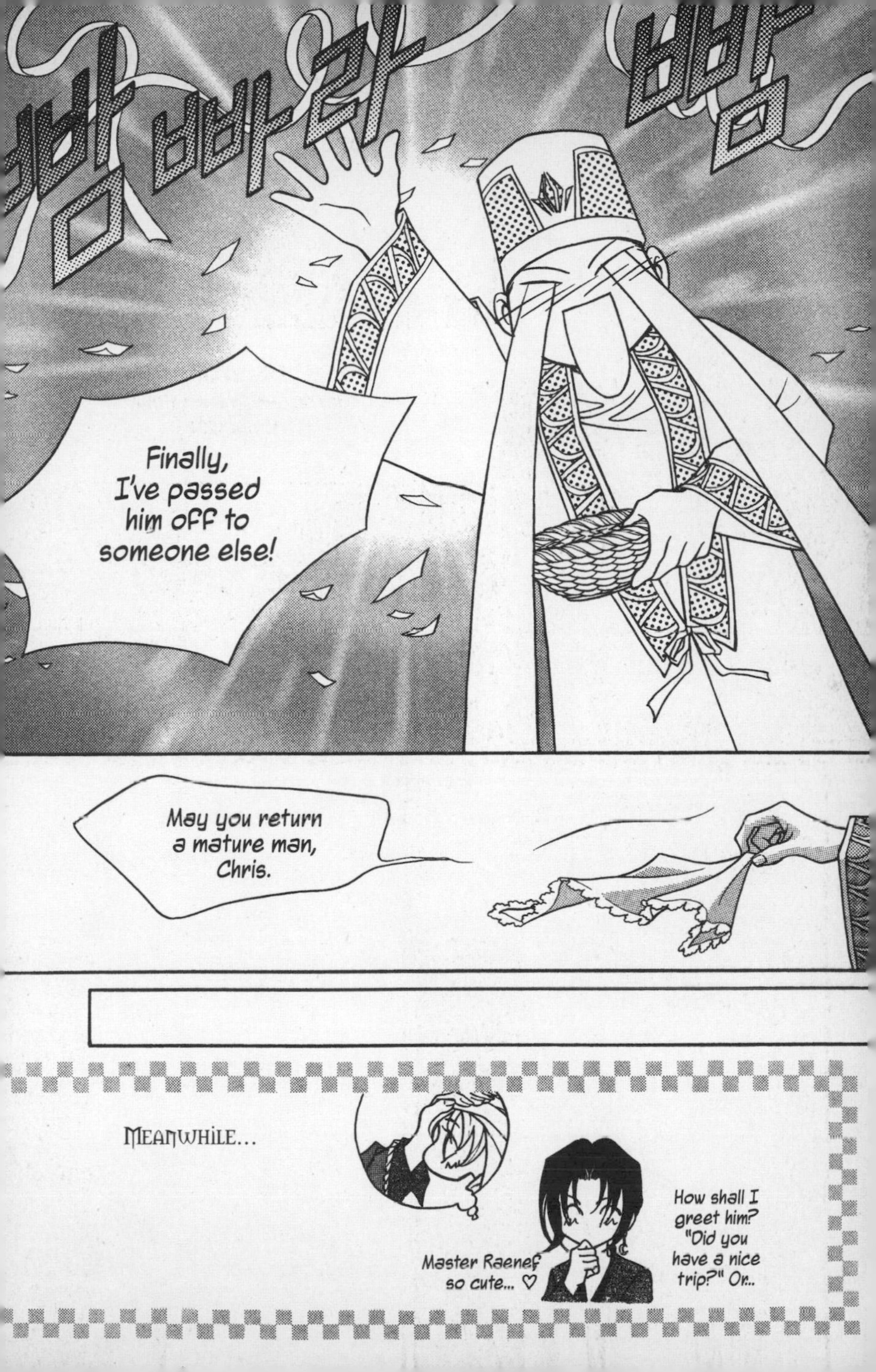

빵 빠바라 빰
Finally, I've passed him off to someone else!
May you return a mature man, Chris.
MEANWHILE...
How shall I greet him? "Did you have a nice trip?" Or..
Master Raenef so cute... ♡

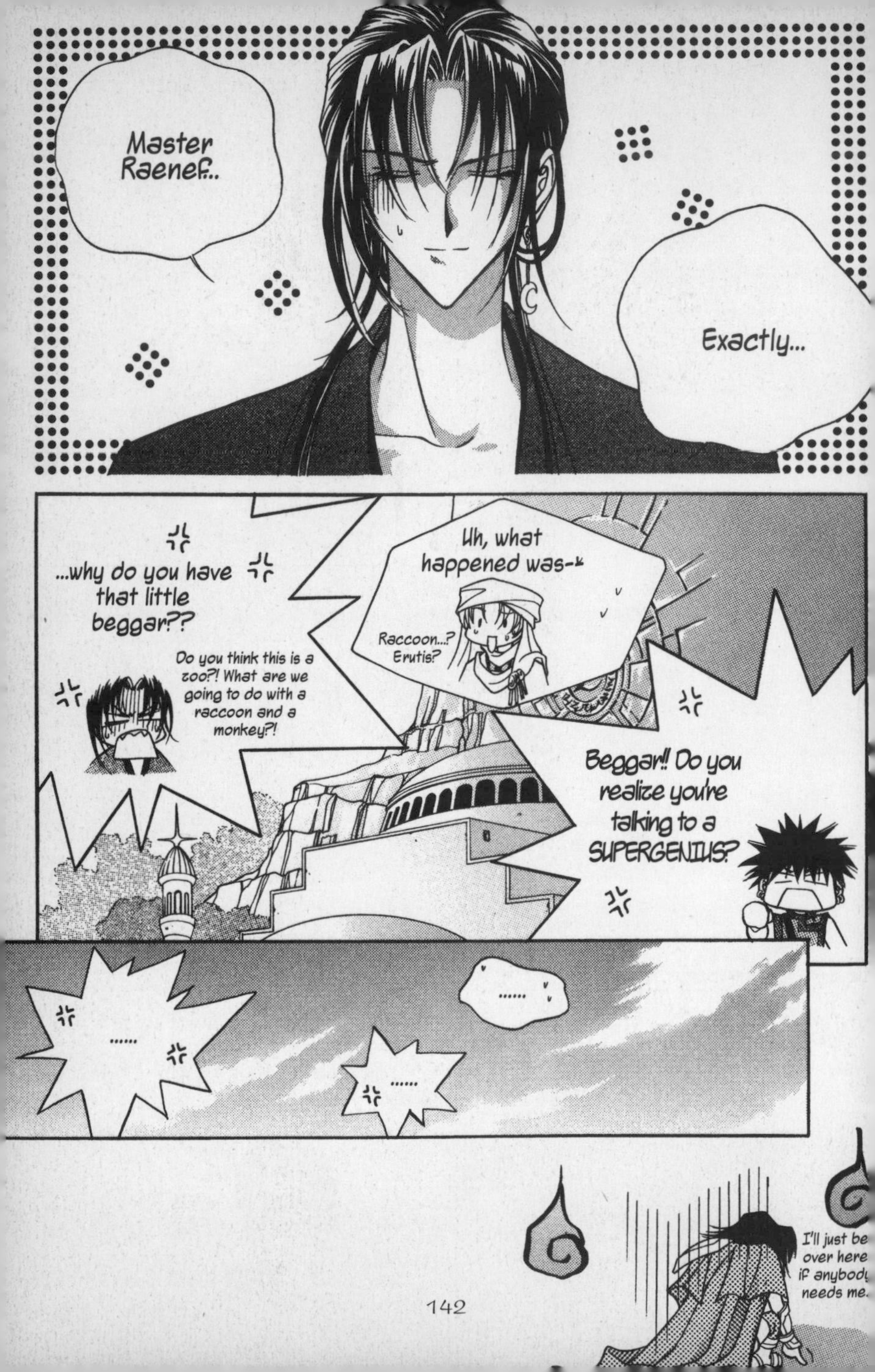
Master Raenef...
Exactly...
Uh, what happened was-
Raccoon...? Erutis?
...why do you have that little beggar??
Do you think this is a zoo?! What are we going to do with a raccoon and a monkey?!
Beggar!! Do you realize you're talking to a SUPERGENIUS?
......
......
......
I'll just be over here if anybody needs me.

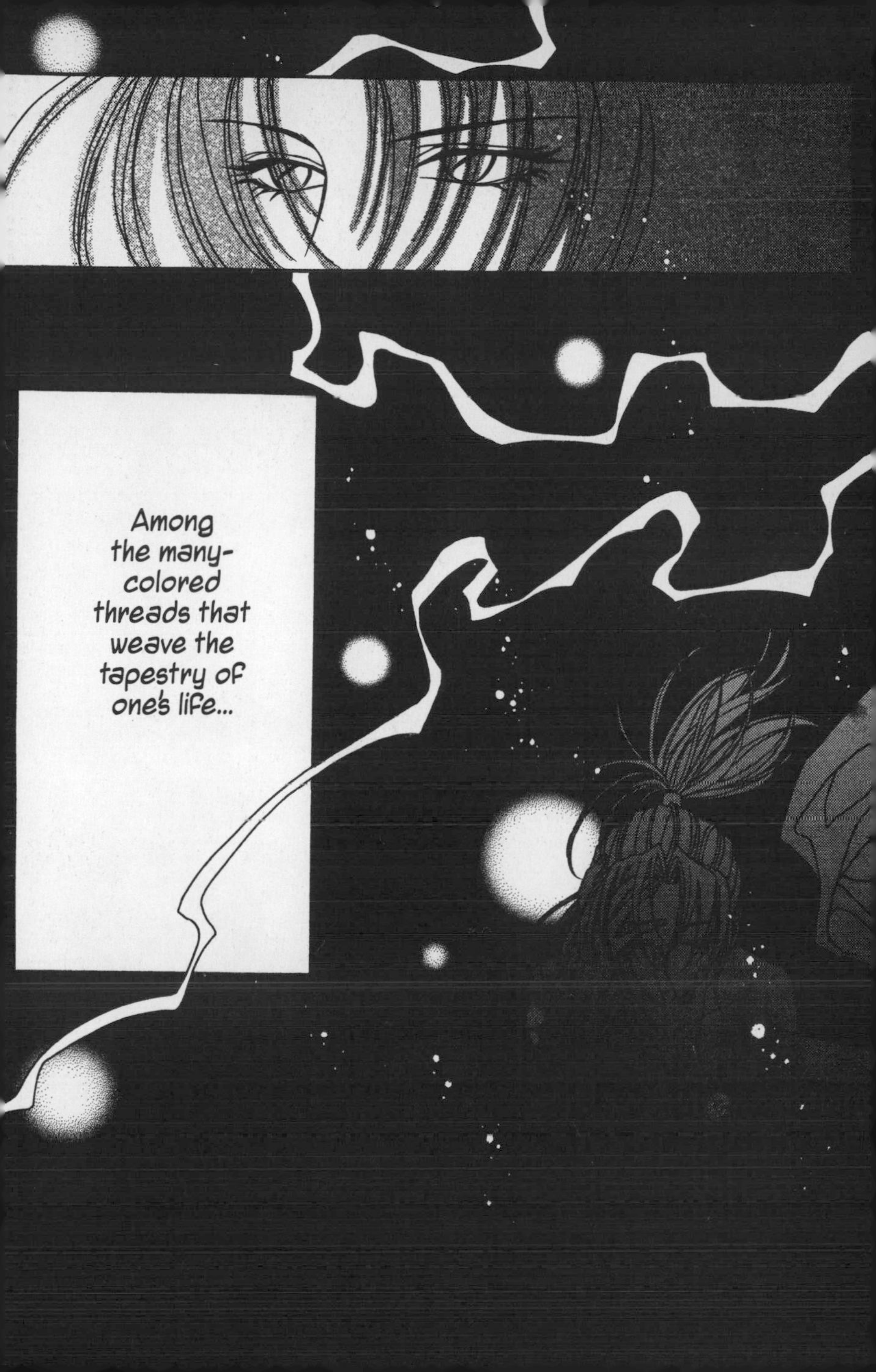
Among the many-colored threads that weave the tapestry of one's life...

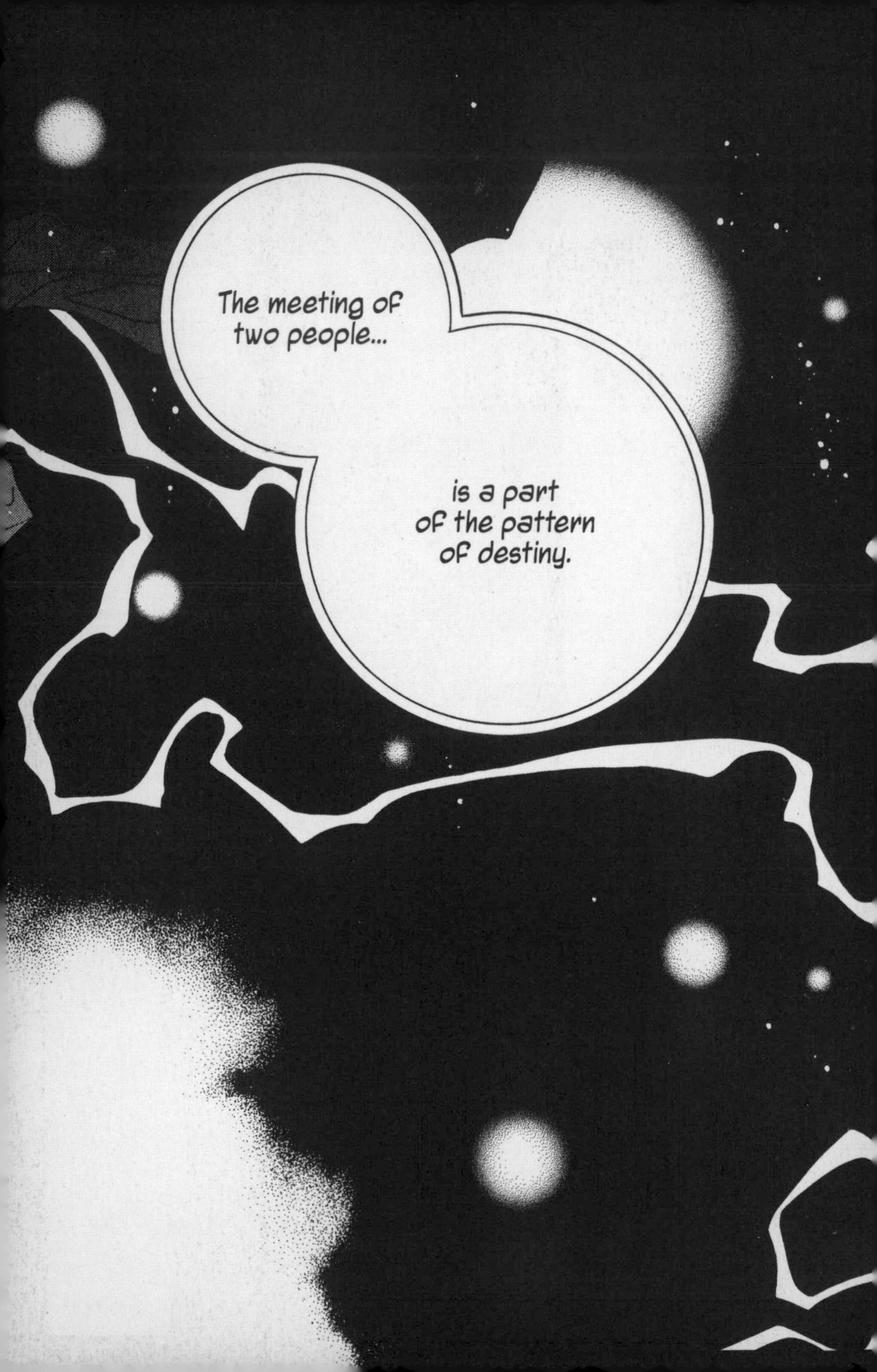
The meeting of two people...
is a part of the pattern of destiny.

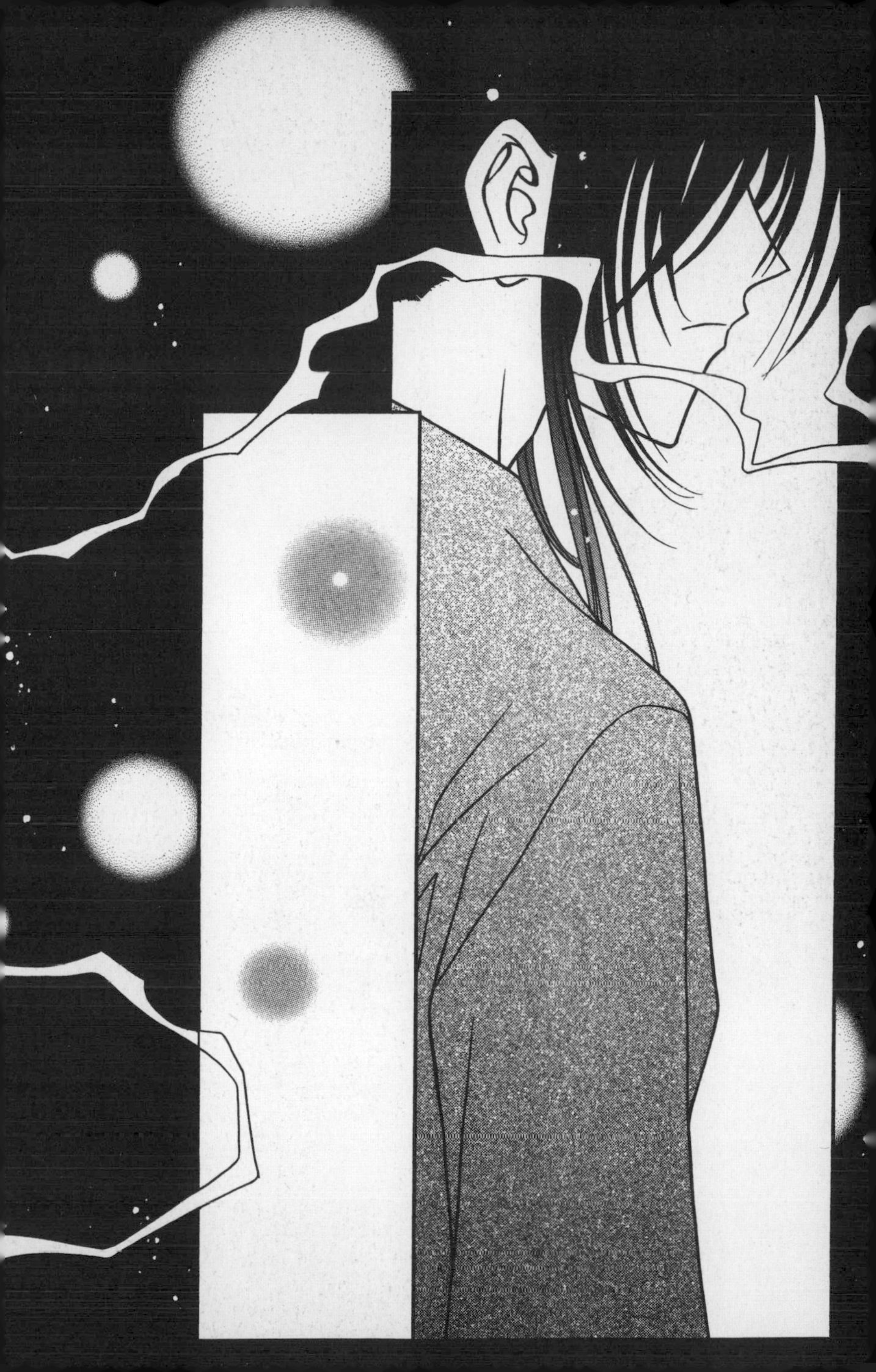

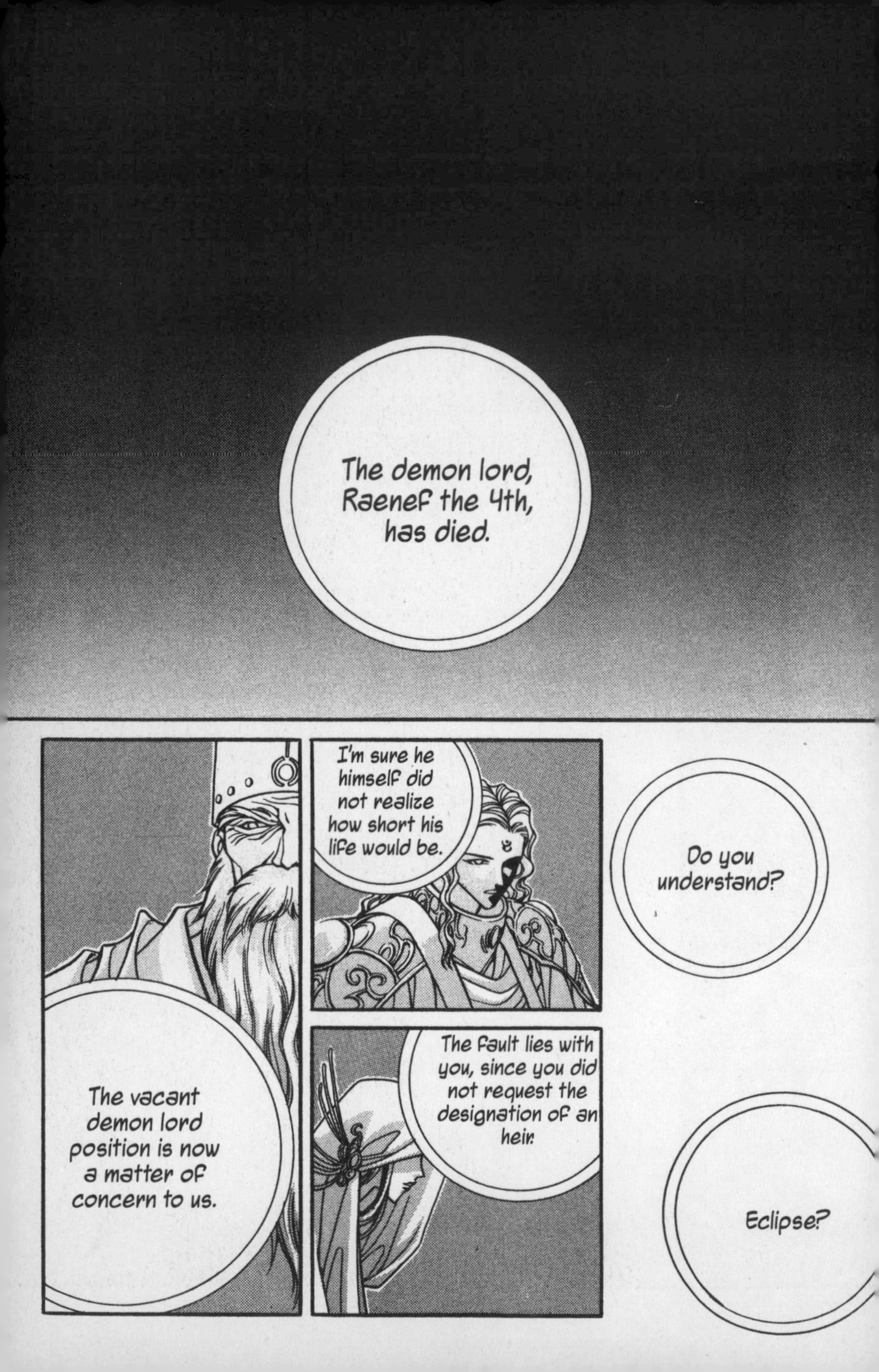
The demon lord, Raenef the 4th, has died.
The vacant demon lord position is now a matter of concern to us.
I'm sure he himself did not realize how short his life would be.
The fault lies with you, since you did not request the designation of an heir.
Do you understand?
Eclipse?

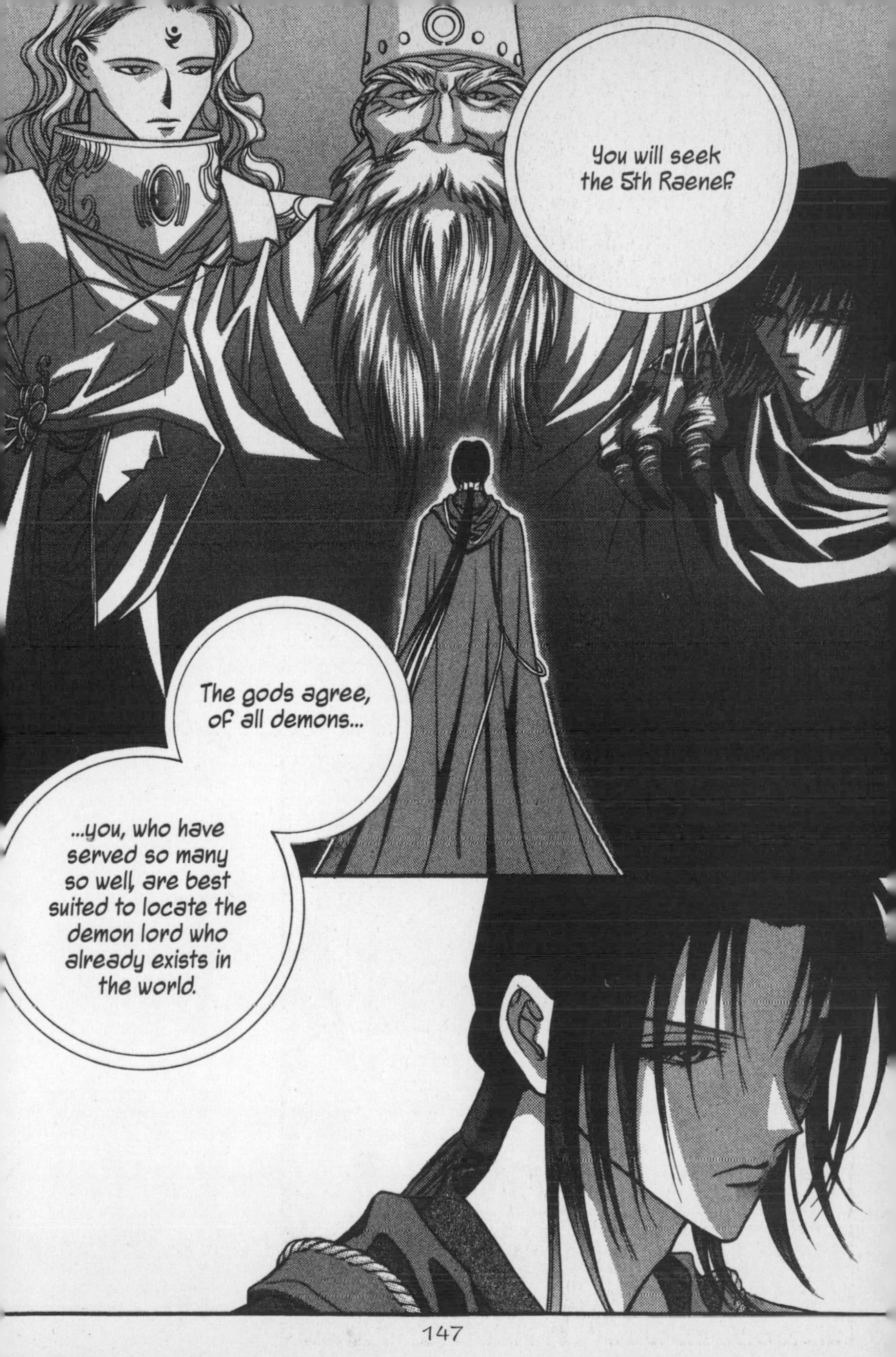
You will seek the 5th Raenef.
The gods agree, of all demons...
...you, who have served so many so well, are best suited to locate the demon lord who already exists in the world.

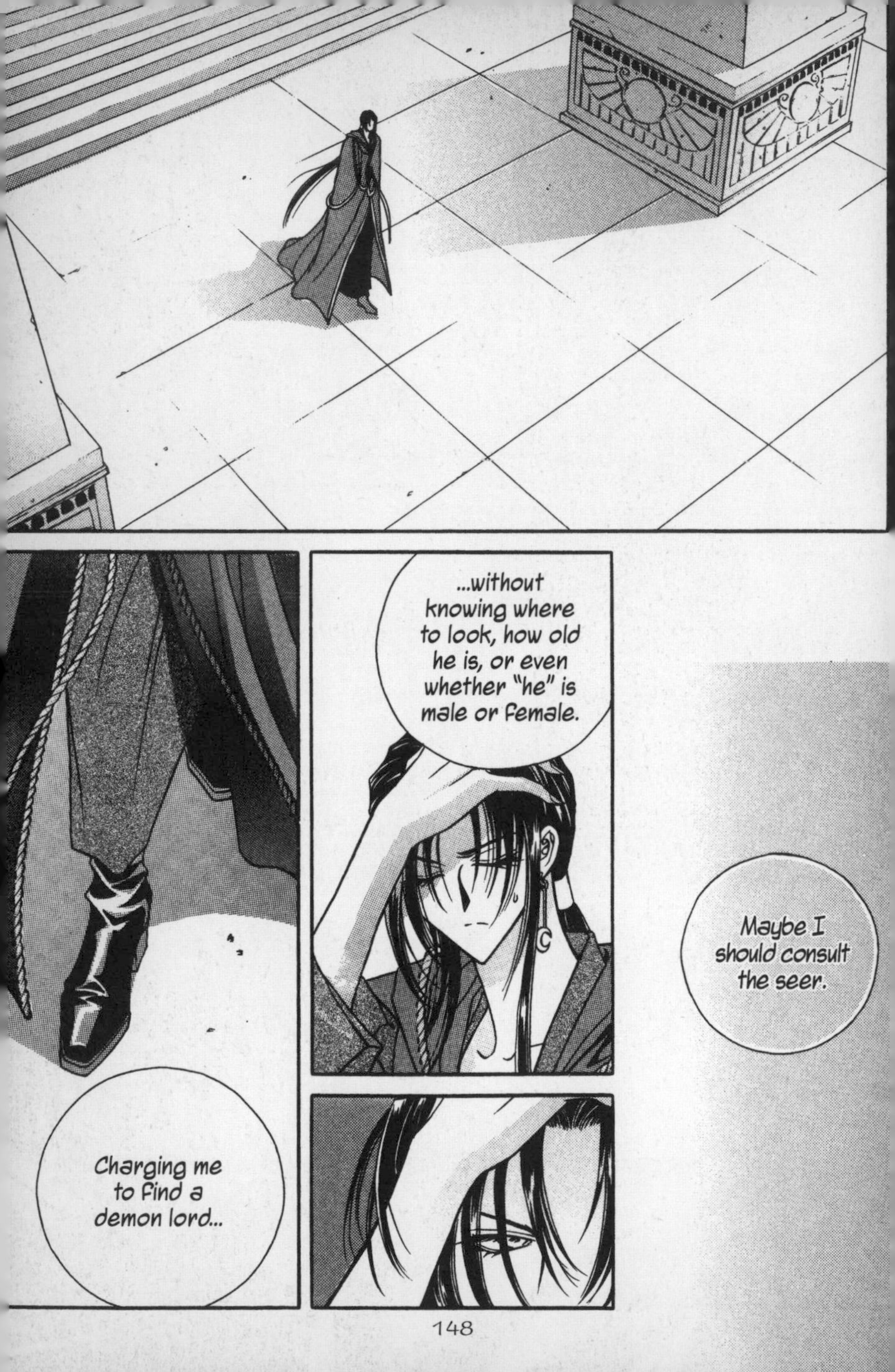
Charging me to find a demon lord...
...without knowing where to look, how old he is, or even whether "he" is male or female.
Maybe I should consult the seer.

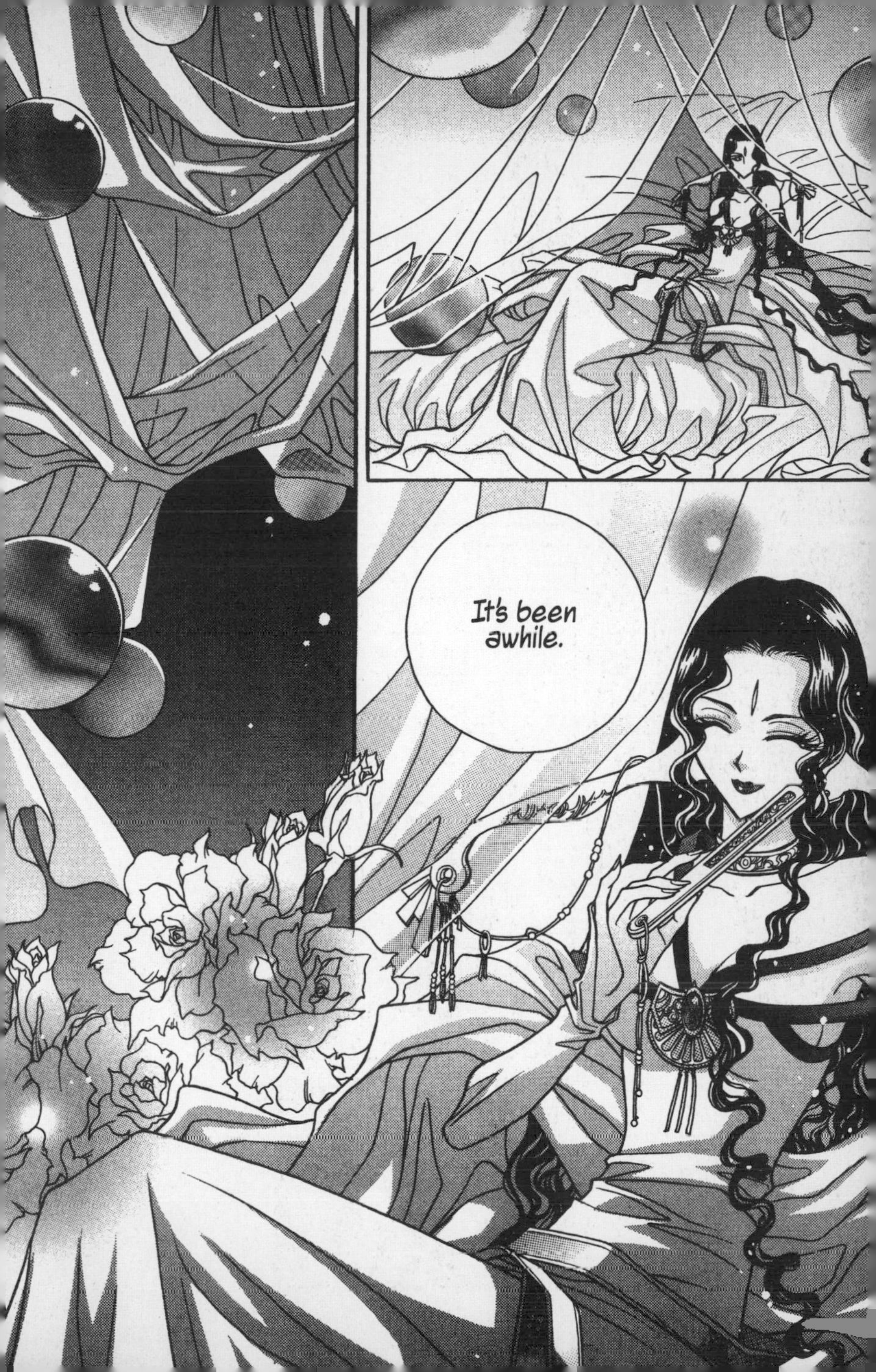
It's been awhile.

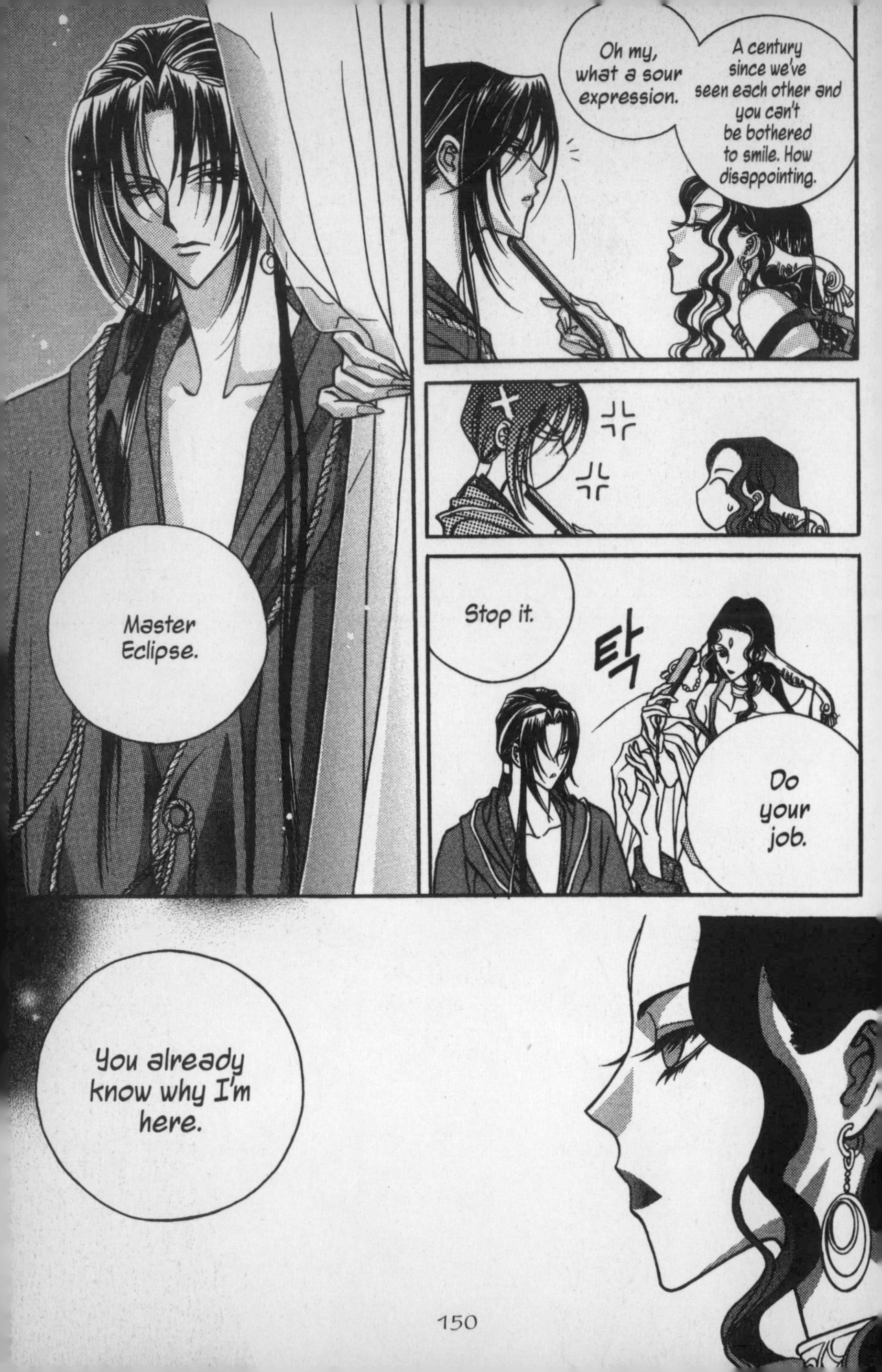
Master Eclipse.
Oh my, what a sour expression.
A century since we've seen each other and you can't be bothered to smile. How disappointing.
Stop it.
탁
Do your job.
You already know why I'm here.

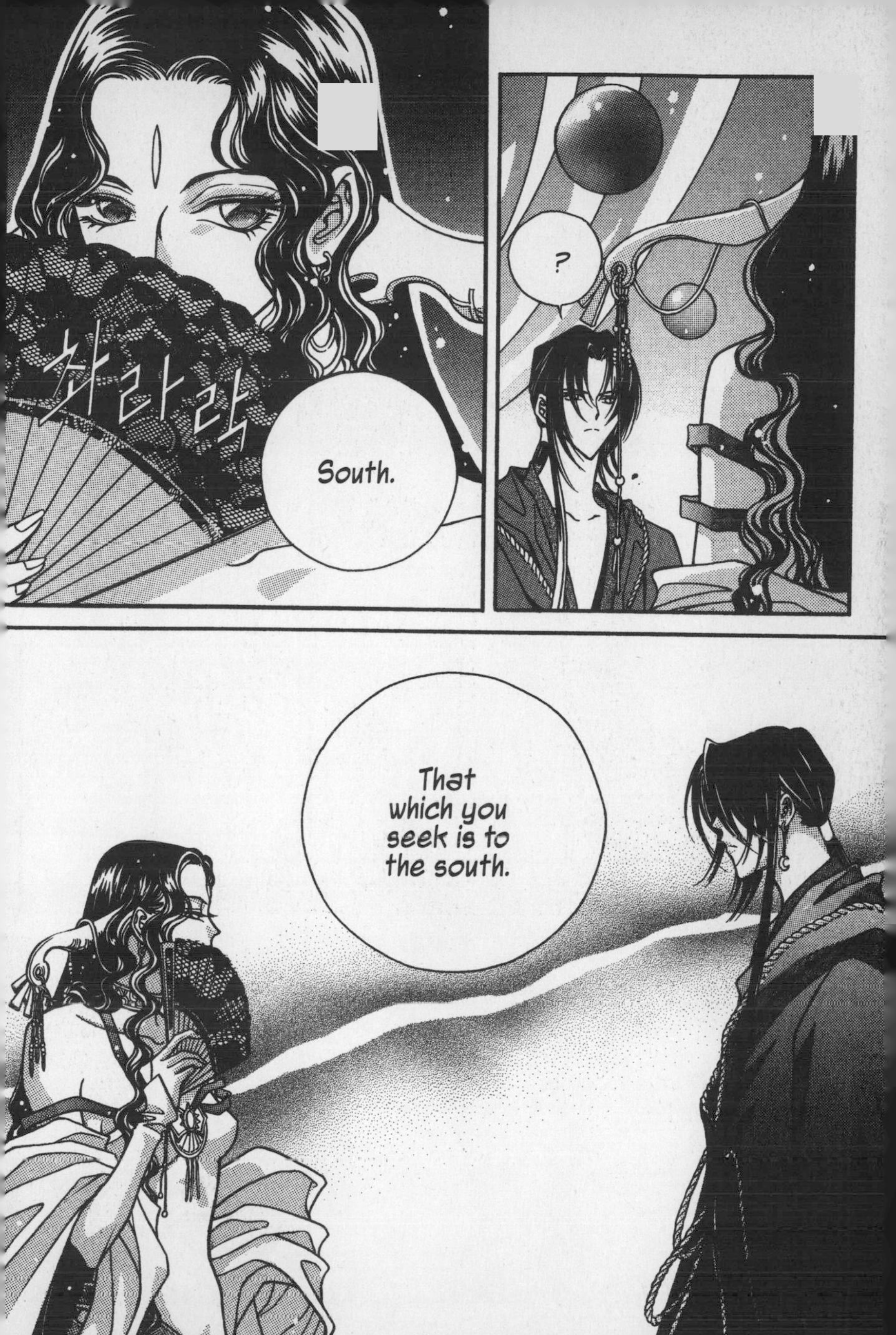
촤라락
South.
?
That which you seek is to the south.

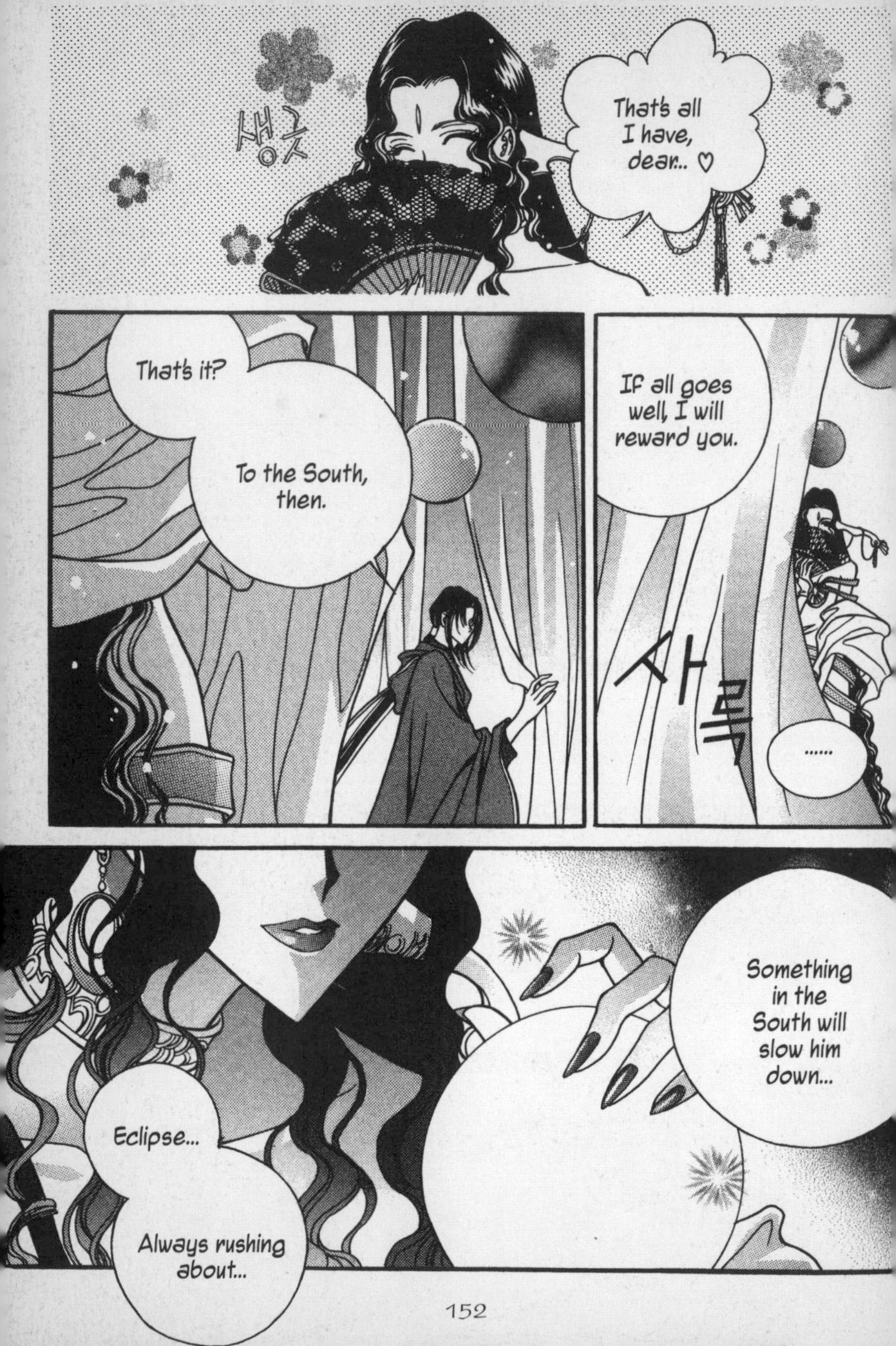
생긋
That's all I have, dear.. ♡
That's it?
To the South, then.
If all goes well, I will reward you.
사르륵
......
Something in the South will slow him down...
Eclipse...
Always rushing about...

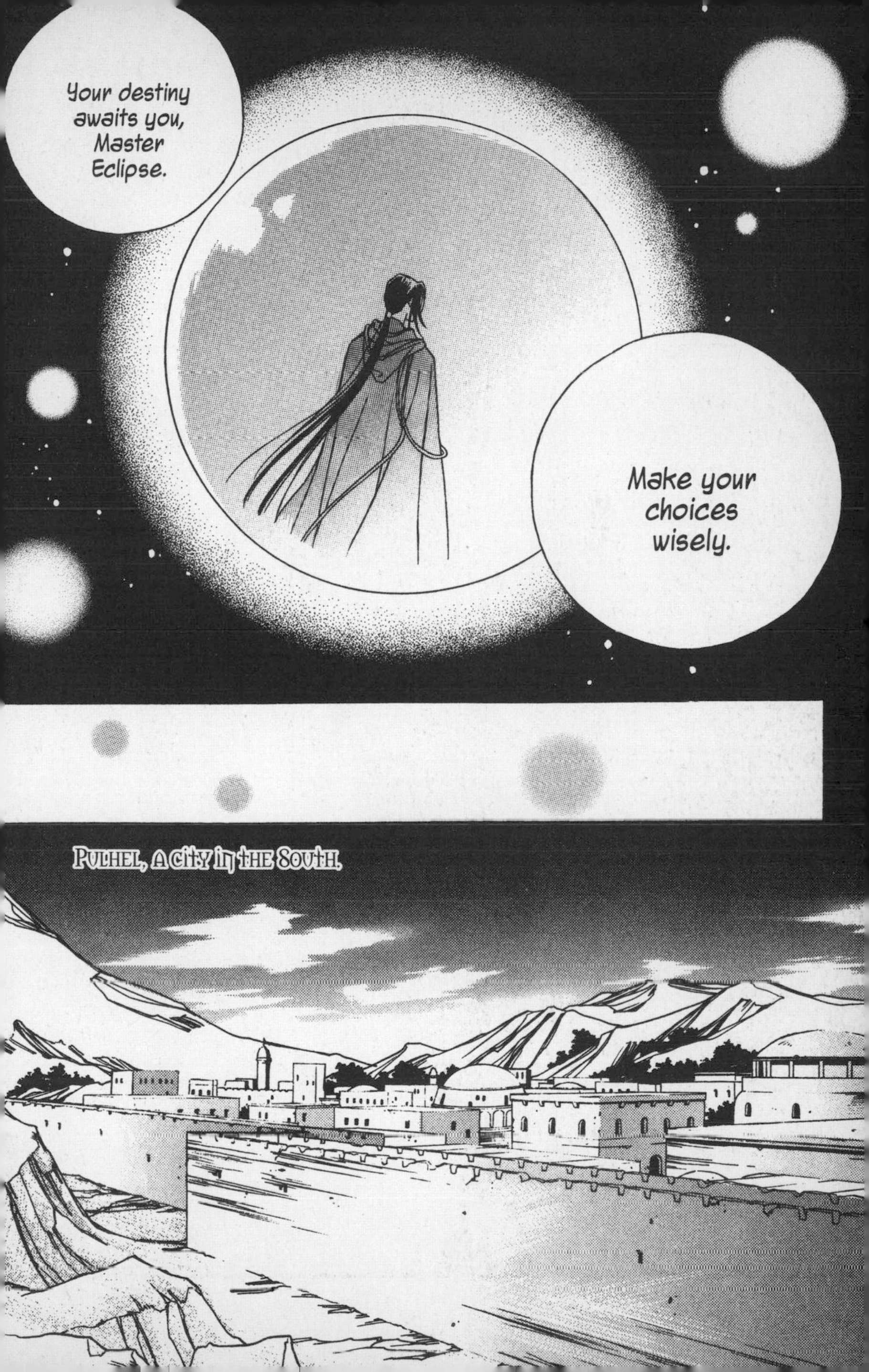
Your destiny awaits you, Master Eclipse.
Make your choices wisely.
Pulhel, a city in the South.

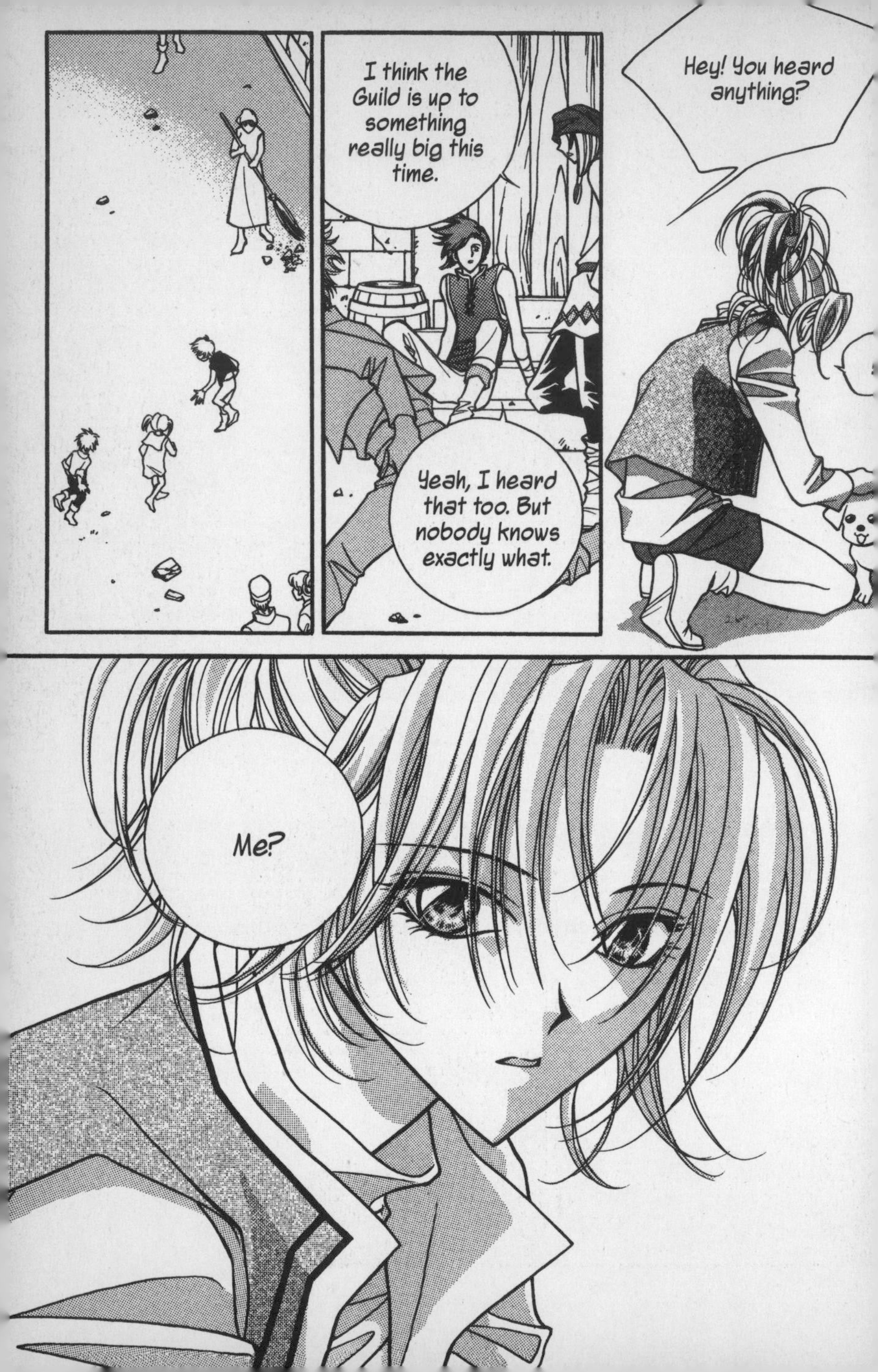
Hey! You heard anything?
I think the Guild is up to something really big this time.
Yeah, I heard that too. But nobody knows exactly what.
Me?

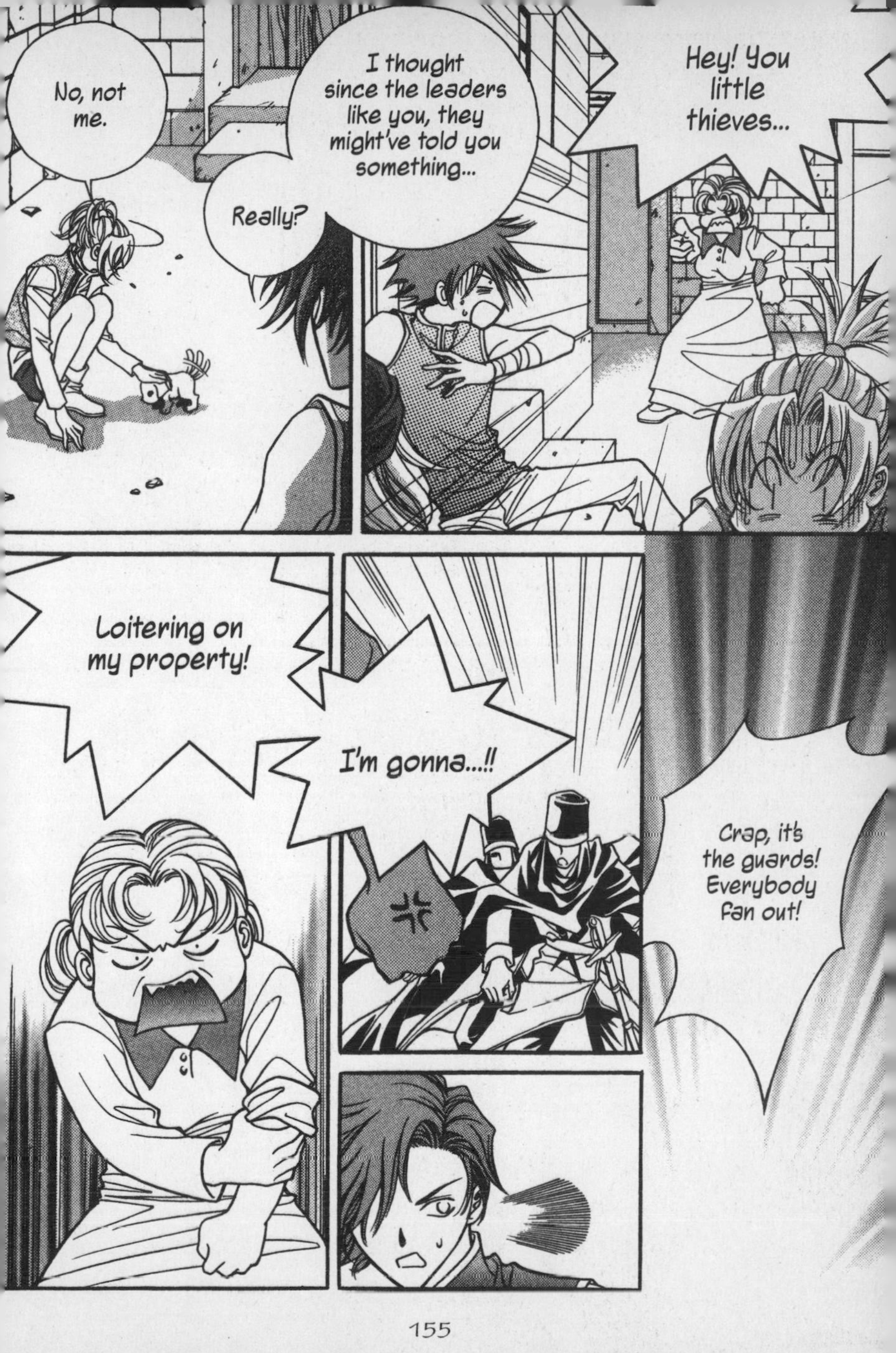
No, not me.
Really?
I thought since the leaders like you, they might've told you something...
Hey! You little thieves...
Loitering on my property!
I'm gonna...!!
Crap, it's the guards! Everybody fan out!

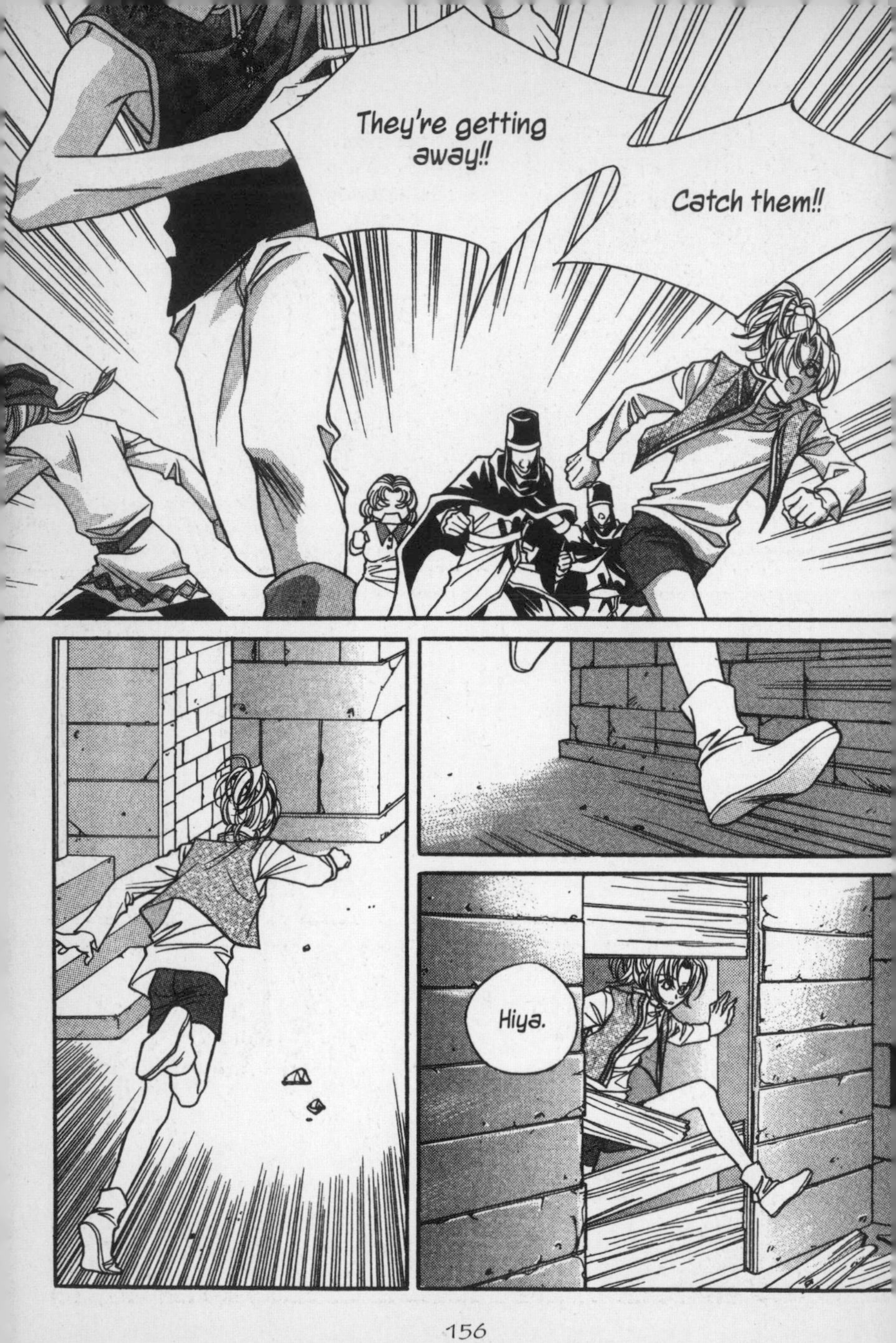
They're getting away!!
Catch them!!
Hiya.

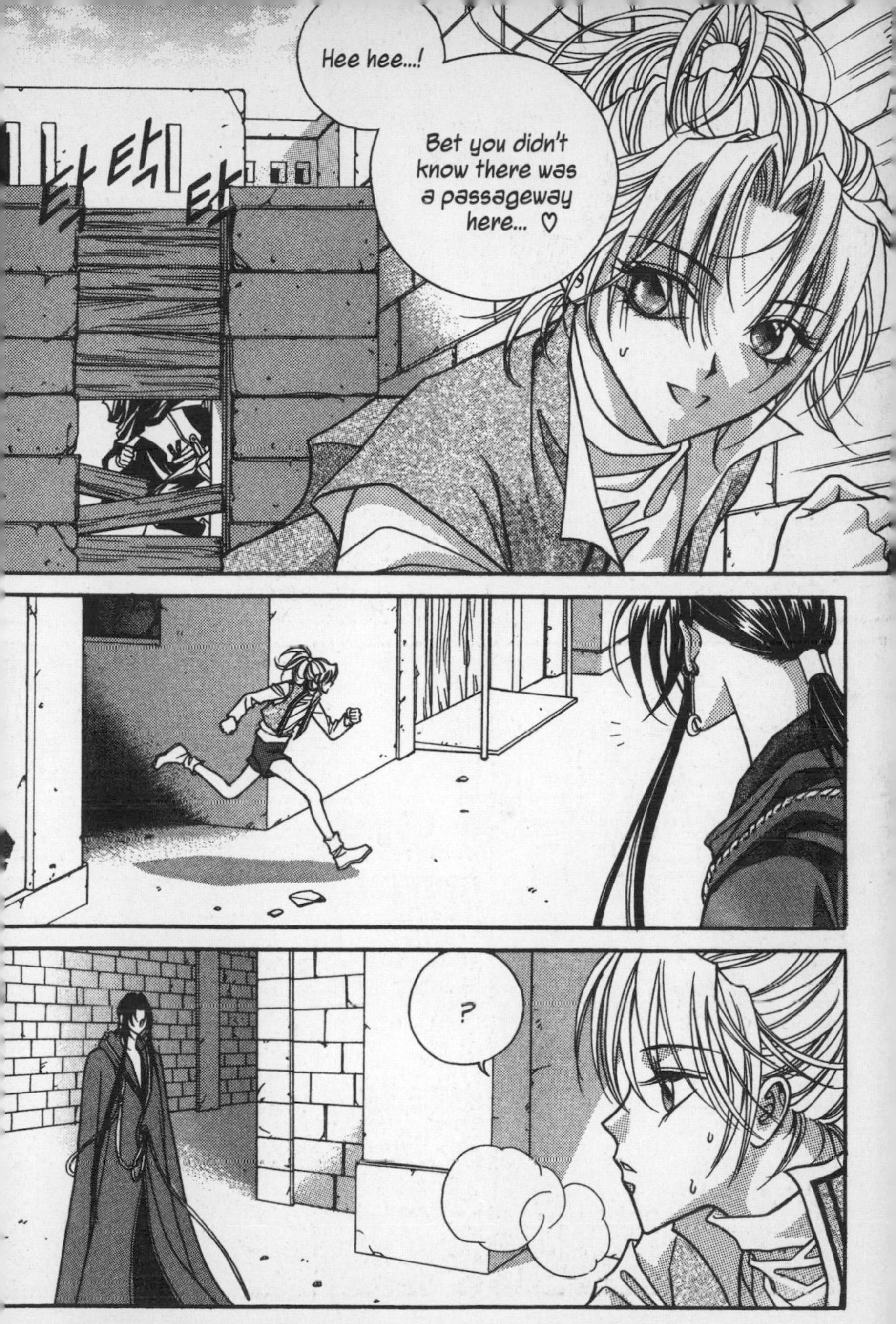
탁 탁 탁
Hee hee...!
Bet you didn't know there was a passageway here... ♡
?

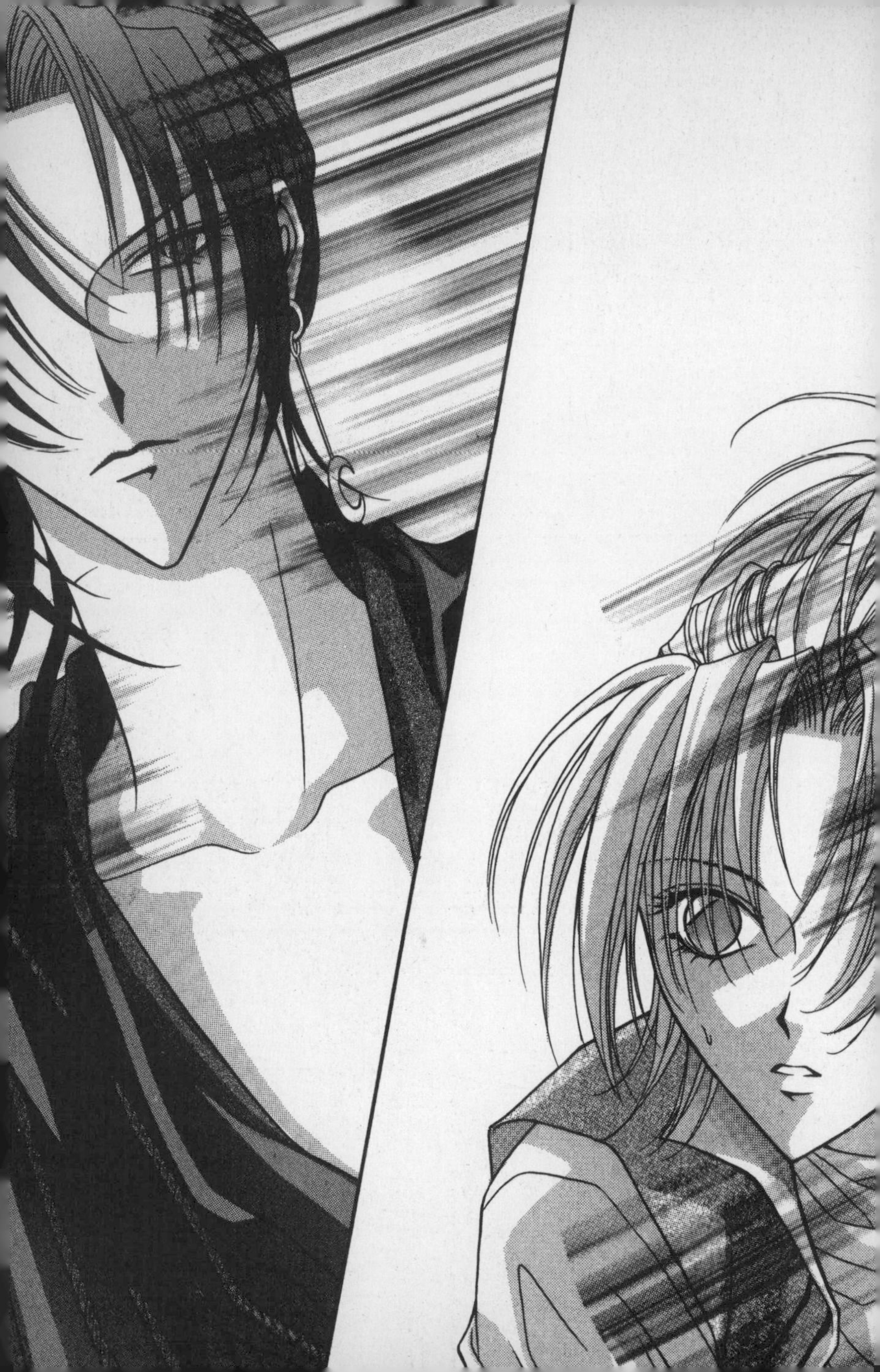

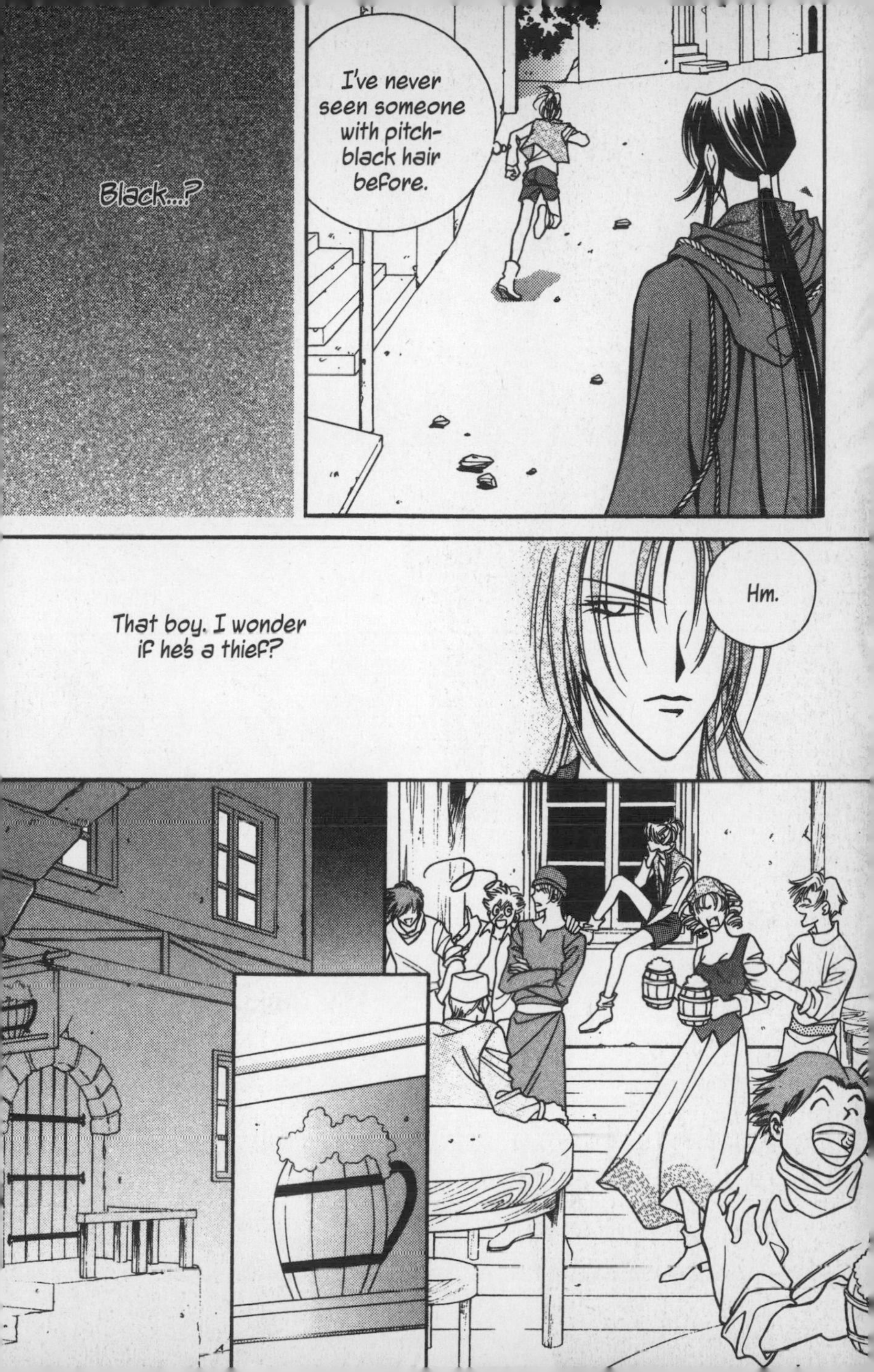
I've never seen someone with pitch-black hair before.
Black...?
Hm.
That boy. I wonder if he's a thief?

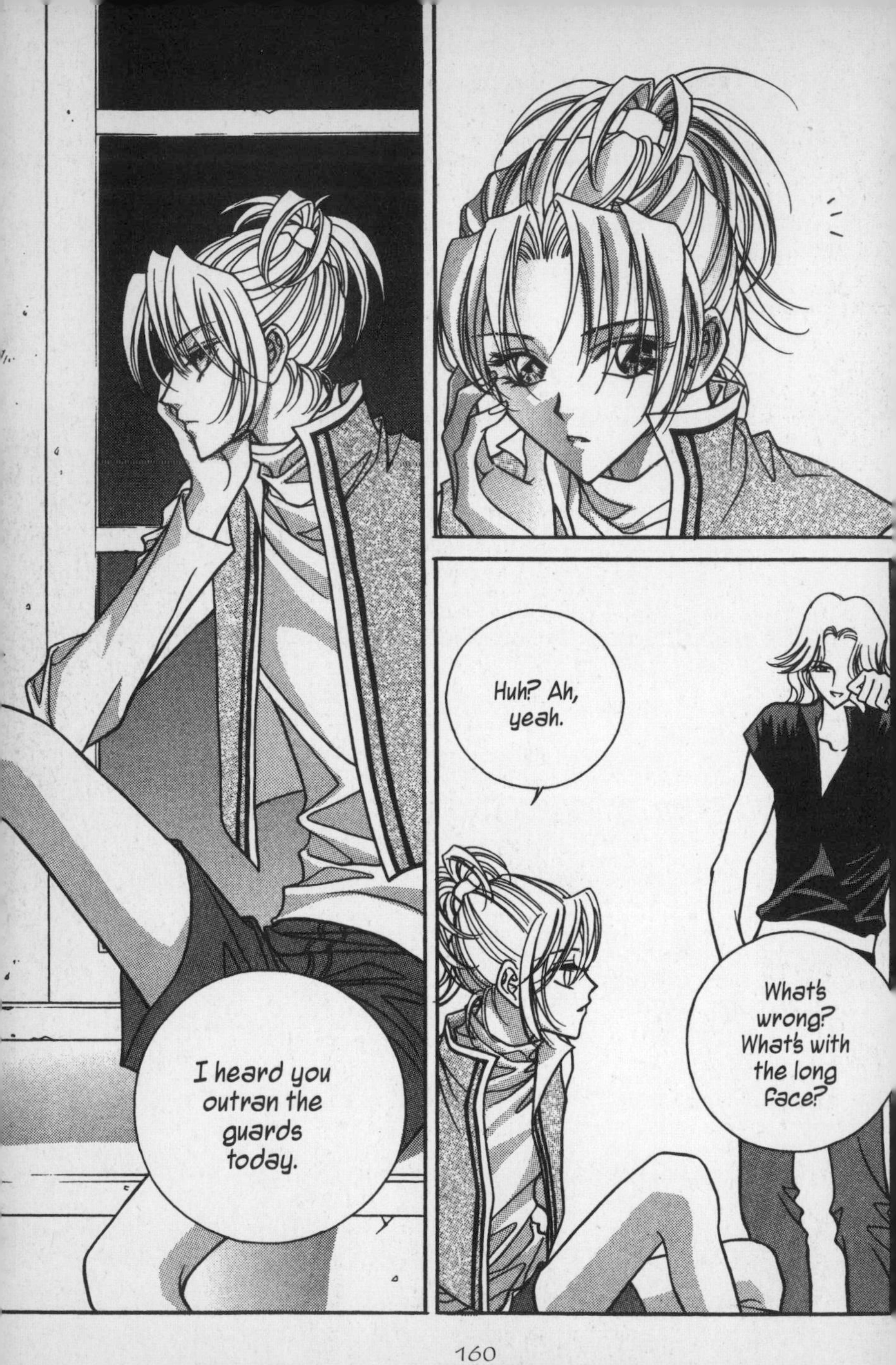
I heard you outran the guards today.
Huh? Ah, yeah.
What's wrong? What's with the long face?

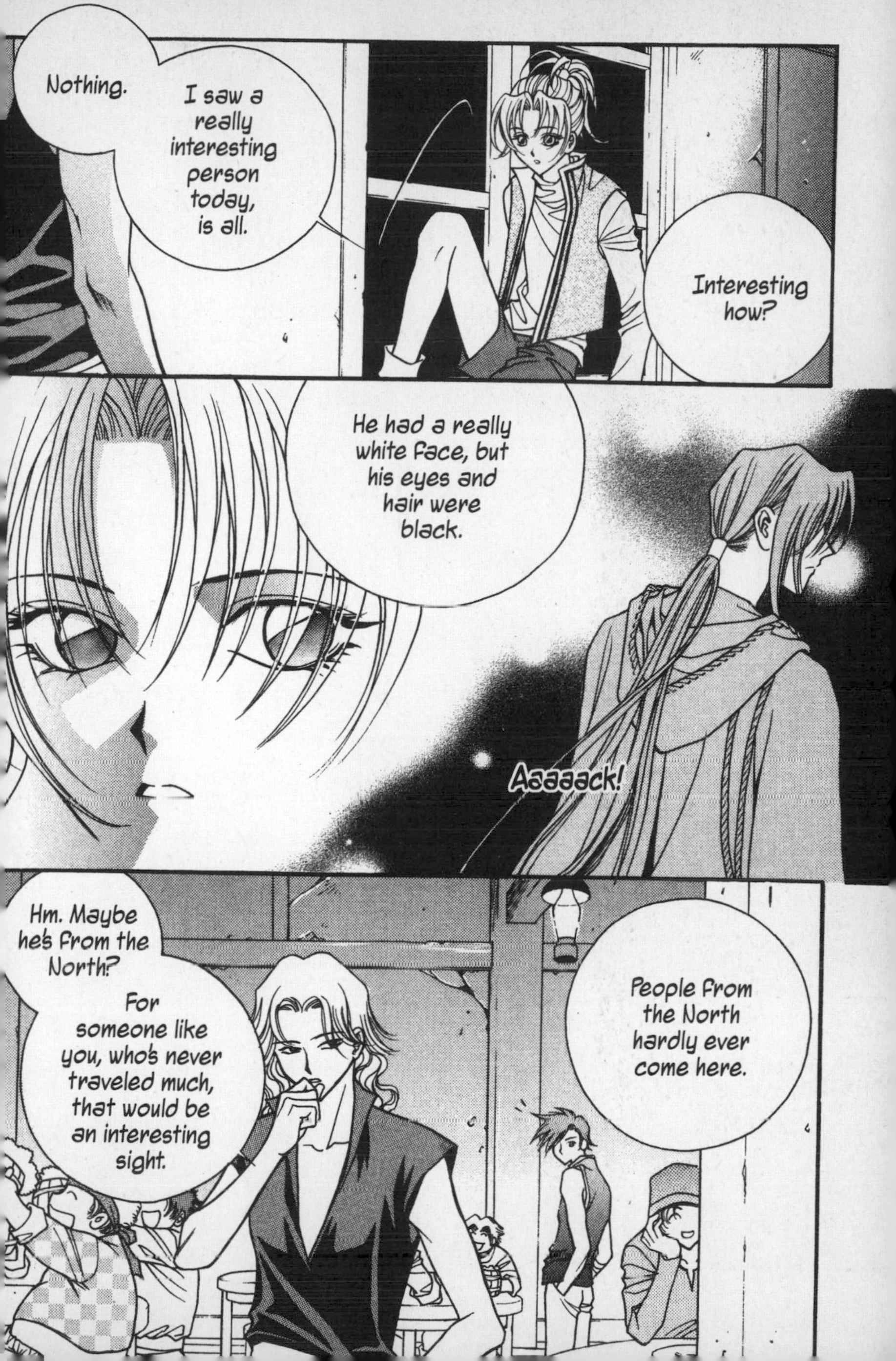
Nothing.
I saw a really interesting person today, is all.
Interesting how?
He had a really white face, but his eyes and hair were black.
Aaaaack!
Hm. Maybe he's from the North?
For someone like you, who's never traveled much, that would be an interesting sight.
People from the North hardly ever come here.

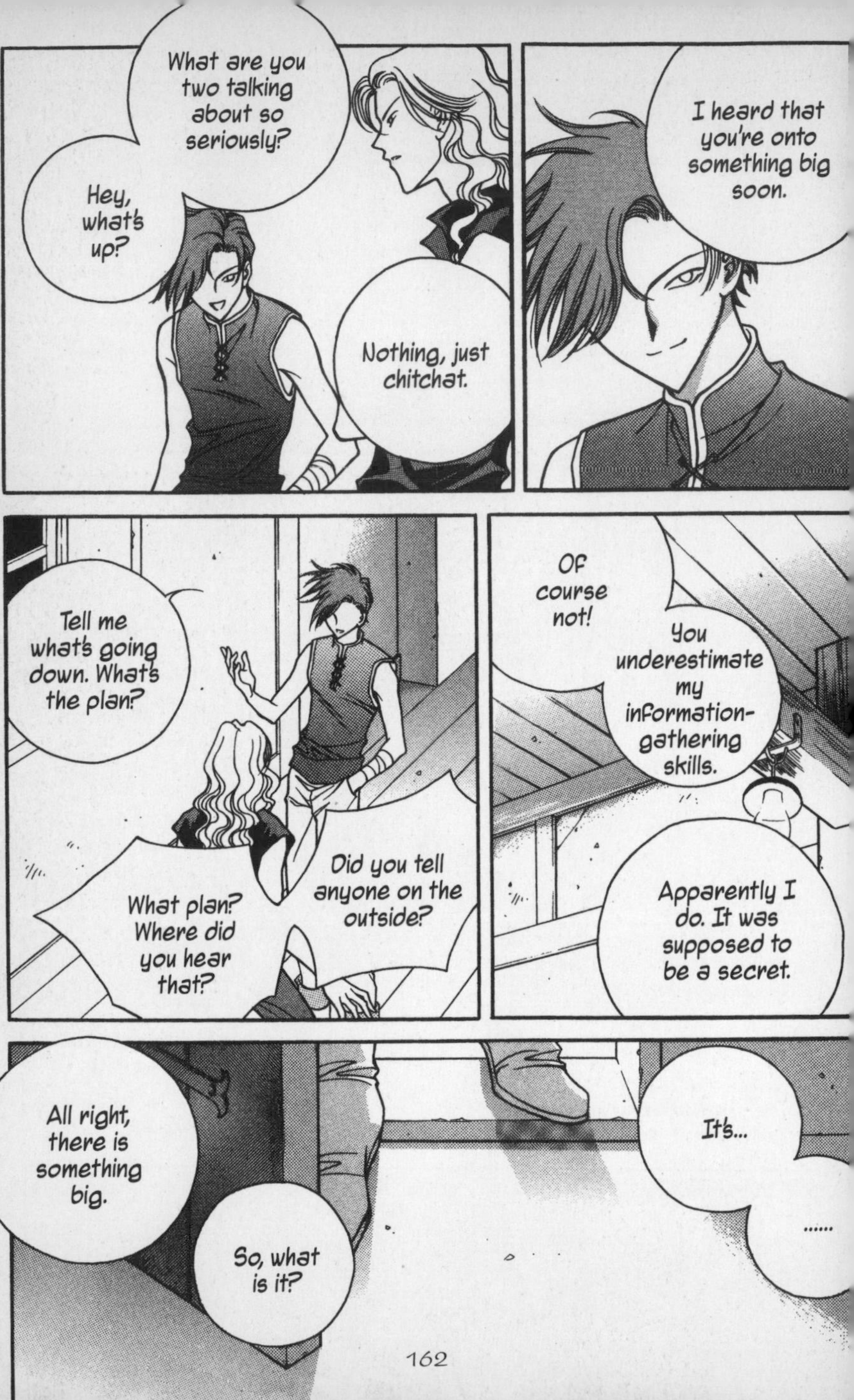
Hey, what's up?
What are you two talking about so seriously?
Nothing, just chitchat.
I heard that you're onto something big soon.
Tell me what's going down. What's the plan?
What plan? Where did you hear that?
Did you tell anyone on the outside?
Of course not!
You underestimate my information-gathering skills.
Apparently I do. It was supposed to be a secret.
All right, there is something big.
So, what is it?
It's...
......

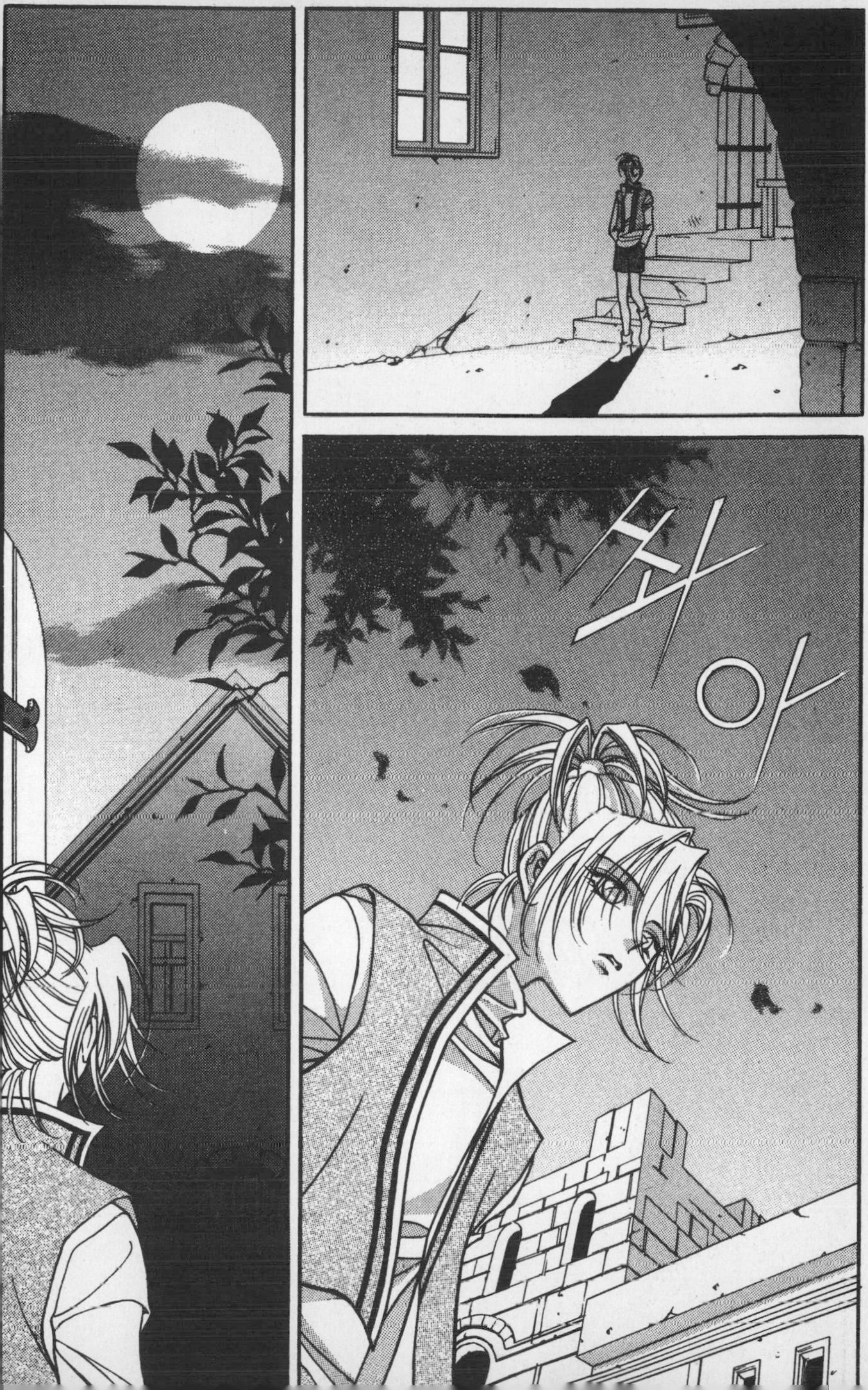
쏴아

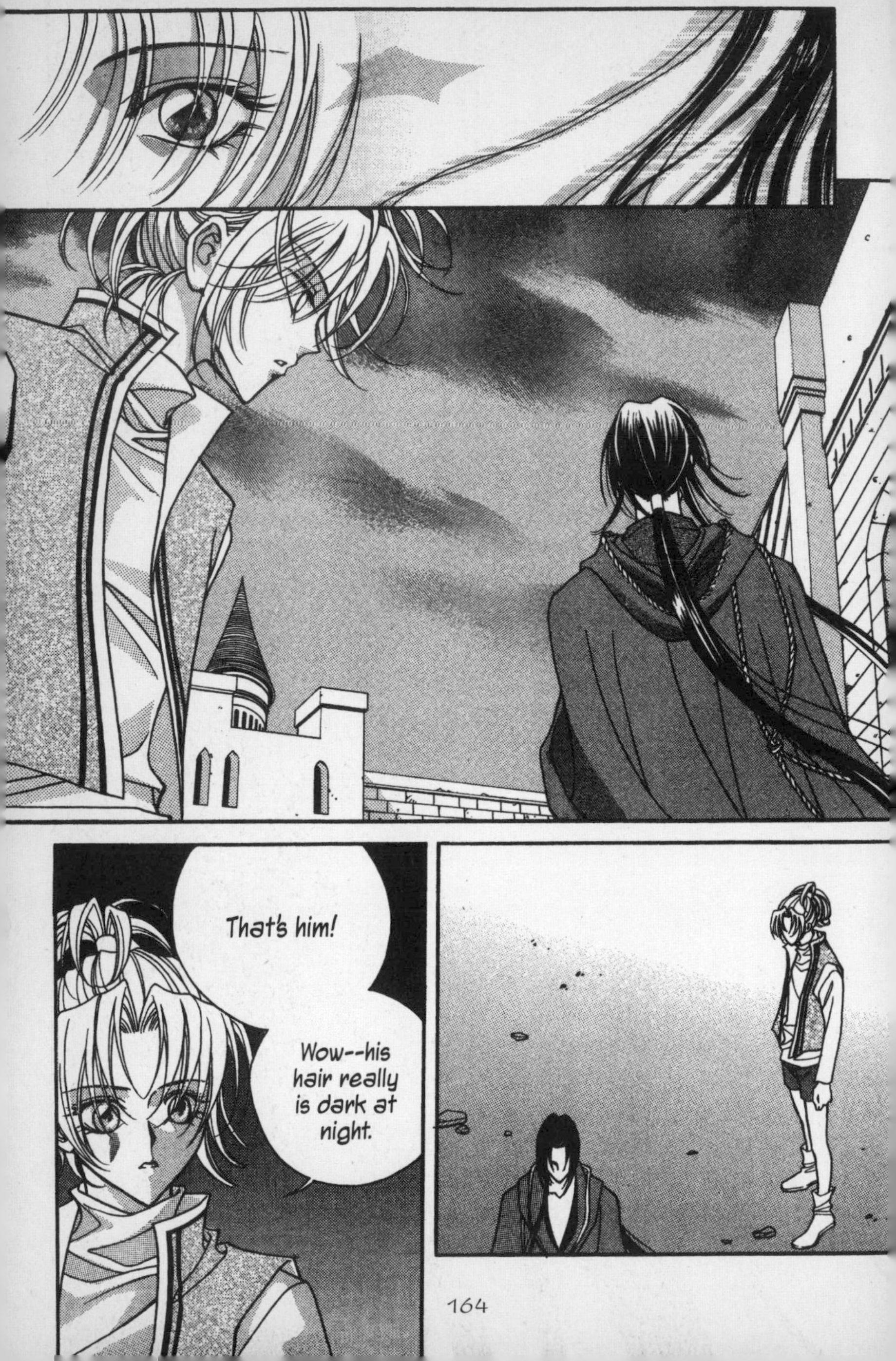
That's him!
Wow--his hair really is dark at night.

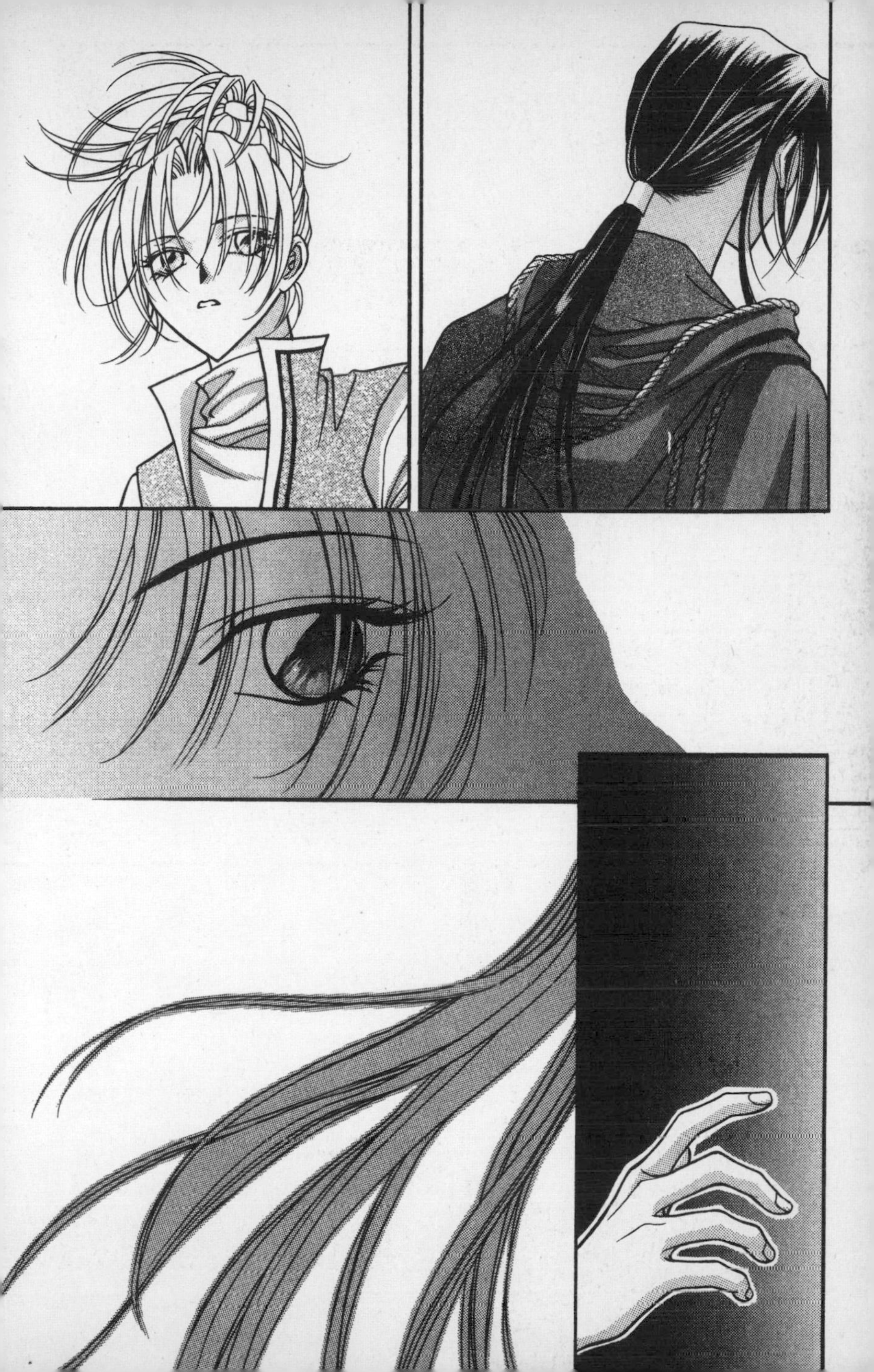

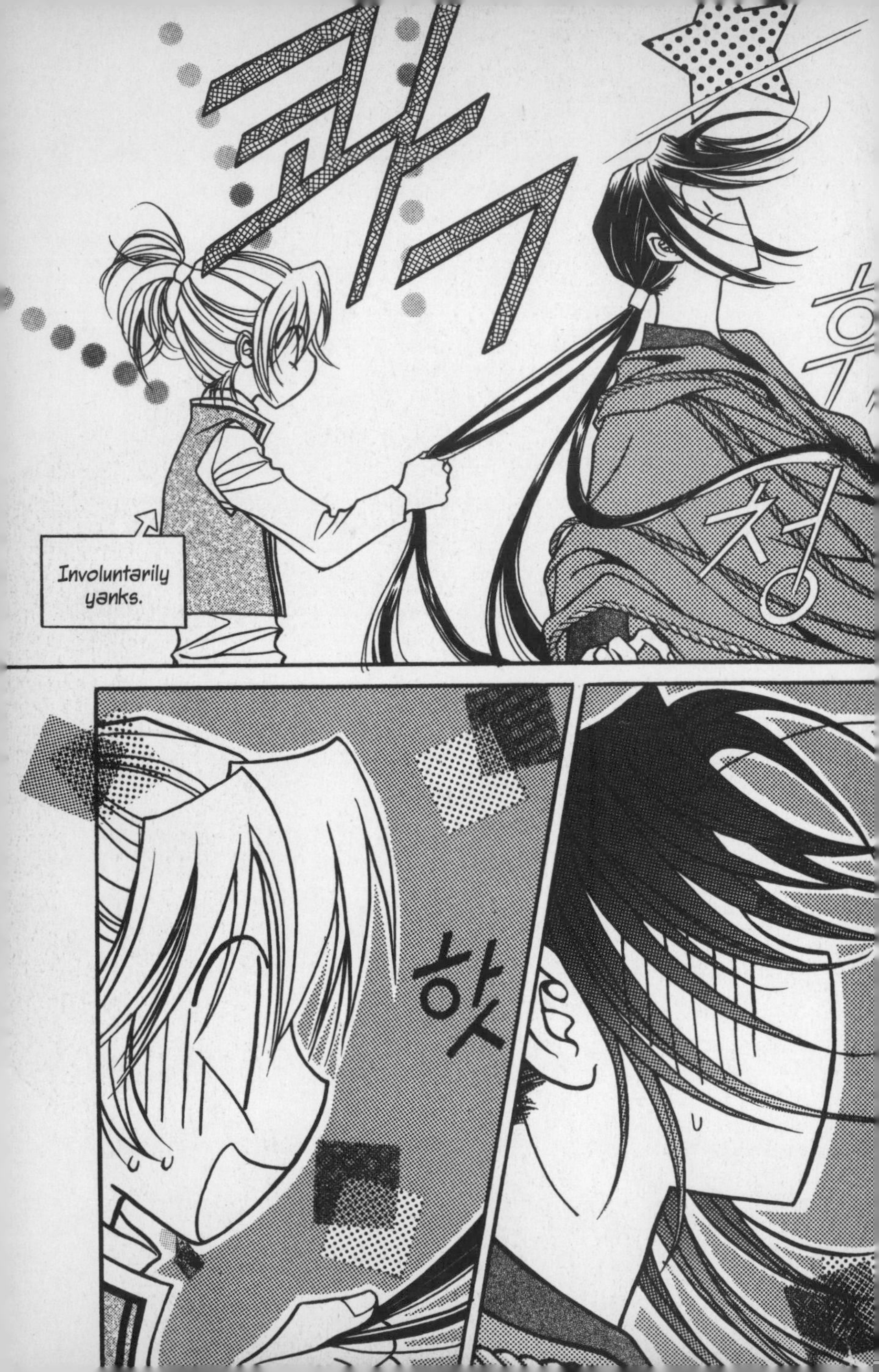
콱
Involuntarily yanks.
핫

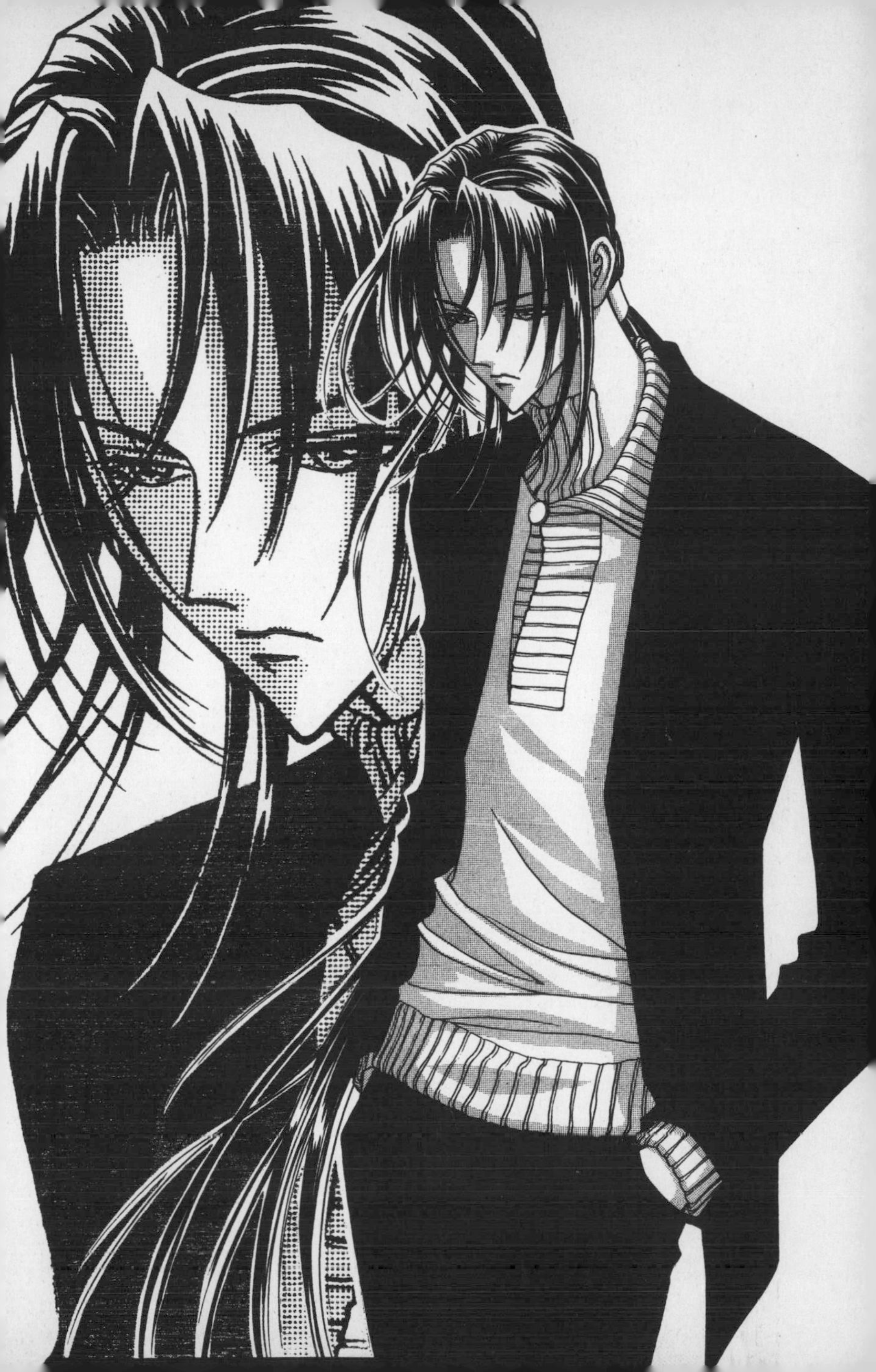

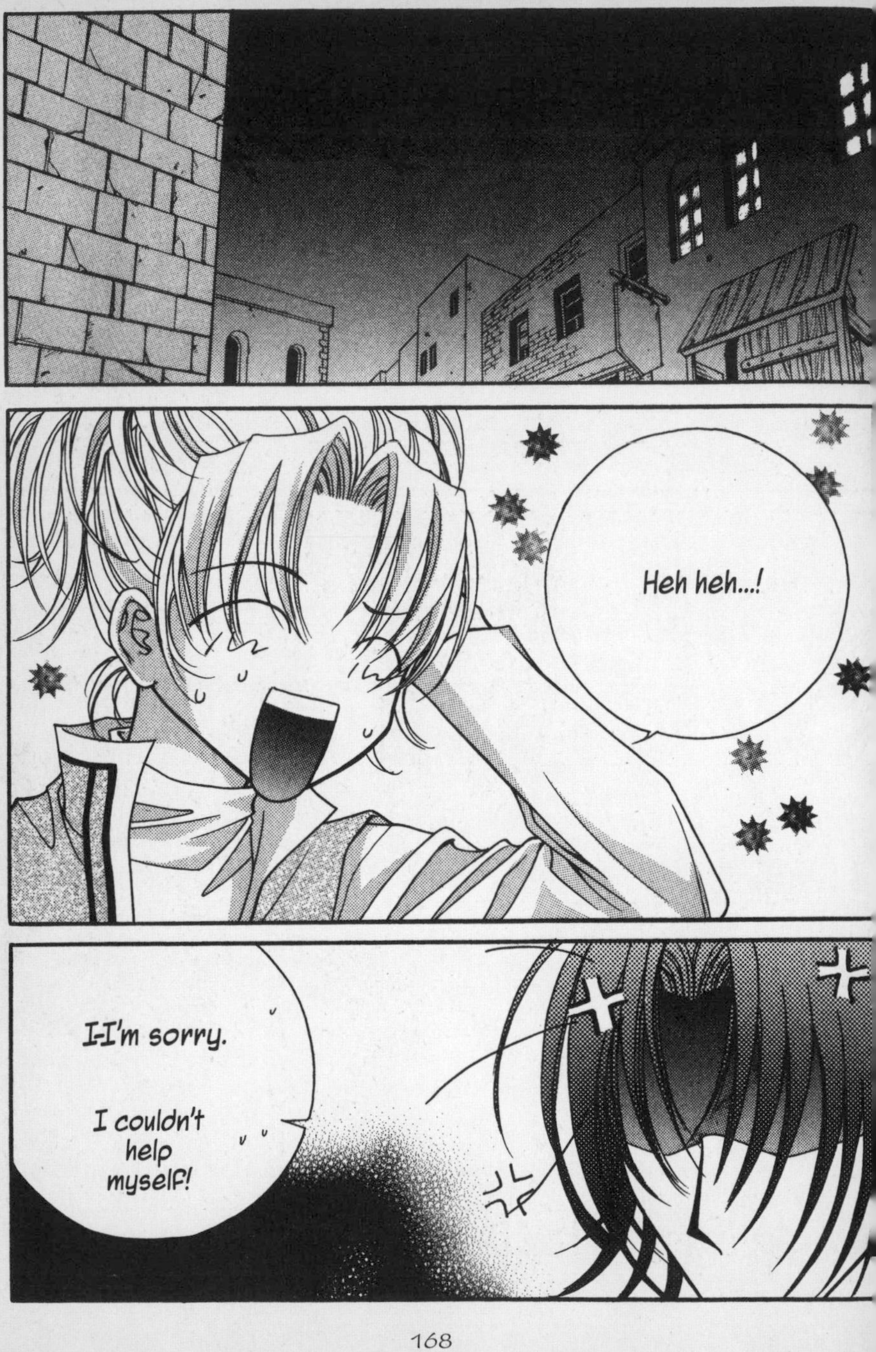
Heh heh...!
I-I'm sorry.
I couldn't help myself!

I really didn't mean anything by it. And I really didn't mean to make you mad!

I grabbed it before I realized what I was doing. Sorry!

Uh...mister we met earlier today, didn't we?

Let's change the topic!

......

I remember because of your black hair. I've never seen anything like it, and I found it really interesting.

방

그스

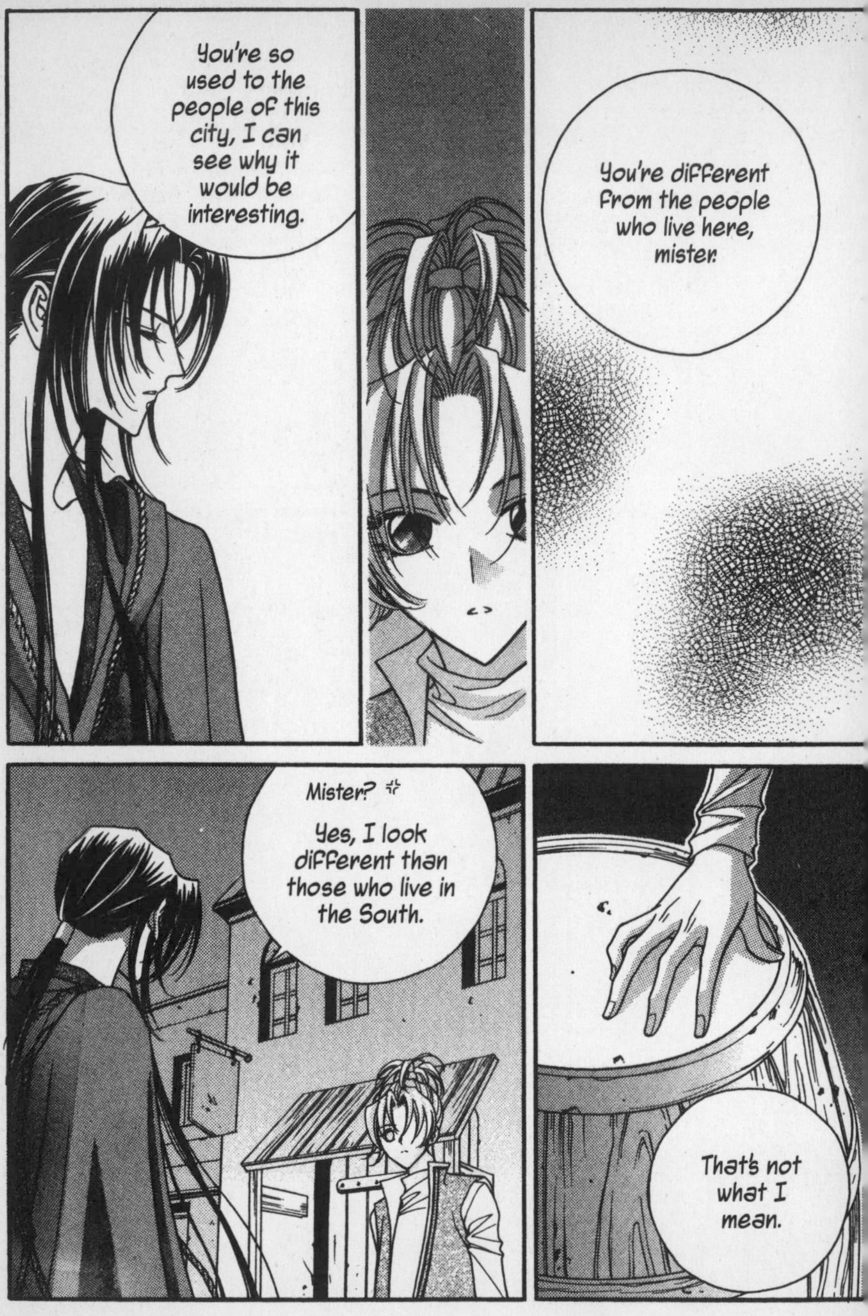
You're different from the people who live here, mister.
You're so used to the people of this city, I can see why it would be interesting.
That's not what I mean.
Mister?
Yes, I look different than those who live in the South.

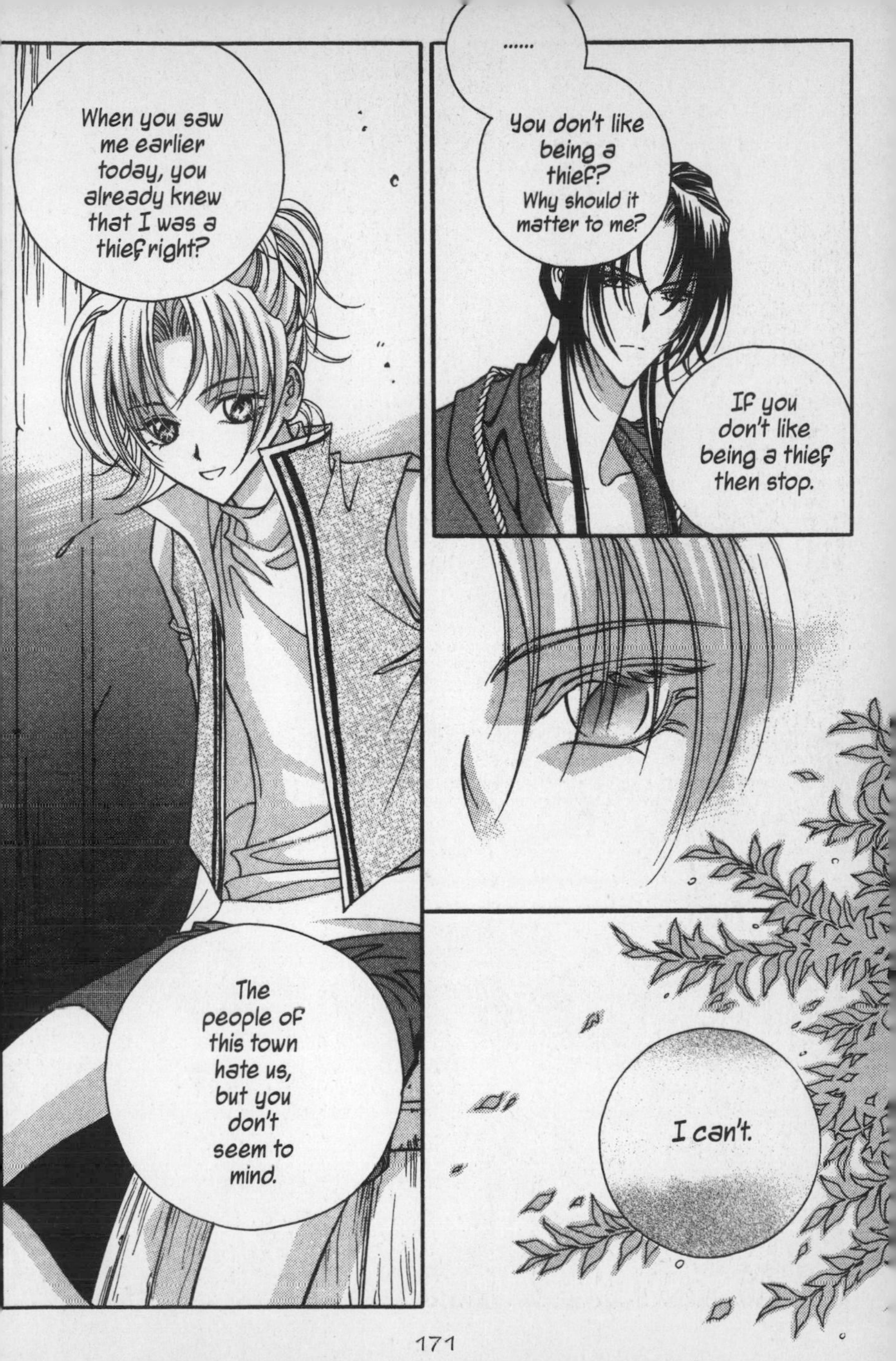
When you saw me earlier today, you already knew that I was a thief right?
The people of this town hate us, but you don't seem to mind.
......
You don't like being a thief? Why should it matter to me?
If you don't like being a thief then stop.
I can't.

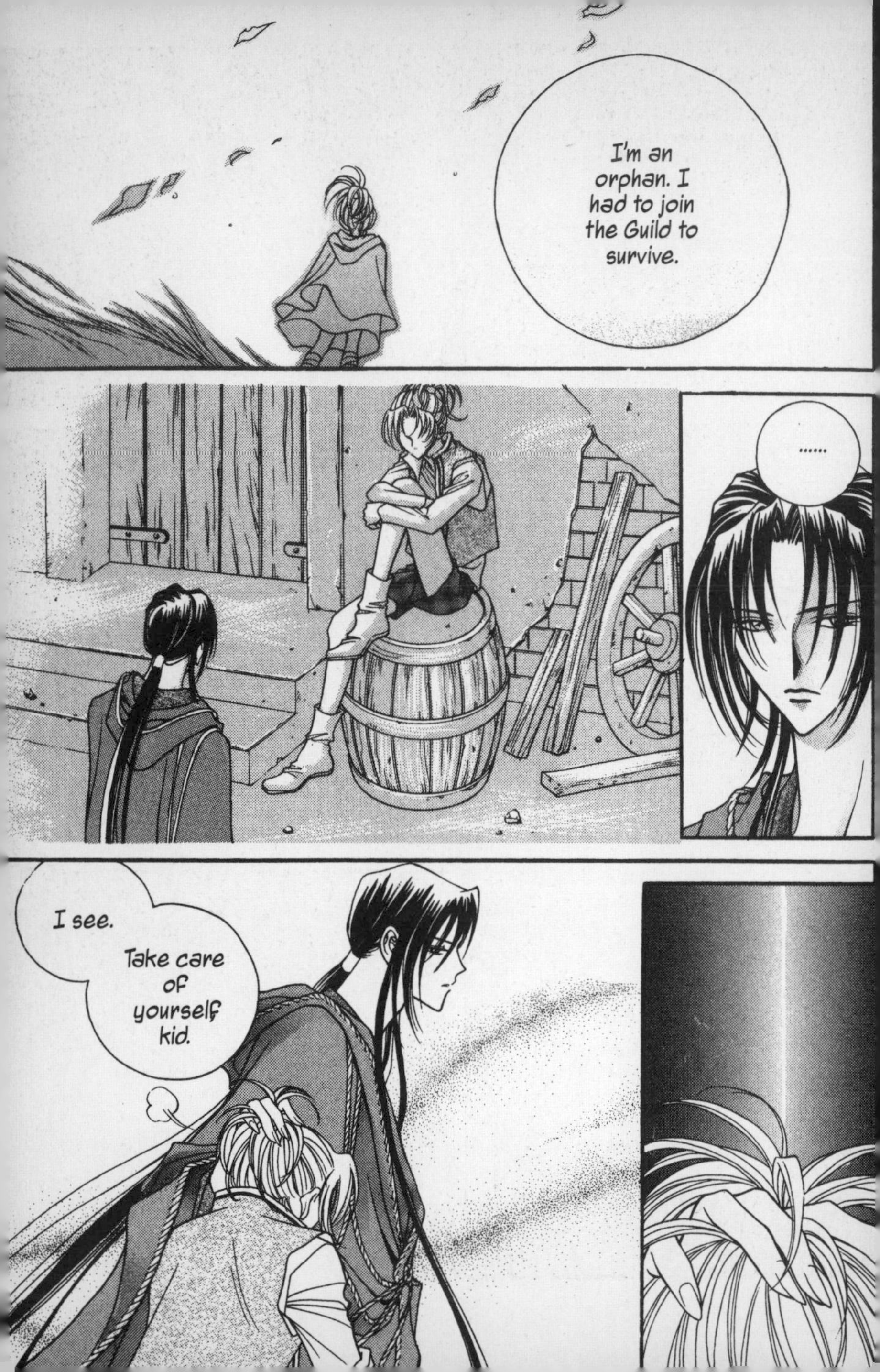
I'm an orphan. I had to join the Guild to survive.
......
I see.
Take care of yourself kid.

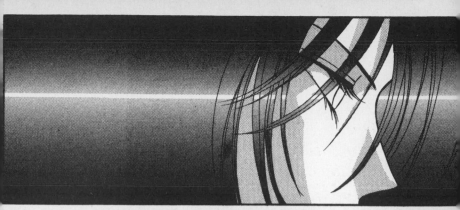

Wait, you...

Hey--what are you doing?

You're gonna be late for the meeting!

!

I'd better go.

Hee!

It was nice meeting you.

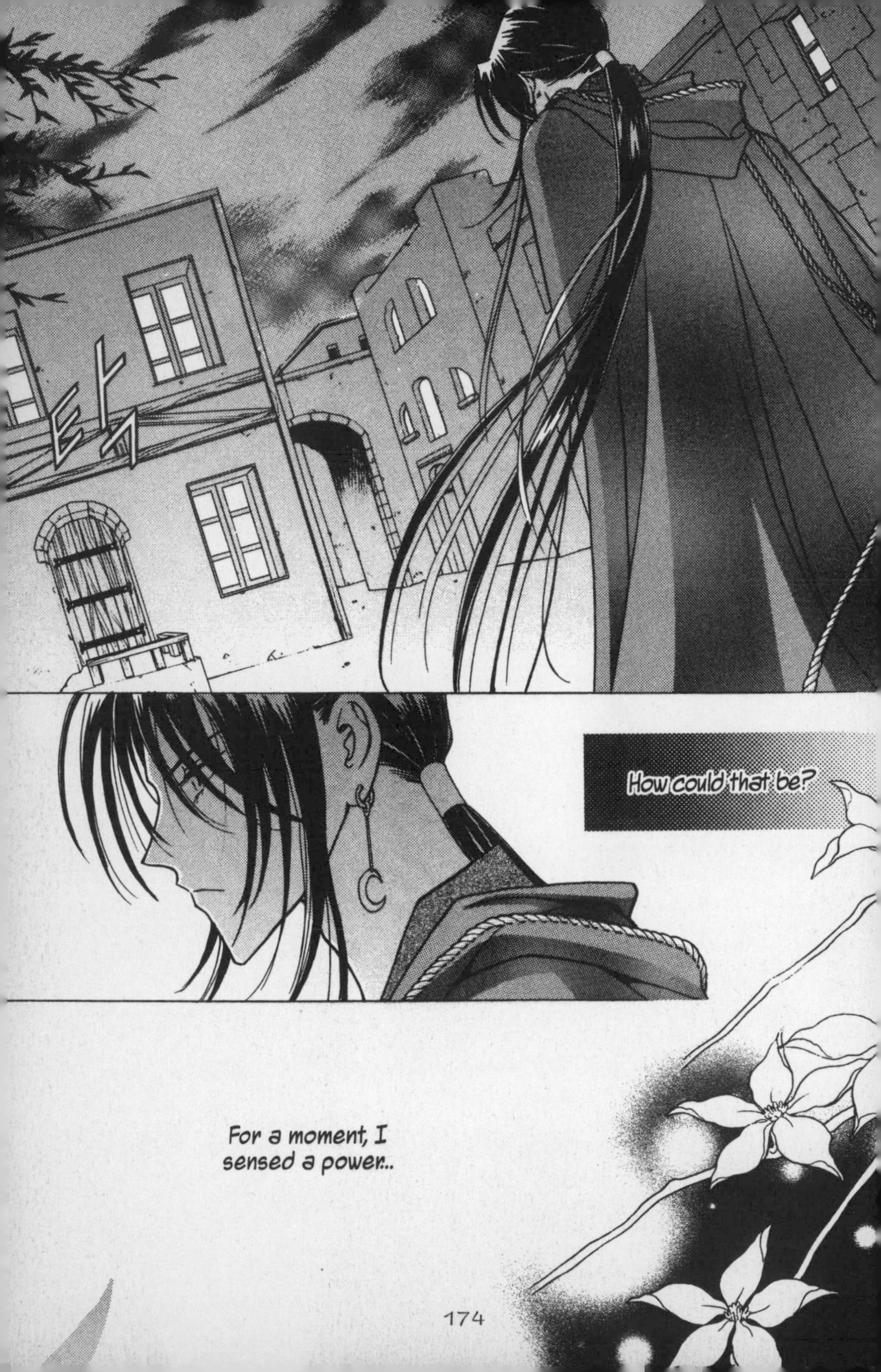
How could that be?
For a moment, I sensed a power...

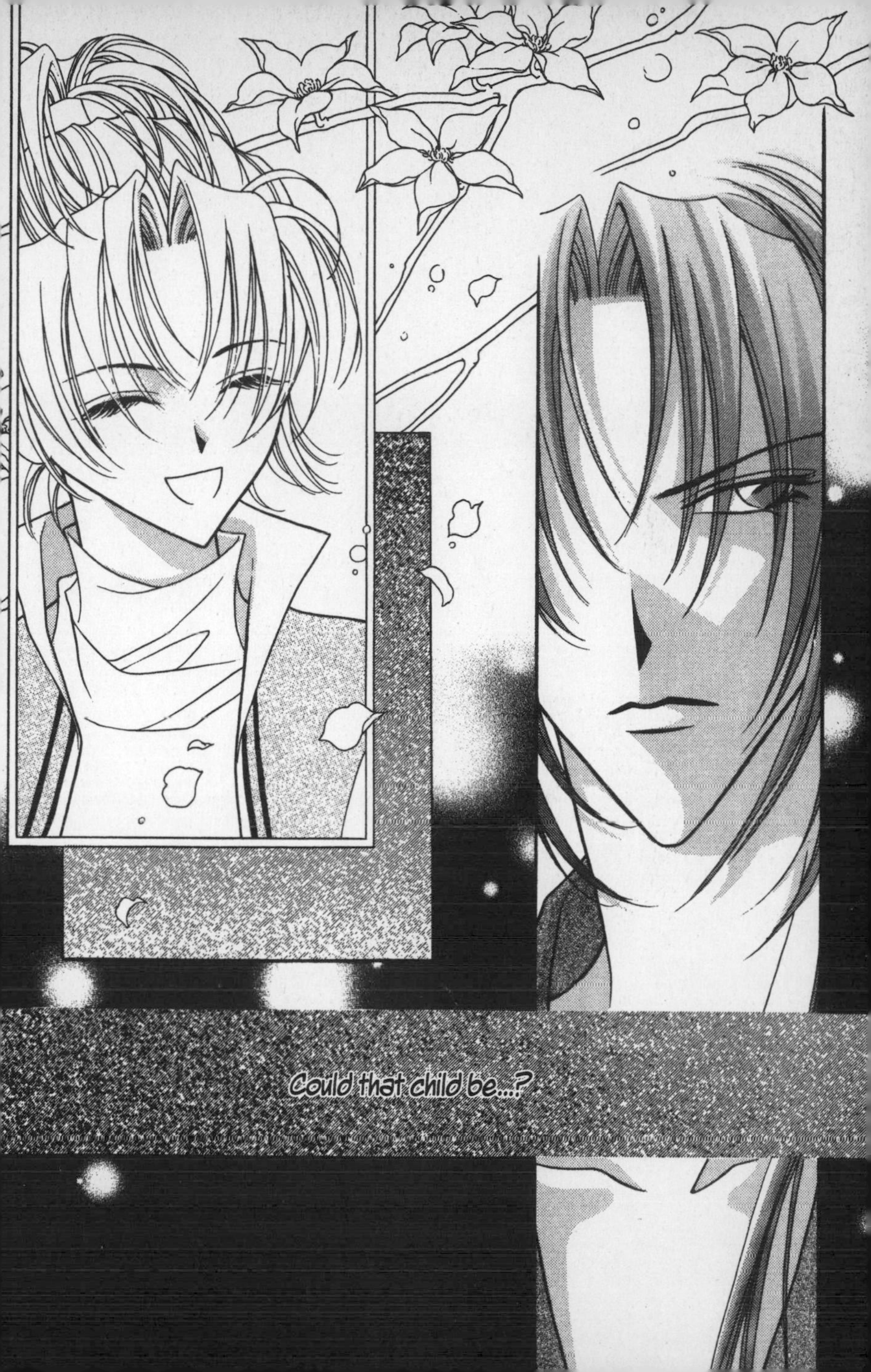
Could that child be...?

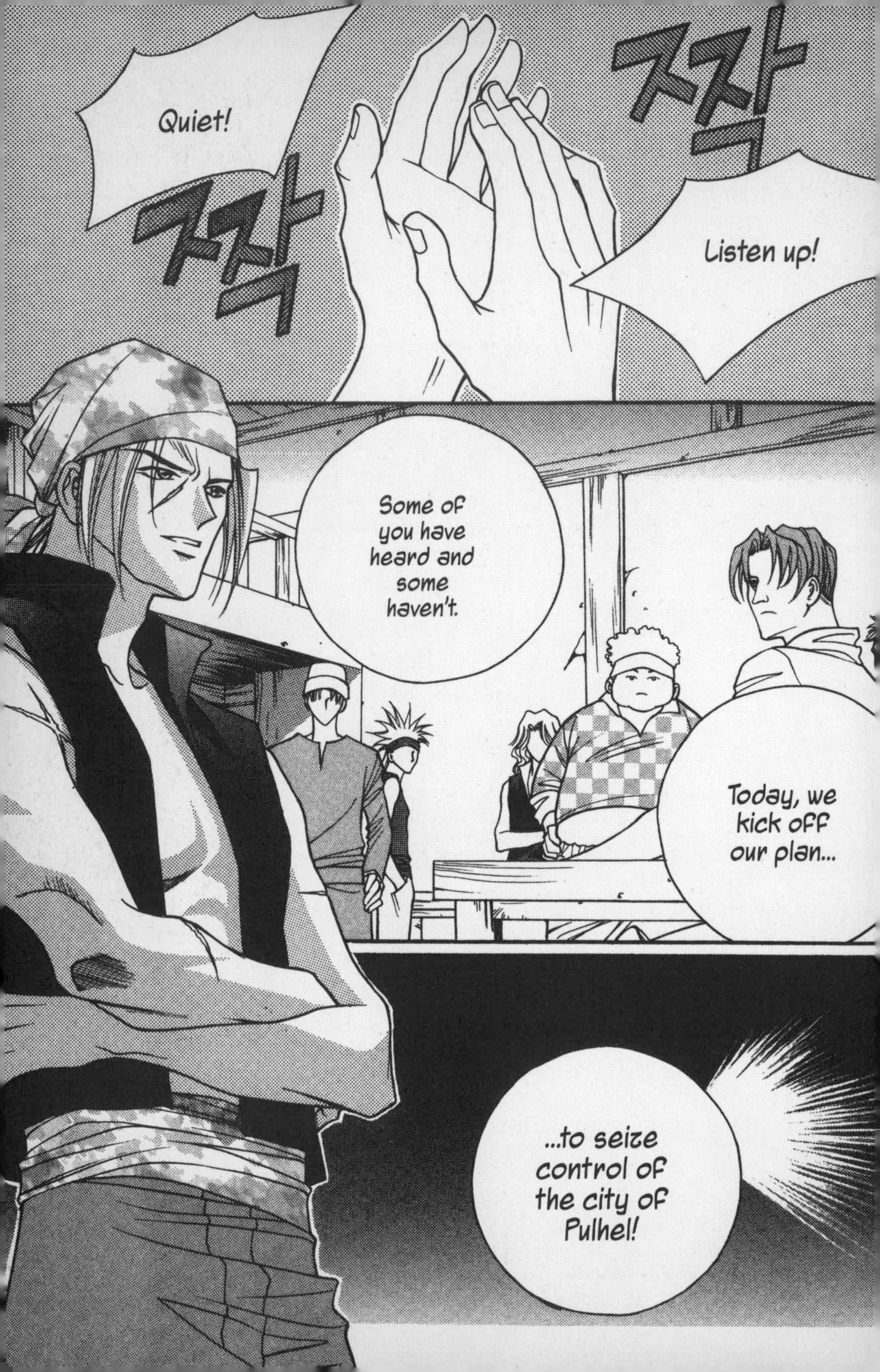
Quiet!
짝
짝
Listen up!
Some of you have heard and some haven't.
Today, we kick off our plan...
...to seize control of the city of Pulhel!

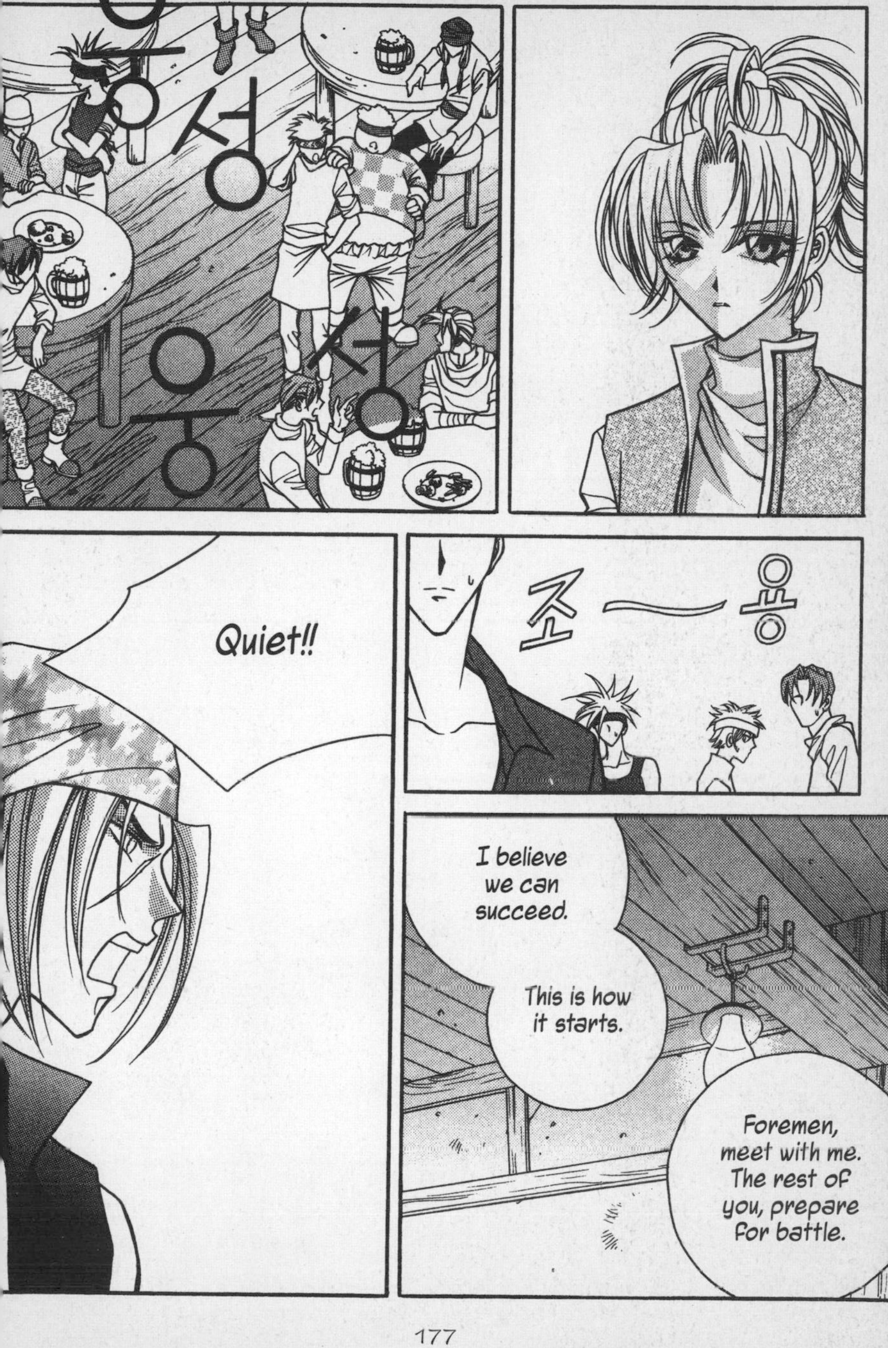
웅성 웅성
Quiet!!
조―용
I believe we can succeed.
This is how it starts.
Foremen, meet with me. The rest of you, prepare for battle.

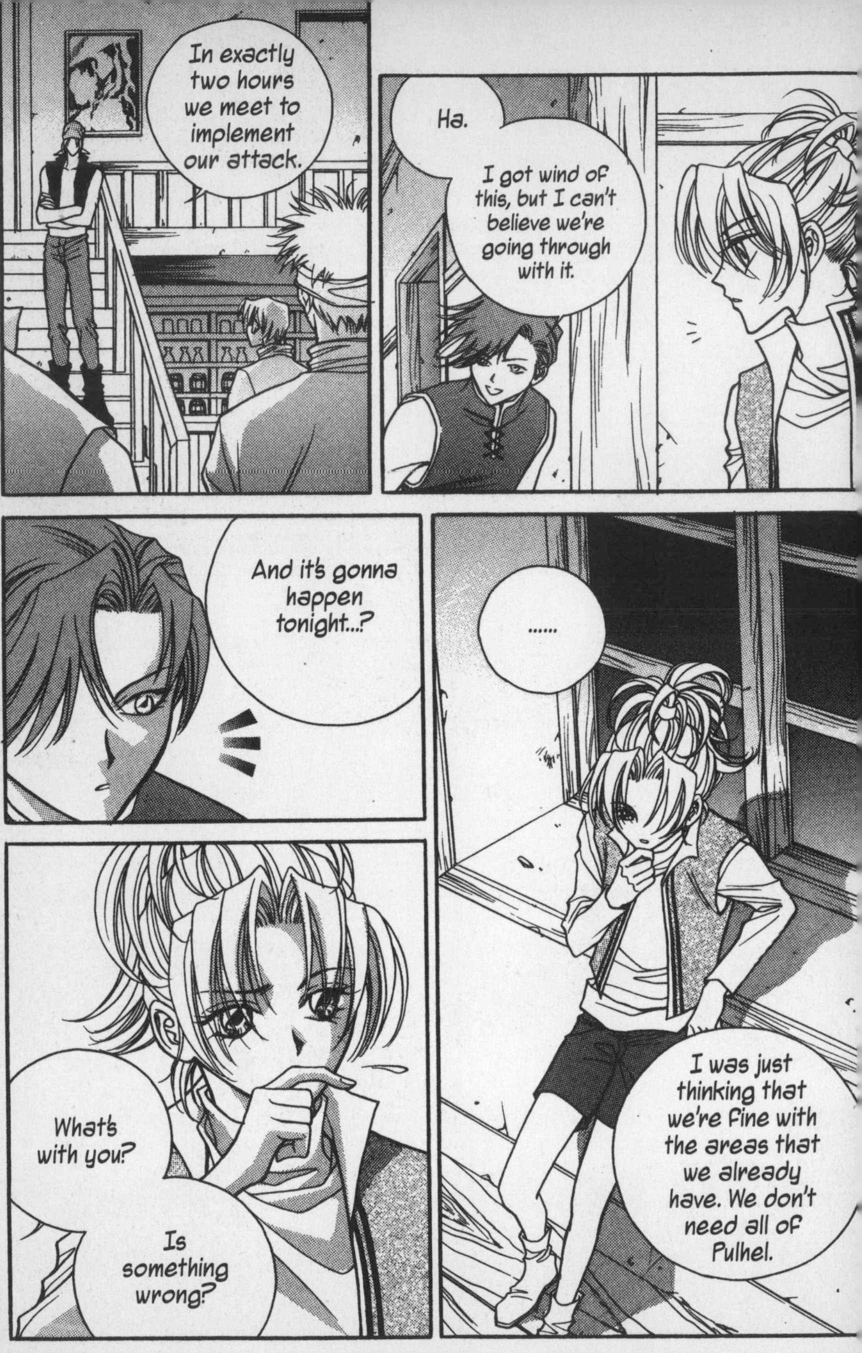
In exactly two hours we meet to implement our attack.
Ha.
I got wind of this, but I can't believe we're going through with it.
And it's gonna happen tonight...?
......
What's with you?
Is something wrong?
I was just thinking that we're fine with the areas that we already have. We don't need all of Pulhel.

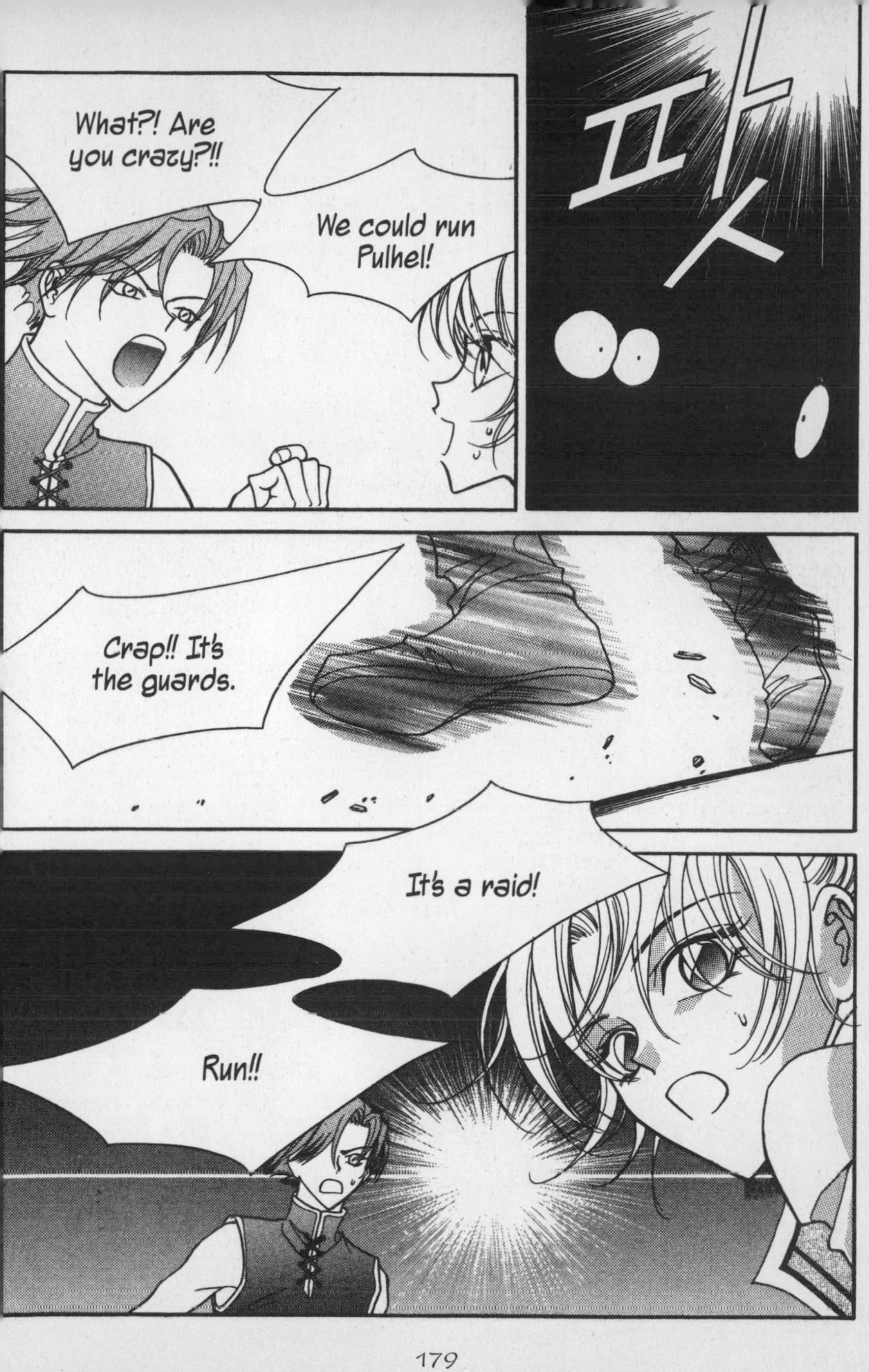
What?! Are you crazy?!!
We could run Pulhel!
Crap!! It's the guards.
It's a raid!
Run!!

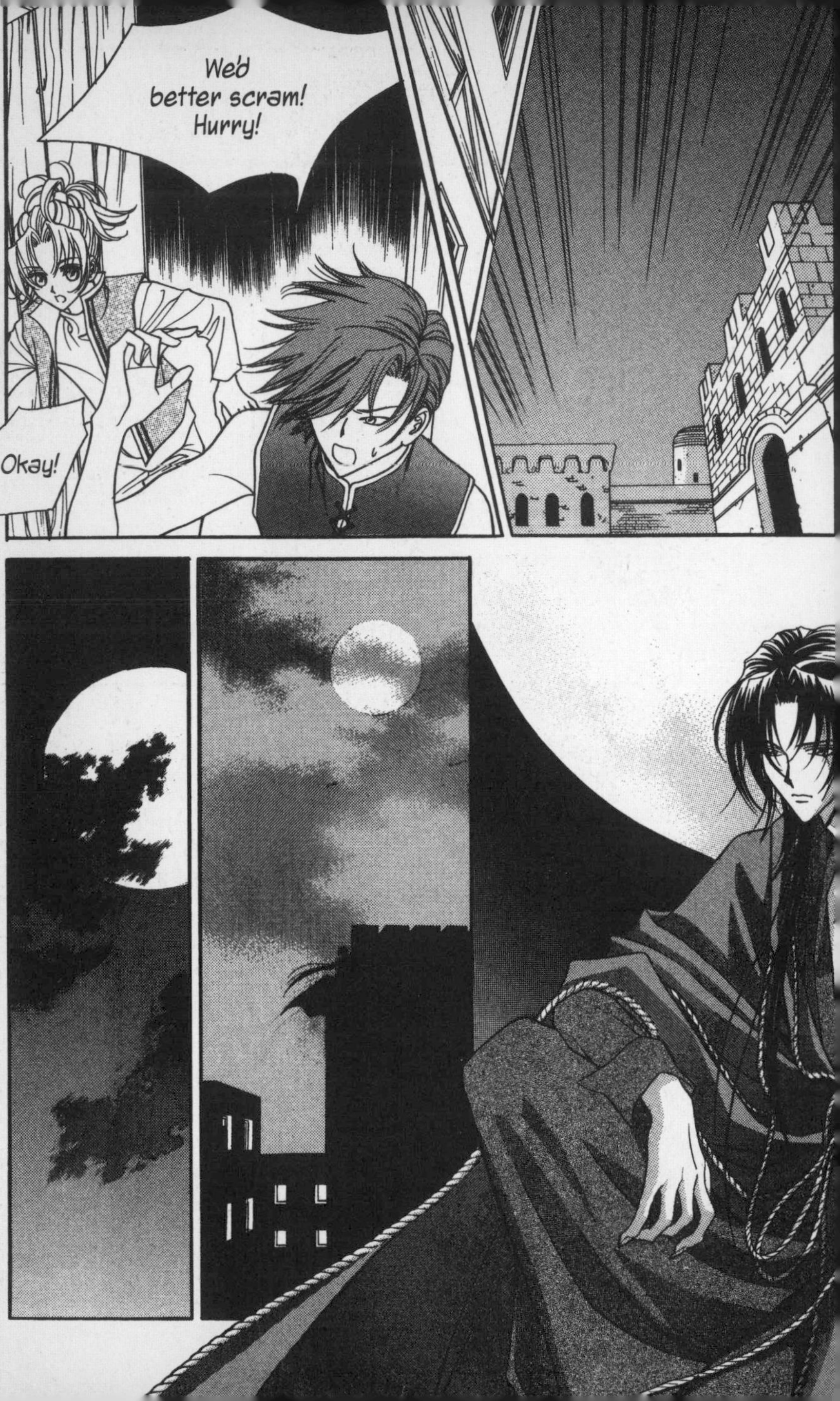
We'd better scram! Hurry!
Okay!

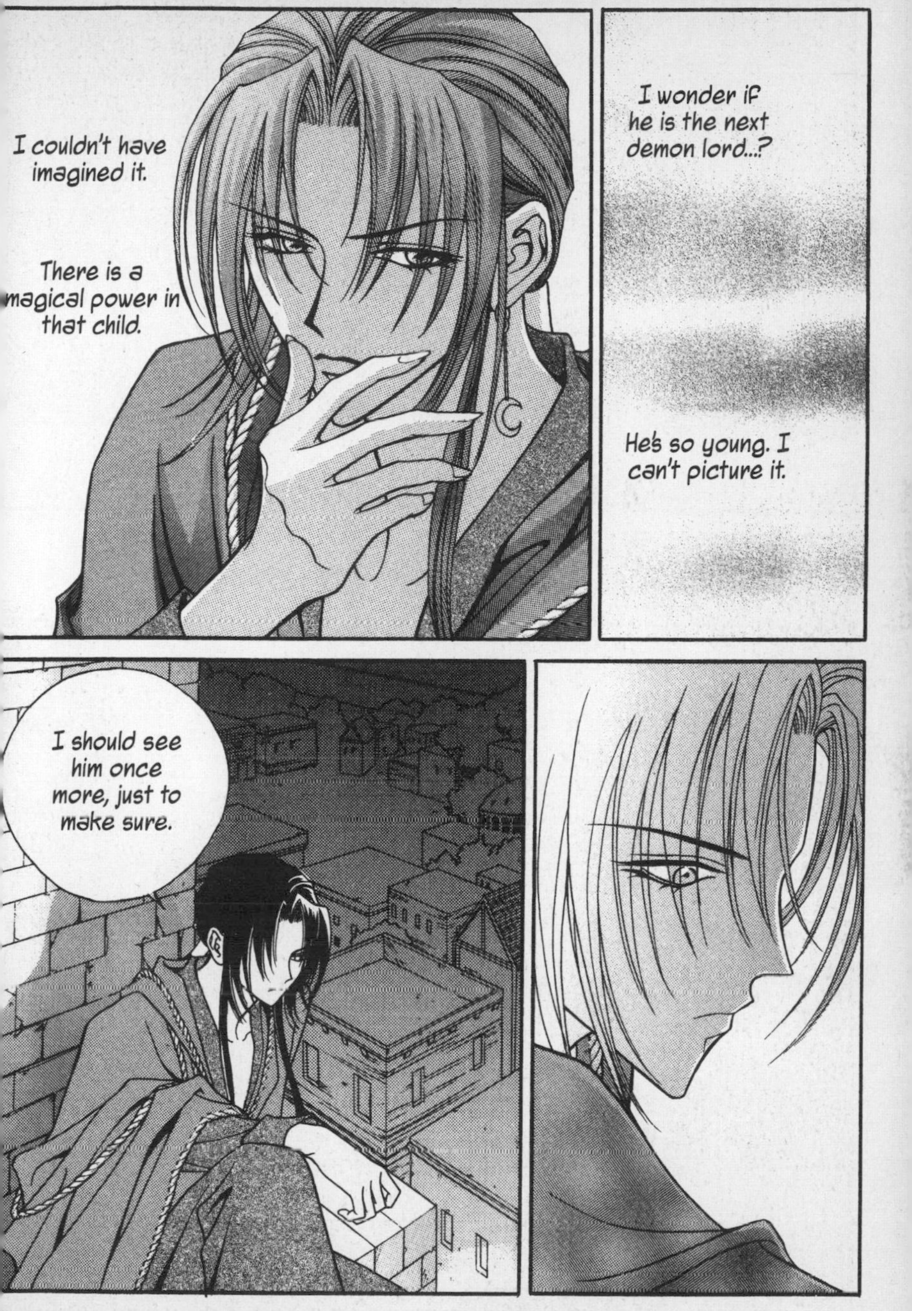
I couldn't have imagined it.
There is a magical power in that child.
I wonder if he is the next demon lord...?
He's so young. I can't picture it.
I should see him once more, just to make sure.

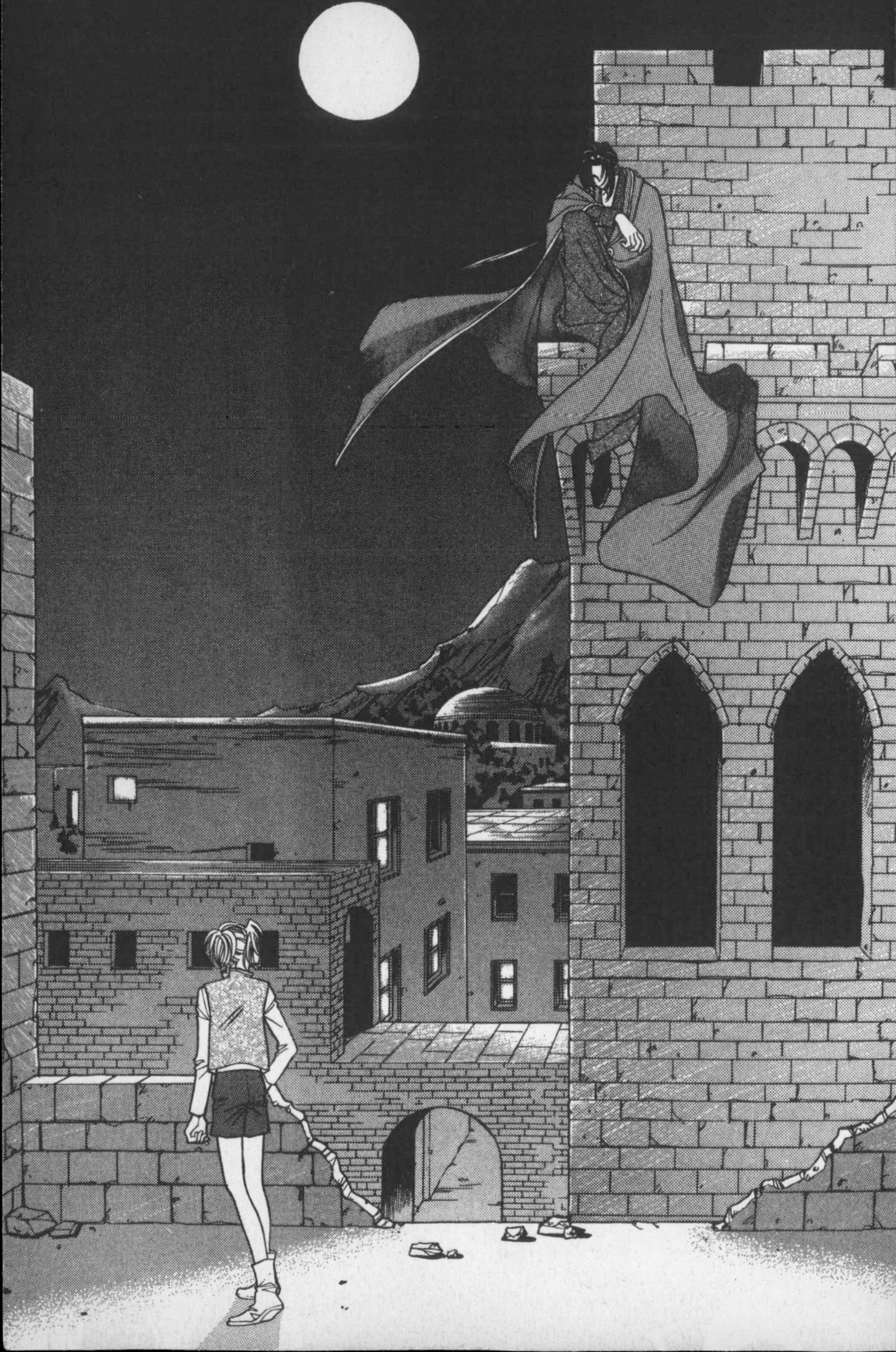

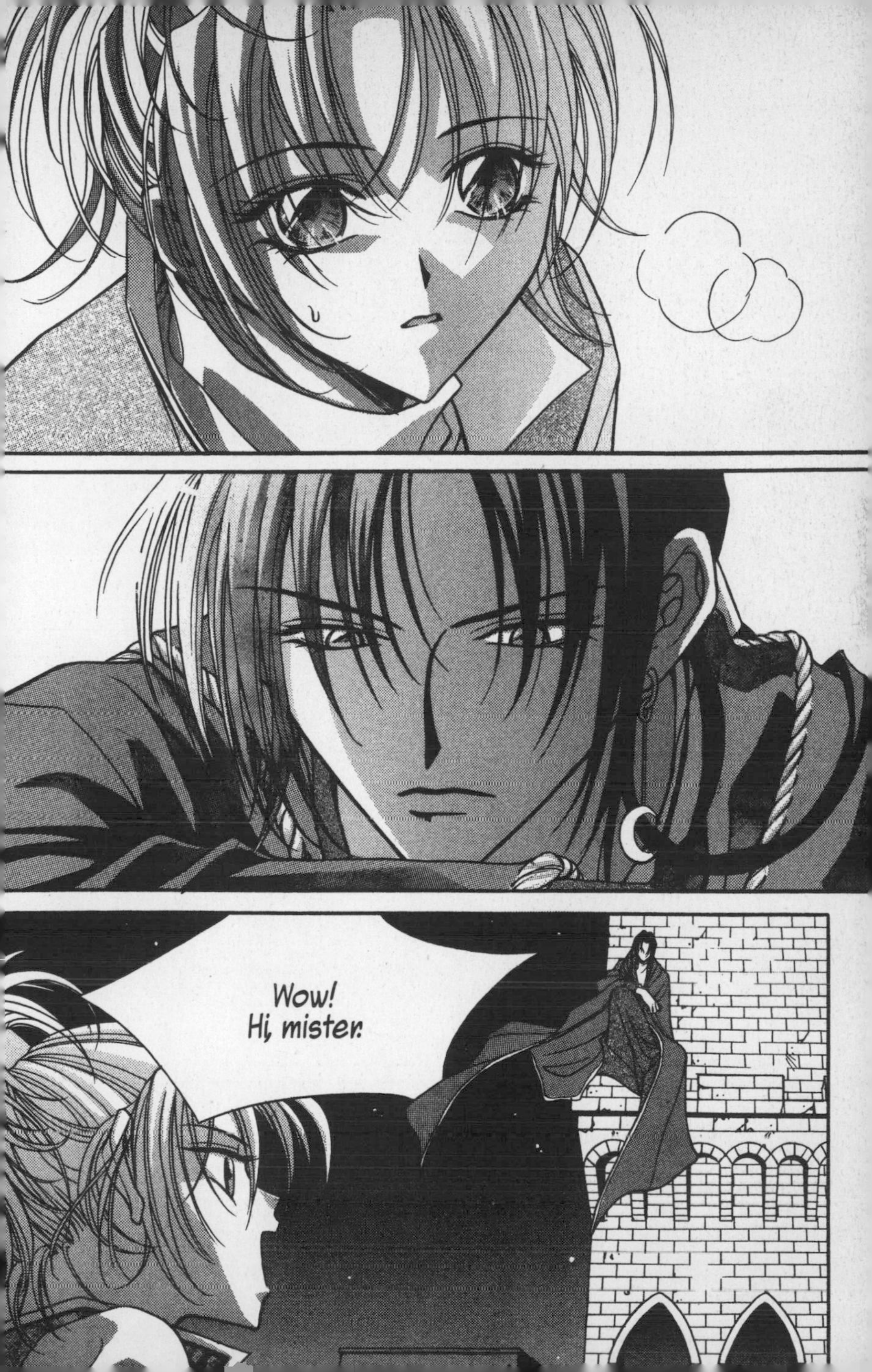
Wow!
Hi, mister.

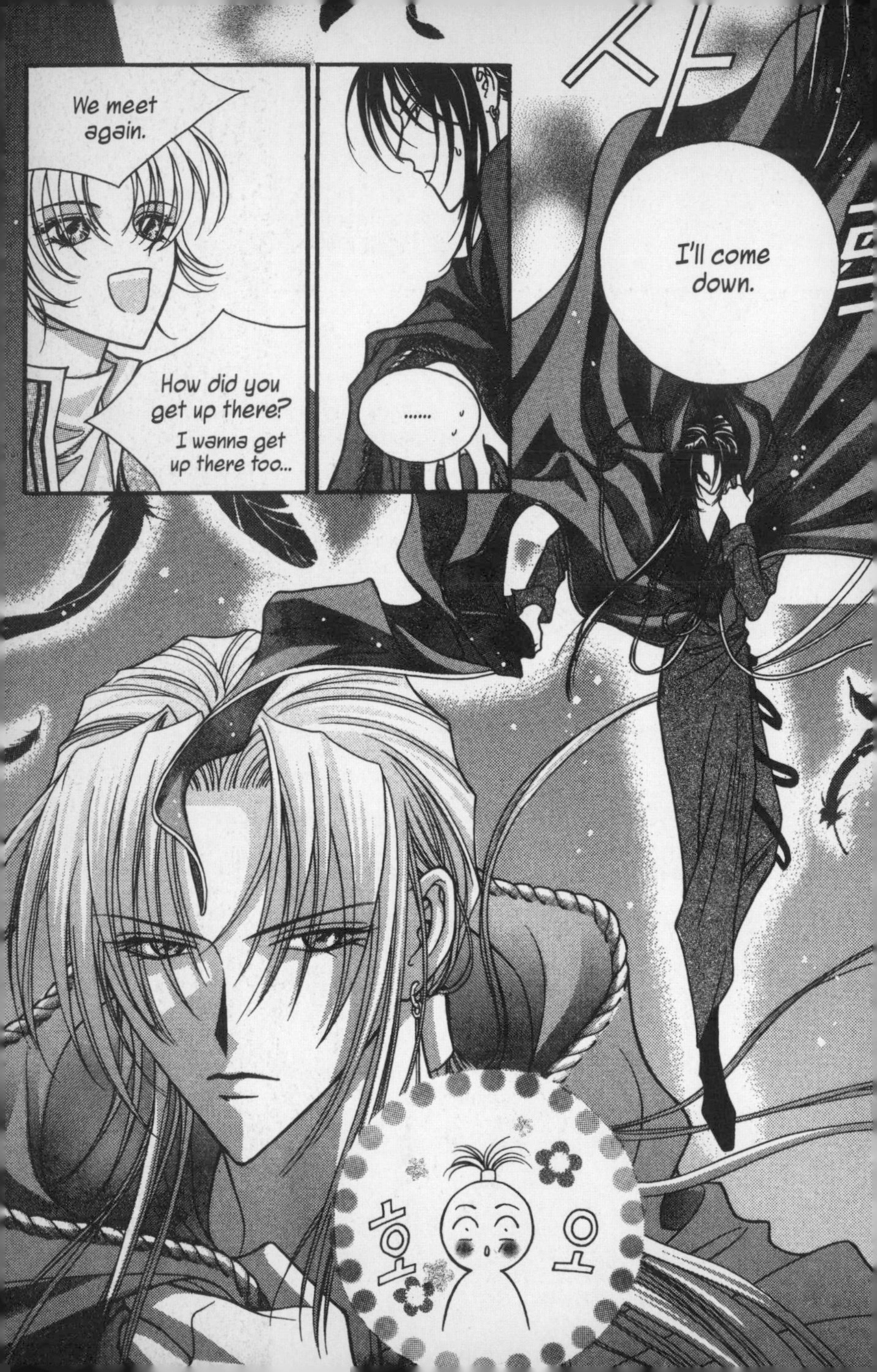

We meet again.
How did you get up there?
I wanna get up there too...
......
I'll come down.

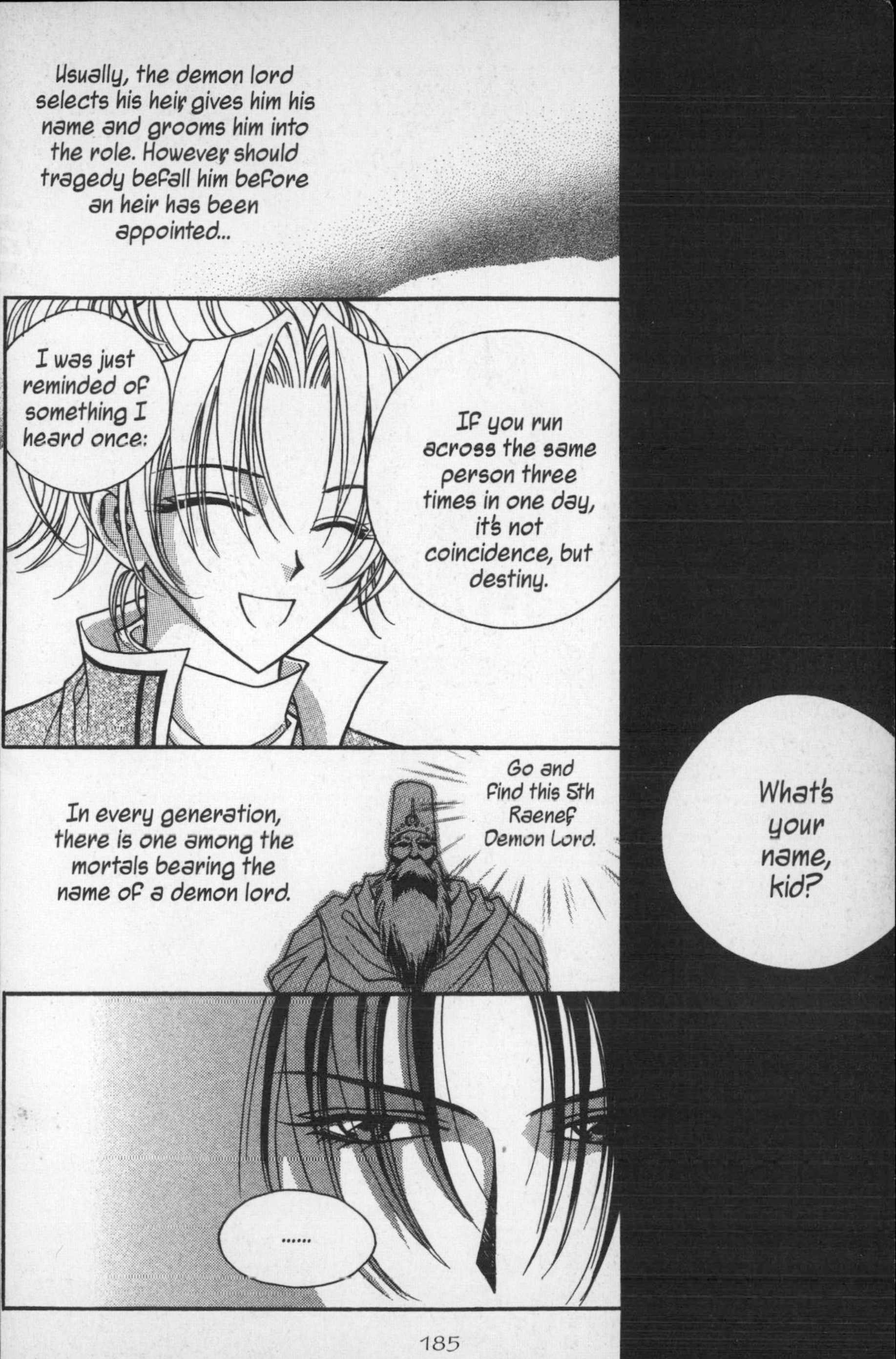
Usually, the demon lord selects his heir, gives him his name and grooms him into the role. However, should tragedy befall him before an heir has been appointed...
I was just reminded of something I heard once:
If you run across the same person three times in one day, it's not coincidence, but destiny.
In every generation, there is one among the mortals bearing the name of a demon lord.
Go and find this 5th Raenef Demon Lord.
What's your name, kid?
......

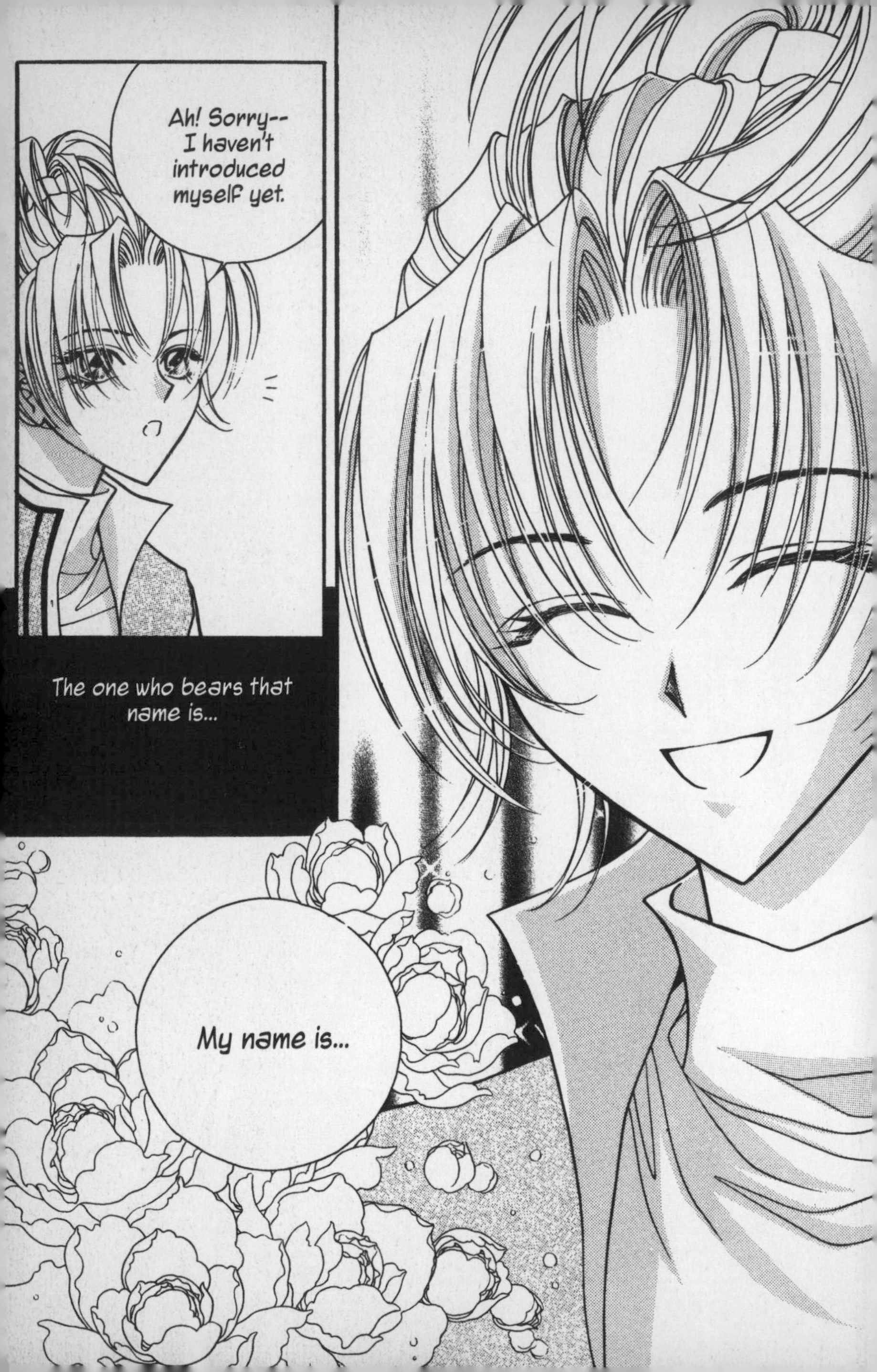
Ah! Sorry-- I haven't introduced myself yet.
The one who bears that name is...
My name is...

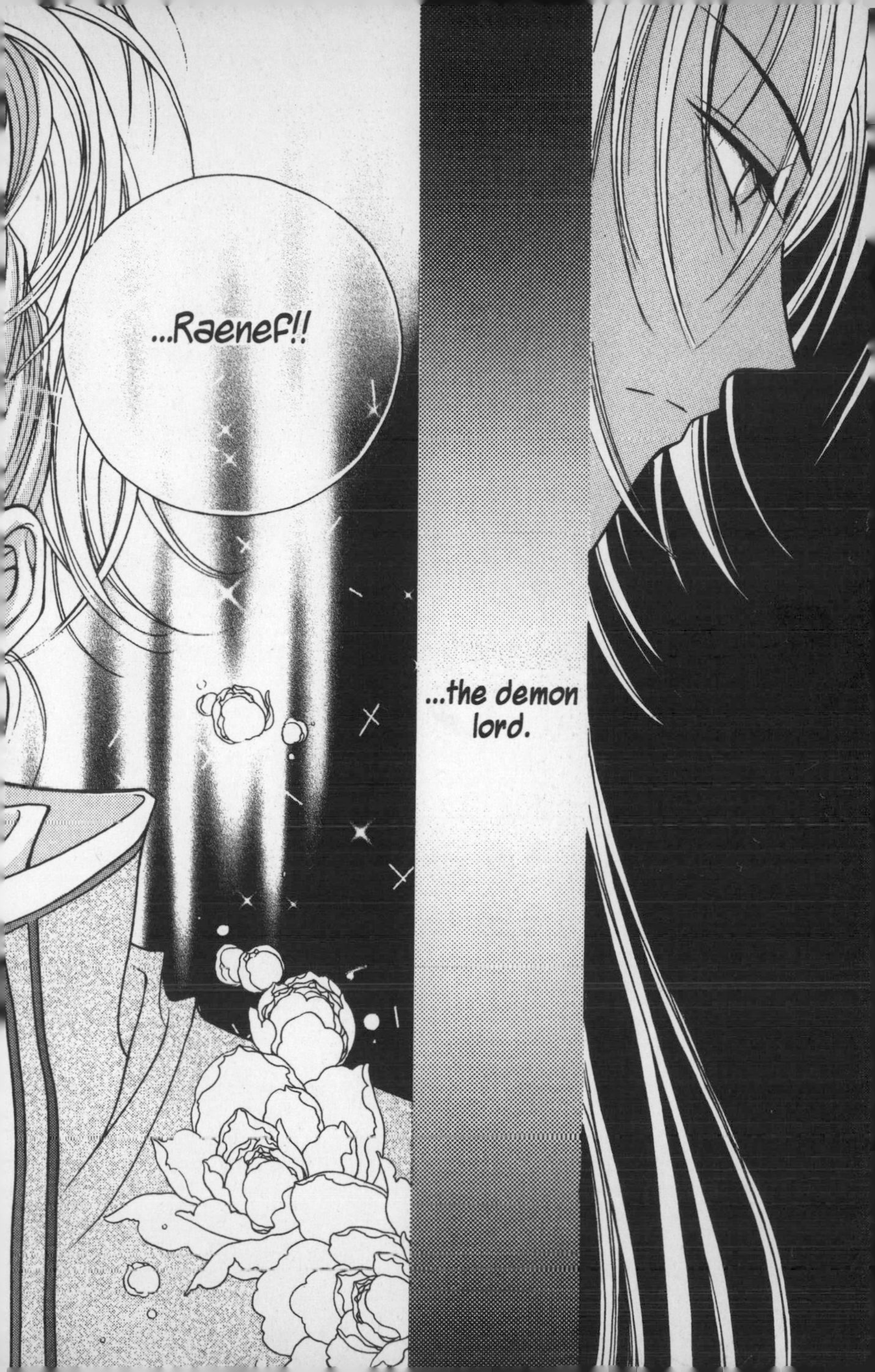
...the demon lord.
...Raenef!!

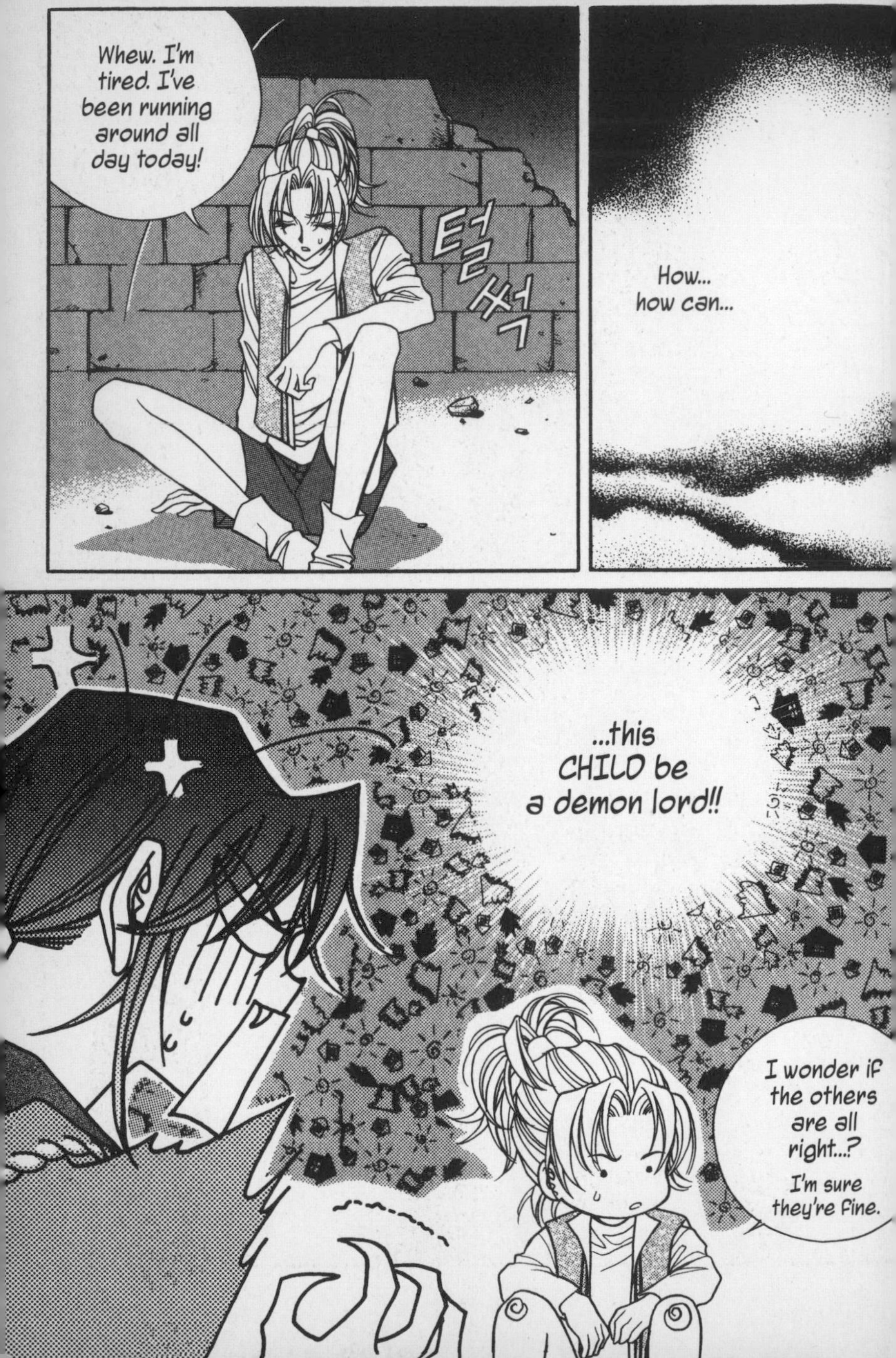
Whew. I'm tired. I've been running around all day today!
털썩
How... how can...
...this CHILD be a demon lord!!
I wonder if the others are all right...?
I'm sure they're fine.

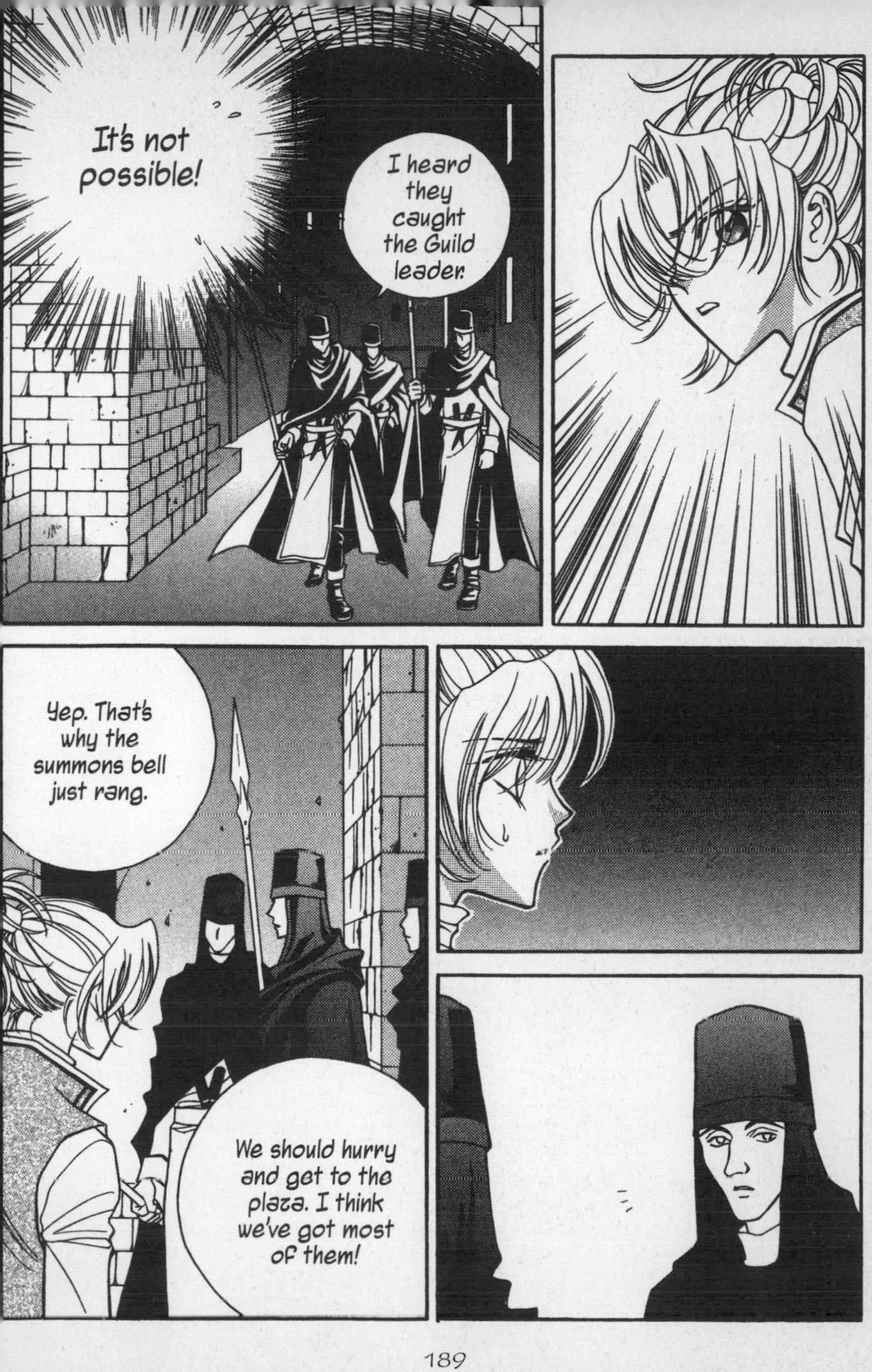
It's not possible!
I heard they caught the Guild leader.
Yep. That's why the summons bell just rang.
We should hurry and get to the plaza. I think we've got most of them!

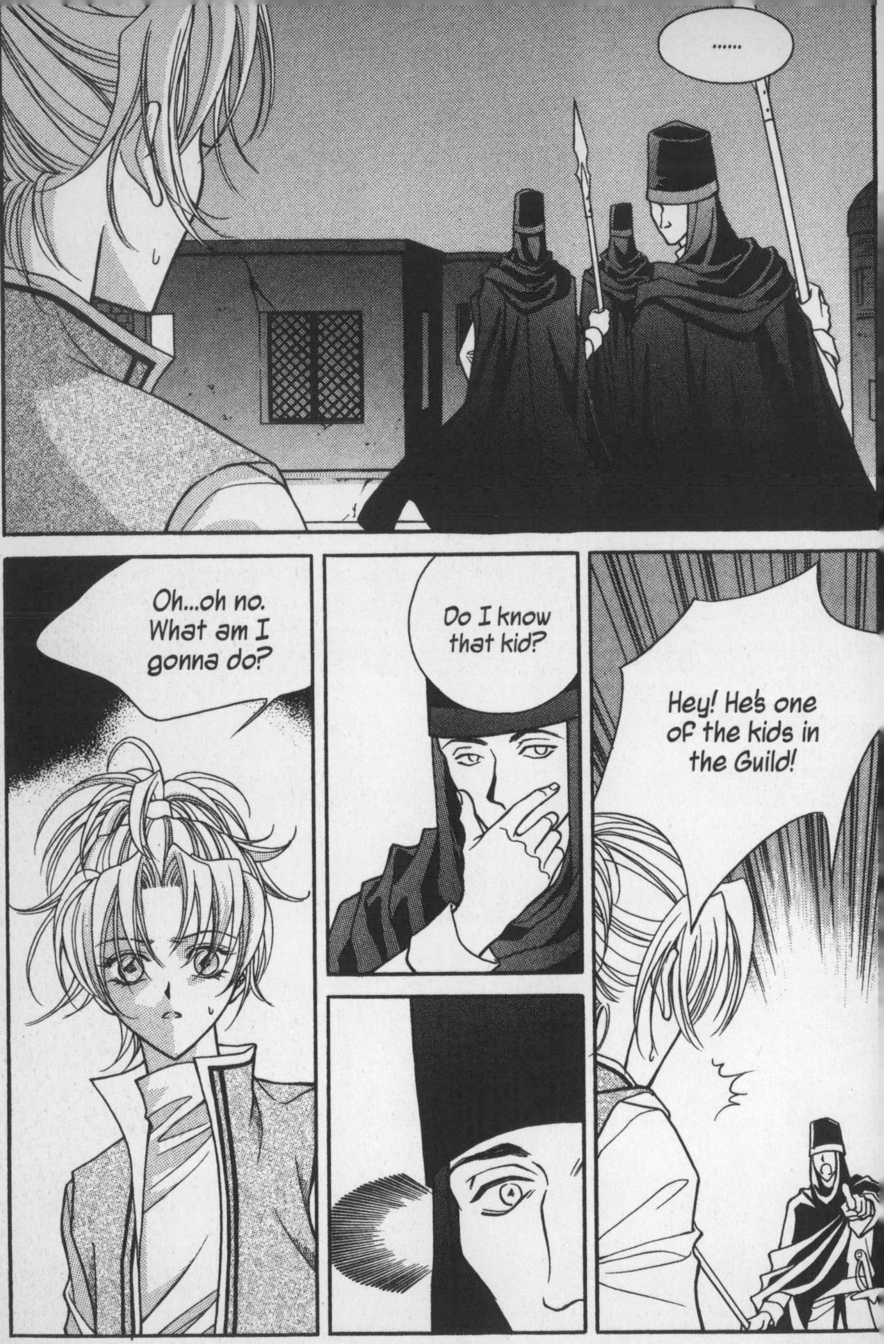
......
Oh...oh no. What am I gonna do?
Do I know that kid?
Hey! He's one of the kids in the Guild!

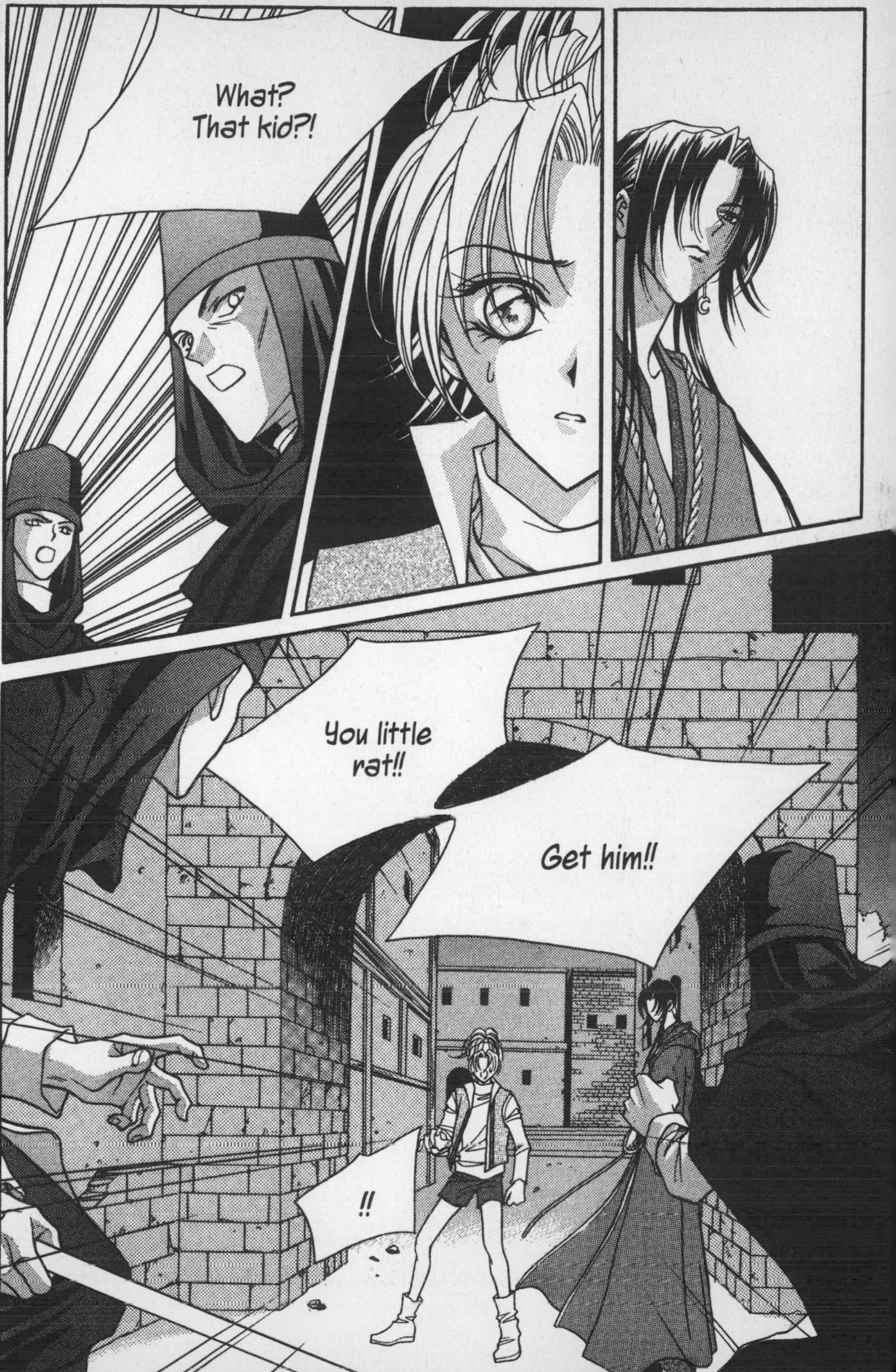
What? That kid?!
You little rat!!
Get him!!
!!

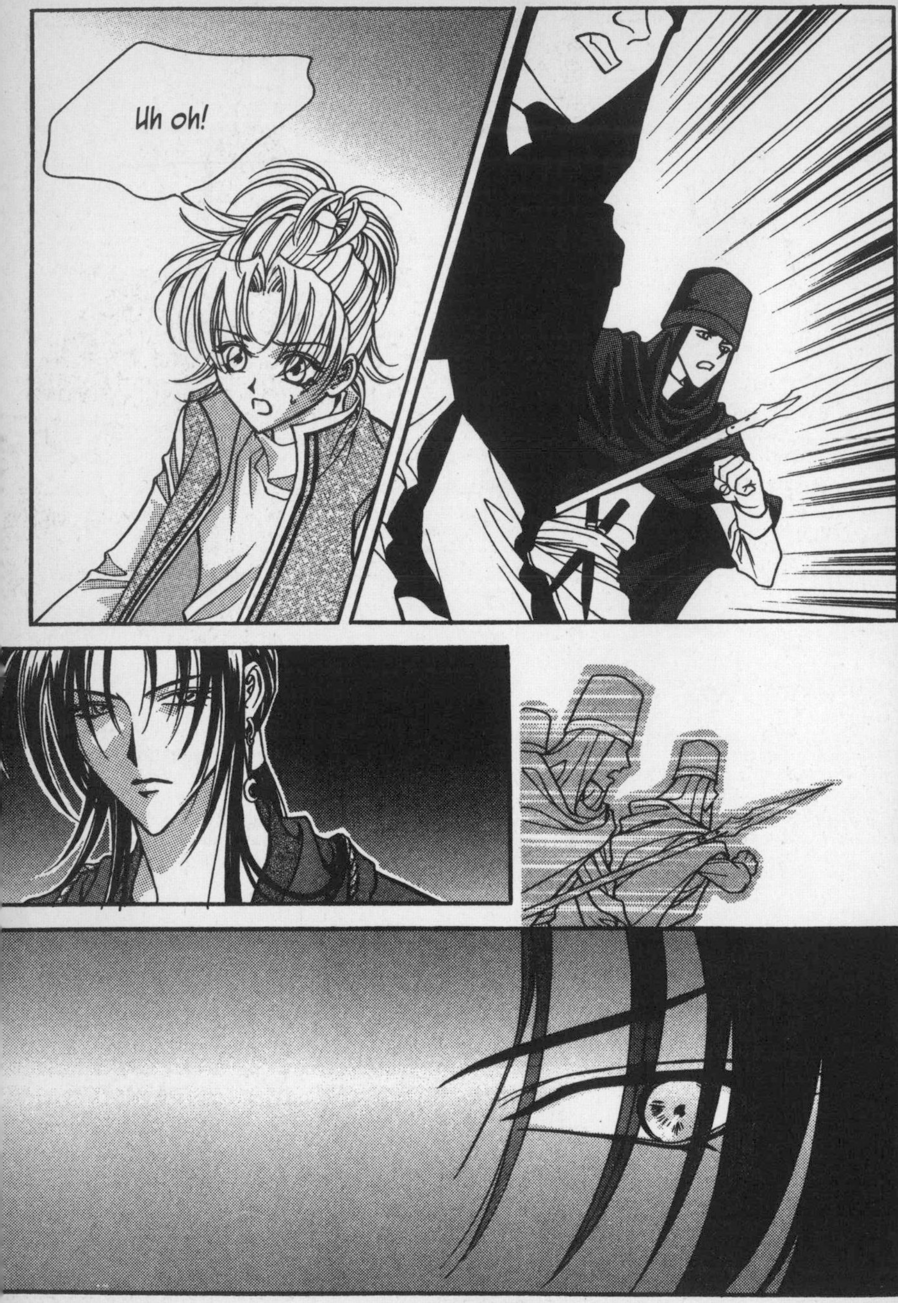
Uh oh!

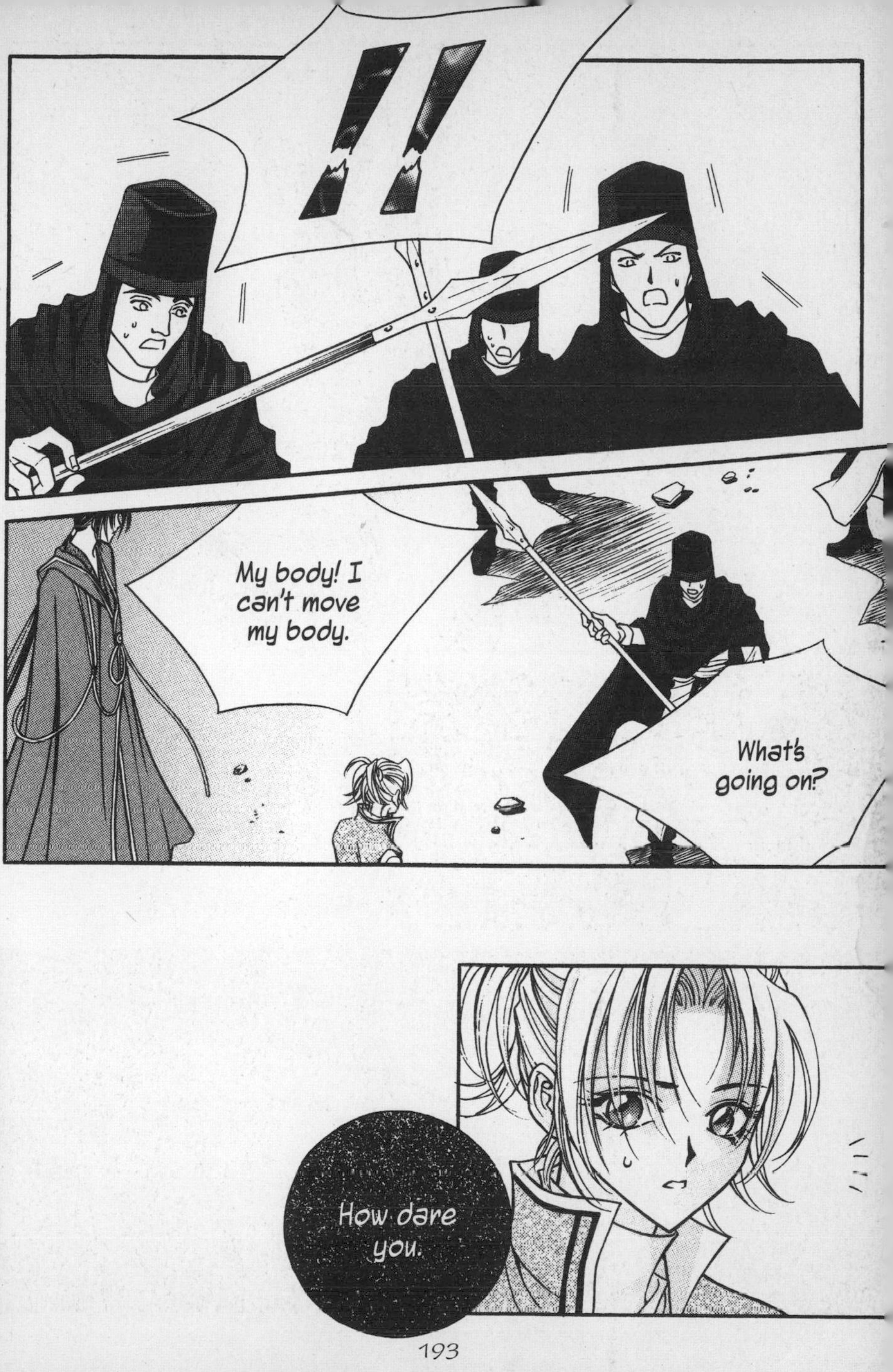
!!
My body! I can't move my body.
What's going on?
How dare you.

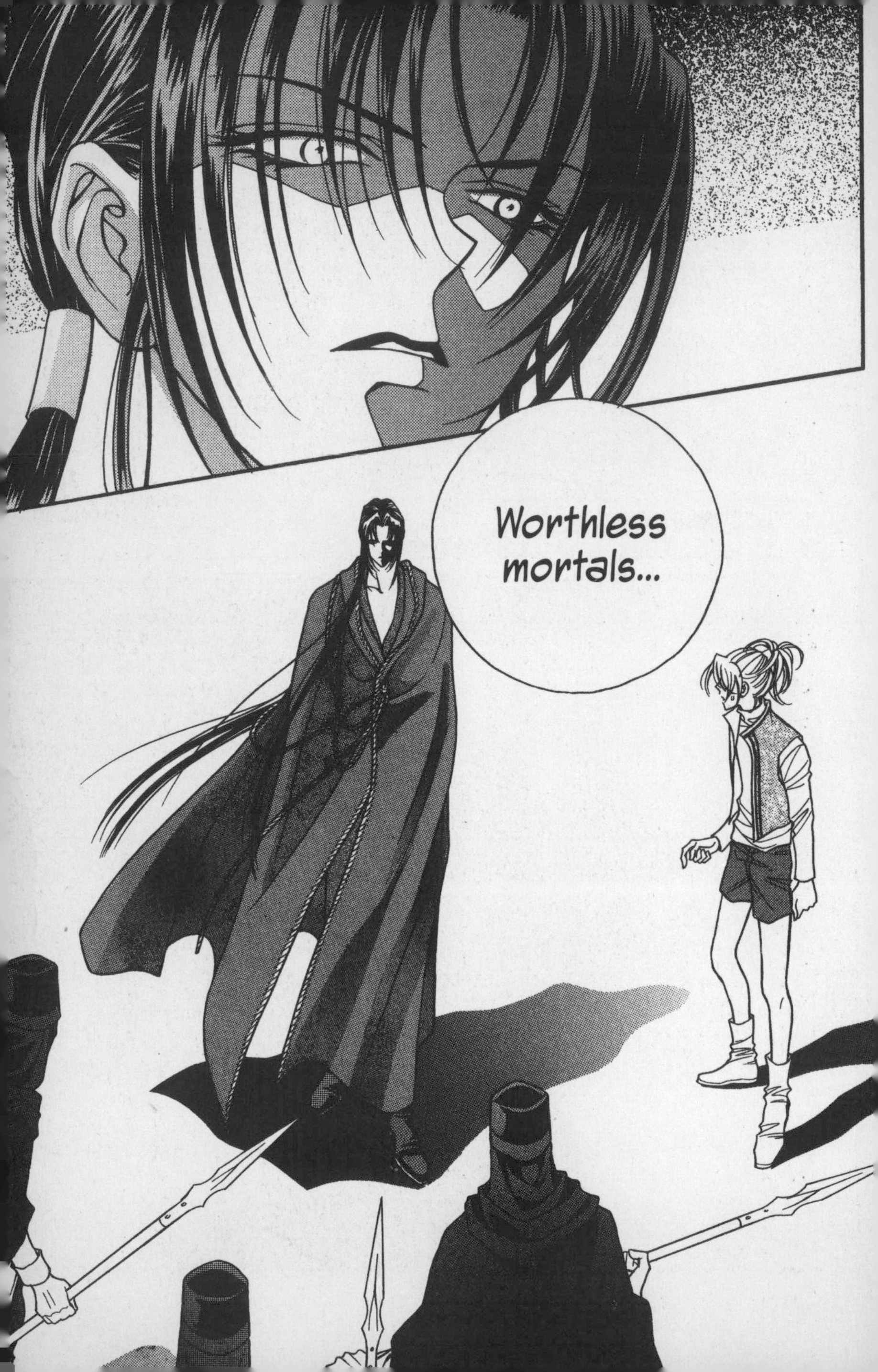
Worthless mortals...

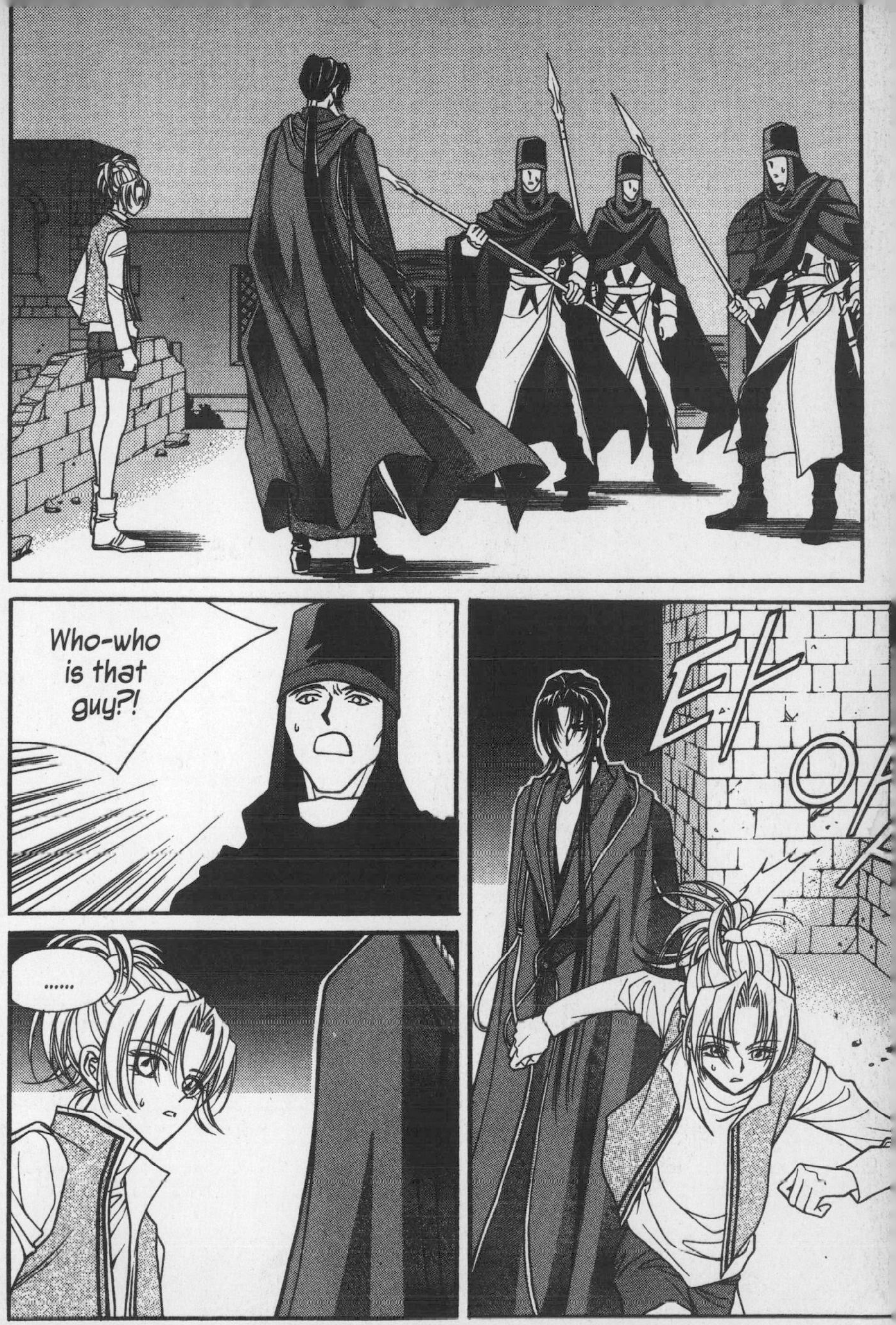
Who-who is that guy?!
......
EF
OA

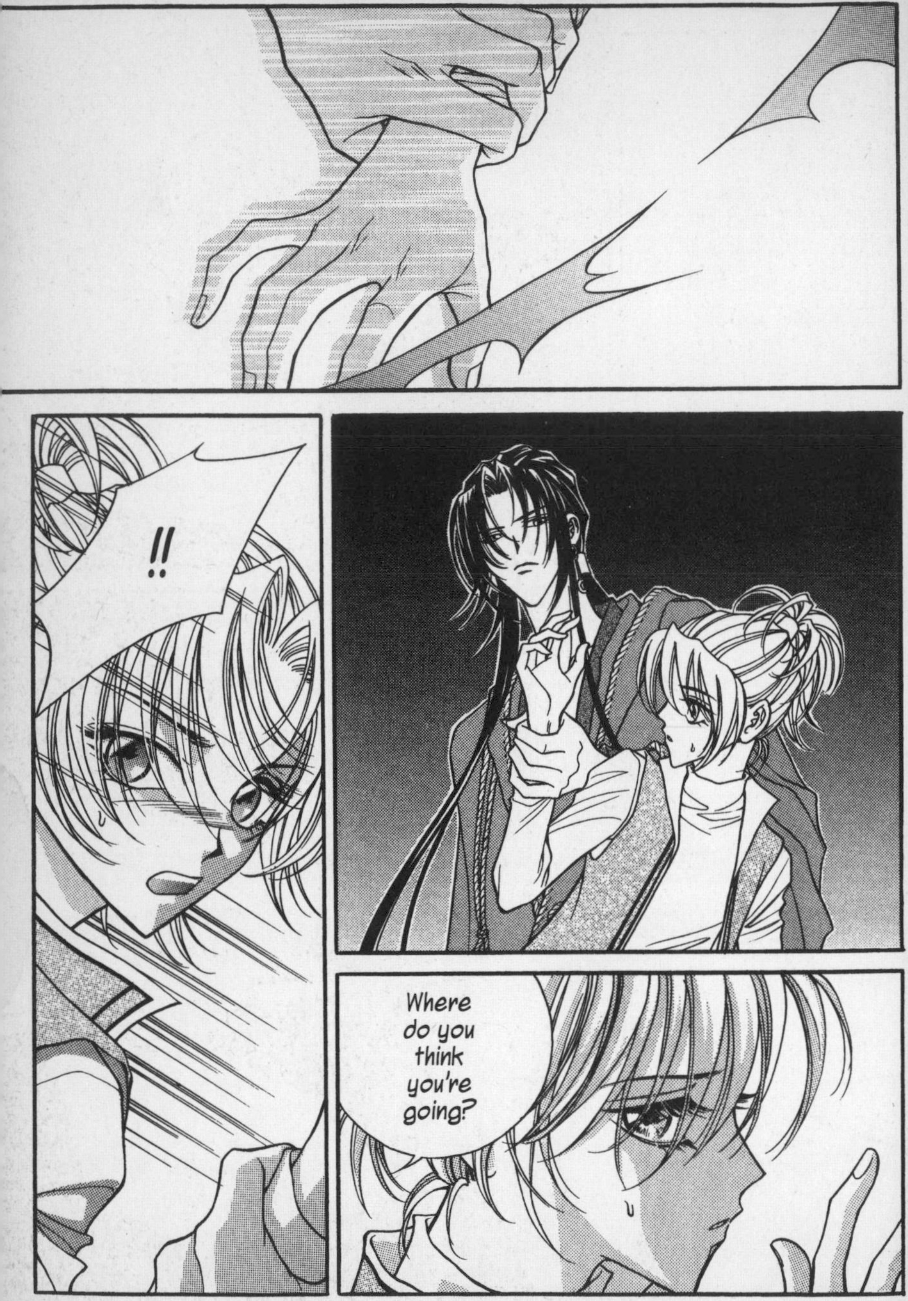
!!
Where do you think you're going?

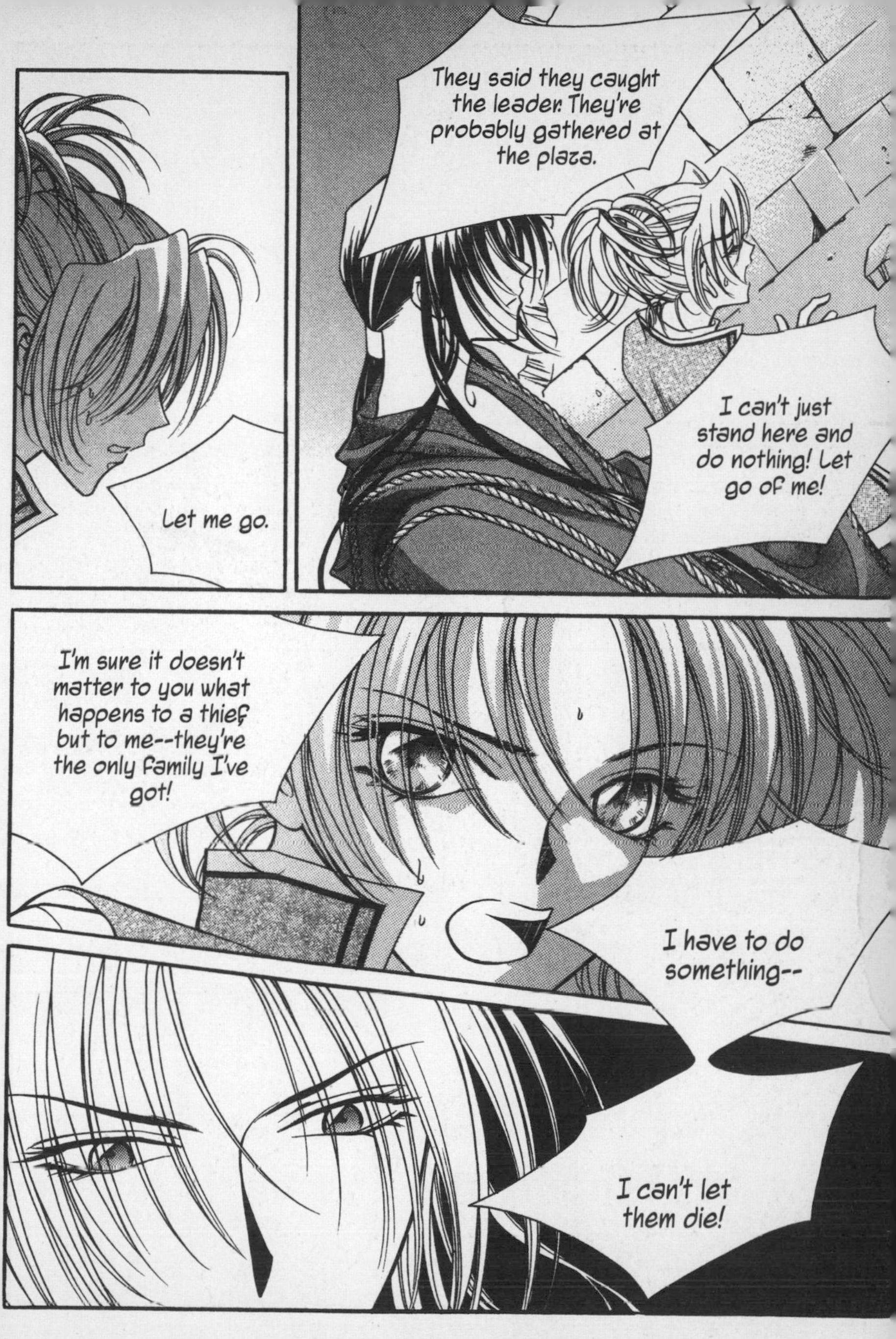
They said they caught the leader. They're probably gathered at the plaza.
I can't just stand here and do nothing! Let go of me!
Let me go.
I'm sure it doesn't matter to you what happens to a thief but to me--they're the only family I've got!
I have to do something--
I can't let them die!

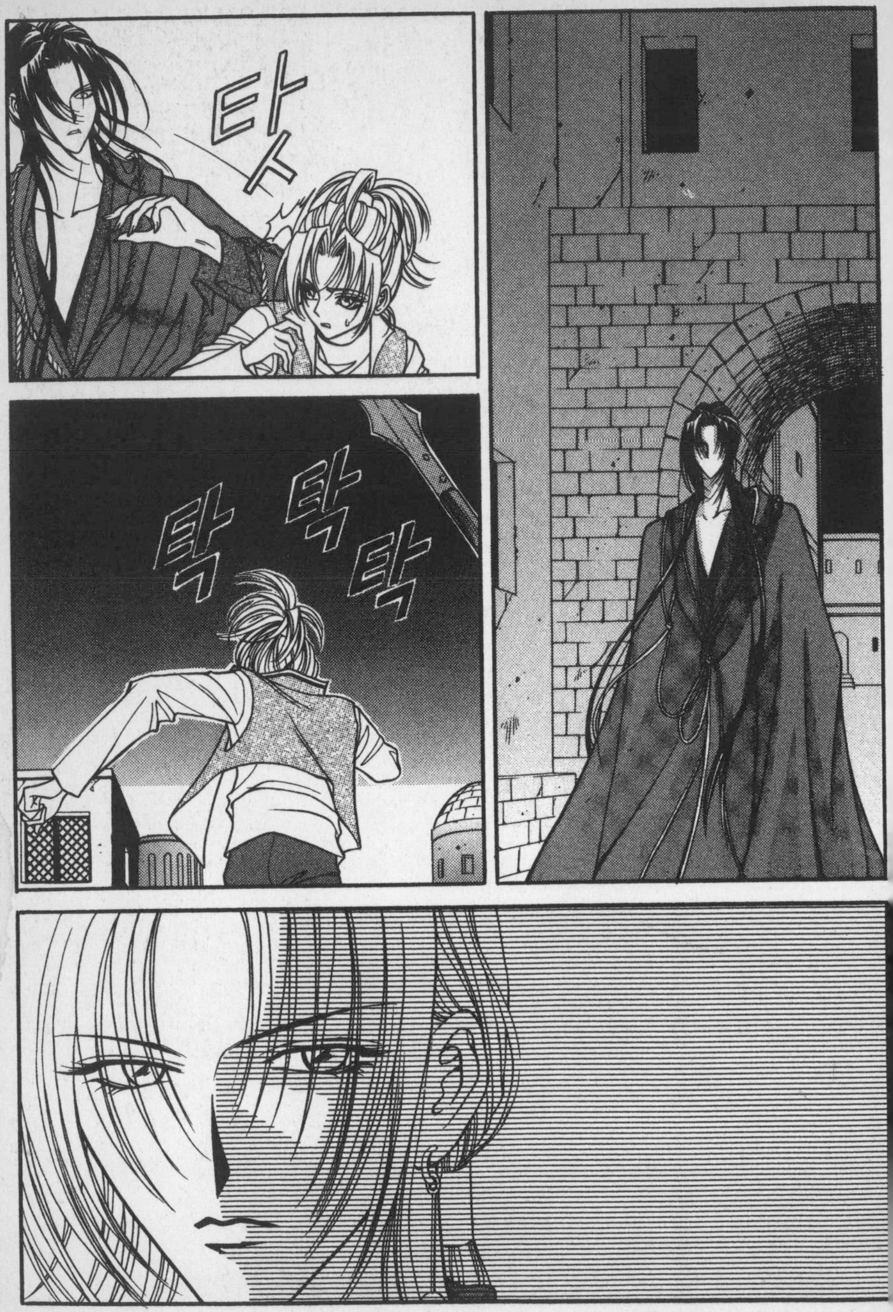
타-ㄱ
탁
탁
탁

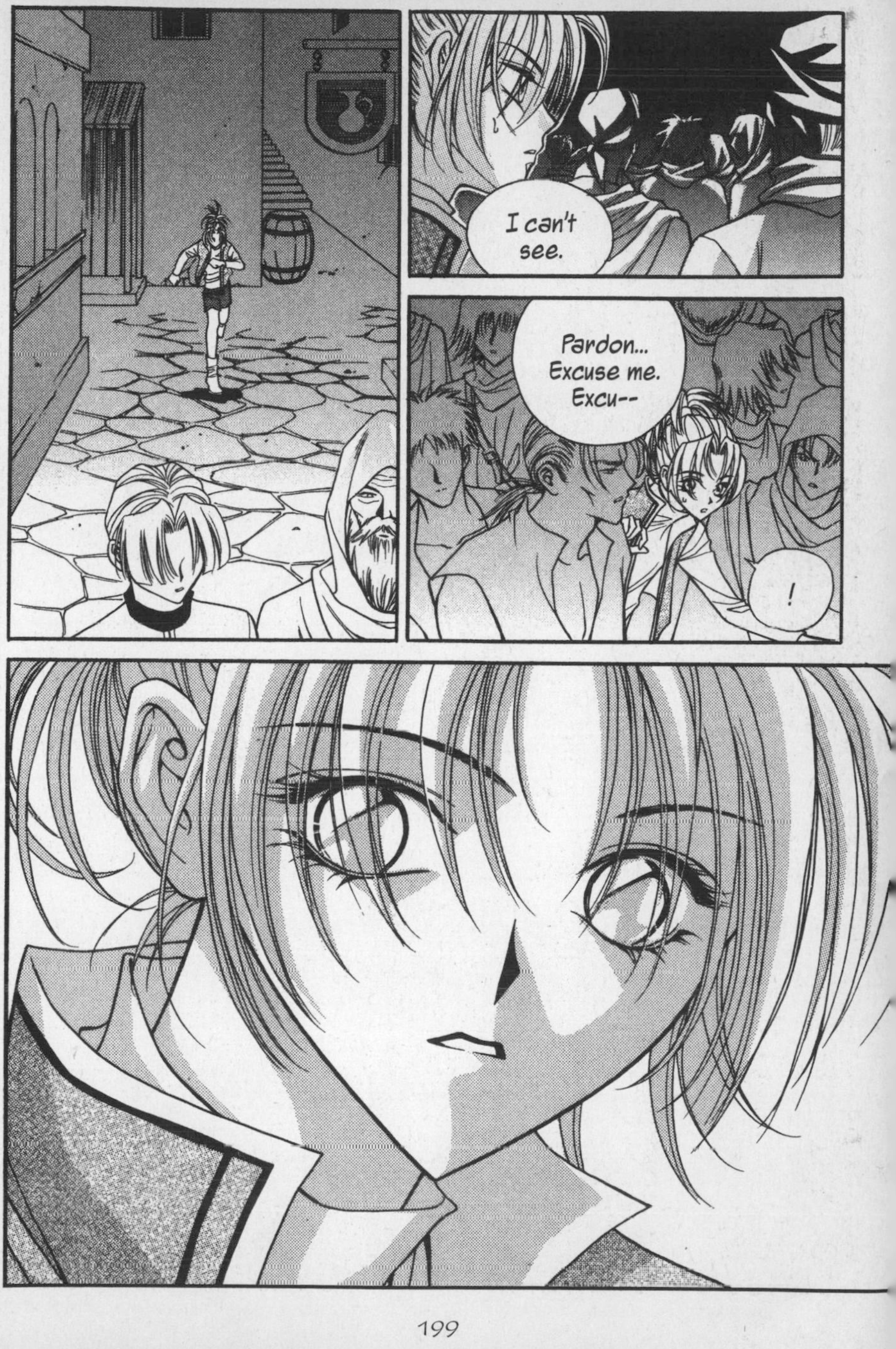

I can't see.
Pardon... Excuse me. Excu--
!

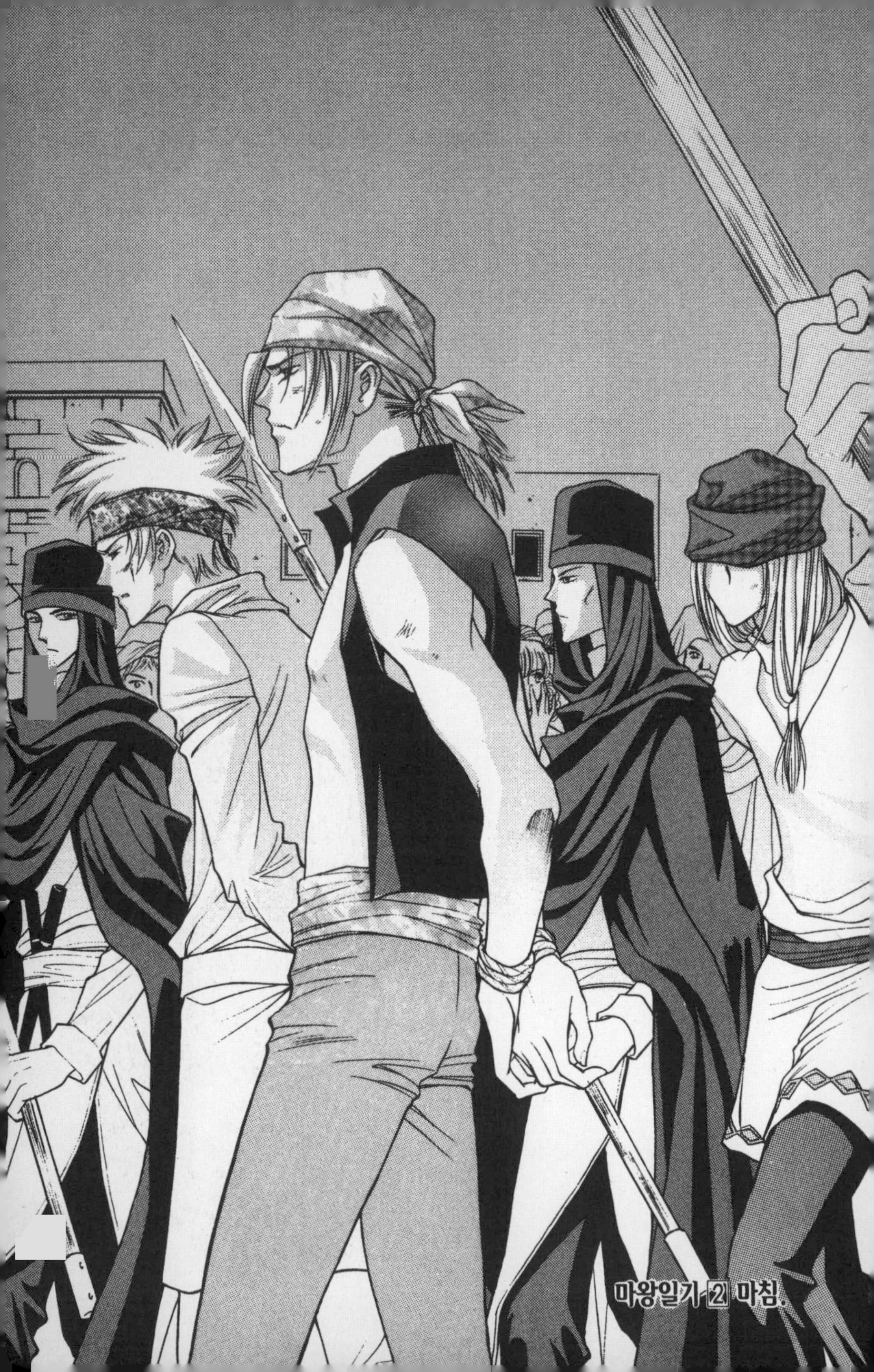
마왕일기 ② 마침.

Preview for Volume 3

Eclipse discovers that Raenef is truly a demon lord and invites him to come with him. Raenef, happy to give up his life as a thief and psyched about the prospect of three square meals a day, agrees. Later, Eclipse goes to see Hejem to complain about getting Chris dumped on him. Hejem explains Chris's past and his future as the head of the Temple of Rased. Finally, Rased appears before Hejem to announce that there are big changes afoot in the demon world--and Chris plays a key role.

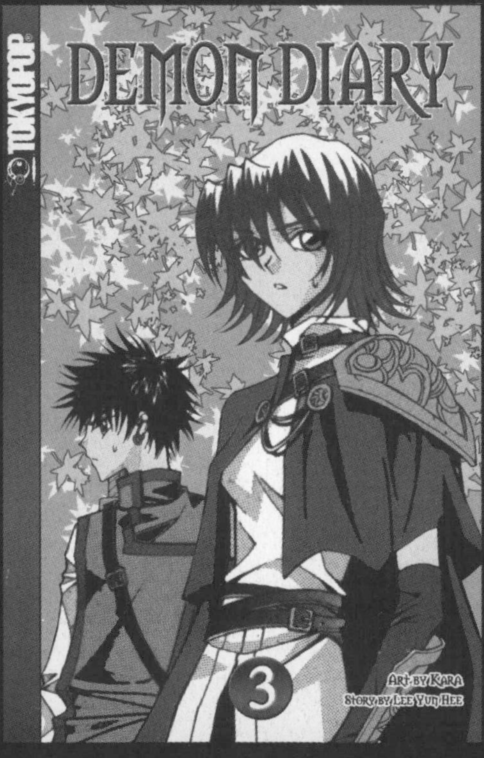

TOKYOPOP
DEMON DIARY
3
ART BY KARA
STORY BY LEE YUN HEE

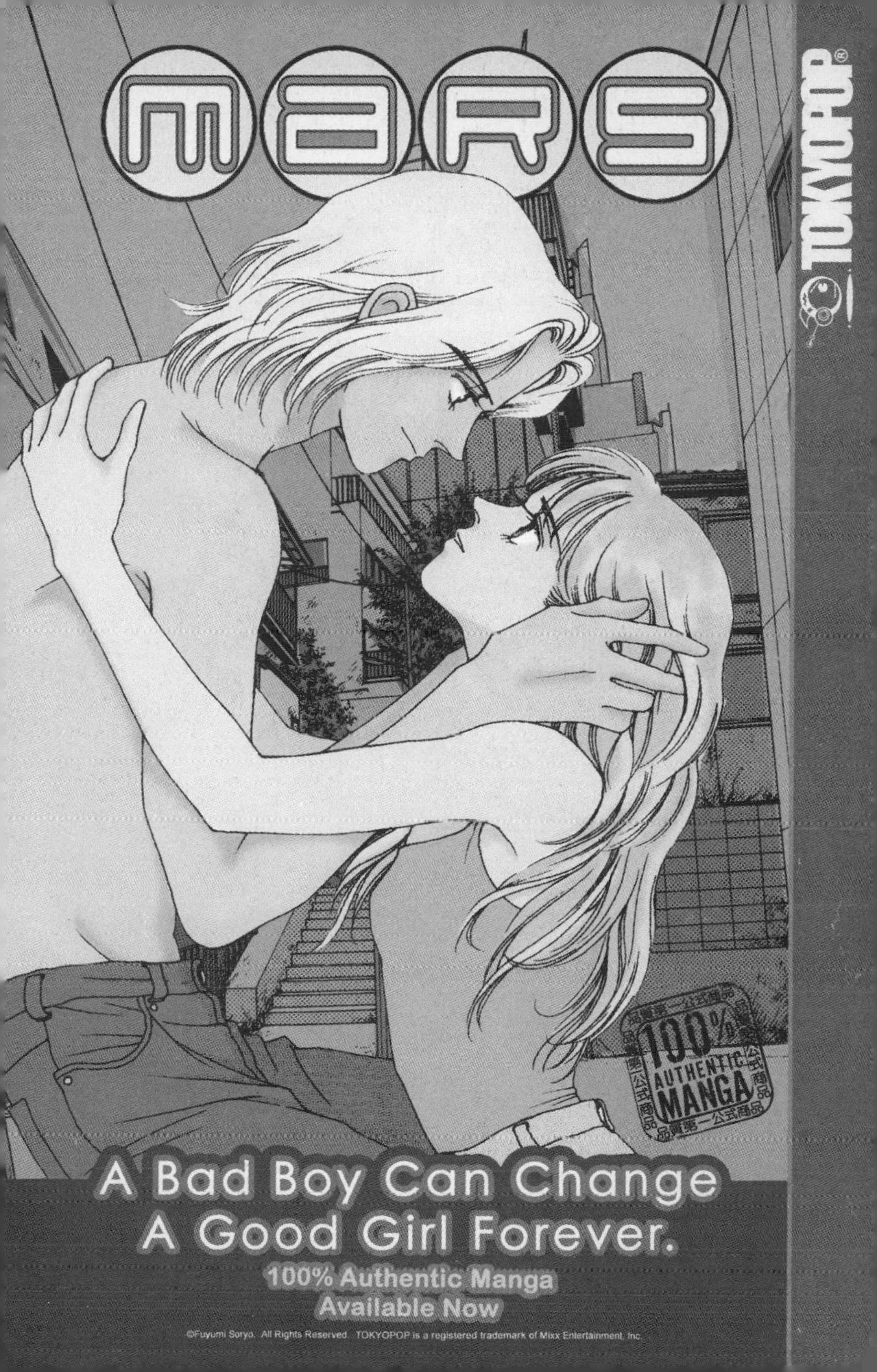
MARS
TOKYOPOP®
100% AUTHENTIC MANGA
A Bad Boy Can Change
A Good Girl Forever.
100% Authentic Manga
Available Now
©Fuyumi Soryo. All Rights Reserved. TOKYOPOP is a registered trademark of Mixx Entertainment, Inc.

TOKYOPOP®

Chobits

BY CLAMP

America's
must-have
manga

"Chobits…
is a wonderfully
entertaining story
that would be a
great installment
in anybody's
Manga collection."
— Tony Chen,
Anime News Network.com

100%
AUTHENTIC
MANGA

OT
OLDER TEEN
AGE 16+

www.TOKYOPOP.com

CLAMP SCHOOL DETECTIVES

The Hit Comedy/Adventure

Fresh Off the Heels of Magic Knight Rayearth

Limited Edition
Free Color Poster Inside

(while supplies last)

100% AUTHENTIC MANGA

From the creators of Angelic Layer,
Cardcaptor Sakura, Chobits,
Magic Knight Rayearth , Wish,
The Man of Many Faces,
Duklyon: CLAMP School Defenders,
Miyuki Chan in Wonderland
and Shirahime-syo: Snow Goddess Tales

AVAILABLE AT YOUR FAVORITE BOOK AND COMIC STORES NOW!

A ALL AGES

www.TOKYOPOP.com

TOKYOPOP